걸프 사태

미국 동향 4

_____

걸프 사태

미국 동향 4

한국학술정보

| 머리말

　걸프 전쟁은 미국의 주도하에 34개국 연합군 병력이 수행한 전쟁으로, 1990년 8월 이라크의 쿠웨이트 침공 및 합병에 반대하며 발발했다. 미국은 초기부터 파병 외교에 나섰고, 1990년 9월 서울 등에 고위 관리를 파견하며 한국의 동참을 요청했다. 88올림픽 이후 동구권 국교 수립과 유엔 가입 추진 등 적극적인 외교 활동을 펼치는 당시 한국에 있어 이는 미국과 국제사회의 지지를 얻기 위해서라도 피할 수 없는 일이었다. 결국 정부는 91년 1월부터 약 3개월에 걸쳐 국군의료지원단과 공군수송단을 사우디아라비아 및 아랍 에미리트 연합 등에 파병하였고, 군·민간 의료 활동, 병력 수송 임무를 수행했다. 동시에 당시 걸프 지역 8개국에 살던 5천여 명의 교민에게 방독면 등 물자를 제공하고, 특별기 파견 등으로 비상시 대피할 수 있도록 지원했다. 비록 전쟁 부담금과 유가 상승 등 어려움도 있었지만, 걸프전 파병과 군사 외교를 통해 한국은 유엔 가입에 박차를 가할 수 있었고 미국 등 선진 우방국, 아랍권 국가 등과 밀접한 외교 관계를 유지하며 여러 국익을 창출할 수 있었다.

　본 총서는 외교부에서 작성하여 30여 년간 유지한 걸프 사태 관련 자료를 담고 있다. 미국을 비롯한 여러 국가와의 군사 외교 과정, 일일 보고 자료와 기타 정부의 대응 및 조치, 재외동포 철수와 보호, 의료지원단과 수송단 파견 및 지원 과정, 유엔을 포함해 세계 각국에서 수집한 관련 동향 자료, 주변국 지원과 전후복구사업 참여 등 총 48권으로 구성되었다. 전체 분량은 약 2만 4천여 쪽에 이른다.

2024년 3월

한국학술정보(주)

| 일러두기

· 본 총서에 실린 자료는 2022년 4월과 2023년 4월에 각각 공개한 외교문서 4,827권, 76만 여 쪽 가운데 일부를 발췌한 것이다.

· 각 권의 제목과 순서는 공개된 원본을 최대한 반영하였으나, 주제에 따라 일부는 적절히 변경하였다.

· 원본 자료는 A4 판형에 맞게 축소하거나 원본 비율을 유지한 채 A4 페이지 안에 삽입 하였다. 또한 현재 시점에선 공개되지 않아 '공란'이란 표기만 있는 페이지 역시 그대로 실었다.

· 외교부가 공개한 문서 각 권의 첫 페이지에는 '정리 보존 문서 목록'이란 이름으로 기록물 종류, 일자, 명칭, 간단한 내용 등의 정보가 수록되어 있으며, 이를 기준으로 0001번부터 번호가 매겨져 있다. 이는 삭제하지 않고 총서에 그대로 수록하였다.

· 보고서 내용에 관한 더 자세한 정보가 필요하다면, 외교부가 온라인상에 제공하는 『대한 민국 외교사료요약집』 1991년과 1992년 자료를 참조할 수 있다.

| 차례

정 리 보 존 문 서 목 록

기록물종류	일반공문서철	등록번호	2012090507	등록일자	2012-09-17
분류번호	772	국가코드	US/XF	보존기간	영구
명 칭	걸프사태 : 미국 의회 동향, 1990-91. 전5권				
생 산 과	북미1과	생산년도	1990~1991	담당그룹	
권 차 명	V.4 1991.3-4월				
내용목차	* 걸프사태 관련 미국 의회에서의 각종 논의, 법안, 결의안, 청문회 개최 동향 등 * 3.7 하원 세출위원회, 걸프전 관련 추가 세출 예산 법안 통과 및 걸프전 재정 공여국들의 기여금 제공 촉구 하원 결의안 채택 3.19 상원 본회의, 걸프전비 추가 지출안 통과 3.22 상.하원 본회의, 걸프전비 추가 지출법안 통과 4.6 Bush 대통령 걸프전비 추가 지출을 위한 수권법안 서명, 발효 4.8 하원 군사위원회, 우방국들의 걸프전비 지원현황에 관한 Aspin 위원장 명의 보고서 작성, 배포 4.10 Bush 대통령, 상기 법안 지출 법안 서명, 발효				

0001

외　무　부

종　별 :

번　호 : USW-1026

일　시 : 91 0305 1443

수　신 : 장　관(미북, 미안)

발　신 : 주　미　대사

제　목 : 걸프전 기여금 관계 의원 발언

　1. 최근 방한한바 있는 PATRICIA SCHROEDER 하원의원은 1.25. 걸프전 기여금 관련, 한국, 일본, 독일의 기여금 수준이 부족하다는 요지의 본회의 발언을하였음을 보고함.

　2. 동 발언 내용은 팩스편 송부함

　(대사 박동진 - 국장)

미주국　　미주국

PAGE 1

주 미 대 사 관

번호 : USV(F)-0262
수신 : 장관(미복, 미안)
발신 : 주미대사
제목 : 걸프전 기여금 관계 의원 발언

배부처	장관신	차관실	一차보실	二차보	기획실	의전장	아주국	미주국	구주국	통아국	국가국	경제국	통상국	정문국	영교국	총무과	감사관	공보관	외연원	청외대	총미실	안기부	문공부
	/	/	/	/		㉗	/		/		/						/	/	/				

GERMANY, JAPAN, AND SOUTH KOREA MUST CONTRIBUTE MORE TO DESERT SHIELD

(Mrs. SCHROEDER asked and was given permission to address the House for 1 minute and to revise and extend her remarks.)

Mrs. SCHROEDER. Mr. Speaker, on this very ominous day, when we hope things continue to go so well, I want to say to our allies, especially three of them—Germany, Japan, and South Korea—that there are no three countries on this planet that owe their prosperity and well-being more to the United States than those three countries. Yet when we look at the cost of this war, those three countries are really doing the least compared to what they could do.

Mr. Speaker, this is terribly disappointing to me. Their attitude has been that after all of their people have health care, which our people do not have in the United States, that after all of their young people are educated in college or whatever they want, which our people do not get in the United States, and after many more programs that they fund, if there is anything left, they will throw some change in the tin cup.

You cannot be a superpower and a super debtor very long. I think we have to say to these allies, especially these three, our patience is running out, and we really expect a whole lot more than loose change. I think that is very, very important. Congress is going to be talking about this as we look at the cost of this war and start trying to pay the bill, which is going to be very difficult, in the next few months.

Patricia Schroeder
(민주, Col)
군사위 소속

0003

외 무 부

종 별 :

번 호 : USW-1045   일 시 : 91 0305 1823

수 신 : 장관(미북)

발 신 : 주미대사

제 목 : 걸프전 종전 관련 의회 동향

1. 미의회는 걸프전의 종료에 제하여 부시 대통령과 SCHWARZKOPF 사령관등 전쟁지도자들에 대한 치하와 각종 영예 수여를 추진하고 있는바, 주요동향을 아래 보고함.

가. 부시대통령 양원 합동 연설

- 부시 대통령은 3.6(수) 저녁 (21:00 EST) 의회의 요청으로 상하양원 합동 연설을 행할 예정인바 FOLEY 하원의장은 3.1(금) 부시 대통령에 대한 연설 초청시 의회가 미국민을 대표하여 부시 대통령의 역사적인 지도역량에 대하여 경의와 축하를 보내고 자한다고 밝힌바 있음.

- 부시대통령의 연설에 대해 민주당 지도부는 통상관례로 행하던 TV 대응 연설 계획이 없는것으로 알려짐.

나. 영예 수여

- TRENT LOTT 상원의원(R-MISS.) 은 SCHWARZKOPF 사령관에 대해 대통령의 금장(국가적 영웅에 대한 국민훈장) 수여권한을 부여하는 법안을 발의함.

- ALFONSE M. D'AMATO 상원의원(K-N.Y)은 부시 대통령에게 SCHWARZKOPF 사령관과 POWELL 합참의장의 오성장군 승진을 촉구하는 서한을 발송.

- JOSEPH I. LIEBERMAN(D-CONN) 상원의원은 SCHWARZKOPF 사령관의 양원 합동 연설 추진.

2. 부시 대통령의 상원 합동 연설 내용 추후 보고예정임.

(대사 박동진-국장)

미주국	차관	1차보	2차보	중아국	정문국	정와대	안기부

관리 번호 M-461

외 무 부

원 본

종 별 :

번 호 : USW-1046　　　　　　　　　　일 시 : 91 0305 1823

수 신 : 장관(미북)

발 신 : 주 미 대사

제 목 : 한국의 걸프전 기여도 관련 SOLOMON 하원의원 발언

연 : USW-1026

1. SOLOMON 하원의원(R-NY)은 2.25 연호 SCHROEDER 의원의 독일, 일본, 한국의 걸프전 기여도 부족 비난 발언에 대한 반박 발언을 통하여, 독일과 일본의 비난에는 동조하나 한국의 경우 세계 자유와 민족 자결을 위한 부쟁에 전폭적으로 참여해왔으므로 한국을 비난 대상에서 제외할것을 촉구한바, 동 의원 발언문 전문을 별첨 FAX 송부함.

2. 본직은 SOLOMON 의원의 상기 발언에 대해 감사 서한 발송등 적의 사의를표명할 예정임.

(대사 박동진-국장)

91.12.31 까지

미주국	장관	차관	1차보	2차보	중아국	정문국	정와대	안기부

PAGE 1　　　　　　　　　　　　　　　　　　91.03.06　09:00

주 미 대 사 관

보안
통제

번호 : USW(F) - 766

수신 : 장 관(미북,미안)

발신 : 주미대사

제목 : Solomon 의원 한국관계 발언문

H 1144   CO

SOUTH KOREA HAS CONTRIBUTED TO CAUSE OF WORLD STABILITY

(Mr. SOLOMON asked and was given permission to address the House for 1 minute.)

Mr. SOLOMON. Mr. Speaker, on this floor a few minutes ago the gentlewoman from Colorado [Mrs. SCHROEDER] criticized three countries, namely, Germany, Japan, and the Republic of Korea, for not participating fully in Operation Desert Storm. Let me concur with her on the first two countries, Germany and Japan, but let me suggest to her that she delete the name of South Korea, because South Korea has participated and continues to participate fully in the struggle for freedom and national self-determination around the world.

Let me point out to the gentlewoman that it was South Korea, standing shoulder to shoulder with the United States of America, that stopped communism dead in its tracks back in 1950. That was the turning point against that deadly, atheistic philosophy—communism—that is even worse than that of Saddam Hussein. The Republic of Korea has stood as a staunch ally of the United States in the fight against communism ever since.

Let me suggest that the gentlewoman from Colorado ought to withdraw the name of South Korea and put in its place that of the Soviet Union, which has contributed not one dollar, which has contributed not one life, to this important cause for which we are all fighting for in Saudi Arabia.

Since joining with the United States to vote for the creation of the United Nations, the Soviet Union has more often than not been a stumbling block for the cause of freedom by means of the votes it cast in that international organization. At last—after more than 40 years—the Soviet Union did cast a truly constructive vote for freedom when it supported the international coalition against Saddam Hussein's occupation of Kuwait. Now, however, it has reverted to form, offering diplomatic escape hatches for Saddam Hussein that, while currying favor for the Soviet Union in the Middle East, work against the allies' efforts to bring long-term stability to the region.

Again, Mr. Speaker, let me suggest that the gentlewoman from Colorado delete her criticism for a good, staunch ally, the Republic of Korea, and aim that criticism where it is well deserved.

외 무 부

종 별 : 지 급

번 호 : USW-1083

일 시 : 91 0306 1840

수 신 : 장관(미북,미안,통일)

발 신 : 주 미 대사

제 목 : 미 경제 관련 하원 세입위 청문회

1. 하원 세입위(위원장 DAN ROSTENKOWSKI 의원)는 작 3.5 오후 DARMAN 예산국장을 출석시킨 가운데 미 경제 현황, 연방 예산 정책, 걸프전비등에 관한 청문회를 개최한바, ROSTENKOWSKI 위원장은 모두 발언에서 금후 미 예산 정책 결정에영향을 미칠수 있는 불확실 요소로서 경기 침체, 무역 적자, 의료 제도, 극빈 아동률 및 대외 분채등을 지적하였음.

2. DARMAN 국장은 부쉬 대통령의 2.22 자 걸프전 수행을 위한 추가 예산 요청서를 경제관련 서면 증언에 대신하고, 걸프전비와 우방국 지원 약속 금액 545 억불중 현재 169 억불을 수령하였으며, 남은 금액도 수령하게될것으로 기대한다고 증언함.

3. 이에 진행된 질의 응답은 주로 의료 제도, 사회 보장 제도등 국내 문제와 걸프전배에 집중되었는바, 이중 걸프전비 관련 질의 응답 요지는 다음임.

O BILL ARCHER 의원(R-TX)이 국별 걸프 전비 지원 약속 금액및 기지불액수, 잔액 지불 전망및 미국의 부담액을 질의한데 대해 DARMAN 국장은 국별 지원 약속금액및 기지불액(괄호안 숫자)을 사우디 168 억(60.2 억), 쿠웨이트 160 억(45.1 억), UAE 40 억(20.1 억), 독일 66 억(29.6 억), 일본 107 억(13.2 억), 한국 3.85 억(7,100 만)을 밝힘.잔액 지불 전망에 대해서는 대부분 약속을 지킬것으로 기대되나 일본의 경우 아직 불확실(A BIG AREA OF UNCERTAINTY)하다고 답변함. 한편, 미국의 자체 부담액은 약 150 억불에 이를것으로 전망하였음.

O RAYMONT MCGRATH(R-NY)의원의 대만에 대한 지원 요청 여부 질의에 대해 동 국장은 미 행정부가 지원을 요청한 사실도 없고 지원을 받은일도 없다고 답변함.

(대사 박동진-국장)

91.12.31 까지

전 토 필(1991. 6.3.   )
예고문에의거 재분류(1991.12.31)
직위   사무관 성명

미주국 안기부	장관	차관	1차보	2차보	미주국	중아국	통상국	정와대

원 본

외 무 부

종 별 : 긴 급

번 호 : USW-1088   일 시 : 91 03062327

수 신 : 장관(미북,미안)

발 신 : 주 미 대사

제 목 : 하원 외무위 아태 소위 청문회

연 USW(F)-780,781

1. 하원 외무위 아태 소위(위원장 SOLARZ 의원)는 금 3.6(수) 오후 SOLOMON국무부 동아태 담당 차관보, CARL FORD 국방부 국제 안보 담당 부차관보등을 출석시킨 가운데, 부쉬 대통령의 아태지역 국가에 대한 92 회계년도 원조 요청안에 관한 청문회를 개최함.

2. SOLOMON 차관보는 상기 증언에서 동아태 지역에대한 미국의 정책을 개관하면서, 동 지역이 전세계에서 가장빠른 경제 성장을 보이고 있으며, 미국과의 쌍무 교역도 서구와의 교역량보다 1/3 이 많은 3,000 억불에 달하고 있다고 말하고, 미국의 대 동아태 지역 정책을 다음과같이 밝혔음

   가. 지속적안 지역 안보를 보장할수 있도록 동 지역에서의 미군사력 조정 및 유지

   나. 일본과의 세계적 동반 협력 관계 발전

   다. 중국과의 강력한 정치.전략적 이해 관계 추구

   라. 필리핀과의 지속적 방위 협력 구축을 위한 새로운 관계 모색

   마. 한국의 새로운 경제, 군사력에 상응하는 지도적 역할 분담을 고무하는 가운데 한국과의 동맹 관계 강화

   바. 캄보디아 분쟁의 평화적, 포괄적 해결 추구

   사. APEC 를 통한 지역 경제 협력 촉진

3. 아국 관련 동인의 증언 요지는 아래와같음(상세 별전 증언문 FAX 참조)

   가. 걸프전 지원

   0 아국의 걸프전비 지원 내역을 상세히 밝히고, 특히 걸프전 발발후 수송기를 최초로 지원하고 의료진을 파견해준것을 평가

   나. 방위비 분담 및 주한 미군 감축

미주국	장관	차관	1차보	2차보	미주국	정와대	안기부

PAGE 1

O 동아 지역 미군 감축 계획의 일환으로 92 년말 7 천명의 주한 미군이 감축될 예정이며, 한국의 자체 방위력 증강과 더불어 미군은 지원 역할로 바뀌게 될것이라고 증언하고, 이와 관련,90.12. 주한 미군에 대한 한국의 노무비 지원 협정및 91.1.25 특별 비용 분담 협정 서명 사실언급.

다. 북한의 비핵 지대화 제안

O 북한이 85 년 핵확산 금지 조약에 가입하고도 IAEA 의 핵 안전 협정 서명을 거부하고 있다고 말하고, 미국은 북한의 한반도 비핵지대화 제안을 수락할수 없으며, 만일 한반도에 핵확산 문제가 있다면 이는 북한의 책임이라고 언급.

라. 남북 대화

O 남북 대화는 한반도의 안정을 위해 비핵지대화 문제보다 훨씬 중요하며, 미국은 남북 대화를 계속 지지해 왔다고 말하고 90.8 월 이래 세차례의 남북 총리 회담을 개최 사실만으로도 의의가 크나 북한이 최근 팀 스피리트 훈련을 이유로 대화를 중단한것은 불행한 일이라고 언급.

4. 이어 진행된 질의 응답중 한국관련 발언 요지는 아래임(상세 연호 FAX 참조)

가.FOGLIETTA 의원은 최근 한국의 민주화 노력이 후퇴하고 있다고 지적하고,1500 명의 정치범 수감문제, 주한 미군 감축 계획, 북한의 핵무기 개발설에 대한 미국의 평가등에 관해 질의한바, 이에 대해 SOLOMON 차관보는 한국정부가 북한의 위협으로 민주화를 신중히 추진해가고 있으며, 최근 수백명의 정치범이 석방된 사실과 이문제에 대한 미국의 한국정부에 대한 지속적인 관심 표명및 주한 미군의 7,000 명 추가 감축계획등을 설명함. 북한의 핵무기 개발문제에 대하여는이를 사실로 보고 있으며, 크게 우려하고 있다고 답변함.

나.SOLARZ 의원은 일본과 비교하여 한국의 주한미군 주둔 비용 분담 비율에관해 질의한바, FORD 차관보는 계산 방법의 차이는 있으나 일본은 대략 총 미군 주둔비의 50 프로 이상을, 한국은 20 프로 정도를 부담하고 있다고 답변함.

(대사 박동진-국장) 예고: 91.12.31 까지

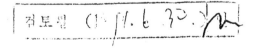

PAGE 2

報 告 事 項

報 告 畢

1991. 3. 7.
美 洲 局
北 美 課(15)

題 目 : 美 下院 外交委 亞.太 小委 聽聞會

下院 外交委 亞.太 小委는 FY02 對外 援助 豫算審議에 關聯 聽聞會를 ~회계년도

開催하여 Solomon 國務部 東亞.太 次官補 및 Carl Ford 國防部 國際安保 이 로부는 3.6 에서 미리의 東아.太정책에 관해 증언하면서,

擔當 副次官補 證言을 聽取하였는 바, 同證言 主要 內容 및 韓國關聯 質疑 을

應答 內容을 아래 報告드립니다.

| 솔로몬 次官補 證言 內容 |

(韓.美 安保協力 關係)

o 美國은 90년대 對 東亞.太 地域 政策 推進에 있어 韓國의 새로운 經濟.
  軍事力에 相應한 指導的 役割 分擔下에 韓國과의 同盟關係를 強化할 것임.

o 韓.美 兩國間 安保協力 關係는 美軍의 前進 配置를 통해 世界 安保는 물론
  域內 均衡者, 誠實한 仲裁者로서의 役割 遂行을 可能케 함.

0010

(걸프戰 支援)

○ 걸프戰 關聯 韓國은 1차로 多國籍軍 支援 1億2千万弗, 周邊國 經濟支援
  1億弗等 總 2億2千万弗을 支援하고 2차로 2億8千万弗을 追加로 支援키로
  決定함.
  - 걸프戰 勃發後 最初로 輸送 支援을 提供하고 醫療 支援團 및 軍 輸送
    支援團을 派遣

(駐韓美軍 減縮 및 防衛費 分擔)

○ 議會에 提出한 넌-워너 報告書 內容과 같이 92년 년말까지 東亞.太 地域
  駐屯 15,000명의 美軍 減縮 計劃의 일환으로 7,000명의 駐韓 美軍이 減縮될
  豫定임.
  - 90.12. 駐韓美軍에 대한 韓國의 勞務費 支援 協定(91년중 4,300만불
    韓國側 負擔) 締結
  - 91.1. 特別 費用 分擔 協定 및 龍山基地 移轉 諒解 覺書(한국측
    10-20억불 부담) 締結 사실 언급
  - 91년중 韓國의 總 負擔額은 1億5千万弗

(北韓의 韓半島 非核地帶化 제안)

○ 北韓의 韓半島 非核 地帶化 提案은 核 억지력과 기존 安保協力 關係를 沮害
  하므로 受諾할 수 없음.
  - 北韓은 85년 核擴散 禁止 條約에 加入하고도 IAEA의 核 安全協定 署名을
    거부중
  - 韓半島에서 核 擴散問題 發生時 北韓의 責任임을 강조

0011

(南．北 對話)

o 南．北對話는 韓半島 非核地帶化 提案보다 韓半島의 安定을 위해 매우 중요한
  문제임.
  - 南．北 對話 進展에 대한 美國의 계속적 지지 사실 언급

o 90년중 3차례에 걸친 南．北 總理會談을 開催 사실만으로도 큰 의미가 있음.
  - 北韓側이 팀스피리트를 구실로한 對話 中斷을 慨歎

(APEC)

o 美國과 東亞．太 地域 國家와의 交易 規模가 大幅 增加하고 있는 가운데 自由
  貿易 原則을 바탕으로한 APEC과 같은 多者間 地域 經協機構의 發展은 매우
  고무적인 사실임.
  - UR의 年內 妥結에도 寄與 期待

┌─────────────────────┐
│ 對東亞．太 地域 政策 │
└─────────────────────┘

* 90년중 美國과 東亞．太 地域과의 交易額이 3,000억불을 上廻함에 따라 90년중
  美國이 推進할 東亞．太 地域 政策 目標를 言明

o 持續的인 域內 安保를 保障하되 美國 및 同盟國의 防衛力 增強에 相應한
  東亞．太 地域 駐屯 美 軍事力의 調整, 日本과의 同伴 協力 關係 發展, 中國
  과의 强力한 政治.戰略的 理解 關係 追求, 필리핀과의 지속적 防衛協力
  構築을 위한 새로운 관계 모색, 캄보디아 紛爭의 解決 및 APEC을 통한 地域
  經濟協力 促進等을 提示함.
  - 美國의 希望하는 東亞．太 地域 國家들의 原則으로 繁榮의 利益을 공유하는
    多元的 民主體制, 市場 開放의 原則, 美 政治.軍事力 駐屯을 통한 安保
    環境 提供 및 地域 紛爭의 抑制 및 解決을 提示

0012

ㅇ 폴리에타 議員(民主, 펜실바니아)은 北韓의 核開發 與否를 질의하는 한편,
政治犯 1,500여명의 收監等 最近 韓國의 民主化 努力이 後退하고 있다고
지적하고, 與黨은 3당 統合을 통해 內閣制로 改憲 與黨의 一黨 統治를 圖謀
하고 있다는 憂慮를 標示함.

 - 솔로몬 次官補는 韓國 政府가 北韓의 威脅에도 불구 86년이래 民主化를
   愼重히 推進中임을 強調하고 최근 韓國 政府의 政治犯의 釋放 사실 및
   美國 政府의 韓國內 政治犯에 대한 지속적 관심 표명을 언급

 - 北韓의 核武器 開發 추진 事實을 認定하고 우려 표명

 - 포드 次官補도 金大中 總裁의 大統領 중심제 선호 사실등을 지적하고
   韓國이 過去와 같은 一人 統治로의 復歸는 어려울 것임을 언명

ㅇ 솔라즈 議員의 駐韓美軍 駐屯 費用分擔 比率에 관한 質疑에 대해서 포드
副次官補는 韓國이 20% 정도를 負擔하고 있다고 答辯함.   끝.

0013

美 下院 外交委 亞.太 小委 聽聞會

91. 3. 7.

外 務 部

美 國務部 솔로몬 東亞.太 次官補와 포드 國防部 國際 安保
副次官補는 3.6. 下院 外交委 亞.太 小委에서 美國의 東亞.太
政策에 관해 證言한 바, 主要內容을 아래 報告드립니다.

1. 솔로몬 次官補 韓國 關聯 證言 要旨

o 美國은 韓國의 經濟.軍事力에 相應한 主導的 防衛 役割
   擔當을 장려하면서, 韓國과의 同盟關係를 強化할 것임

o 美軍의 前進 配置를 통해 世界安保는 물론 東亞.太 地域의
   均衡者로서의 役割을 遂行할 것임

o 韓國은 걸프戰에 있어 1, 2차에 걸쳐 總 5億弗의 支援을
   提供함.
   - 걸프戰 勃發後 最初로 輸送機를 提供하고, 醫療 支援團
      및 輸送 支援團을 派遣함

0014

o 北韓의 「韓半島 非核 地帶化」 提案은 核 억지력과 既存
   安保協力 體制를 沮害하므로 受諾할 수 없음.
   - 北韓이 IAEA의 核 安全 協定 署名을 거부하고 있으므로
      韓半島에서 核 擴散問題 발생시 북한의 책임임

o 90년중 3차례에 걸친 南.北 總理會談 開催는 고무적임
   - 그러나 北韓側이 팀스피리트를 구실로 對話를 中斷한
      것은 慨嘆스러움

o 自由貿易 原則을 바탕으로한 APEC과 같은 多者間 地域 經濟
   機構의 發展은 매우 고무적임

2. 質疑 應答 要旨

o 폴리에타 議員(民主, 펜실바니아)이 最近 韓國의 政治犯 問題
   等 民主化 努力이 後退하고 있다고 指摘하고, 與黨이 3黨
   統合을 통해 內閣制로 改憲, 一黨 統治를 圖謀하고 있다는
   憂慮를 表示함

o 이에 대해 솔로몬 次官補는, 韓國 政府가 北韓의 威脅에도
   불구, 86年以來 民主化를 推進中임을 強調하고, 最近 韓國
   政府의 政治犯 釋放과 美國 政府의 韓國內 政治犯에 대한
   持續的 關心 表明 事實을 言及함

0015

o 또한 포드 副次官補는 韓國이 過去와 같은 一人 統治로 復歸
   하기는 어려울 것이라 答辯함

o 솔라즈 議員이 韓國의 駐韓美軍 駐屯 費用分擔 比率을 質疑한
   데 대해, 포드 副次官補는 韓國이 20% 정도(日本은 약 50%)를
   負擔하고 있다고 答辯함

3. 美國의 東亞.太 政策 基調 提示

o 솔로몬 次官補는 7個項의 90년대 東亞.太 地域 政策 基調를
   아래와 같이 提示함
   - 地域安全 保障에 必要한 水準의 美 軍事力 調整 및 維持
   - 日本과의 世界的 同伴 協力關係 發展
   - 中國과의 强力한 政治.戰略的 關係 追求
   - 필리핀과의 持續的 防衛協力 構築을 위한 새로운 關係의
     樹立
   - 韓國의 防衛分擔 增大 및 韓.美 同盟關係 强化
   - 캄보디아 紛爭의 平和的, 包括的 解決
   - APEC를 통한 地域 經濟協力 促進   끝.

0016

관리
번호 91-651

외 무 부

종 별 : 지 급

번 호 : USW-1087   일 시 : 91 0306 2220

수 신 : 장관(미북,미안,중근동)

발 신 : 주 미 대사

제 목 : BUSH 대통령 대의회 연설

연: USW(F)-0779

1. 금 3.6 저녁 9 시 BUSH 대통령은 GULF 전에서의 승리를 보고하기 위한 대의회 연설을 가졌음(연설 전문 연호 FAX 참조)

2. 부쉬 대통령은 금일 저녁 연설도중 민주.공화를 막론하고 의원들로부터 수많은 환호와 박수를 받았으며, 의회 연설장(하원 CHAMBER)은 미국의 승리를 자축하고 대통령의 리더쉽에 경의를 표하는 애국적 분위기로 충만되었음.

3. 최근 미국 조야는 걸프전 종전과 함께 미국이 주도하는 새로운 세계 질서의 내용과 그간 소홀히 취급되어온 국내 문제에 대해 보다 구체적인 해답이 필요하다는 의견을 제기 하였었는바, 금일 부쉬 대통령은 동 2 가지 문제에 대해 나름대로 자신감있는 답변을 제시하고 향후 국제 문제를 이용한 민주당측의 역공가능성을 사전 봉쇄하는 효과를 기였다고 관찰됨.

-유엔의 창설 당시의 취지와 기능 회복, 정의와 인권이 보장되는 세계관 제시

-미국의 승리와 저력을 계속적인 미국의 발전과 국내 문제 해결에 연결, 자신감 표시

4. 한편, 그간 미 행정부는 이락의 쿠웨이트 침공과 이스라엘-아랍분쟁의 연계를 단호히 거부 해왔으며, 중동 지역의 여타 문제는 별도로 해결되어야한다는 입장을 취해 왔는바, 금일 부쉬 대통령은 최초로 동 분쟁을 해결할 시간이 도래했다는 미국의 전향적 정책 방향을 분명히 밝혔음.

5. 현재, 부쉬 대통령은 각종 여론 조사에 90 프로를 상회하는 지지도를 얻고 있으며, 차기 선거에서 부쉬 대통령의 승산은 확고하다는것이 현지 분위기인바, 이러한 분위기는 금일 연설에 대한 의회의 반응에서 잘 보여지고 있음.

6. 본직은 금일 여타 외교단과 함께 동 연설회에 참석하였음.

미주국	장관	차관	1차보	2차보	미주국	중아국	청와대	안기부

PAGE 1   91.03.07   13:40

(대사 박동진-국장)
91.6.30 까지

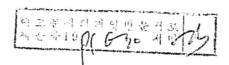

0018

걸프전의 대 미국정치 영향

(3.6.자 WP Broder 칼럼 및 NYT Wicker 칼럼 요약)

91. 3. 7.
북 미 과

o 걸프전 미국의 압승으로 끝난 이후 부쉬 대통령의 인기도는 90%이상으로 상승
하고 있으나 민주당에 대해서는 부쉬 대통령의 군사력 사용 승인 결의안 신청에
대한 민주당측 반대 투표 사실을 놓고 최근 민주당에 대한 신뢰성 및 통치 능력에
대한 미국민들의 의구심이 팽배하고 있음.

- 대의회 무력사용 결의안 승인 표결시 68%의 미국민이 무력사용을 지지했음
에도 불구, 민주당 상원의원 45명(55명중), 하원의원170명(267명중)이 반대
표결

o 월남전에서의 굴욕이후, 지난 20여년간 민주당은 국가안보 문제에 미온적이고
공화당측은 적극적이라는 미국민 일반의 인식이 증명된 대표적 사례가 금번
걸프전임.

o 민주당측은 상기 이미지 불식을 위해 Sam Nunn(GA) 상원 군사위원장, Lloyd
Bentsen(TX) 상원 재무위원장 및 Richard Gephardt(MO) 민주당 하원 원내총무가
주도하는 민주당 지도위원회(Democratic Leadership Council)을 중심으로 강력한
국방정책과 세계문제에 대한 적극적 개입 정책을 주창해 오긴 하였음.

0019

- 그러나 금번 걸프전시 부시 대통령의 정책에는 반대의사 표명

о 민주당측의 금번 잘못된 정책 결정은 민주당내 다음 인사들에 의해 재검토 되고
미국민들에 대한 해명이 이어져야 할 것임.
- Dante Fascell(Fla) 하원 외무위원장, Les Aspin(Wis) 하원 군사위원장 및
Albert Gore(Tenn), Bob Graham(Fla), Charles Robb(Va) 상원의원등

о 걸프전의 압승이후 92년 대선시 Bush 대통령의 러닝메이트로 Powell 합참의장이
좋을 것이라는 보도가 나오고 있음.
- WSJ/NBC News 합동 여론조사 결과

о 92년 대선시 Bush 대통령의 러닝메이트 결정시 가장 중요한 요소는 96년 대선시
공화당 후보로 등장이 가능한 인사라는 고려가 제일 중요함.
- 최근 대선시 대통령 후보가 부통령 후보 결정시 최우선 고려 요소
- 88대선시 Bush 대통령이 Quayle 부통령은 자신이 러닝 메이트로 결정하게
된 결정적 고려 요소는 레이건 행정부내 실속없는 2인자 위치에 염증을 느낀
나머지 자신보다 인기도나 능력면에서 출중치 않은 인사를 선택한다는 고려가
크게 작용
- Powell 의장이 정치력에 있어서는 아이젠하워 대통령 타입으로 전락할
가능성도 배제 불가하며, 부쉬대통령도 88년 자신의 결정이 잘못임을 인정치
않을것이므로 Quayle 의 재지명 가능성도 큼.

0020

: USW(F) - *0774*

: 장   관 (미불,총리)   '발신 : 주미대사

: 걸프戰 (美國 國內 政論)   (*6* 매)

— Bush 강력한 리더십
— Broder의 분석
Tom Wicker의 분석
4시내 → 국장실

Bush Popularity Surges With Gulf Victory

By David S. Broder and Richard Morin
Washington Post Staff Writers

President Bush goes before Congress and the country tonight as the most popular president in more than four decades but with voters still expressing great uncertainty about where he intends to lead the nation in the years ahead.

The president's overall job approval rating in the latest Washington Post-ABC News Poll, completed Monday, surged to 90 percent with the end of the Persian Gulf War, more than a 10-percentage-point increase since late January.

But as the Democratic-controlled Congress prepares tonight to give Bush accolades for his leadership in the war against Iraq, many in the national television audience indicate they are waiting to hear what comes next.

One out of five of those questioned in the poll (22 percent) said they had a "good idea" about where "Bush plans to lead the nation in the next two years," while 40 percent said they had little idea. Another 37 percent were

President Bush's address will be broadcast on the major networks tonight at 9.

in between, saying they had "just some" idea of what Bush wants to accomplish during the remainder of his first term.

The survey showed that domestic economic issues already have replaced the Persian Gulf crisis atop the public's list of the most important problems facing the country. Bush receives significantly lower ratings in that policy area, with only 49 percent expressing confidence in his handling of the economy and 47 percent saying they disapprove.

"He has an historic opportunity to define his goals," said Richard Fenno, a University of Rochester authority on the presidency and Congress. "We've had six weeks in which he set very clear objectives and exercised very strong leadership. Now is the time for him to expend some of the popularity he has gained in pursuit of a comparably large cause at home."

White House officials said yesterday that tonight's speech will be mainly about the war and foreign policy. The section on domestic policy, expected to be brief, may call on Americans to tackle social and economic problems in their communities with the same fervor and unity the war evoked. But these sources said it will not offer new proposals or new initiatives.

0774-1

While nine out of 10 of those polled said they think the economy is either stagnant or declining right now, seven out of 10 said they think the end of the war will have a positive effect in reviving its growth.

Bush's current approval rating tops the 87 percent peak for President Harry S. Truman shortly after the end of World War II, as recorded by the Gallup Organization, using a different survey method that may have slightly underestimated presidential support. Presidents Lyndon B. Johnson, John F. Kennedy and Franklin D. Roosevelt all had peak approval ratings in the low 80s in Gallup polls.

The support for Bush is strong and deep among virtually all demographic groups. He scored 90 percent among men and 89 percent among women; 85 percent among self-described liberals; 84 percent among Democrats; and 77 percent among blacks, who as a group were sharply divided over the war. In all these categories, large majorities characterized their support for the president as strong.

Follow-up interviews with persons questioned in the poll suggest Americans were most impressed with Bush's confident, deliberate and determined style of leadership following Iraq's invasion of Kuwait in August.

"I didn't vote for him but I would now," said Anna Hensley, 63, a lifelong Democrat who lives in Valrico, Fla. "He was always so positive. He wasn't going to take no for an answer. He was alway very serious and determined, and always made you feel he was so full of confidence."

Bush also made many Americans feel good about their country—and about politicians—again.

"I wanted to wear red, white and blue for the first time since the second World War," Hensley said. "I've never really felt strong about any politicians in a long time—not since Kennedy. . . . I do about Bush."

"I was really surprised how strong he was in making his decisions and not letting politics interfere," said Ray Guynes, 60, of Ca-

WP

manche, Iowa.

"I was in the service back in the 'Nam era," said Al Sharps, 41, of Boston, "It was good to see . . . the country behind the war, everyone behind the troops saying, 'Go out and get the job done.'"

But now that the war is over, most respondents in the poll remain unsure about what Bush sees as the job

> *"I didn't vote for him but I would now. He was always so positive."*
> —lifelong Democrat Anna Hensley

at hand. Even members of his own party are in the dark on their leader's agenda: Only 30 percent of the Republicans questioned said they clearly understood what the Bush administration wants to accomplish.

Still, the poll indicates most Americans appear willing to give the administration the benefit of the doubt on what Bush himself has called "the vision thing"—at least for the immediate future.

"I trust him, but no, I don't have a clear picture of what's ahead of us," said Marilyn Field, 50, of Chico, Calif. "But he has good people around, and he lets those good people around him handle things and he doesn't interfere."

Many expressed newfound confidence in Bush's ability to deal with the country's largest domestic problems.

The Post-ABC poll found that 70 percent of those questioned said the war with Iraq has made them more confident in "Bush's ability to handle the country's other big problems"—with nearly half saying the war has greatly increased their confidence in Bush.

0021

"I think he's a real problem solver," said Robert Murray, 28, of Dunkirk, N.Y. "He proved it with this war. If he could do this, he will have no problem working with other issues. He's one in a million and

Mar 6. 1991

and a challenge for Bush. "There's clearly a sense that when he knows what he wants to do, he knows how to do it," said Kirk O'Donnell, an aide to former speaker of the House Thomas P. "Tip" O'Neill Jr. and a longtime legislative strategist. "The question is whether he will attempt to translate the momentum he's developed in foreign affairs into change at home."

Kenneth Duberstein, White House chief of staff under President Ronald Reagan, said: "The window of opportunity is not very long, because the stage is moving quickly toward the politics of the campaign and all its divisiveness. He has to decide if he wants to be revered for his domestic accomplishments—or just for what he's done abroad."

By 60 to 28 percent, those surveyed said they regard Bush as a better hope than Congress to "do the things that are needed." And 84 percent said Bush is able to deal with the big issues facing this country, while 60 percent expressed similar confidence in Congress.

Continuing a pattern established in the early months of his presidency, Bush received his highest scores on foreign affairs, not domestic issues. According to the poll, 85 percent said they approved of the way Bush was managing foreign affairs, up from 76 percent in January. And 84 percent said they supported Bush's handling of the Soviet Union, up from 77 percent in the January survey. The numbers in the current poll represent new highs for the Bush administration.

The country's current mood of relief and euphoria has, at least temporarily, pulled up the president's ratings on a number of domestic problems other than the economy. The survey showed that 68 percent approved of the way Bush is handling race relations and 63 percent approved of his performance on environmental issues. Again, those results equal or surpass the administration's best showing on those issues in Post-ABC surveys.

Yet the nation's domestic agenda remains filled with difficult problems the public feels are not likely to be solved as quickly or convincingly as the war with Iraq.

The survey found that 81 percent of those questioned said the country was not making enough progress on the federal budget deficit. Another 81 percent said the country was moving too slowly against poverty; 79 percent said the country wasn't moving fast enough against crime; and 76 percent expressed displeasure over progress dealing with the drug problem.

And even in a time of peak popularity, not everyone is enthusiastic about Bush or the war. "George Bush is not good for the country" said Michelle Thompson, 32, of Queens, N.Y. "He worries me. He's quick to go to war. He just did it to boost the economy."

0774-2

0022

: USW(F) ‑

: 장   관   발신 : 주미대사

| 보안 | |
| 묵제 | |

(예)

WASHINGTON POST-ABC NEWS POLL

Q. Do you approve or disapprove of the way George Bush is handling his job as president?

	Approve	Disapprove
March 4, 1991		9%
Jan. 27, 1991	79	11%
Dec. 2, 1990	63	33%
Oct. 28, 1990	70	
Aug. 20, 1990		21%
July 24, 1990		
Jan. 16, 1990	74	14%
Feb. 14, 1989	64	22%

Q. Do you approve or disapprove of the way Bush is handling foreign affairs?

(Graph shows only the percentage who said they approve.)

5/23 6/19 10/3 1989 1/16 7/24 9/9 1990 1/27 3/4 1991

Q. Do you approve or disapprove of the way Bush is handling the nation's economy?

	Approve	Disapprove	Don't know
Mar. 4, 1991	49%	47%	4%
Jan. 27	45	49	6
Oct. 14, 1990	38	58	4
Sept. 9	53	41	6
July 24	46	51	3
Jan. 16	61	34	5
Oct. 3, 1989	64	31	5
June 16	61	34	5
May 23	61	35	4

Q. Now I want to ask you about a few issues facing the country. Please tell me whether you think the country is making enough progress or is not making enough progress on each one.

(Figures show only the percentage who think the country is "not making enough progress.")

	Mar. 4
Federal budget deficit	81%
Poverty	81
Crime	79
Illegal drugs	75
Health care	73
State of the country's economy	71
Public schools and education	70
Environment	61
Race relations	46
Respect for the United States abroad	26

Q. Do you think the Congress is able to deal with the big issues facing this country, or not?

	Mar. 4, '91	Oct. 7, '90
Yes	60%	54%
No	37	42
Don't know	3	4

Q. Do you think Bush is able to deal with the big issues facing this country, or not?

	Mar. 4
Yes	84%
No	15
Don't know	1

Q. Do you think you have a good idea, just some idea or not much of an idea of where Bush plans to lead the nation in the next two years?

	Mar. 4, '91	Feb. 4, '90	Apr. 3, '89	Jan. 16, '89
Good idea	22%	21%	19%	22%
Just some idea	37	44	31	30
Not much of an idea	40	34	48	45
Don't know	1	1	2	3

Q. Has the war with Iraq made you more confident in the ability of Bush to handle the country's other big problems, less confident, or hasn't it made much of a difference?

	Mar. 4
More confident	70%
Less confident	5
Not made much difference	24
Don't know	1

Q. When you think of the kinds of things you would like to see done in Washington, which of the following is closest to your view: A) President Bush will do the things that are needed but Congress won't; or B) Congress will do the things that are needed but President Bush won't?

	Mar. 4
Bush will do what is needed but Congress won't	60%
Congress will do what is needed but Bush won't	28
Neither of those things	5
Both of those things	5
Don't know	2

Note: Figures do not add to 100% in the first question because the percentage "don't know" is not shown. March 4 figures are based on a nationwide Washington Post-ABC News telephone poll of 1,215 randomly selected adults conducted March 1-4. All other polls are Washington Post-ABC News polls with samples ranging from 758 to 1,518. Margin of sampling error is plus or minus 3 percentage points for the March 4 poll, and plus or minus 3 to 5 percentage points for the other polls. Sampling error is, however, only one of many potential sources of error in these or any other public opinion polls. Interviewing was conducted by International Communications Research of Media, Pa., and Chilton Research of Radnor, Pa.

BY MICHAEL OREW—THE WASHINGTON POST

Mar. 6, 1991 0023

0774-3   WP

House Panel Approves $15.8 Billion To Help Cover Added Gulf War Costs

Israel Granted $650 Million Under Administration Request

By John E. Yang
Washington Post Staff Writer

The House Appropriations Committee yesterday voted to spend $15.8 billion to begin paying the U.S. share of the additional military and civilian costs of the Persian Gulf War, including $650 million in aid for Israel at the request of the Bush administration.

Before finally passing the supplemental spending measures on voice votes, the lawmakers also voted 37 to 12 to order Defense Secretary Richard B. Cheney to continue production of 12 F-14D Tomcat carrier-based fighter planes this year at a cost of $987 million. Cheney has been trying to kill the Navy program for two years.

The panel also approved $3.3 billion in extra fiscal 1991 spending for programs from food stamps and the unemployment insurance administration to cleaning up nuclear waste at military facilities.

The additional aid to Israel was approved by voice vote after only about two minutes of discussion, belying arduous negotiations over the matter among Secretary of State James A. Baker III, Israeli officials and congressional leaders.

The money is intended to help pay extra military costs related to the Persian Gulf War. As part of the deal, Israel has agreed not to seek additional U.S. assistance until after Sept. 2, only 28 days before the end of the current fiscal year.

"This is an agreement the administration supports and the government of Israel supports," said Rep. Mickey Edwards (Okla.), ranking GOP member of the House Appropriations subcommittee on foreign operations.

The money has been declared emergency spending and so would not count against the strict spending limits imposed by last year's budget agreement.

Baker had sought to pare the original Israeli request for about $1 billion in aid to $400 million in cash plus a gift, valued at between $400 million and $500 million, of the four Patriot missile batteries the United States sent there as protection against Iraqi Scud missiles, according to congressional officials. Israel

REP. MICKEY EDWARDS
... U.S., Israel back aid agreement

countered by asking for $750 million in cash and two Patriot batteries, the officials said.

Yesterday's agreement does not address the matter of the Patriots. "I'm sure they'll get them," said Rep. David R. Obey (D-Wis.), chairman of the foreign operations subcommittee. "I don't know how, but they'll get them."

Lawmakers had wanted to include money for Israel, but wanted the administration to request it. "Congress didn't want to take the lead," said Rep. Lawrence J. Smith (D-Fla.), a strong supporter of Israel. "Now it's a bipartisan issue."

Rep. Robert J. Mrazek (D-N.Y.) used the measure to tend to concerns closer to home, offering the language to protect the F-14 program. The carrier-based aircraft, which flew thousands of combat missions in the Persian Gulf War, is produced by Grumman Corp. near his Long Island district.

Mrazek, whose father worked at Grumman for more than 30 years, said he offered the amendment "in the name of simple fairness, in the name of simple justice." The planes were included in this year's military spending bill, but were canceled by Cheney.

Backing Mrazek, Rep. Joseph M. McDade (Pa.), the Appropriations Committee's ranking Republican, argued that cancellation of the project would leave only one company—McDonnell Douglas Corp.—in the business of producing Navy aircraft. "We want to make sure all the doors are not closed," he said.

Work on the F-14 is also done at a Grumman facility in Salisbury, Md.

The Persian Gulf War supplemental spending measure appropriates $15 billion as a down payment on the nation's war bills until more of the $54.5 billion in foreign pledges of cash, equipment and services comes in. As of late last month, allies had paid the United States $12.2 billion in cash and $2.7 billion in equipment and services for the war effort; $39.6 billion remained to be paid.

Although no final tally of costs is yet possible, the measure would appropriate as much as $42.6 billion in U.S. funds and foreign gifts. That figure uses an estimate of $6.3 billion for combat costs by the House Appropriations subcommittee on defense. However, Office of Management and Budget Director Richard G. Darman, speaking with reporters in a break during testimony to the House Ways and Means Committee, yesterday set the combat figure at about $30 billion.

Although putting the amount in two separate bills, the panel fully funded the Army's request for $324 million to buy 500 additional Patriot missiles.

The regular supplemental bill unrelated to the war includes $609,000 so the Agriculture Department can take over meat and poultry inspection services in Maryland. The state is ending its inspection services April 1.

The panel also added language, offered by Rep. Harold Rogers (R-Ky.) that would prohibit prisoners from collecting witness fees. "If we can't get honoraria, they damn well shouldn't either," quipped Rep. Joe Skeen (R-N.M.). **0024**

Staff writer Steven Mufson contributed to this report.

0774-16   Mar. 6 1991   110

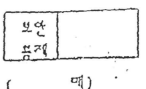

: USW(F) –

: 경 관   발신 : 주미대사   보안 / 품질

(매)

David S. Broder

Think Again, Democrats

The Democrats reacted with understandable anger last week when Sen. Phil Gramm (R-Texas), the chairman of the Republican Senatorial Campaign Committee, charged that their votes in January against authorizing the use of force in the Persian Gulf "showed the nation once again that Democrats cannot be trusted to define the destiny of America."

Rep. Vic Fazio (D-Calif.), the chairman of the Democratic Congressional Campaign Committee, predicted there would be "a backlash" against Gramm's effort "to wring partisan advantage out of an issue which was debated with great conscientiousness. . . ."

But Gramm was not impressed. "Saying it was 'a matter of conscience,' " he told me, "just makes it more important in judging where Democrats would lead the country. On the most important foreign policy vote in years, the entire leadership and the vast majority of the membership on the Democratic side voted to deny the president his request for authority to use force against Saddam Hussein. That is something they have to explain."

Gramm has a point. The Democratic opposition to this war was deep and passionate. It was rooted in conscience and in conviction. It was not simply political. In the week of the congressional vote last January, a Washington Post-ABC News Poll showed 63 percent of those interviewed favored going to war with Iraq once the Jan. 15 deadline for withdrawal from Kuwait had passed, and 68 percent wanted Congress "more actively supporting" President Bush's policy, against 20 percent who wanted it to show more opposition.

Nonetheless, even in the face of public opinion and the president's request, 45 of 55 Democratic senators voted against the use of force, as did 179 of 265 Democrats in the House. So much has happened since that Jan

... withdraw to include Israel, Turkey or other allies; the long-term American occupation of Iraq; increased instability in the Persian Gulf region; long-standing Arab enmity against the United States; a return to isolationism at home. All of those risks are there."

Those were not idle words, any more than this was a routine vote. Constituents will ultimately judge for themselves the weight they give to this particular vote against all the rest of their representative's or senator's service. But there are at least two good reasons why the Democrats need to revisit this issue now, rather than sweep it under the rug or try to shift the focus immediately to domestic policy, as so many of them are doing.

The first reason has to do with their credibility and their capacity to govern. It is historical fact—not partisan rhetoric—that the Vietnam War sundered the Democratic Party and rendered it incapable of governing for close to 20 years. It drove Lyndon Johnson from the White House in 1968 and so divided the party that—with one exception—no Democrat since has been able to win the presidency. Jimmy Carter their only winner ...

... five years ago, many Democrats recognized the need to come to terms with the legacy of Vietnam. Leading congressional figures—notably Sens. Sam Nunn (D-Ga.) and Lloyd Bentsen (D-Texas) and Rep. Dick Gephardt (D-Mo.)—formed the Democratic Leadership Council as a voice for Democrats who favored a strong defense and an active U.S. involvement in the world.

But in the Gulf crisis, those Democratic leaders—and many others—opposed the president when he said the time had come to use force. At a minimum, those in that camp—and they include the top leaders of the Senate and the House—need to reexamine their own thinking and explain to the public what they have learned from the war.

They can be led in that reevaluation by those whose judgment has been vindicated—by the chairmen of the House Foreign Affairs and Armed Services committees, Reps. Dante Fascell (D-Fla.) and Les Aspin (D-Wis.) and by such senators as Albert Gore (D-Tenn.), Bob Graham (D-Fla.) and Charles Robb (D-Va.). It may be that they grasp some things that ...

... Republicans alone.

The concern many Democrats expressed in the Gulf debate may have been misplaced, but they are relevant to other situations in other parts of the world. The question of whether, when and how the United States should intervene remains a critical decision. The Democrats were wrong on the Gulf. They need to think again—and then rejoin the national debate.

02211-5   WP March 6, 1991 0025

: USM(F) -

: 장 관   발신 : 주미대사   보안 품?

(매)

IN THE NATION | Tom Wicker
The Dream Ticket

The Dream Ticket, that perennial fantasy of American politics, is again showing a pretty face and an alluring smile. This time the dream has President Bush paired with Gen. Colin Powell, the black Chairman of the Joint Chiefs of Staff, as his running mate in 1992.

Now that General Powell has directed the military to its runaway victory in the Persian Gulf war, this Dream Ticket is even more attractive than when first proposed in 1988. The general was then only Ronald Reagan's national security adviser.

Before that, the last real Dream Ticket was conjured up in 1968 — Gov. Nelson Rockefeller of New York paired with Gov. Ronald Reagan of California, left and right, East and West, the two biggest states, victory guaranteed. There were only two problems — the two Governors, neither of whom wanted any part of the other or second place on the ticket.

The Bush-Powell entry would not have such problems, since the two principals obviously admire each other and Mr. Bush is already President. As is usually the case with Dream Tickets, however, this one may look better in the airy precincts of imagination than in real political life.

General Powell is certainly an attractive figure, an able and popular man. His presence at Mr. Bush's side would emphasize Republican claims to greater reliability on national security issues. He probably would lure a number of black voters away from their strong allegiance to the Democrats; but his military background would reassure Republicans who might be wary of supporting a conventional black politician.

General Powell's service in two Republican Administrations should allay any lingering doubts about his political affiliation; and a Wall Street Journal/NBC News poll showed heavy Republican support for him on the 1992 ticket. But attractive though it undoubtedly is, the Dream Ticket has its problems — both in itself and in the practicalities of putting it together.

For one thing, Mr. Bush — from the evidence of the polls — needs neither another man's popularity nor a general's backing. George Bush himself was Commander in Chief during the gulf war, and his conduct of it has left him with exceptionally high political standing, to which General Powell can add little.

A Bush-Powell ticket might even be considered a cynical exploitation of the war's political spoils and an implicit promise of a militaristic foreign policy. Republicans hardly need a general on their ticket to claim that they're tough and the Democrats soft on national security; they've success-

fully touted that line for 20 years and now can adduce as evidence the gulf war and Democratic opposition to it.

The Dream Ticket also would give greater credence to the Democrats' certain charge that Mr. Bush has no interest in or program to cure the nation's domestic ills. And black voters are unlikely to be swayed massively by one black on one Republican ticket, against Mr. Bush's poor record on civil rights issues.

General Powell campaigning as a Republican in 1992 — how much bloom would that take off the military rose? — might win over enough blacks who otherwise would have voted Democratic to swing a close election; but a close election doesn't appear to be in the cards. And Republicans who care about the black vote need a long-term party approach to serving blacks' needs and interests, not one spectacular gesture of questionable sincerity.

One reason Dan Quayle was chosen for the Bush ticket in 1988, moreover, is reported to have been that Mr. Bush was tired of being second banana in the Reagan Administration

Bush-Powell in '92? Not likely.

and did not want a running mate of equal or greater stature. If so, that does not augur for dropping Mr. Quayle and supplanting him with the impressive General Powell this time around; nor can Mr. Bush want to invite the charge that his judgment was wrong in 1988.

If recent history is a guide, Mr. Bush's second-term Vice President may well be the party's Presidential nominee in 1996. Would the powerful Republican right wing, which regards Mr. Quayle as its voice in the Administration, prefer General Powell as a future Presidential nominee? How do they know he won't turn out to be more like Dwight Eisenhower than Ronald Reagan?

President Bush saw to it, moreover, that Mr. Quayle was pictured constantly with the inner circle that ran the gulf war; and in recent decades the visibility and standing of the Vice Presidency itself has been greatly enhanced. For all these reasons, dropping Mr. Quayle might be too costly to be offset by anything that even Colin Powell could add to a Bush ticket. 0026

0774-6 (END)

Mar. 6, 1991 NYT

외   무   부

종   별 :

번   호 : USW-1117   일   시 : 91 0308 1532

수   신 : 장 관(미북,미안,중동일)

발   신 : 주 미 대사

제   목 : 걸프전 관련 추가 세출 예산법안 하원 통과

1. 하원 세출위는 3.7. 걸프전비 지출 및 대이스라엘 원조를 위한 158억불 규모의 추가 세출 예산법안 (SUPLLEMENTAL APPROPIRATIONS BILL:HR 1281 ,1282) 을 각각 찬반 380:19 및 365:43 으로 통과시켰음. 동법안에 의하면 상기 금액중 150억불은 국방부의 직접적 전비 지출을 위해, 나머지 8억불은 기타 관련 민간경비 지출에 사용될것이 라함.

2. 상기 2개법안 통과후 JIM CHAPMAN 의원 (D-TEX) 의 발의로 여타 걸프전 재정 공여국들의 기여금 제공을 촉구하는 내용의 별도 하원결의안 (SENSE OF CONGRESSRESOLUTION) 이 채택되었는바, 동결의안은 재정 공여국들이 기 약속한 기여금을 4.15 까지 제공치 않을 경우 의회가 적절한 조치를 취할 것이라 (THE CONGRESS MAYCONSIDER APPROPRIATE ACTION) 는 경고를 담고 있으나, 동 조치의 구체적 내용에 관해 서는 명시하고 있지 않음.

3. 상기 법안 통과 관련 기사와 결의안 사본별전 FAX 송부함.

첨부 : USW(F)-799

(대사 박동진 국장)

미주국   1차보   미주국   중아국   정문국   안기부

PAGE 1   91.03.09   09:35 WG

외신 1과 통제관

0027

CHAPMA023

[3/4/91]

AMENDMENT TO H.R. 128, AS REPORTED
OFFERED BY MR. CHAPMAN

At an appropriate place in the bill, insert the following new section:

1   SEC. ____. (a) The Congress finds that--

2   (1) United States and coalition armed forces devoted

3   enormous human and financial resources to the successful

4   effort to free Kuwait from illegal Iraqi occupations,

5   enforce United Nations resolutions, and preserve the

6   territorial integrity of the Gulf States;

7   (2) Americans take great pride in the troops who won

8   this historic victory and honor those who gave their

9   lives to liberate Kuwait and turn back aggression;

10   (3) major trading nations of the world will benefit

11 substantially and directly from the coalition victory in

12 this strategic area;

13   (4) six nations have pledged $53,500,000,000 in

14 contributions to help meet the costs of the coalition

15 effort;

16   (5) some nations have been slow to honor those

17 commitments for 1990; and

799-3   0028

CHAPMA023

2

1   (6) the 1991 commitments are agreed to be due on

2   March 31, 1991.

3   (b) Having appropriated significant supplemental funding

4   for the United States Armed forces in the Gulf region in a

5   time of recession and budget deficits, it is the sense of the

6   Congress that--

7   (1) these pledges of financial support from the

8   allied nations are appreciated;

9   (2) nations that have made such pledges are urged to

10 comply with them at the earliest possible time, with

11 substantial compliance or an agreed upon payment schedule

12 no later than April 15, 1991;

13   (3) these commitments shall be ~~upheld~~ Fulfilled; and

14   (4) if these commitments are not met the Congress may

15 consider appropriate action.

791-4   0029

報 告 事 項

報告畢 ✓

1991. 3. 9.
美 洲 局
北 美 課(16)

題 目 : 걸프戰 追加 歲出法案 美 下院 通過

美 下院은 3.7(木) 158億弗 規模의 걸프戰 關聯 追加歲出法案 通過시켰는
바, 關聯事項 아래 報告드립니다.

---

1. 걸프戰 關聯 追加歲出法案(380:19로 通過)

   o 規 模 : 158億弗(걸프戰 戰費 150億弗, 기타 民間費用 8億弗)

   o 545億弗 規模의 友邦國 寄與 約束額을 優先 使用後 158億弗의 美 豫算은
     차후 使用한다는 걸프戰 戰費使用 節次를 명시
     - 우방국 약속 545억불중 현재 169억불만 입금

   o Jim Chapman(民主, TX)議員 發議에 따라 91.4.15 이전 友邦國이 寄與를
     約束한 支援額 未 執行時 美 議會는 적절한 措置를 講究할 것이라는
     修正案을 첨부함.
     - 우방국들의 기여 약속액 집행 지연에 대한 의회내 불만 분위기 반영

2. 對이스라엘 追加援助

   o 美 議會는 동시에 91 會計年度 追加歲出法案中 6億5千万弗 규모의
     對이스라엘 追加援助를 包含, 通過시킴.
     - 미국은 이미 이스라엘에 대해 매년 30억불 규모의 원조를 제공중

                                                              - 끝 -

0030

House, Voting $15 Billion for War, Warns Allies to Pay Their Part

By ADAM CLYMER
Special to The New York Times

WASHINGTON, March 7 — The House of Representatives voted tonight to appropriate $15 billion to pay for the Persian Gulf war after warning other countries to pay up on their pledges of aid and promising that Congress "may consider appropriate action" if those commitments were not fulfilled.

The sense of Congress resolution was added to a $4.3 billion supplemental appropriation bill intended to pay some of the non-domestic costs of the gulf war, provide aid to Israel, and pay for a variety of programs from Food Stamps to nuclear waste cleanup to veterans pensions.

The $15 billion measure, adopted by a 380-to-19 vote, also spelled out procedures for using those contributions from other countries first and the United States dollars last.

The warning to other nations was adopted on a voice vote, despite a cautioning by Representative Jamie L. Whitten, Democrat of Mississippi and chairman of the House Appropriations Committee, that "we'll get more money if we don't threaten them."

Complaints on Pledges

The resolution was proposed by Representative Jim Chapman, Democrat of Texas, who complained about "allied pledges that the checks are in the mail." Other countries have pledged $54.5 billion in contributions to help pay for the war, but only $16.9 billion of it has been paid so far. Neither his proposal nor the debate offered any suggestions about what Congress might do if other countries did not meet the demand to achieve "substantial compliance of an agreed upon payment schedule no later than April 15."

After passage by a vote of 365 to 43, the supplemental appropriation bill went to the Senate, where complaints about slow payments from allies have also been voiced angrily and frequently.

On the aid for Israel, there were about two hours of debate before the 397-to-24 vote for $650 million for that country came. Most of the speakers supported the aid and wanted to get on record with their arguments that Israel, a steadfast ally of the United States, had suffered losses of at least that much because of the war — from damage by Scud missiles to a continual air force alert to the distribution of gas masks.

On Israelis' Defense

The opponents generally insisted that they were supporters of Israel. But they said the $3 billion Israel now gets annually was enough. Representative Tim Valentine, Democrat of North Carolina, who offered the amendment, said more aid for Israel was inappropriate "when we are struggling under the weight of a recession."

But Representative Charles E. Schumer, Democrat of Brooklyn, insisted, "The Israelis simply want the wherewithal to defend themselves as the rest of the world turns against them."

And Representative David R. Obey, the Wisconsin Democrat who heads the appropriations subcommittee on foreign operations, said he supported the aid. He said the Administration needed support as it sought peace in the Mideast.

He did complain that the original Israeli request for $3 billion was "outlandish."

The aid to Israel was adopted under a provision of last year's budget act, under which "emergency" needs were exempt from the spending limits set at that time. Representative Robert H. Michel of Illinois, the House Republican leader, voted for the aid to Israel, but warned against using the concept too loosely: "Let's not let the word 'emergency' fall victim to semantic inflation."

The $650 million for Israel was included in a grab-bag $4.3 billion appropriations bill which also included $151 million to offset various domestic costs arising out of the war, especially security expenses for the F.B.I., the Secret Service, the Capitol Police and the District of Columbia police force.

There were also war-related appropriations of $200 million for maintenance of military depots and $270 million for health care costs for the military and their dependents.

The other big items in the bill were $1.5 billion for food stamps, $601 million for nuclear waste cleanup, $302 million for veterans pensions, $232 million for supplemental security income payments by the Social Security Administration, $200 million to help states pay the costs of administering the unemployment compensation program, and $100 million for an increased Federal payment to the District of Columbia.

The bill also directed the Department of Defense to go ahead with a $988 million program of modernizing 12 Grumman F-14A aircraft, a plan the Pentagon seeks to cancel. It also told the department to spend previously appropriated funds on the vertical takeoff Osprey aircraft, another project the Pentagon resists.

Tourism and Public Housing

The House did move to cut spending on one matter. At the urging of Representative Jim Slattery, Democrat of Kansas, it voted 271 to 111 to repeal one of the most embarrassing items Congress financed last year, a $500,000 appropriation to develop a tourist center around the restored birthplace of Lawrence Welk in Strasburg, N.D. "No issue caused us more grief last year," complained Representative Dan Glickman, also a Kansas Democrat.

Despite Wednesday night's appeal by President Bush for fast Congressional action on his domestic agenda, the House rejected, by a 246 to 177 vote, an effort to start spending money quickly on various new housing programs he pushed last year, including one that would enable public housing tenants to buy the housing they now rent.

Representative Newt Gingrich, the Georgian who serves as Republican whip, urged passage of a plan to shift $779 million in funds already appropriated for other housing programs to these plans. "How can you turn the President down." But Representative Bill Green, Republican of Manhattan, said local communities were not ready to implement the new legislation and the proposal would "start the program off on the wrong foot by trying to force feed them."

House Votes Funds to Pay for War

$15.8 Billion From U.S. Allocated; Efforts to Cut Israel Aid Rejected

By John E. Yang
Washington Post Staff Writer

The House voted yesterday to spend $15.8 billion to begin paying the U.S. military and civilian costs of the Persian Gulf War after overwhelmingly rejecting attempts to cut aid to Israel.

The twin supplemental spending bills would allocate $42.6 billion—$15 billion in U.S. funds and the rest from foreign gifts—to pay the Pentagon's costs of the war, and about $800 million to pay various civilian expenses.

The bills include $3.3 billion in extra fiscal 1991 spending for such domestic programs as food stamps, higher-than-expected unemployment insurance costs and $30 million in drought relief for California.

The military spending bill passed 380 to 19 and the companion measure was approved 365 to 43.

During yesterday's day-long House consideration, lawmakers voted 397 to 24 to defeat a move by Rep. Tim Valentine (D-N.C.) to strip the bill of $650 million in additional aid to Israel that the Bush administration has sought.

"I do not believe the majority of Americans share the wish of this Congress to grant [the money] to the government of Israel... when we are struggling under the weight of a recession," Valentine said. "We cannot afford to support the economies of other nations when our own economy is hurting."

Valentine said the target of his amendment was foreign aid, not Israel. "Foreign aid is completely out of control and an overwhelming majority of Americans are disgusted," he said.

But other lawmakers argued that the aid for Israel, the target of more than three dozen Iraqi-launched Scud missiles during the gulf war, was needed to help bring peace to the troubled region.

"Israel's security, Israel's strength are essential to peace in the Middle East," said Rep. Mickey Edwards (Okla.), the ranking Republican on the House Appropriations subcommittee on foreign operations.

"This is part of the price we're going to have to pay," said Rep. David R. Obey (D-Wis.), chairman of the subcommittee.

On voice votes, lawmakers subsequently defeated a series of attempts by Rep. James A. Traficant Jr. (D-Ohio), a strident opponent of foreign aid, to cut the Israel funding to $400 million, $600 million and then $637 million.

Israel had sought as much as $1 billion to meet its additional military costs resulting from the war. As part of a deal with the Bush administration, worked out after long negotiations, Israel has agreed not to seek additional U.S. aid until after Sept. 2, only 28 days before the end of this fiscal year.

Despite lobbying from Housing and Urban Development Secretary Jack Kemp, the House voted 240 to 177 to reject an amendment offered by Reps. Jim Kolbe (R-Ariz.) and James P. Moran (D-Va.) to shift nearly $800 million from public housing programs in order to fund new Kemp initiatives designed to help the poor buy their own housing and have more choice in rental housing.

Rep. Bill Green (N.Y.), the ranking GOP member of the House Appropriations subcommittee on HUD, argued that it would be better to consider funding these programs in fiscal 1992, which begins Oct. 1, rather than rush to implement them now.

Bandleader Lawrence Welk fared no better. On an unusual standing vote, the House adopted, 71 to 11, an amendment offered by Rep. Jim Slattery (D-Kan.) killing a $500,000 federal grant that would have tried to make a tourist attraction out of the Strasburg, N.D., sod farmhouse where Welk was raised.

The Persian Gulf War supplemental spending measure appropriates $15 billion in U.S. funds as a down payment of the nation's war bills until more of the foreign pledges—now in excess of $50 billion—are fulfilled. The administration's most recent accounting shows $14.2 billion in cash on hand from the allies.

The report accompanying the legislation notes: "The American people have a right to expect that all financial commitments will be honored expeditiously."

In addition, the House on a voice vote adopted nonbinding language offered by Rep. Jim Chapman (D-Tex.) to set an April 15 deadline for the foreign contributions. If that date is not met, "Congress may consider appropriate action," the amendment said.

W.P.
3/8/91

799-2

0032

관리 번호	91-718

외 무 부

종 별 :

번 호 : USW-1213   일 시 : 90 1315 1141

수 신 : 장관(미북,미안,중동일,기정)

발 신 : 주 미 대 사

제 목 : 걸프전 이후 중동정세 관련 상원 외교위 청문회(1)

　　상원 외교위(위원장:PELL 의원) 는 3.13(수) 오후 걸프전 이후 중동정세와 미국의 정책방향에 관한 청문회를 개최한바, 동 청문회에 출석, 증언한 PHEBE MARR 국방대학 전략연구소 연구원, JOSEPH NYE 하바드대 국제문제 연구소장 및 WILLIAM QUANDT 브루킹스 연구원의 발언요지 아래 보고함(증언문 차파편 송부 예정)

　　가. 걸프전후 이락의 장래(PHEBE MARR 증언)

　　1)걸프지역 일반 정세 전망

　　0 사우디의 정치, 사회적 변화를 기대해 볼수도 있으나 변화의 정도는 미미할것임. 중산층으로 부터의 개방과 참여 요구가 증대될 것이나, 아직은 이슬람 보수 세력의 영향력이 강하므로 사우디 지배층은 결국 이들 양세력간 균형을 유지하는 정책을 취하게 될것임.

　　0 이란은 전후 걸프지역의 새로운 안보체제에서 나름대로의 역할을 기대할것이며, 미국-사우디 동맹에 의한 주도권 행사를 견제하고자 할것인바, 이란이 새로운 안보체제에서 배제될 경우 동 체제의 붕괴를 기도하거나 이 지역에서의 미군사력 제거 또는 감축을 위한 외교 공세를 취할것임.

　　0 역내 대부분의 국가(특히 이락) 에서 인종, 종파간 분쟁이 증대 될것이며, 이슬람 재건운동(ISLAMIC REVIVALISM)도 활발한 정치적 움직임의 하나가 될것임. 그러나, 무엇보다도 이락과 쿠웨이트의 체제변혁 가능성과 그 여파는 이 지역정세 불안의 가장 큰 요인이 될것임.

　　2) 이락의 장래와 미국의 정책방향

　　0 전후 이락의 장래와 관련, 가능한 시나리오는 다음과 같음.

　　- 후세인이 추종세력을 규합, 내분을 진압하고 정권유지 (단, 후세인의 계속 집권은 미국과 참전국의 협조하에서만 가능)

미주국 안기부	장관	차관	1차보	2차보	미주국	중아국	정문국	청와대

- 군사 쿠테타에 의한 후세인 제거(이락 정규군, 특히 수니파 장교들이 쿠데타 가능세력이나 아직은 집권 기반 취약)

- BATH 당내 민간 세력의 집권(후세인에 대한 신뢰 추락은 필연적으로 당의 영향력 약화를 초래 하였다는 점이 취약 요인)

- 지속적 민중 봉기로 인한 체제 변화(이란의 영향력 증대 가능성 및 이락의 내부 분열 촉진 위험 상존)

O 상기 어느 경우가 되든 미국의 대이락 정책은 아래 사항이 고려된 것이어야 함.

- 이락의 내부 분열과 혼란은 걸프지역의 불안은 물론 조속한 미군 철수에도 장애가 되므로 미국의 국익을 위해서는 이락의 영토 보전을 최대한 지원해야 함.

-외부 세력을 업고 등장한 집권 세력이 안정을 유지하고 권력을 공고히 할 가능성은 거의 없으므로, 이락 내부 문제에 대한 공개적 개입은 피해야 하며, 이락의 장래는 이락 국민에게 맡겨야 함.

-막대한 전쟁 피해로 상당수 이락 국민의 대미 감정이 악화되었을 가능성을 고려, 인도적 차원에서 대이락 원조를 통해 이를 무마하는 노력이 필요함.

- 이락내 특정 집권 기도 세력을 지원도 반대도 하지 않으면서 미국이 원하는 방향으로 신정부의 노선을 이끌어 갈수 있는 방안을 모색해야함.

3)쿠웨이트 의 장래와 미국의 정책 방향

O 쿠웨이트 내 정치세력의 분열과 상호 대립으로 다소 파란은 예상되나 전후 쿠웨이트의 정치체제 변화와 개방된 사회로의 발전 가능성은 충분히 있음. 미국은 신중하고 사려깊게 이러한 방향으로의 발전을 지원해야함.

O 쿠웨이트와 이락, 요르단, 팔레스타인과의 긴장 관계는 상당기간 지속될것이나, 쿠웨이트가 보다 관용적 자세를 취하도록 미국의 막후 후원 역할이 바람직함.

나. 걸프 지역의 군비확산 봉제(JOSEPH NYE 증언)

O 걸프전의 승리로 미국이 지나친 자만심에 빠져 장기적 국익을 간과하는 위험을 경계해야 함. 군사력과 경제력에 의존한 HARD POWER 와 지휘 보다는 공동모색(CO-OPT. RATHER THAN COMMAND)하는 능력, 즉 SOFT POWER 를 적절히 활용할때 미국의 국익 증진을 기할수 있음.

O 걸프 사태에 직면, 미국이 사우디에 조속 군대를 파견할수 있을만큼 HARDPOWER 를 보유하고 있었다는 것도 중요하지만, 유엔의 대이락 제재 결의안을 이끌어 낼수 있는 SOFT POWER 를 겸비하고 있었다는 것도 그에 못지않게 중요한것임.

O 군사기술의 확산 방지와 여타 외교목표 사이에는 항상 TRADE-OFF 가 있게마련이므로 , 일단기술이 확산된후 그여파(DESTABILIZING EFFECT)를 줄이기 위한 보다 현실적인 목표에 촛점을 맞추어야 함.

O 이를 위해서는 NPT, IAEA 와 같은 기존협력 체제를 통한 통제 노력과 병행하여 인접 핵 위협국간 상호 신뢰 증대를 위한 지역협력 및 정보 수집 능력 제고, 조기 경보체제, COCOM 과 같은 수출통제 체제의 확대 노력등이 긴요함.

다. 아랍. 이스라엘 분쟁해결(WILLIAM QUANDT 증언)

O 걸프전은 과거 냉전 체제하에서의 제약 요소에 벗어나 아랍. 이스라엘 분쟁해결을 도모할수 있는 유리한 환경을 조성 하였음.

O 그러나, 사다트 와 같은 지도자 가 현재 아랍권에 없다는 점과 대부분의 아랍국가들이 대이스라엘 평화 협상에 참여를 꺼릴 것이라는 점, 걸프전으로 인한 팔레스타인과 요르단의 정치적 발언권 약화(IN THE POLITICAL DOGHOUSE) 및 현 이스라엘 정권의 강경 노선등이 협상에 장애 요인이 될것임.

O 미국의 리더쉽과 이집트의 역할, 팔레스타인, 요르단의 PEACE PROCESS 에의 참여가 협상 성패의 관건이 될것임.

(대사대리 김봉규- 국장)

91.12.31. 까지

검보필 (1. 0(. 6

외 무 부

관리번호 91-716

종   별 : 지 급

번   호 : USW-1214

일   시 : 91 0315 1141

수   신 : 장관(미북, 미안, 중동일, 기정)

발   신 : 주 미 대사

제   목 : 걸프전 이후 중동 정세 관련 상원 외교위 청문회(2)

연 USW-1213

연호 청문회 증언에 이어 진행된 질의 답변 요지 아래임.

1. 아랍, 이스라엘 잠정 협정 전망(PELL 위원장 질의)

0 요르단과 팔레스타인이 공동 협상팀을 구성하고, 이스라엘이 WEST BANK 에서의 지방 선거 또는 GAZQA STRIP 에 대한 영유권 문제 협상 용의등 전향적 태도를 보일 경우, 가능하다고봄(QUANDT)

2. 협상 성공시 결과 전망(PELL 위원장 질의)

0 이스라엘, 팔레스타인, 요르단 3 국간 느슨한 연합체(THREE-WAY ENTITY WITH THEIR DILUTED OPLITICAL LINES)형태의 국가를 상정할수 있을것임(QUANDT)

0 전통적인 주권 국가와는 다른 형태가될것으로 보나 현재로서는 협상의 결과 보다는 시작에 더 큰 중요성을 부여해야함(NYE)

3. 협상에서 KURDS 를 배제한 미 행정부의 결정이 옳은것이지(PELL 위원장 질의)

0 미국은 모든 정치 세력과 대화해야하며, KURDS 도 PEACE PROCESS 에 참여시켜야함(QUANDT, NYE, MARR)

4. 대중 H 동 무기 수출구간 카르텔 구성필요 여부(BIDEN 의원 질의)

0 무기 수출에 대한 모라토리움이 필요한 시점이며, 이란과 이락이 우선 고려 대상이라고봄(NYE)

5. 중동 평화 협상을 위한 고위 사절 파견 필요여부(SIMM 의원 질의)

0 미국이 진지한 자세로 회담에 임하고 있음을 보여주기 위해 고위급 사절이 파견되어야함(QUANDT)

0 SIMON 의원은 자신이 최근 행정부측에 슐차 전 국무장관을 추천한바 있다고 언급.

미주국	장관	차관	1차보	2차보	미주국	중아국	청와대	안기부

PAGE 1

91.03.16   05:21

외신 2과 통제관 CE

0036

6. 이락과 쿠웨이트에서의 미국의 역할(PRESSLER 의원 질의)

0 미국은 이락을 MICRO-MANAGE 해서는 안되며, 그렇게 될 경우 이락 내부의결과에 대한 책임을 져야하는 위험 부담을 안게 될뿐 아니라 이락을 또하나의 레바논화 하는 결과를 초래할지도 모름(QUANDT)

0 미국이 쿠웨이트의 민주화를 위해 압력을 행사해야 한다는 주장(NYE) 에 대해, QUANDT 는 압력 보다는 막후에서 조용히 지원하는것이 바람직하다고 반박함.

(대사 대리 김봉규-국장)

예고:91.12.31 까지지방 선거 또는 GAZQA STRIP 에 대하

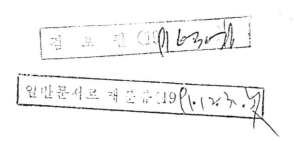

PAGE 2

주 미 대 사 관

미국(의) 700- 585

1991. 3. 15.

수신 : 장 관
참조 : 미주국장, 중동국장
제목 : 걸프전 이후 중동정세 관련 의회 청문회

연 : USW - 1213, 1214

　　연호 청문회 증언문 2부 (Quandt 브루킹스 연구원은 텍스트 없이
증언) 와 Pell 상원 외교위원장의 모두발언문을 별첨 송부하니 참고하시기
바랍니다.

첨부 : 상기 증언문 2부 및 Pell 위원장 모두발언문.　　　끝.

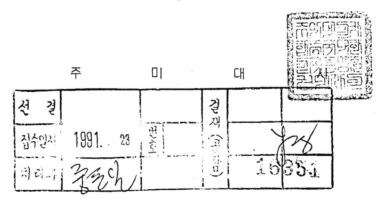

0038

Chairman's Opening Statement
Post War Issues in the Middle East
March 13, 1991

Today the Foreign Relations Committee begins a series of
hearings on the post-war situation in the Persian Gulf and the
new world order sought by President Bush. After the recess we
will hear from Secretary Baker. Other hearings will address
regional security issues, war crimes, third world
militarization, the future of the United Nations and the
international environmental agenda for the 1990's.

Today's hearing will cover three critical issues emerging
from the post-war situation in the Middle East. These are: (1)
the political future of Iraq, (2) the prospects for containing
a new arms race of both conventional and unconventional
weapons, and (3) the opportunity for a new effort to settle the
Arab-Israel dispute. We have a panel exceptionally well
qualified to discuss these issues.

As to the future of Iraq, I hope we will support a more
pluralistic and democratic alternative to Saddam Hussein and to
the Ba'ath party regime. For most of its modern history Iraq
has been ruled by dictators from the 15 percent Sunni Arab
minority. A more pluralistic system could better accommodate
the interests of the long repressed non-Arab Kurdish population
and the majority Shi'a population.

0033

I understand Saudi Arabia is promoting its own alternative to Saddam Hussein. While I have great respect for our Saudi allies, democracy is not one of their areas of expertise. The Saudi alternative should not necessarily be ours. And in this connection, I regret the Administration's decision not even to speak to the representatives of the Iraqi Kurds or of the Iraqi opposition coalition.

It is interesting to note that all the countries that supplied Saddam Hussein's armies were part of the coalition against Iraq. Unrestrained arms sales to Iraq may have made the regime more aggressive; it certainly made it more dangerous. I would hope we could take advantage of the cooperation that existed among the major weapons suppliers to move to a new regime in which restraint is the watchword for arms sales in the Middle East and in the third world.

Finally, I note that U.S. relations with Israel and with the key Arab states have never been better. I hope this creates an opportunity for a new peace initiative that might provide some hope for a resolution of the too long simmering Arab-Israeli conflict.

I look forward to the testimony of our distinguished panel on these and other regional issues.

0040

TESTIMONY ON THE FUTURE OF THE PERSIAN GULF TO SENATE FOREIGN
AFFAIRS COMMITTEE

Dr. Phebe Marr

Senior Fellow

Institute for National Strategic Studies

National Defense University

March 13, 1991

Mr. Chairman, I welcome the opportunity to testify before
the Committee and to explore with you the prospects for stability
in the Gulf in the wake of the recent war. My expertise lies in
the modern history and politics of the Arab world, with
particular emphasis on Iraq and the Gulf. In addition to my
research, I travel to the region frequently and keep in touch
with government officials, academics, journalists and other
opinion makers. The views expressed here are my own and not that
of NDU or the administration.

The US and its coalition allies have just prosecuted a
remarkably successful war in the Gulf with minimal losses to US
treasure--human and material. As a result, the US has emerged

1

0041

with renewed credibility in the region, and a brief window of opportunity to help construct a post war environment more conducive to long term stability. Nevertheless, despite the military successes of the coalition, the war has left some unfinished business. I propose to deal with some of the social and political consequences of the war for the future of the Gulf. Specifically, I would like to address three questions: the prospects for stability in the Gulf: where we are likely to see major changes in the near future, and the impact of these on US interests.

In general, the prospects for stability in the Gulf are most favorable in Saudi Arabia and the GCC states, except for Kuwait. As victors in the war, they will benefit from a shared sense of accomplishment. A major threat to their security, Iraqi military power, has been remove, and they will be able to look to regional Arab states and to the US and its coalition partners for military protection against external aggression in the coming decade. Although we may expect some domestic social and political changes in Saudi Arabia, in my view, they are likely to be modest. While the regime faces pressures from a small, but vocal Western educated middle class for greater participation in government and a more open society, it also faces demands from Islamic groups for a return to more traditional behavior and norms. Indeed, if Saudi Arabia is to play a new more assertive role in foreign policy, particularly in the Arab-Israeli arena,

2

0042

it may have to lean more heavily on its Islamic credentials and to propitiate conservative elements at home. In any event, the ruling family can be espected to maintain a delicate political balance between the two groups.

Iran may also fall on the stable side of the ledger. Iran has been a major beneficiary of the outcome of the Gulf war, but thus far has not played a disruptive role. Iran showed considerable caution in resisting Iraq's attempts to involve it in the war, and, thus far, has maintained that caution in the face of the uprising in Iraq. Iran is still recuperating from the devatating effects of its Islamic revolution and eight years of war with Iraq. Rafsanjani, a pragmatist, seems firmly in control and reluctant to jeopardize Iran's gradual raprochement with Europe and the GCC states on which its future economic development depends. With an expected population increase in the next decade and the slow recovery of its oil resources, Iran's population may see a stagnation or even a gradual reduction of its per capita income during the decade. For this reason, Iraq will probably emphasize domestic affairs and a continued, but gradual, rapprochement with the West.

Nevertheless, Iraq's defeat has now left Iran in a better position to assert its interests in the Gulf. Iran expects a role in the newly emerging Gulf security system and fears US-Saudi hegemony. If it is excluded from the new arrangements, it could exhibit disruptive behavior and focus on diplomatic efforts

3

0043

to remove or reduce the US military presence in the Gulf. It could also play a destabilizing role in Iraq, encouraging rebellion rather than exercising caution. If Iran's interests in the Gulf are taken into account, however, Iran under Rafsanjani, seems more likely to follow a policy of cautious pragmatism in the future, than a return to messianic zeal or strident nationalism.

In two other countries, Kuwait and Iraq, however, uncertainty and instability are likely to prevail. It is on these countries that I would like to concentrate. Before doing so, however, I would like to sketch, briefly, some general trends that will affect the Gulf in the next few years, and may be destabilizing, rather than the reverse.

1. The countries of the Gulf--along with others in the Middle East--are undergoing accelerated population growth expected to double their populations by the year 2010. Iran, for example, will have over 100 million; Iraq, 35 million. Over 50 percent of the population will be below the age of 15, requiring greatly expanded education facilities and increased job opportunities. While the sparcely populated oil states of the Arabian peninsula will be able to absorb their increase, most have pro-natal policies), others--Iran, Oman, Yemen-- will have difficulty keeping up with population growth. In the near term, there is likely to be less revenue. The costs of war

4

0044

reconstruction, allied to the residual costs of the eight year Iran-Iraq war, are astronomical. Once Kuwait and Iraq resume oil production, oil revenues are likely to be lower, rather than higher. This will leave fewer funds to cushion the effects of population growth and social change.

2. The region may see increased ethnic and sectarian strife, particularly in Iraq, but possibly in Iran as well. As the central government weakens in Baghdad, Kurdish separatism will increase, with the potential to affect Kurdish areas in Turkey and possibly in Iran. Shi'i sectarianism may also get a second wind in Iraq, with some spill over into shi'i communities in Bahrain, Kuwait and the Eastern Province of Saudi Arabia. Most important of all is the still uncertain impact of the disintegration of the Soviet empire across the border from Iran. Growing separatist movements in Islamic regions of the USSR, particularly Azerbaijan, could affect Iran's stability as well.

3. Islamic revivalism, both in its sunni and shi'i form, is likely to be the most dynamic political movement in the region. Islamic movements are by no means monolithic, nor should they be regarded as implacably hostile to the West. The aims of most groups are directed toward reform of their domestic societies and are a matter of indifference to Western security interests. Nevertheless, these movements do constitute an umbrella under which opposition to established regimes can and does operate. In

5

Saudi Arabia, in Iraq, and even in Iran, Islamic revivalism may be a force for instability even if it is unable, as seems likely, to unseat regimes.

4. Lastly, the Persian Gulf is likely to experience changes of regime, accompanied by social upheaval, in two key states, Iraq and Kuwait. Since these changes are the most likely sources of instability, and will provide the most serious challenges for policy makers, I would like to concentrate on them.

Let me begin with Iraq, the second largest state in the Gulf and one of critical importance to the US. As is clear from the current upheaval, Iraq's future is acutely uncertain, and no hard and fast predictions can be made. In this fast moving situation, one can only sketch a range of possible outcomes and their implications for US interests.

1. First, it is possible that Saddam Husain and the Ba'th Party may succeed in quelling the current uprising, giving the regime a lease on life. In prosecuting this aim, Saddam Husain can count on his family and on a small group in the ruling elite, whose personal loyalty to him is beyond question, on the several security services, on leading members of the Ba'th Party, and, probably, on the remaining organized units of the Republican Guard. To these may be added the Regular Army, although the loyalty of some units off the Regular Army, with

6

0046

large numbers of shi'i recruits, may be suspect. Loyalists in these units may hang together because they fear to hang separately should Saddam and his regime fall. Nonetheless, the milita;ry units available to Saddam are few and thinly spread, and in the case of the Regular Army, may be subject to defections.

Even if the regime should succeed in restoring order, its future is uncertain and its lease on life insecure. Saddam Husain's long term survival is possible only if the US and its coalition partners cooperate in the effort, an unlikely eventuality. If the UN removes all economic sanctions on Iraq; if Saudi Arabia and Turkey cooperate in opening the oil pipeline across their territory; if OPEC countries make room for Iraqi oil production in their quotas; if European states are willing to offer credit to help revive Iraq's economy, and if foreign technocrats are willing to participate in Iraq's recuperation, then Saddam Husain may still be with us by the middle of the decade. Just to list these conditions, however, indicates how precarious is his long term position. Indeed, it is far more likely that, should Saddam surmount this immediate crisis, the US and its regional allies will continue to place severe constraints on Iraq's economy, if not by economic sanctions, then by other means. These will gradually increase pressure on the population-- and the leadership--to remove Saddam Husain by one means or another.

7

0047

2. Second, it is possible that Saddam Husain may be replaced by a military coup. The Regular Army is one of the few, relatively independent institutions, remaining in Iraq, although it has been badly mauled in the war. As an institution dating back to the founding of the state in the 1920s, it has, traditionally, seen its role as a protector of the state and its territorial integrity rather than the supporters of a particular regime. While its upper reaches have been Ba'thized and Party cadre are installed at virtually every level, rumors of failed military coup attempts through the years indicate that the regime has had trouble keeping the military in line. Today, the elements of a military coup are present in a disasterous defeat in a war for which Saddam is almost single handedly responsible; in the potential for retribution by Saddam against military leaders in its aftermath; and in strong military motivation to save the country from disintegration. Indeed, the rebellion among shi'ah and Kurds may be intensifying this motivation among mainly sunni officers.

However, there are also problems with this scenario. The destruction of much of the military and massive desertions have left the the Regular Army a very weak instrument on which to depend for a a change of regime. Use of the military to restore order by harsh measures may discredit them as future leaders. There may be potential splits between senior officers, still loyal to the regime, and junior officers willing to work for a

8

0048

change if the occasion offers itself. Above all, officers may be unwilling to undertake an act that could prove suicidal for themselves and their families as long as the security apparatus remains intact with Saddam Husain in control.

3. Third, Saddam Husain could be replaced by civilian members of the Ba'th Party, possibly in conjunction with military elements. Some Party members might move the country in a more pragmatic direction and hold out the promise of some power sharing. Although the Party as an institution has been downplayed in recent years in favor of Saddam's personal dictatorship, it has some strength in the country. Prior to the Iran-Iraq war, it was estimated to have about 50,000 full members--a substantial cadre--and up to a million supporters. Although this support is undoubtedly weak at the base, new leadership at the top of the party might generate sufficient support, if backed by the military and the security services, to tide the country over a transition period, and might even provide some new direction. Indeed, under any new administration it may prove difficult to remove and replace the party personnel. After 23 years of rule they dominate the ubiquituous security services, the bureaucracy, the military structure and the academic world.

However, there are also difficulties with this scenario. Much of the discredit that now adheres to Saddam Husain also afflicts the party which is probably unacceptable to those now in revolt. Moreover, the party leadership is civilian and has

9

0049

little coercive means at its disposal; most of the force is now in the hands of the military. Like senior military leaders, party members may feel that if Saddam goes, they will go too; meanwhile, they could be subject to severe retribution if their attempts fail.

4. The fourth outcome is continued upheaval from below. Although information on the extent and depth of the rebellion is sparse and often unreliable, several generalizations may be made about it thus far. First, it has been spontaneous and indigenous, sparked in part by the disasterous defeat in the war; deteriorating social and economic conditions, and the return of hungry and demoralized soldiers. Second, it lacks leadership and organization. The strongest groups are opposition forces left over from pre-war rebellions--the Kurdish Democratic Party (KDP) and Patriotic Union of Kurdistan (PUK) among the Kurds and the Da'wah (Religious Call) among the shi'ah, but these do not necessarily control a majority of their communities. Third, while the authority of the central government may be eroding, there is no local authority to replace it. Fourth, the rebels may be joined by soldiers, individually and in units, eroding the authority of the army to keep order, even if a successor regime should emerge in Baghdad.

The outcome of the rebellion is uncertain. It may be put down by Saddam Husain, leaving him once again in control of the country, but greatly weakened. It is my assumption that

10

government forces still have the coercive edge, especially in the south. The longer the rebellion lasts, however, the greater Saddam's weakness at its end, and the more likely is an eventual change. A second outcome is an increase of Iranian influence in Iraq, particularly in the south. If Saddam's authority is greatly eroded there, pockets of radical shi'i influence, supported from Iran, could be established, as was the case with the Hizballah in southern Lebanon and the Bekaa. Third, and least likely, the rebellion could result in the gradual fragmentation of Iraq. Saddam Husain could maintain control in Baghdad and the central part of the country, but gradually lose control over areas of the Kurdish north and the shi'i south. Indeed, fears of this outcome may be strengthening his hold over his military in the short term. Lastly, the rebellion could succeed in forcing a change of regime or a change of policy in Baghdad.

A few caveats are in order here about Iraq's fragmentation. The shi'ah in the south of Iraq who constitute about 55% of the population are Arab; they have no desire to be ruled from Iran nor to be separated from the government in Baghdad. In fact, the border between Iraq and Iran is one of the true cultural divides in the Middle East, separating as its does, Persians from Arabs. Second, the hold of the shi'ah clergy over their flock in Iraq is weaker than it is in Iran. Hence, a religious autocracy among the Iraqi shi'ah is far less likely than it was in Iran.

It is also important to note that 23 years of Ba'th

11

·dictatorship have left the country with no organized alternatives to the regime inside the country. All opponents have been executed, jailed or exiled. A large Iraqi exile community, centered mainly in London and Tehran, has generated numerous groups vigorous in their opposition to the regime. These include offshoots of the shi'i Da'wah (the main Da'wah group is located in Tehran); Kurdish groups, including representatives of the KDP and the PUK; remnants of the Iraqi Communist Party, and assorted Western educated Iraqis with a secular liberal bent. Some of these groups--notably those devoted to Kurdish separatism and to the shi'ah--have some roots inside Iraq, but other individuals represent little beyond themselves. Over 20 of these groups are presently meeting in Lebanon with a view to charting future policy in the event of Saddam's fall.

The weaknesses of this opposition are many. First, most have resided outside the country for years and it is not clear how much of a constituency they represent at home or how they would adjust to a totally new reality on their return. Second, their aims and their potential constituencies are so far apart that it is doubtful whether their cohesion would last in the face of any kind of pressure. Third, even if they could lay claim to some legitimacy, there is no mechanism for their accession to rule nor any means of getting them inside Iraq. Lastly, with the exception of some Kurdish groups, they have no force at their disposal with which to confront the regime. Under these circumstances, it appears chimerical to expect them to replace the regime or to

12

0052

constitute a force which could rapidly or automatically assume a
governing role in an economically devestated society unable to
keep law and order.

How are these outcomes likely to affect US interests?

First, it is not in US interests that Iraq fragment or
descend into chaos. Such an eventuality, though unlikely, would
have a very destabilizing effect on the Gulf. A revival of shi'i
activism in the south of Iraq could threaten Kuwait's emerging
stability and spill over into Bahrain and the Eastern Province of
Saudi Arabia where large shi'i populations exist. And it could
also affect US plans to drawn down its forces as rapidly as
possible. The US should support, and to the best of its ability,
uphold the territorial integrity of the Iraqi state.

Second, Iraq's future is best left in the hands of Iraqis.
While a more responsible government in Baghdad that puts the
interests of its citizens, rather than its leaders, first is in
everyone's interest, leadership imposed by outside forces will
have little chance of achieving stability or consoldiating power.
To this end, aggression or overt interference by Iraq's
neighbors in its internal affairs, should be discouraged.

Third, the war has inflicted intense hardships on the Iraqi
people, who are inclined to blame the US, at least in part, for
their difficulties. In order to rectify some of this hardship and

13

0053

prevent social collapse, the US should collaborate with international bodies to provide humanitarian aid to Iraq. This aid could include food (rice); medicines (to prevent cholera and typhoid epidemics); and help with environmental problems such as water pollution. This aid should be accompanied by international agents who can monitor its distribution to the populace; it should not be distributed in a way that supports Saddam Husain's government.

Fourth, while not supporting or rejecting any contenders for power in Iraq, US government spokesmen can articulate the direction we would like any future Iraqi government to take. This direction should include a far better human rights record, greater civil rights for its citizens, a more open society, to include freedom to travel, freedom of expression and freedom of assembly, and reasonable and prompt progress toward a more accountable government with greater participation by all its citizens. The US and its coalition allies can make it clear that until such policies emerge, Iraq's economic recovery is likely to be slow and painful. Progess on these issues would warrant reconsideration of economic constraints on the regime and more international cooperation in Iraq's economic development.

2. A second Gulf country with the possibility of a change of regime is Kuwait. Here, however, the change may be evolutionary and accomplished with an minimum of instability. Repair of

14

Kuwait's war damage will, of necessity, provide a focus of energy for its people.

More important, however, will be the repair of Kuwait's social and political structure. Kuwait has a number of fundamental questions to face. First is the demographic issue. What will be the composition of its population and who will be given the vote? Will certain national groups be excluded and if so, on what grounds? Second, is the issue of foreigner workers. If foreigners are to be drawn into Kuwait's new work force, where will they originate? Will Kuwait continue to rely primarily on foreign labor for work it does not want to do, or will a new work ethic take shape among Kuwaitis? Last and most importantly, is the issue of Kuwait's political institutions and the democratization of its structure. Will the dominant role of the ruling family be maintained, or will a process of political reform take place? And with what speed? At least four groups are contending for political influence: the ruling family that has traditionally controlled the political system but has now come under severe pressure for reform; the secular political opposition, consisting mainly of middle class professionals and intellectuals, like Ahmad al-Khatib, who have long sought the establishment of a genuine parliamentary government; the Kuwaiti resistance movement, consisting of those who stayed in Kuwait to face death and hardship during the occupation, and are now adament about political change that gives them a say in

15

government, and lastly, Kuwait's Islamic movement, recently in decline. The thorough disruption of Kuwaiti society, the radical shift in its demography, and the bitter events of the last eight months make some political change likely. Given the divisions among the groups in Kuwait, particularly between those who left and those who stayed, the change is likely to be contentious, if not volatile. Moreover, the resistance movement shows signs of vigilantism hardly conducive to democratic reform. But Kuwait has considerable potential for movement toward a more open, accountable government, that could provide an attractive model for other Gulf states, including Iraq. It is in US interests to encourage and foster this process with discretion and tact, and hopefully with a minimum of tension and instability.

Kuwait will also face tensions with some of its neighbors, notably Iraq, Jordan and the Palestinians. Bitterness toward those who sided with Saddam Husain is likely to be deep and relatively long lasting. A policy of retribution, however, could prolong, rather than heal, these cleavages. Here, too, the US can play a role behind the scenes in encouraging a more benign attitude toward the citizens of these countries who , through no fault of their own, found themselves caught in this tragedy.

16

0056

Testimony of
JOSEPH S. NYE, JR.
Director, Center for International Affairs
Harvard University

Senate Foreign Relations Committee
March 13, 1991

The most intangible, but perhaps the most important of the American interests in responding to the Gulf events was the idea of a "new world order," a phrase that President Bush had already begun using in February 1990 to describe the end of the Cold War. Throughout the five centuries of the modern state system, order in world politics has been associated with the outcome of major wars and the treaties associated with their settlement. For the last half century, the balance of power in world politics reflected the outcome of World War II, and the bipolar preponderance of the United States and the Soviet Union. Although the standoff between the two superpowers meant that the collective security provisions of the United Nations Charter of 1945 could not be fully implemented, the Cold War balance did provide a degree of order. The decline of the Soviet Union spelled the end of bipolarity and a weakening of Soviet constraints on its regional client states. Saddam Hussein publicly recognized the Soviet decline in a speech in Amman in February 1990, but he drew the wrong conclusions. In that sense, Kuwait was the first victim of the post Cold War order. Note that order is not the same as justice, but order which is perceived as just is more likely to be stable.

Can the United States construct a just order in the postwar period? That question is hotly debated between declinists and revivalists as part of America's global role. In his best selling book, *The Rise and Fall of the Great Powers*, the eminent Yale historian Paul Kennedy argued that the United States is following other empires suffering from imperial overstretch

1

and is declining more rapidly than should be expected. In my book, *Bound To Lead: The Changing Nature of American Power*, I show that America's postwar decline in its share of world product ended by the early 1970s, and that contrary to theories of imperial overstretch, the burdens of the military today are less than half what they were at the height of the Cold War. Nor is this trend altered by the Gulf War.

In 1989, polls showed that half the American people believed the country to be in decline and that Japan had a larger economy than the United States. Early polls suggest that the Gulf War corrected this tendency to exaggerate American weaknesses. The danger now, however, is that American self-estimates will overshoot in the other direction. If Americans learn the wrong lessons from the Gulf War, they could do real damage to their long term national interests. Such would be the case if they conclude, for example, that they can police the world alone.

The problem for the United States -- and other countries -- in shaping a new world order lies less in the traditional danger of battles for first place in the rank of great powers than in the diffusion of power to weak states and private transnational actors in a world of increasing interdependence. Military power premains relevant in such a world. The trendy proclamations of Japan and Germany as the new superpowers early in 1990 began to wilt after August. But in a world where the sources of power become more diffuse, military power alone will not be enough.

America's capacity to promote its national interests will have to rest on both hard and soft power. Hard power is based on the familiar resources of military and economic might. Soft power, the ability to co-opt rather than command, rests on intangible resources such as culture, ideology, and the ability to use international institutions to determine the framework

2

of debate. In the Gulf crisis, it was important to get the hard power of the military to Saudi Arabia quickly, but it was equally important to have the soft power to shape the United Nations resolutions that defined Iraq's entry into Kuwait as a violation calling for sanctions. Without such resolutions, it might have been impossible for the Saudis to accept American troops, for other Arab countries to have sent forces, and for allied countries to have paid some three quarters of the financial costs. And while America's hard power was critical to winning the war, winning the peace will require investments in such soft power initiatives as a regional development fund to redistribute the oil wealth and further steps to forward the Arab-Israeli peace process.

This morning, however, I have been asked to focus on the question of proliferation of advanced weaponry in the region, particularly weapons of mass destruction. In 1990, every dollar change in the price of oil was worth a billion dollars a year to Iraq. Not only was annexing Kuwait like capturing a gold mine, but had Saddam gone unchallenged in his use of force, he would have been able to cow Saudi Arabia and the smaller states into cutting their oil production and jacking up the world price. It would be nice to believe that the additional income would have been devoted solely to economic development, but that belief is inconsistent with Saddam's past behavior aimed at building Iraq into the dominant military power in the region. The additional revenues would have permitted a dramatic increase in Iraq's already impressive ability to import modern weapons and the technology necessary for production of weapons of mass destruction.

Saddam had already demonstrated his chemical weapons capability against Iran and against his own Kurdish civilians. In addition, he was developing biological weapons, extending the range of his ballistic missiles, and covertly importing components for a nuclear weapons

3

0059

program. Despite alarmist reports, Iraq in 1990 was probably still some five years away from a deliverable nuclear weapon. If Saddam wanted to become the Bismarck of the Arabs, eliminating those friendly to the West and finaly confronting Israel, the next decade in the Middle East would have seen escalating violence and loss of life. Facing such prospects, those who believed that a conflict with Saddam Hussein was highly likely concluded that the proliferation of weapons of mass destruction meant that sooner was better than later. Can we avoid such a situation arising again?

There is both good news and bad news. As the following table shows, the barriers to chemical weaponry are lower, and the taboos against use have been violated. On the other hand, the taboos against biological weapons are enshrined in a treaty. Treaty limits exist for nuclear, chemical, and biological weapons, but not ballistic missiles. Supplier agreements exist for nuclear and ballistic missile technology.

Proliferation Problems

	States (Global)	States (Mid-East)	Treaty Bans	Suppliers Limits	Technical Complexity
Nuclear	9	1	NPT	NSG	High
Chemical	20	6	--	Australia Group	Low
Biological	10	6	BWC	--	Medium
Missile	15	8	--	MTCR	Medium

What can be done about the diffusion of military power and the proliferation of the technologies of mass destruction?

4

0060

The first step is to be realistic about goals. Stemming proliferation is only one aspect of foreign policy. There will always be trade-offs between efforts to slow the spread of dangerous technology and other foreign policy objectives -- witness the vacillating U.S. performance in trying to slow Pakistan's nuclear weapons development in the 1980s, when Pakistan provided the critical supply route for American assistance to the Afghan resistance. Moreover, we have to think about what steps to take after technology has spread. Cliches about horses being out of the barn are misleading; it makes a difference how many horses remain in the barn and how quickly they are fleeing. Our goal should be to slow the rate of spread of dangerous technologies in order to better manage their destabilizing effects. With this goal we buy time, but we also need to use that time to seek political settlements. Multilateral arms control agreements will be an important part of the mix of policy instruments but they cannot stand alone.

In the area of nuclear nonproliferation, we need to deal with the covert proliferators without weakening our efforts to discourage further proliferation. The greatest danger to our security is that one of these covert proliferators may lose control of its nuclear weapons because of inadequate technical safeguards or domestic political turmoil. Once a nation can build nuclear weapons, we should try to persuade it to freeze or halt the level of its development, rather than proceeding to produce and even to deploy a large nuclear arsenal. While we may not be happy about countries that have bombs in their basements, a bomb in the basement is less dangerous than bombs spread all over the front lines where they are susceptible to military revolt, theft, or leakage into terrorist hands.

We need to supplement our traditional support for the NPT, the IAEA, and the nuclear suppliers' agreement with regional efforts to encourage greater confidence among

5

0061

threatening neighbors. In the Middle East, on the other hand, it is hard to imagine effective arms control agreements without progress in the Middle East peace process. Moreover, progress in limiting chemical weapons in the region may also be linked with both the nuclear and general peace issues.

Halting or slowing chemical, biological, and missile technology will also require the use of multiple instruments. Even an imperfect chemical weapons convention strengthens barriers against the possession and use of chemical weapons. It could reinforce export controls and legitimate the use of force in self-defense against chemical threats by reaffirming the stigma against chemical weapons. Finally, good intelligence collection and early warning will be an important part of the package of policy instruments. The official inspection scheme will complement rather than replace national intelligence efforts in this area. In the area of biological weaponry, negotiation of a protocol relating to verification would help to reinforce the existing stigma against biological weapons and would serve as a basis for the other instruments such as export controls, sanctions, and intelligence.

In containing missile technology, the next step should be to broaden the acceptance of an export control regime. This may require renegotiation because of Soviet and Chinese concern about not being included in the early stages of the development of the current MTCR. Once again, however, the agreement must be developed in the context of other instruments, including intelligence collection.

What are the prospects for broader arms restrictions in the Middle East? The need is certainly great. The Middle East is the world's principal market for arms and military equipment with 31 percent of the total in 1988. From 1984 to 1988, Iraqi arms imports were $30 billion, Saudi Arabia's $20 billions, and Iran's $11 billion. Eight of the 18 countries that

6

68 걸프 사태 미국 동향 4

spent more than 10 percent of the their GNP on defense in 1988 were located in the Middle East. These figures show the extent of insecurity in the region. Again, there is good and bad news. The bad news is that insecurity remains high and demand persists. The good news is that capacity to pay is temporarily reduced.

There are two difficult trade-offs involved in restricting weapons sales to the region: whether to cover the whole spectrum of technology and how to define the region. A broad definition of the region would prevent sales to countres like Israel, Egypt, Saudi Arabia and Kuwait -- countries that look to us for security. A broad definition of technology runs afoul of the larger number of suppliers for low tech weapons.

One way around these problems would be to focus on high technology (i.e., jet engines, sensors, advanced electronics) where the number of suppliers is limited and where there is experience with applying the COCOM rules. Another way around the problem would be to start by focusing on restraints of arms sales to Iraq and Iran, two countries that spent most of the last decade at war, and where we have export constraints in place.

7

외 무 부

종 별 :

번 호 : USW-1276

일 시 : 91 0319 1836

수 신 : 장 관(미안,미북,동구일,동구이,중동일,기정,국방부)

발 신 : 주 미 대사

제 목 : 하원 외무위 대외 안보 원조 예산 관련 청문회

1. 하원 외무위 (위원장 DANTE FASCELL) 는 금 3.19 체니 국방장관을 출석 시킨 가운데 미 행정부의 '92 대외 안보 원조 예산안 (SECURITY ASSISTANCE) 에 관한청문회를 개최한바, 체니 장관의 증언 요지 아래 보고함. (증언문 FAX 참조)

가. 세계 안보 상황의 변화

미국의 새로운 방위 전략은 다음의 4가지 세계안보 상황 변화를 감안하여 수립되어야함.

1) 소련및 동구권의 변화

0 소련에 의한 기습적 세계 대전 발발 가능성감소

0 소련의 대외 군사 배치 능력 감소 추세

0 소련 국내 정세 불안정 심화 (동구권에 대한불안 요소로 파급 위험)

2) 국지전 위협의 변화

0 대쏘 대결 체제 감퇴로 국지전의 세계 대전비화 위험 감소

0 양극 체제 종식으로 국지 분쟁 발발 위험증대

3) 동맹국과의 관계 변화

0 유럽에서의 미국의 안보 중점이 소련 봉쇄 대신동구권의 불안 방지로 전환

4) 매래 전쟁 양상의 변화

0 고도 군사 기술 혁명으로 군사 작전 개념의 변화초래

0 미군사 전략도 이러한 군사 기술 혁명에 맞추어발전 필요

나. 미국의 안보 목표

상기 세계 아노 상항의 변화에도 불구, 미국의 아래안보 목표는 불변

1) 안보 억지력 지속

2) 세계 민주화 및 번영 추구

미주국 국방부	1차보	2차보	미주국	구주국	구주국	중아국	정문국	안기부

3) 미국의 세계적 지도 역할 유지

다. 신방위 전략

상기 안보 목표 달성을 위한 새로운 방위 전략은 90.8.2 이락의 쿠웨이트 침공시 , 부쉬 대통령의 연설에서 이미 밝힌바와 같이 다음의 6가지 로 요약됨.

1) 세계적 동맹 체제 유지

2) 미군의 전진 배치 (FORWARD DEPLOYED FORCES)체제 유지

3)국지전 위협 대처 및 전진 배치 부대 증강을 위한 기동성 강화

4) 해상권 통제를 위한 강력한 해군력 유지

5) 군사력 감축 계획을 수행해 나가는 한편 유사시 신속한 군사력 증강 능력 유지

6) 강력한 공격및 방어 능력 보유

라.국방 예산

92-95년간 국방 예산은 연간 약 2,780 억불로 동결될것인바, 이는 91년 국방 예산 11.3프로 실질 감소분을 포함하여 96년까지 국방비가 연평균 3 프로 실질 감소됨을 의미하며, 96년에는 GNP대비 국방 예산이 3.6 프로 (2차 대전 이후 최저 수준)선으로 떨어질것으로 예상됨.

마.걸프전배 추가 예산

부시 대통령의 92-93 회계 년도 국방 예산 요청서에는 걸프전 수행 경비가 포함되어 있지 않은바, 기 요청한 추가 예산 150억불에 우방국 재정 부담 545억불을 합하면 DESERT SHIELD/STORM 총 경비를 충분히 충당할수 있을것임.

바.걸프전에 대한 우방국 지원

걸프전을 지원한 50 개국중 35 개국이 군사 또는 비군사 요원을 파견하였으며, 재정 지원 약속 금액 545억불중 현재까지 196 억불을 수령함.

2.상기 증언에 이어 진행된 주요 질의 응답 요지.

가.향후 걸프 지역에 주둔할 미군 병력과 기간 및 사우디등 역내 국가 방위를 위한 미국의 구체적공약 유무 (HAMILTON 의원)

0 병력의 규모와 기간은 이지역 안보에 대한 위협의 성격 (NATURE OF THREAT)에 따라 결정될것이나, 장기 주둔할 의도는 없음 (NOT INTERESTEDIN LONG-TIME PRESENCE) 그러나 해군력과 공군력은 유지될것이며, 이집트등 역내 국가와의 정기적공군 합동 훈련등도 계속될것임.

이문제에 대한 정책 결정은 최근 베이커 국무장관의 중동 순방 결과에 대한 평가와

PAGE 2

영,불등여타 우방과의 협의등을 거쳐 장기적 안목에서 이루어질것이나, 지역 안보에 직접적 영향을 받는역내 국가 (특히 GCC)의 역할에 보다 중점이주어질것임.

0 터어키와는 조약상 의무를 부담하고 있으나 사우디에 대하여는 공식 협정에 의한 의무 부담은 없음. (NO FORMAL ARRANGEMENT) 그러나, 사우디 안보는 미국 국익을 위해 극히 긴요하므로 사우디에 대한 안보지원은 계속될것임.

나.무기 수출 통제등 걸프 지역 군비 확산 방지를 위한 구체적 조치 계획 (WOLPE, GEDJENSON, BERMAN,SOLARZ 의원)

0 대 이락 무기 수출은 현재 매우 효과적으로 통제되고 있음. 이락의 군사 장비와 기술은 대부분 유엔 안보리 상임 이사국에 의존하고 있으므로 제 3국을 통한 무기 수출에도 큰 문제는 없다고보나, 이를 통제하기 위한 노력은 배가될것임.

0 대중동 무기 수출 통제를 위한 주요 무기 수출국간 협력 필요성에 대해, 이지역 안정을 위한 군비통제의 필요성에 는 동의하나, 무기 수출 통제와 여타 외교 목표 사이에는 TRADE-OFF 가 있게 마련이므로 신중한 접근이 필요하다고 답변함. (이스라엘을 대표적 예로 언급)

0 북한의 대시리아 무기 수출설, 영, 독, 소련, 중국등의 대 중동 무기 수출 규모, 이집트에 대한 미국의 추가 무기 수출 여부 관련 질의 (GEDJENSON의원)에 대하여는 비공개 회의에서 논의할 문제라고 답변을 회피하고, 미국의 대 이스라엘 추가 무기수출 계획 유무에 대하여는 현재로서는 구체적인 계획이 없다고 답변함.

0 이락이 보유하고 있는 화학 무기 및 핵무기 개발잠재력을 제거하기 위한 규정을 대이락 종전 협정에 포함시킬 용의가 없느냐는 질의 (SOLARZ의원)에 대해, 이는유엔 결의를 기초로 안보리이사국들과 협의, 결정할 문제이나, 미국으로서는, 이문제에 적극 대처 (FAIRLY AGGRESSIVE RESPONSE)할것이라고 답변함.

다.후세인 처리및 전범 재판(SNOWE 의원)

0 미국은 후세인이 물러나게 되기를 원하나 이를군사 목표로 삼지는 않았음. 미국은 이락 내부문제에 관여할 의도는 없으나, 후세인 이 물러날경우 여타 국가와의 정상관계 회복이 더욱 순조로울것임을 이락 국민들이 깨닫게 되길기대함.

0 후세인 전범 재판 문제에 대하여는, 유엔 결의안에 관련 규정도 없고, 현재후세인의 신병을 확보하고 있지도 않다고 (NOT IN OUR CUSTODY)만 답변함.

라.대 동구권 군사 원조 문제 (MEYERS 의원)

0 동구권 국가 (특히 폴란드)가 미국의 군사 원조를 기대하고 있다는 정보와 이에

PAGE 3

0066

대한 미 행정부 방침에 관한 질의에 대해 현재로서는 대동구권 군사원조 계획이 없으나 장래에 검토해 볼수 있는문제라고 답변함.

　마.소련 집권층의 군부 통제력 여부(SNOWE의원)

　0 과거보다 군사정책 결정과정에서 군부의 영향력이 커지고 있으며, 고르바쵸프가 개혁파 보다는군부 및 보수파와 연합하고 있다는 징후가 있는것은 사실이라고 답변함.

　0 또한 소련 군부대 CFE 협정에 대한 비판 세력이 있고, 그로인해 동 협정 시행이 지연되고 있다고 부언함.

　바.소련내 각 공화국 정세 불안으로 인한 핵무기확산 우려에 대한 안전 장치 (SMITH 의원)

　0 미국은 소련측에 이러한 우려를 수차 표명한바 있으나, 이에 대한 소측은 대부분의 관련 핵무기 및 시설들이 러시아 공화국에 배치되어 있고, 발트 3국과 같이 정정이 불안한 지역에는 배치되어 있지않으므로 완벽한 안전 장치가 마련되어 있다고 재다짐하였으며, 체르노빌 사건 이후 소련이 이문제에 더많은 주의를 기울이고 있으므로 효과적으로 이를통제할수 있을것으로 본다고 답변함.

　(대사 현홍주-국장)

-56

STATEMENT OF SECRETARY OF DEFENSE DICK CHENEY
HOUSE FOREIGN AFFAIRS COMMITTEE
MARCH 19, 1991

    Mr. Chairman, members of the Committee, thank you for this opportunity to appear before you. In my prepared statement, I would like to discuss our new U.S. defense strategy in the context of the changing security environment, highlight the budget request and force structure we are recommending to support that strategy, and comment on several budgetary and burdensharing issues surrounding our Persian Gulf operations.

    Even though we are just beginning to redeploy U.S. armed forces after their magnificent performance in the Gulf War, we are at the same time proceeding with restructuring and reducing those forces to adapt to changes in the global strategic environment. Underpinning this formidable task is a new strategy for America's defense. This strategy was first set forth publicly in a speech by President Bush last August 2--the very day Saddam Hussein invaded Kuwait. This is ironic, because the strategy President Bush presented directs attention away from a global war beginning in Europe--the contingency that had necessarily preoccupied America's planners for four decades. The new strategy focuses our efforts instead on regional contingencies and on sustaining the forward military presence in peacetime necessary to deter the outbreak of regional wars.

    This new strategy also emphasizes that technological breakthroughs will change military art, just as our Stealth fighters carried a disproportionate role in the Gulf air war. It calls for ballistic missile defense, much as American Patriot units performed in the Middle East. It directs resources for increased mobility, very appropriate considering that we just conducted one of the largest and most rapid military deployments in our history. Finally, the strategy recognizes potential new roles for America, for our allies, and for the Soviets, even in light of the unprecedented international effort that was forged for the Gulf effort.

    But it is also a strategy that recognizes the importance of continuing historic roles for America's defense. It cites the continued importance of the quality of our armed forces and the critical need to maintain and modernize our strategic capabilities. And it warns of the continued need for caution in an uncertain world, the need to be ready to rebuild, even as we plan to reduce dramatically over the next several years.

    Today I would like to discuss this new strategy, the elements that underlie it, and its implications for our defense budget. For an effective strategy for America's defense requires first a sound understanding of the challenges and opportunities ahead of us, a clear sense of our interests and

930-1

goals, and an honest appreciation of our strengths and
characteristics as a nation. On these sound bases the President
has built America's defense strategy for the 1990s, a strategy
fully reflected in the force structures and programs contained
in the defense budget recently submitted to the Congress.

THREATS AND OPPORTUNITIES

The remarkable changes of 1989 in Europe and the Soviet
Union brought to the fore the need to reexamine the strategy of
containment that had guided us from early post-World War II
days. But there are other changes afoot, as well, partly as a
consequence of the end of the Cold War, and partly from other
historical trends. These have interlocking effects on our
purposes as a nation and on the resources we will devote to our
defense. Let me discuss briefly problems and opportunities
presented in four categories:

- Changes in the Soviet Union and Eastern Europe.
- Changes in future regional threats.
- Changes in relations with our allies.
- Changes in the nature of future warfare.

Changes in the Soviet Union and Eastern Europe

The past two years have seen extraordinary, historic changes
in the strategic environment. The revolutionary change in the
nations of Eastern Europe has been more wide-ranging and
sweeping than anything we have seen in the last forty years.
Noncommunists now lead most of the former non-Soviet Warsaw Pact
states. Germany has been unified in NATO. The Soviet Union has
agreed to withdraw its troops from Czechoslovakia, Hungary and
Germany, is negotiating withdrawals from Poland, and is
unilaterally reducing its general purpose forces at home. The
military structure of the Warsaw Pact is set to be dissolved by
April 1. In short, the West has achieved a great strategic
success.

The Soviets have played a responsible and helpful role in
many of these developments. Communism collapsed in Eastern
Europe and is under siege elsewhere because it failed to nurture
the spirit and innovation of its individual citizens. Democracy
and free market economies have proven more durable, more
successful and more responsive to the aspirations of the
majority of mankind. But the Soviets helped change along and in
the past two years took some steps toward reform at home as
well. Significantly, the Soviets also joined with the
overwhelming majority of the international community in
supporting 12 UN Security Council resolutions condemning Iraq's
wanton aggression in the Persian Gulf. In this sense it is now
common to say, at last, "the Cold War is over."

Last fall, during trips to Poland and the Soviet Union, I
witnessed some of these advances first hand. In Moscow, I

930-2

0069

addressed a joint meeting of the Defense and State Security and International Affairs committees of the Supreme Soviet, and this experience in particular left me with a sense of the great changes taking place in the Soviet Union.

But the moves towards democracy and demilitarization of the Soviet Union that we all welcomed now appear to be in doubt. Recent, worrisome events raise questions about the prospects for needed economic and political reform and the Soviet Union's future course.

The economic situation in the Soviet Union today is as bleak as it has been since the end of World War II. In October 1990, just about the time I visited the Soviet Union, the central government rejected the Shatalin plan, the only economic program that had any real prospect to reform the Soviet economy. The Soviet government has taken other steps that make any significant improvement in the Soviet economy less likely, including reasserting the priority of state orders in the economy, authorizing the KGB to search business enterprises for economic data, and otherwise countering the movement toward free markets and prices. These actions are certain to trouble western businessmen contemplating investment in the Soviet Union. In short, the Soviet central government has for now abandoned economic reform and in turn has been abandoned by the most prominent economic reformers, many of whom are now working with the government of the Russian Republic.

As a result of the center's policies, the Soviet economy is collapsing. There only remains the question of how rapidly the shrinkage is occurring. Estimates for 1990 range from an official Soviet estimate of some 2 percent reduction in Soviet economic activity to at least a 10 percent reduction in the 12 months ending in February 1991. Many experts and Soviet officials anticipate that 1991 will see a further contraction of the Soviet economy.

Mr. Gorbachev's success in the eyes of many hinged upon his ability to deliver economic reform, to move the Soviet Union into the modern era so that it could compete with the West. Success depended first and foremost upon his ability to dismantle the old structures that clearly did not work, and put new structures in their place. In my view, to date, he has clearly not yet achieved that transformation. Given this failure, we have to anticipate that there will continue to be economic decline and increased prospects for significant unrest. If the government pursues additional anti-reform steps, Moscow will find itself locked in a vicious cycle. It is hard to discern, at this point, a strategy at the center for dealing with these problems or regenerating a process of reform.

Political reform in the Soviet Union is also under attack. Leading liberal political figures have left the government, most notably former Foreign Minister Shevardnadze, whose resignation

930-3

speech warned of an impending dictatorship. Shortly thereafter,
Gorbachev resorted to and sanctioned a crackdown on the freely
elected governments in the Baltic states. There has been a
reversal of progress in human rights and a broad campaign
attacking press freedoms. Political conflict is worsening.
There are vigorous campaigns of public criticism by both
reactionary Communist figures and leading reformers. Over the
past few weeks, large pro-reform demonstrations have been held
in Moscow. Similar demonstrations have been held in a number of
other cities of the Russian Republic. The central government,
in response to these public assemblies, has denounced the
"pseudodemocratic" opposition.

     Finally, just a word about Sunday's referendum in the Soviet
Union. There are only fragmentary returns available today from
that vote. And one soon learns in politics not to draw too many
conclusions from fragmentary returns. Yet whatever the results
on the artfully worded question about a looser confederation,
the same questions will confront the Soviet Union:

     • How can the economic problems confronting the Soviet Union
     be corrected?

     • What will be the relationship of the center to the
     Republics? One particular aspect of this will be the
     relationship of the center to the Russian Republic, which
     may soon have a popularly elected President.

     During his recent swing through Byelorussia, Gorbachev has
tried to reposition himself at the center of the Russian
political spectrum. Nonetheless, in recent weeks, rather than
moving toward greater openness to resolve the underlying
problems, Gorbachev appears ready to rely on the security
services and the military and their use of force to maintain
order inside the Soviet Union. He has issued a decree
establishing joint Interior Ministry-Army patrols. There is now
a widespread consensus among Soviet observers that the central
government is increasingly influenced by the military and the
security services, as well as the Communist party bureaucracy.
We will have to see if the aftermath of the recent referendum
will reverse these trends.

     In the absence of ongoing reform there is no prospect for a
permanent transformation in U.S.-Soviet relations. Experience
shows that ultimately U.S.-Soviet relations are driven by how
the Soviet Union governs itself. Except at the margins, long-
term improvement depends on the democratization and
demilitarization of Soviet society. The failure of reform would
not necessarily mean a return to the worst days of the Cold War,
but it would prevent movement to thoroughgoing, across the board
cooperation with the Soviet Union.

930 - 4

0071

Reform need not fail. Our President has said many times that we want the process of reform in the Soviet Union to succeed. We still hope that it will be successful, and the central government, we believe, may still be able to take steps to return to the path of reform.

But what do these conflicting trends mean for our long-term defense requirements? Five implications must be weighed.

First, the Warsaw Pact is dead as a military organization. I do not see any possibility of resurrecting it. Even though the Soviet military will remain, by a wide margin, the largest armed force on the continent, the threat of a short-warning, global war starting in Europe is now less likely than at any time in the last 45 years. The USSR will, very likely, continue withdrawing forces from Eastern Europe. The withdrawals from Hungary and Czechoslovakia are well on their way to completion; and, despite some recent difficulties, we anticipate that withdrawal from Germany and Poland will be completed some time thereafter.

Second, the Soviet ability to project conventional power beyond its borders will continue to decline, whether that decline is part of a broad strategy of improving relations with the West or is simply an unintended effect of the continued economic collapse of the Soviet Union. For the moment there does not appear to be a constituency for a revanchist policy toward Europe or a forward policy in the Third World. More generally, as many Soviets have noted, the Soviet Union has a sick economy, and it is getting sicker. The military is not able to insulate itself completely from this broader social illness, and as a consequence some of its capabilities inevitably will be degraded. Thus, I think overall the Soviets are going to find it increasingly difficult to project power beyond their borders, and that obviously reduces the threat we have been faced with for the past 40 years.

Third, there is enormous uncertainty about developments inside the Soviet Union, and this should be reflected in our planning. Absent a return to the course of reform, I believe the Soviet decline will continue. Growing unrest and violence in the Soviet Union would threaten its neighbors in Central and Eastern Europe since some of the turmoil may well spill over the borders of the Soviet Union. This unrest will be particularly troubling to the Soviet Union's neighbors since, as former Foreign Minister Shevardnadze said not long ago:

[N]o one can calculate the consequences of a social explosion capable of igniting not only befogged minds but also the giant stockpiles of nuclear and chemical weapons and nuclear power stations and the zones already weakened by environmental and natural disasters and regions shaken by interethnic strife.

As the situation deteriorates in the Soviet Union,
anticommunist democrats and ethnic nationalists could well take
to the streets in protest or flee. Large flows of refugees to
Europe are possible. This will only heighten the concerns of
Eastern European nations, as they seek solutions to their
longer-term security needs.

Fourth, and a key point, the Soviets not only retain
significant strategic capability but are modernizing it
virtually across the board. It is expected that Soviet nuclear
forces will be fully modernized by the mid-1990s, including
Typhoon/Delta IV submarines, SS-24 and SS-25 missiles and
follow-ons to each, and a new highly accurate version of the SS-
18 missile. They will also modernize their air-breathing forces
with the ALCM-carrying Bear-H, Blackjack and Backfire bombers,
among other improvements. In all, we see five or six new Soviet
long-range ballistic missiles under development. The USSR also
continues to modernize its strategic defenses. While we seek to
capitalize on the significant reductions in conventional
capabilities, we must recognize the continued importance of
maintaining robust strategic offensive and defensive
capabilities.

Fifth, the prospects for arms control are in doubt. We have
serious, unresolved differences with Moscow over the agreement
to reduce Conventional Forces in Europe (CFE). There is still,
at this time, no resolution on START, although at various times
there has been reason to believe we were close to finishing a
START agreement. These setbacks in arms control demonstrate the
spillover effects of Soviet domestic unrest and the resurgent
role of the military. Nevertheless, we remain hopeful that we
may yet conclude meaningful arms control agreements with the
Soviets.

Changes in Future Regional Threats

The cooling of the superpower rivalry has implications for
the regional conflicts we confront as well. The containment
strategy dictated that part of our regional interests derived
directly from Moscow's expansionist strategy, and our own
efforts to counter that expansionism. U.S.-Soviet rivalry did
not create U.S. regional interests, but gave them a special
context and urgency. A new era holds the prospect for treating
regional issues independent of the East-West context.

A true demise to the Cold War therefore promises many
positive effects on regional conflicts, including greater
superpower cooperation, with the most dramatic example to date
being the Soviet support in the United Nations against Iraq.
The cooling of superpower rivalry decreases the chances that a
regional conflict will escalate into global war--a worrisome
concern throughout the Cold War. This shift drains many
regional insurgencies of their most common source of military
and economic support, and undercuts adherents to Communist

930 - 6

0073

ideological fervor. On the other hand, there is a risk that the
end of the bipolar world could unleash local, destructive forces
that were previously kept in check. For example, there is some
thought that Saddam Hussein saw the end of the Cold War as an
opportunity to pursue his own expansionism.

Whatever the positive consequences of Soviet "new thinking"
on foreign affairs, we face the sobering truth that local
sources of instability and oppression will continue to foster
conflicts small and large virtually across the globe. The Gulf
conflict illustrated once again that these regional crises and
conflicts are likely to arise, or to escalate, unpredictably and
on very short notice. This will require that we be able to
respond if necessary, very rapidly, often very far from home,
and against hostile forces that are increasingly well-armed with
conventional and unconventional capabilities.

The Middle East's post-crisis political and military
relationships remain uncertain, but we are confident of a more
favorable future there. Secretary Baker's recent trip was a
first step in this direction. As we pursue progress on one
important aspect of such a future, regional security
arrangements, several points will guide our approach. First,
the security structure that was in place on August 2 failed; we
need a new structure which can maintain the peace. Second, our
friends in the gulf will have to take the lead; they are most
directly affected by conflict there. Third, we have major
interests in that part of the world; we must remain engaged to
protect those interests, consistent with the wishes of our local
friends. Fourth, we are prepared to increase our presence
compared to the pre-crisis period. We will want to have the
capability to return forces quickly to the region should that
ever be required. We will want to do much more prepositioning
of heavy equipment in the region than was the case before, while
seeking to minimize any long-term, large U.S. presence.

The Gulf war presaged very much the type of conflict we are
most likely to confront again in this new era--major regional
contingencies against foes well-armed with advanced conventional
and unconventional weaponry. In addition to Southwest Asia, we
have important interests in Europe, Asia, the Pacific and
Central and Latin America. In each of these regions there are
opportunities and potential future threats to our interests. We
must configure our policies and our forces to effectively deter,
or quickly defeat, such future regional threats.

Iraq's forces were considerable, but not entirely unique:
there are other regional powers with modern armored forces,
sophisticated attack aircraft and integrated air defenses, anti-
ship cruise missiles, and even modern diesel submarines. The
problem will be exacerbated by post-Cold War phenomenons:
transfers of Cold War surplus armaments, increasing economic
pressures on international arms dealers, and growing indigenous
technical capabilities in the Third World. Opponents in

930 — 7

regional conflicts are unlikely to possess the across-the-board
technical sophistication of the USSR. It will not be uncommon,
however, for U.S. forces to face sophisticated systems
containing high technology in regional confrontations.

Iraq also illustrates the growing problem of the
proliferation of weapons of mass destruction. For the first
time in more than 70 years, we face the possibility of the use
of chemical and biological weapons against us in a conflict.
The use of such capabilities would require a devastating
response. We must respond resolutely not only because of
current combat requirements, but also to deter future use. Only
a few years hence, had it continued on its same path, Iraq could
well have credibly threatened a nuclear weapons capability as
well. By the year 2000, it is estimated that at least 15
developing nations will have the ability to build ballistic
missiles--eight of which either have or are near to acquiring
nuclear capabilities. Thirty countries will have chemical
weapons, and ten will be able to deploy biological weapons as
well.

One implication for future regional conflicts emerging from
Hussein's aggression is the need for tighter arms transfer and
proliferation controls. Those responsible for violations of
such control should be held strictly accountable. We cannot
allow the end of cold-war-level hostilities to open further the
door to transfer of unconventional or ballistic systems.

A second implication for future regional conflicts that
clearly emerges from the current crisis is the military and
political importance of enhancing defenses to counter missile
proliferation. Patriot missiles have demonstrated the technical
efficacy and strategic importance of missile defenses. This
underscores the future importance of developing and deploying a
system for Global Protection Against Limited Strikes (GPALS) to
defend against limited missile attacks--whatever their source.
As President Bush has said, "Thank God that when the Scuds
came--the people of Israel and Saudi Arabia, and the brave
forces of our coalition had more to protect their lives than
some abstract theory of deterrence."

A third implication is the importance of being able to focus
intelligence efforts more on specific regional threats in the
post-Cold war world. This is not simply a matter of redirecting
our intelligence specialists from the study of the Soviet Union
to concentration on other areas. We will need, if anything, to
continue our close attention to the Soviet Union and the
increasingly diverse activity we must understand as we also
track developments in other regions.

Separate and apart from the broad regional conflicts
discussed above, there is another set of demanding threats.
They are low intensity conflicts, including insurgencies,
terrorism, and drug trafficking. Some of these challenges

930 - 8

require uniquely tailored military capabilities. Countering
such challenges deserves our attention and support.

Changes in Relations with Our Allies

The third area of change is our relations with key allies.
Europe is experiencing fundamental changes. In security terms,
the challenge from the Warsaw Pact has disintegrated, and the
military capability of the Soviet forces that remain in Eastern
Europe is diminishing. The countries of Eastern Europe are
seeking to reweave themselves back into the larger political and
economic fabric of Europe. A unified Germany stands at the
center of the continent. Economic change is also underway: the
United States supports European efforts to create a single
unified market by 1992. As the continent works through the
political, economic and security challenges of this new era, and
discovers a new identity, there will be pressures and
temptations to question fundamental elements of our trans-
Atlantic commitments. These ties must not weaken: the U.S.
shares with its allies in Western Europe a common history and
heritage--a shared commitment to freedom and individual rights.
The continued strength of NATO remains critical.

As our concerns shift from the containment of the Soviet
Union to possible instability in Europe, a substantial American
presence and continued cohesion within the Western alliance
remain vital to furthering our interests. A U.S. presence will
provide reassurance and stability as the new democracies of
Eastern Europe mesh themselves into a larger and evolving
Europe. The Soviet Union will retain the largest army in Europe
by far even after its forces are pulled back within its borders
and projected conventional force reductions are completed.
While its mission may be changed in this new era, the North
Atlantic Alliance remains indispensable to peace and stability
in Europe. To keep the Alliance strong and viable in a new
environment, we must recognize that there are important tasks
beyond the changed--but still important--task to balance and
deter Soviet military power. In this regard, it is important to
note that both our new friends in Eastern Europe and the leaders
of the Soviet Union have made it clear to me in my visits that
they consider a continued U.S. presence in Europe and a strong
NATO to be essential to overall European stability.

We expect to share more equitably with our increasingly
strong allies and partners the worldwide responsibilities that
go with leadership. Operation Desert Shield/Storm is a good
model for dealing with future crises.

Changes in the Nature of Future Warfare

For some time the Soviets have been writing about a military
technological revolution that lies just ahead. They liken it to
the 1920s and 1930s, when revolutionary breakthroughs--such as
the blitzkrieg, aircraft carriers, and amphibious operations--

930 — 9

changed the shape and nature of warfare. We have already seen
the early signs of this revolution in the recent breakthroughs
in Stealth, information, and other key technologies. This
revolution will present enormous challenges, not just
technologically, but in the development of doctrine and
operational concepts. Whatever we do, the Soviets and others
will be pursuing this revolution diligently. Revolutionary
military capabilities are a reality with which our future
strategy must deal.

The military technological revolution will have political,
as well as military import, both in our competition with the
Soviets and more broadly in the military arena. The recent
changes in the Soviet Union reflect in no small degree the
Soviet perception of this military technological revolution. In
large part the Soviet leadership accepted the changes Gorbachev
sought because they perceived they could not keep pace in this
technological revolution. By the same token, the technological
revolution could be used as justification to devote more
resources to Soviet defense spending, further inhibiting
economic prospects. The technological edge we have shown in
Desert Storm and the promise of breakthroughs tomorrow will have
an even greater effect on the calculations of regional powers.
Staying ahead in this technical revolution will help shape the
future security environment in ways favorable to us and will
help give us capabilities that we are comfortable employing for
deterrence or defense against tomorrow's regional aggressors.

ENDURING U.S. SECURITY OBJECTIVES

In the first exhilaration of the dramatic changes of 1989,
some began to question the nature of enduring U.S. interests.
Let me review briefly some broad American purposes that
persist--even in this changed world I have described.

Security. Security is the first requirement upon which all
our individual and national aspirations depend. We must accept
that even after historic Cold War successes we live in a
dangerous world. The Soviet strategic nuclear arsenal is the
most dramatic example of our vulnerability because the USSR
continues to possess, and indeed has a modernized capability, to
destroy this country with little warning. This is not to imply
that we believe a bolt from the blue attack is likely, but to
note our vulnerability. We must also ensure the safety of our
commerce and of our people at home and abroad as they pursue the
normal conduct of their daily affairs. Thus our security
requires maintaining capabilities for deterrence and defense
across the broad spectrum, from low intensity threats and
noncombatant evacuation efforts to strategic nuclear threats.

Democracy and Prosperity. Second, we seek to promote a
world environment in which societies with values similar to our
own--political and economic freedom, human rights, and
democratic institutions--can flourish. We engage in such

350— 10

0077

efforts because they benefit our friends abroad, but also
because we know our own security and prosperity are well-served
when we are surrounded by friends and allies who share our
fundamental values and aims. We know we cannot long remain
secure in isolation.

The President, in his State of the Union address, spoke of
these "universal aspirations of mankind: peace and security,
freedom, and the rule of law." For 200 years we have served
such ends through our example. But it is also necessary from
time to time to help others in providing for their own
security, to join in security alliances, and to promote regional
military and political stability through economic and social
development and the pursuit of just resolutions of persistent
regional conflicts.   And, at times, where our interests merit
the sacrifice, it will be necessary to use force to deter
aggressors or defend freedom. In the Persian Gulf today, in
Panama last year, and in our longstanding commitments in Asia,
the Pacific and Europe we have demonstrated our readiness to
bear the burdens our interests demand.

Leadership. The President clearly outlined his view of
America's role in the world in the State of the Union address:
"Today, in a rapidly changing world, American leadership is
indispensable....Among the nations of the world, only the United
States of America has had both the moral standing and the means
to back it up. We are the only nation on this earth that could
assemble the forces of peace." Our experience in the Persian
Gulf demonstrates once again the continued importance of
American leadership. In my recent discussions with world
leaders, I have been struck by how unique a role America plays
in furthering the President's vision of a world "where diverse
nations are drawn together in common cause," and "aggression
will meet collective resistance."

THE NEW DEFENSE STRATEGY

To meet our aims in the changing and increasingly
interdependent world around us, we must be ready to show moral
and political leadership; to reassure others of our commitment
to protect our interests; and, if necessary, to respond to
threats resolutely with forces for deterrence or defense. These
aims and a close appreciation of the changes and continuities in
today's world give rise to the main emphases of our new defense
strategy.

Let me summarize briefly the key elements of the new defense
strategy outlined by the President last August. First, we need
to maintain a system of alliances worldwide. Second, to give
substance and meaning to those commitments, we want to maintain
US forward deployed forces, although at lower levels than in the
past. Third, we must retain the forces and mobility to respond
to crises and to reinforce those forward units. Fourth, we need
a robust navy to control the world's oceans. Fifth, as we

J30-11

0078

reduce forces deliberately--based on continuing reevaluations of
the strategic environment, we must retain the national capacity
to reconstitute forces, should this be needed. Sixth, we need
to preserve a strong strategic offensive and defensive
capability.

The most important change reflected in this new strategy is
that we no longer are focused on the threat of a Soviet-led,
European-wide conflict leading to global war. Our strategy
continues to recognize the massive conventional capabilities the
Soviets will retain for the foreseeable future. Yet, we judge
that the striking political and military changes in the USSR and
Eastern Europe noted earlier would alter the character of the
remaining Soviet threat from the capability to wage global war
to a threat to a single region in Europe or elsewhere. To size
and shape the forces we will need in the future, the new
strategy therefore shifts its focus to regional threats and the
related requirements for forward presence and crisis response.
We believe we will have sufficient warning of the redevelopment
of a Soviet threat of global war, so that we could reconstitute
forces over time if needed.

Our program of reductions and our budget have thus been
based on certain assumptions about the future strategic
environment. If trends prove less favorable along the way than
we first projected, we may not be able to reduce forces as fast
or as far as we have planned. Remarkably, the reshaping and
reducing of our forces now underway is occurring against the
backdrop of a major war in the Persian Gulf and worrisome trends
in the Soviet Union. I know of no historical precedent for our
country making changes of this magnitude under such conditions.
This in itself is cause for due caution.

Strategic Deterrence

I have earlier noted that the Soviets continue to modernize
their strategic nuclear arsenal at a pace that seems out of step
with their positive actions in other spheres. Given all that is
at stake, this is an area in which we can ill-afford to accept
much risk. America must continue to maintain a diverse mix of
survivable and highly capable offensive nuclear forces, as well
as supporting command and control assets. At the same time as
we modernize, we have planned to scale back our strategic forces
in accordance with our expectations of a START agreement
covering such forces. Negotiations with the Soviets are
continuing intensively but have not yet yielded success in
negotiation. We hope to be able to complete a treaty in the
near future, as we assumed when we formulated our currently
planned reductions.

Future Secretaries of Defense are going to have to be able
to deploy defenses against ballistic missiles--whether against
the kind of theater threat we faced against SCUDs, or the far
more sophisticated threats we anticipate in the future. We will

930- 12

pursue a defensive system for global protection against limited ballistic missile strikes--whatever their source.

Forward Presence

Our new strategy emphasizes the importance of U.S. presence abroad, albeit at reduced levels. This is one of the key roles on which we will size our forces. The success of our historic strategy of forward presence should be carefully recognized. We should be slow to make destabilizing changes. Recent attention has focussed on our plans to reduce our levels of forward deployed forces, especially in Europe under CFE, but also in Asia under last year's strategy initiative.

Despite its historic success, the great importance of maintaining a forward military presence may not be widely appreciated. Our presence sends an unmistakable signal to allies and adversaries alike of our commitment to be engaged in a region. It supports our aim of continuing to play a leadership role in international events. In this era of shifti.., regional power balances, our forward military presence supports our aim of maintaining the stability that lets other nations flourish, by preventing the emergence of dangerous power vacuums or imbalances and by staving off regional arms races. Forward forces also provide an initial capability to respond rapidly to regional crises or contingencies.

Presence can take many forms. The stationing of forces in selected forward bases is perhaps the most tangible demonstration of U.S. commitment in key areas. Periodic deployments, rotations, exercises, and visits provide a flexible operational presence, and may loom larger than before as a way of maintaining our future forward presence. Not least, we must maintain the infrastructure and logistics arrangements that are so essential to being able to sustain a forward presence.

While we will reduce our forward presence, there are risks in reducing too far or too fast. These risks regarding reduced forward presence are sometimes likened to thin ice: you don't know for sure how much is too little, until you've fallen through--and then the consequences can be dire and long-lasting. To keep this risk acceptable, reductions in presence to levels near the minimum acceptable should be gradual and part of a carefully developed and agreed long-term plan. Our phased plan for reductions in Asia, including the agreement with our allies on a 10 percent reduction in our forces there by FY 1992, exemplify this commitment to keeping our forward presence as trim as possible. Let me reemphasize, however, that we cannot withdraw from the world. Our forward military presence will remain a key factor in our overall national defense strategy and in the strategies at our allies as well.

930 — 13

Crisis Response

The need to respond to regional crises is one of the key elements of our new strategy and plays a significant role in how we size our active and reserve forces. We have already noted how important regional threats can be to our interests. Under conditions pertaining during our policy of containment, safety demanded that we assume that a major regional conflict involving superpower interests might not stay limited to that region, but could well escalate to a global conflict. This made any single-regional conflict a "lesser-included case" or a potential precursor to a global war scenario. In contrast, we now focus on a disparate array of possible regional conflicts that we believe are more likely to remain localized.

The regional contingencies we might face are many and varied, including differences in terrain, climate, distance from the U.S., nature of threat forces, potential for outside involvement, and level of infrastructure and host nation support. One trait most of them share, however, is that they will arise on very short notice, and therefore require a highly responsive military capability. As we have learned again most clearly in Operation Desert Shield/Desert Storm, a regional crisis can also mean mounting a very large military operation. Furthermore, the proliferating unconventional threats of ballistic missiles and chemical, biological or even nuclear weapons, plus the potentially confounding threat of terrorism, raise the risks our forces face if deployed to respond to such crises, and raise the stakes involved in forestalling or containing them.

Finally, we must recognize that when the U.S. is engaged (perhaps in concert with others) in responding to a substantial regional crisis, potential aggressors in other areas may be tempted to capitalize on our preoccupation. The requirements of both deterrence and defense dictate that we not reduce forces to a level that would leave us overly vulnerable to this threat.

Force Reconstitution

The dramatic changes of 1989 and 1990 in Eastern Europe and the Soviet Union allow us to plan on dramatic increases in the time available to meet any renewed threat of a massive, theater-wide attack on Europe that could lead to global war. Such long warning of a renewed global threat enables us to reduce our forces in being to levels sufficient to meet the regional threats which are now our focus. This allows us to reduce our forces now, so long as we are prepared to build, as the President has said, "wholly new forces" should the need to counter a global threat reemerge.

Timely reconstitution requires that we take care to preserve the longest-lead elements of our security. This includes particularly our alliance structures, forward deployments and

930—14

0081

access, and the technological and doctrinal edge that comes from vigorous innovation and development. This also includes particular weapons systems or capabilities that take a long time to rebuild, such as large weapons platforms that require long production or recommission times, and highly skilled personnel, like unit commanders and specialized technicians. We can benefit from our defense investments over the last decade by retaining some equipment of disestablished units in laid-up status, and tapping the pool of trained personnel exiting units but still accessible in reserve manpower categories. We also will retain some units in very low-strength, cadre-type status. But our emphasis has been on removing from the force those units needed for a resurgent global threat that could be reconstituted in the expected time available. Moreover, our reconstitution concept is not necessarily simply to recreate the same forces that we "deconstituted." Rather, we would consider what new forces were most needed for a specific reemerging threat.

We recognize that to take major reconstitution measures would require major political decisions, potentially on the basis of early strategic warning indications. We will therefore give increased attention to the intelligence and warning processes that would support such decision making, as well as measures that will provide an early response while minimizing undue escalatory pressures.

Following a strategy of reconstitution prudently accepts some risk during a time of reduced likelihood of global conflict, to permit adequate attention to other concerns. These include capabilities for the more likely regional threats we face now, plus the long-term technological and doctrinal innovation which may be decisive against future threats-- including those in the further future which we cannot now even foresee.

IMPLEMENTING THE NEW STRATEGY

The Administration's FY 1992-93 budget request is the first installment of DoD's comprehensive FY 1992-97 multiyear defense program. That program is the result of the Department's rigorous analysis of the capabilities needed to support the new U.S. defense strategy. The overall goal is to streamline and restructure America's armed forces, in order to provide those needed capabilities within projected fiscal constraints. In essence, U.S. forces are becoming smaller, but still fully capable of securing our nation and its global interests.

The FY 1992-93 DoD budget reflects priorities that flow directly from our new strategy. (Chart 1) Rapid response to global crises requires sustainment of the current high quality and superior capabilities of U.S. forces, especially as their total size is reduced. This in turn requires continued support for the high quality of U.S. military personnel, vigorous defense research and development, the fielding of advanced

military systems as soon as necessary, and the preservation of
critical elements of America's defense industrial and technology
base. These priorities also enable DoD to reconstitute a larger
military posture, if needed.

Other priorities include the ability to project military
power rapidly to areas of U.S. strategic interest. The new
strategy also requires that U.S. forces sustain their
traditional high readiness. To ensure credible nuclear
deterrence, DoD will maintain strong offensive nuclear forces.
We will also pursue strategic and theater defenses to provide
global protection against limited ballistic missile strikes--
regardless of their source.

DoD budget proposals also reflect my commitment to continue
to strengthen defense management and streamline the U.S. defense
infrastructure, to extract the greatest security value from
increasingly scarce resources. Special attention is going
toward efficient acquisition. The goals include funding
sustainable production rates for essential programs and
terminating lower priority programs.

Budget Topline and Trends

DoD budget authority levels for FY 1991 through FY 1995 are
consistent with the discretionary caps for defense in last
fall's budget summit agreement. These topline numbers represent
a nominal freeze in DoD budget authority at about $278 billion,
starting in FY 1992. Total DoD budget authority for FY 1991
through FY 1995 will be $131 billion less than estimated in the
President's January 1990 request. After an 11.3 percent real
decline in FY 1991, DoD budget authority will decline, in real
terms, an average 3 percent per year through FY 1996. (Chart 2)

DoD outlays as a share of America's Gross National Product
(GNP) are expected to fall to 3.6 percent in FY 1996, the lowest
level since before World War II and well below the 4.7 percent
reached during the defense decline of the 1970s. (Chart 3)

Force Structure

The FY 1992-93 request includes reductions in the U.S. force
structure that continue a prudently phased plan for reaching the
force targets established for the new strategy and threat
projections. Our FY 1995 forces will approximate those targets
and be well below FY 1990 levels. (Chart 4)

U.S. strategic forces are programmed to be scaled back in
accordance with expectations regarding arms reductions
agreements and to enable DoD to maintain credible strategic
deterrence at the least cost. Retirement of the Minuteman II
force will begin in FY 1992. Retirements of submarines with the
aging Poseidon missile are to be accelerated. During the 1990s,
the current mix of 34 Poseidon and Trident boats will be reduced

930 — 16

to a force of 18 Trident submarines carrying Trident I (C-4) and
Trident II (D-5) missiles. Strategic bombers will decrease from
268 in FY 1990 to 171 in FY 1993, as older B-52s are retired and
FB-111s are transferred to tactical use.

U.S. <u>conventional</u> forces will be restructured so that they
best support the new strategy. For crisis response, we must be
able to deploy to regions of U.S. interest sufficient forces
with the capabilities needed to counter a wide variety of
contingencies. Thus the restructured force will include a high
airlift and sealift capacity, substantial and highly effective
maritime and amphibious forces, a full and sophisticated array
of combat aircraft, both heavy and light Army divisions, and
appropriate special operations forces.

Because serious contingencies can arise quickly, a timely
U.S. response would require mostly active forces. Reserve
forces would initially provide airlift, sealift, and some other
vital support for deploying forces. When longer preparation
allowed, reserves could provide additional support, plus combat
units that would be needed for larger or prolonged deployments.

In applying the new strategy to our Total Force posture, we
project that reserve forces will decline by about the same
percentage as active forces. That circumstance, however, should
not mask the fact that our future force will <u>not</u> merely be a
proportionally scaled-back version of today's force. We are
planning to eliminate those forces--be they active or reserve--
whose justification has been based on the previous threat of
short-notice global war. We have given priority to preserving a
mix of forces that can best meet our strategy's requirements for
forward presence and crisis response. Some types of reserve
forces will be fully retained or even increased, while others
will be cut considerably. For example, Army reserve (and
active) components will be cut substantially; in contrast, the
Air Force reserve will decline only slightly. The criteria for
such restructuring have come from the new strategy.

To help provide for reconstitution in our new strategy, some
reserve forces will be maintained in "cadre" status. Cadre
units would have greatly reduced manpower and training; but they
would have the equipment and other preparations needed to
facilitate a smooth transition to full strength if required.
Our plans currently include two cadre divisions in the Army (not
counted in the 18 divisions programmed for FY 1995), plus
creation of a new status for some Navy frigates.

DESERT SHIELD/STORM SUPPLEMENTAL APPROPRIATIONS REQUEST

Last fall's budget summit agreement specified that
incremental costs associated with the Persian Gulf crisis would
be treated as emergency funding requirements, not subject to the
defense caps in the agreement. Consequently, the President's
recently submitted FY 1992-93 defense budget request do not

950 – 17

0084

reflect those costs. FY 1990 incremental costs of Desert Shield and increased fuel prices were covered by shifts in previously appropriated DoD funds ($800 million) and by a supplemental appropriation ($2.1 billion). In mid-February, the Administration sent to Congress a request to cover FY 1991 incremental costs of Desert Shield/Storm, at least in part.

Because it was impossible to predict accurately future operational requirements when it was prepared, this supplemental does not purport to estimate definitively or necessarily fund completely what might be the eventual total cost of the war and the subsequent redeployment of U.S. forces. Rather, the primary intent is to obtain approval for a funding plan to cover our immediate and known operational requirements, to include establishing a mechanism for spending foreign contributions most effectively, in order to offset U.S. costs as much as possible.

The FY 1991 Desert Shield/Storm supplemental requests the authorization and appropriation of $15 billion in new budget authority. This and other provisions we are proposing are needed to provide the Department of Defense (DoD) with the necessary funds and flexibility to meet immediate operational requirements until sufficient allied contributions are received, and to accelerate production of essential items. This $15 billion in new budget authority, plus the $54.5 billion pledged by our allies, could prove sufficient to cover all our Desert Shield/Storm incremental costs. But it will be some time before we can estimate if that will be true or not.

ALLIED CONTRIBUTIONS FOR OPERATION DESERT SHIELD/STORM

Operation Desert Shield/Storm was part of an effort that was truly multinational in scope and character. In that spirit, U.S. requirements incident to deploying and sustaining the largest force in the Gulf area will be substantially offset by contributions from our allies. (Chart 5)

Some of this allied cost sharing comes in the form of direct financial assistance. Cash received is deposited in the Defense Cooperation Account, established by Congress as part of the FY 1990 Desert Shield Supplemental Appropriation. Deposits to the Account are invested in 90-day Treasury securities. Account funds do not become available for obligation by DoD until after they are appropriated by Congress.

The other form of allied cost sharing is in-kind contributions--goods and services provided to U.S. forces directly. Most prominently, this includes Saudi Arabia's commitment to provide all host nation support for U.S. forces, both on its soil and in the surrounding waters. This host nation support includes food, fuel, water, facilities, and local transportation. In-kind contributions from other nations include materials, supplies, airlift, and sealift.

930 - 18

0085

Commitments to us from our allies total ~~two billion~~.
According to our latest recapitulation, we have received ~~$19.6~~
billion in allied contributions so far. However, there is a
~~considerable~~ delay between the time in-kind assistance is
rendered and the time we can officially account for it. We
fully expect that our allies will fulfill their commitments.

Also reflecting the responsibility sharing of the Gulf
action, nearly ~~50 nations~~ contributed to the military effort.
Of these, about ~~28 countries had personnel~~ in the area of
operations. Our allies committed nearly 300,000 troops and over
60 warships, 750 combat aircraft, and 1200 tanks to the effort.

CONCLUSION

We are at the dawn of a new era. For much of the past 45
years our primary security concern has been the Soviet threat in
Europe. We met that challenge successfully. The threat to
Western Europe has diminished. But as the war in the Gulf
demonstrated, meeting regional threats can be quite demanding
even when we can marshal international cooperation.

To preserve our unique international role, to consolidate
changes in Europe, and to contain and defeat the many regional
threats we may one day face, we must sustain America's military
might. Military strength like we relied on in the Persian Gulf
cannot be built overnight. Continued investment in America's
defense is a must, as we look forward to the years ahead.

930 — 19

MAR.19 '91 19:01 KOREAN EMBASSY WASHINGTON DC   P.010

0086

92 걸프 사태 미국 동향 4

DEFENSE BUDGET PRIORITIES

- People
- Power Projection/Mobility
- Force Quality
- Readiness
- Strategic Offensive and Defensive Forces
- Technological Advantage
- Efficient Acquisition
- Streamlined Infrastructure

930-20

Chart # 2

DoD BUDGET AUTHORITY
($ in Billions)

	1991	1992	1993	1994	1995	Cumulative 1991-1995
President's Budget January 1990	295.1	300.0	304.4	308.0	311.8	1,519.3
Real Program Decline	-2.6%	-2.0%	-2.0%	-2.0%	-2.0%	-10.6%
Dollar Reduction	-22.1	-21.7	-26.5	-29.8	-31.1	-131.2
President's Budget February 1991	273.0	278.3	277.9	278.2	280.7	1,388.1
Real Program Decline	-11.3%	-0.9%	-3.9%	-3.6%	-2.7%	-22.4%

0088

Chart # 3

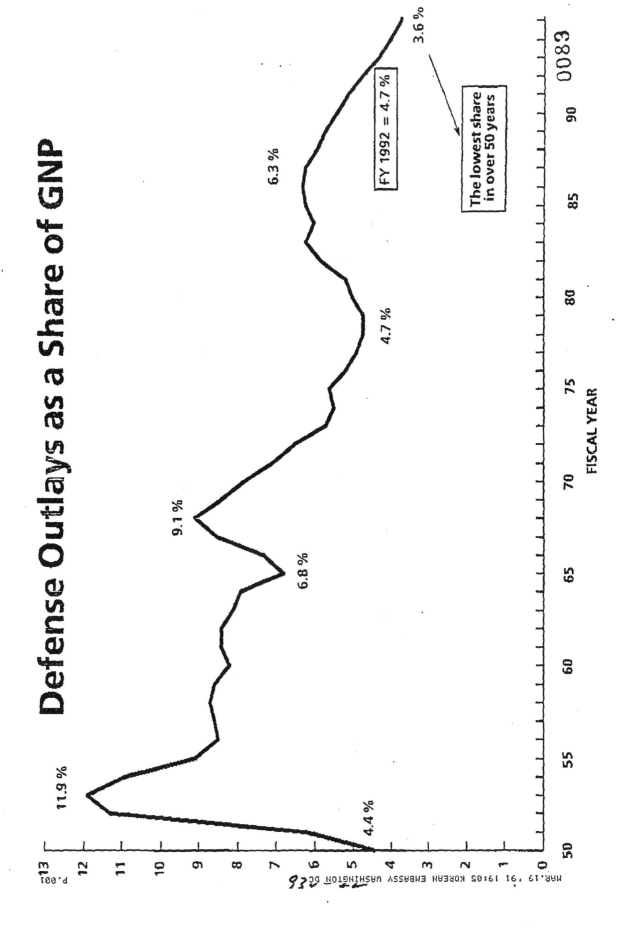

Defense Outlays as a Share of GNP

FISCAL YEAR

11.9 %

9.1 %

6.8 %

4.7 %

6.3 %

FY 1992 = 4.7 %

3.6 %

The lowest share in over 50 years

4.4 %

P.001

MAR.19 '91 19:05 KOREAN EMBASSY WASHINGTON DC

0083

Chart #4

FORCE STRUCTURE

	FY 1990	FY 1995
Army Divisions	28 (18 active)	18 (12 active)
Aircraft Carriers	13	12
Carrier Air Wings	15 (13 active)	13 (11 active)
Battle Force Ships	545	451
Tactical Fighter Wings	36 (24 active)	26 (15 active)
Strategic Bombers	268	181

Chart # 5

DESERT SHIELD
Major Foreign Contributions
(U.S. $ Million)

Contributor	Commitments 1/	Receipts Cash 2/	Receipts In-Kind 2/	Receipts Total
Saudi Arabia	16,839	4,536	1,566	6,102
Kuwait	16,006	5,500	10	5,510
UAE	4,000	1,870	140	2,010
Japan	10,740	866	457	1,323
Germany	6,572	4,092	531	4,623
Korea	385	50	21	71
Others	3	-	3	3
Total	54,545	16,914	2,728	19,642

1/ Commitments are through March 31 and do not include pledges to other countries.

2/ Cash received as of March 15; In-Kind as of January 31.

0091

관리
번호 91-743

외 무 부

종 별 : 지 급

번 호 : USW-1285

일 시 : 91 0319 2040

수 신 : 장관(미북,미안,중동일,기정)

발 신 : 주 미 대 사

제 목 : 상원 걸프전비 추가 지출안 봉과

연 USW-1117

1. 상원 본회의는 금 3.19 걸프전비 관련 추가 지불 법안을 찬성 98, 반대 1 의 압도적 다수로 봉과시켰음. 동 법안은 3.7 하원 봉과법안(H. 1282)과 마찬가지로 걸프전 총 소요 경비를 426 억불로 상정, 외국 기여금에서 우선적으로 충당하고 부족분에 대해서만 미국 자체 예산 150 억불 범위내에서 소요 경비를 지출할수 있도록 하되,150 억불중 잔액이 발생할 경우 국고에 반납하도록 규정하고있음.

2. 한편, 상원 세출위는 3.14 상기 지출법안 심의시 UAE 의 기여 약속 금액(40 억불)이 이락의 인접국으로서 지불능력에 비추어 부족한 액수라고 비난하고UAE 가 기여금 증액을 약속할때까지 행정부가 의회에 대해 대 UAE 무기 판매 승인 요청을 하지 말것으로 촉구하고, 나아가 기여 약속 금액 전액을 지불하지 않는 국가에 대해 미국의 무기 판매를 금지하는 일반 규정을 삽입한바 있음.

3. 한편, 금일 상원 본회의는 걸프전 참전 용사들의 복지 향상과 대 이스라엘 (6 억 5 천만불) 대터키(2 억불) 원조를 포함하는 52 억불 지출 법안(HR 1281)을 아울러 봉과 시킨바 있음.

4. 당관 관찰및 평가

가. 금일 상원 봉과한 걸프전배 지출 예산은 현재까지 공약된 우방국들의 기여금 545 억불 보다 훨씬 하회하는 금액으로 이론상 기여금액이 전액 기탁될 경우 미국 자체 예산 충당은 물론 상당한 액수의 잔액이 발생하는것으로 되어 있으며, 따라서 동 잔액에 대한 처리 문제에 기여국들의 관심이 집중되고 있음.

나. 금일 백악관 기자 브리핑시 관련 질문에 대하여 FITZWATER 대변인은 걸프전을 통하여 미국이 이익(PROFIT)을 남길 생각은 없다는 내용을 가볍게 답변하였으나, 금후 계속 이에 관한 논란이 계속될 소지가 클것으로 보임.

미주국	장관	차관	1차보	2차보	미주국	중아국	청와대	안기부

PAGE 1

91.03.20   11:20

외신 2과   통제관 BN

0092

다. 한편 미 의회는 지난 3.6 하원 CHAPMAN 의원의 발의에 따라 통과된 결의안에서 볼수 있듯이 기여공약분에 대한 조속 기탁을 관련 우방국들에 계속 촉구하는 압력을 가할것으로 예상됨.

(대사 현홍주-국장)

91.12.31 까지

검토필 (19(.6.30.)

일반문서로 재분류 (19(12 31

USW(F) ― 1515
수신 : 장관 (미북)
발신 : 주미대사
제목 : 걸프전비 추정액관련자료

II   ↑b

Calendar No. 42

102D CONGRESS
1ST SESSION

H. R. 1282

[Report No. 102-23]

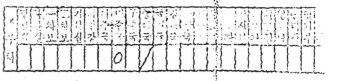

IN THE SENATE OF THE UNITED STATES

MARCH 11 (legislative day, FEBRUARY 6), 1991
Received; read twice and referred to the Committee on Appropriations

MARCH 14 (legislative day, FEBRUARY 6), 1991
Reported by Mr. BYRD, with amendments
[Omit the part struck through and insert the part printed in italic]

AN ACT

Making supplemental appropriations and transfers for "Operation Desert Shield/Desert Storm" for the fiscal year ending September 30, 1991, and for other purposes.

1   *Be it enacted by the Senate and House of Representa-*

2 *tives of the United States of America in Congress assembled,*

3 That the following sums are appropriated, out of any

4 money in the Treasury not otherwise appropriated, to pro-

5 vide supplemental appropriations for the fiscal year end-

6 ing September 30, 1991, and for other purposes, namely:

1515―1   0094

2

1   PERSIAN GULF REGIONAL DEFENSE FUND

2   (INCLUDING TRANSFER OF FUNDS)

3   For incremental costs of the Department of Defense

4   and the Department of Transportation associated with op-

5   erations in and around the Persian Gulf as part of oper-

6   ations currently known as Operation Desert Shield (in-

7   cluding Operation Desert Storm), $15,000,000,000 is ap-

8   propriated to the Persian Gulf Regional Defense Fund,

9   which is hereby established in the Treasury of the United

10   States, and in addition such sums as necessary are appro-

11   priated to such Fund by transfer from current and future

12   balances in the Defense Cooperation Account, such sums

13   so appropriated to the Persian Gulf Regional Defense

14   Fund to be available only for transfer *transfers by the Sec-*

15   *retaries of Defense or Transportation, with the approval of*

16   *the Director of the Office of Management and Budget*, in

17   a total amount not to exceed $42,588,372,000

18   *$42,625,822,000* to the following chapters and accounts in

19   not to exceed the following amounts:

3

CHAPTER I

DEPARTMENT OF DEFENSE—MILITARY

MILITARY PERSONNEL

(TRANSFER OF FUNDS)

MILITARY PERSONNEL, ARMY

For an additional amount for "Military Personnel, Army", ~~$4,862,700,000~~ *$4,849,000,000*.

MILITARY PERSONNEL, NAVY

For an additional amount for "Military Personnel, Navy", ~~$797,400,000~~ *$792,000,000*.

MILITARY PERSONNEL, MARINE CORPS

For an additional amount for "Military Personnel, Marine Corps", ~~$983,400,000~~ *$978,000,000*.

MILITARY PERSONNEL, AIR FORCE

For an additional amount for "Military Personnel, Air Force", ~~$1,278,200,000~~ *$1,271,000,000*.

OPERATION AND MAINTENANCE

(TRANSFER OF FUNDS)

OPERATION AND MAINTENANCE, ARMY

For an additional amount for "Operation and Maintenance, Army", ~~$16,393,750,000~~ *$14,981,400,000~~, of~~ ~~which $350,000 shall be available only for the 1991 Memorial Day Celebration~~.

1515-3

0096

102 걸프 사태 미국 동향 4

4

1   OPERATION AND MAINTENANCE, NAVY

2   For an additional amount for "Operation and Main-

3   tenance, Navy", ~~$3,000,500,000~~ $2,391,000,000.

4   OPERATION AND MAINTENANCE, MARINE CORPS

5   For an additional amount for "Operation and Main-

6   tenance, Marine Corps", ~~$1,330,000,000~~ $1,197,000,000.

7   OPERATION AND MAINTENANCE, AIR FORCE

8   For an additional amount for "Operation and Main-

9   tenance, Air Force", ~~$4,080,000,000~~ $3,026,000,000.

10   OPERATION AND MAINTENANCE, DEFENSE AGENCIES

11   For an additional amount for "Operation and Main-

12   tenance, Defense Agencies", ~~$236,000,000~~ $173,000,000.

13   ~~OPERATION AND MAINTENANCE, NAVY RESERVE~~

14   ~~For an additional amount for "Operation and Main-~~

15   ~~tenance, Navy Reserve", $16,000,000.~~

16   ~~OPERATION AND MAINTENANCE, AIR NATIONAL GUARD~~

17   ~~For an additional amount for "Operation and Main-~~

18   ~~tenance, Air National Guard", $55,000,000.~~

19   PROCUREMENT

20   (TRANSFER OF FUNDS)

21   AIRCRAFT PROCUREMENT, ARMY

22   For an additional amount for "Aircraft procurement,

23   Army", $7,100,000.

1   MISSILE PROCUREMENT, AF

2   For an additional amount for "Missile procurement,

3 Army", $311,900,000.

4   PROCUREMENT OF WEAPONS AND TRACKED COMBAT

5   VEHICLES, ARMY

6   For an additional amount for "Procurement of weap-

7 ons and tracked combat vehicles, Army", $26,300,000.

8   PROCUREMENT OF AMMUNITION, ARMY

9   For an additional amount for "Procurement of am-

10 munition, Army", $~~437,000,000~~ $425,800,000.

11   OTHER PROCUREMENT, ARMY

12   For an additional amount for "Other procurement,

13 Army", $~~30,300,000~~ $26,300,000.

14   AIRCRAFT PROCUREMENT, NAVY

15   For an additional amount for "Aircraft procurement,

16 Navy", $16,000,000.

17   WEAPONS PROCUREMENT, NAVY

18   For an additional amount for "Weapons procure-

19 ment, Navy", $~~1,065,100,000~~ $1,057,300,000.

20   OTHER PROCUREMENT, NAVY

21   For an additional amount for "Other procurement,

22 Navy", $34,600,000.

23   PROCUREMENT, MARINE CORPS

24   For an additional amount for "Procurement, Marine

25 Corps", $~~68,000,000~~ $64,200,000.

HR 1282 RS

1515-5

0098

6

1   AIRCRAFT PROCUREMENT, AIR FORCE

2   For an additional amount for "Aircraft procurement,

3 Air Force", $101,200,000.

4   MISSILE PROCUREMENT, AIR FORCE

5   For an additional amount for "Missile procurement,

6 Air Force", $400,000,000.

7   OTHER PROCUREMENT, AIR FORCE

8   For an additional amount for "Other procurement,

9 Air Force", $419,100,000.

10   PROCUREMENT, DEFENSE AGENCIES

11   For an additional amount for "Procurement, Defense

12 Agencies", $2,700,000.

13   ~~RESEARCH, DEVELOPMENT, TEST AND~~

14   ~~EVALUATION~~

15   ~~(TRANSFER OF FUNDS)~~

16   ~~RESEARCH, DEVELOPMENT, TEST AND EVALUATION,~~

17   ~~ARMY~~

18   ~~For an additional amount for "Research, Develop-~~

19 ~~ment, Test and Evaluation, Army", $1,200,000.~~

20   REVOLVING AND MANAGEMENT FUNDS

21   (TRANSFER OF FUNDS)

22   ARMY STOCK FUND

23   For an additional amount for "Army Stock Fund",

24 ~~$57,000,000~~ *$214,000,000.*

HR 1282 RS   *1515 - 6*

0099

7

1   AIR FORCE STOCK FUND

2   For an additional amount for "Air Force Stock

3 Fund", ~~$214,000,000~~ $57,000,000.

4   COMBAT COSTS OF OPERATION DESERT

5   SHIELD/DESERT STORM

6   (TRANSFER OF FUNDS)

7   For expenses, not otherwise provided for, necessary

8 to finance the estimated partial costs of combat and other

9 related costs of Operation Desert Shield/Desert Storm in

10 the following additional amounts: ~~for Operation and main-~~

11 ~~tenance,~~   ~~$5,000,000,000;~~   ~~for~~   ~~Procurement,~~

12 ~~$1,300,000,000; In all: $6,300,000,000~~ *for Operation and*

13 *maintenance,*   *$7,000,000,000;*   *for*   *Procurement,*

14 *$2,750,000,000.*

15   GENERAL PROVISIONS

16   (INCLUDING TRANSFER OF FUNDS)

17   SEC. 101. (a) In administering the Persian Gulf Re-

18 gional Defense Fund, the Secretary of Defense shall use

19 the corpus of the Fund only to the extent that amounts

20 ~~transferred to the Fund~~ from the Defense Cooperation Ac-

21 count established under section 2608 of title 10, United

22 States Code, are not currently available.

23   (b) If the balance of the corpus of the Persian Gulf

24 Regional Defense Fund is less than $15,000,000,000, the

25 Secretary shall transfer amounts from the Defense Co-

1 operatio——ccount to the Persian Gulf R—¬al Defense

2 Fund, to the extent that amounts are available in that

3 Account, to restore the balance in the corpus of the Fund

4 to $15,000,000,000.

5   (c) For purposes of this section, the term "corpus of

6 the Fund" means the amount of $15,000,000,000 appro-

7 priated by this Act to the Persian Gulf Regional Defense

8 Fund from the general fund of the Treasury, as such

9 amount is restored from time to time by transfers from

10 the Defense Cooperation Account.

11   (INCLUDING TRANSFER OF FUNDS)

12   SEC. 102. (a) The authority provided in this Act to

13 transfer funds from the Persian Gulf Regional Defense

14 Fund *and from the Defense Cooperation Account* is in addi-

15 tion to any other transfer authority contained in this or

16 any other Act making appropriations for the Department

17 of Defense for fiscal year 1991.

18   (b) Amounts transferred from the Persian Gulf Re-

19 gional Defense Fund *and from the Defense Cooperation Ac-*

20 *count* shall be merged with and be available for the same

21 purposes and the same time period as the appropriations

22 to which transferred.

23   (c) Amounts appropriated to the Persian Gulf Re-

24 gional Defense Fund shall remain available until trans-

25 ferred.

HR 1282 RS

/5/5~d

0101

9

1   (d)(1) Upon payment of all incremental costs associ-
2 ated with the purpose for which the Persian Gulf Regional
3 Defense Fund is established, the Fund shall be termi-
4 nated.

5   (2) If the balance in the Fund at the time of the ter-
6 mination is $15,000,000,000 or less, the balance shall re-
7 vert to the general fund of the Treasury. ~~If the balance~~
8 ~~in the Fund at the time of the termination is in excess~~
9 ~~of $15,000,000,000, the amount of $15,000,000,000 shall~~
10 ~~revert to the general fund of the Treasury and the remain-~~
11 ~~ing amount shall revert to the Defense Cooperation Ac-~~
12 ~~count.~~

13   *(e) The Secretary of Defense shall notify the Commit-*
14 *tees on Appropriations and Armed Services of the Senate*
15 *and House of Representatives before making any transfer*
16 *from the Persian Gulf Regional Defense Fund or from the*
17 *Defense Cooperation Account. No transfer may be made*
18 *until the seventh day after such committees receive the noti-*
19 *fication required by this subsection to be submitted for such*
20 *transfer.*

21   (TRANSFER OF FUNDS)

22   SEC. 103. (a) For the purpose of adjusting amounts
23 appropriated to the Department of Defense for fiscal year
24 1991 to reflect changes in expenses due to the order to
25 active duty (other than for training) of members of the

HR 1282 RS   /5/5-9   0102

10

1 National Guard and Reserves in connection with oper-
2 ations in and around the Persian Gulf as part of oper
3 ations currently known as Operation Desert Shield (in-
4 cluding Operation Desert Storm), the Secretary of De-
5 fense may during fiscal year 1991 transfer not to exceed
6 $446,000,000 among the fiscal year 1991 Military Per-
7 sonnel appropriation accounts of the Department of De-
8 fense.

9   (b) Amounts transferred under subsection (a) shall
10 be merged with and be available for the same purposes
11 and the same time period as the appropriations to which
12 transferred.

13   (c) A transfer of funds under subsection (a) is subject
14 to regular congressional reprogramming notification re-
15 quirements.

16   (d) The transfer authority in subsection (a) is in ad-
17 dition to any other transfer authority contained in this or
18 any other Act making appropriations for the Department
19 of Defense for fiscal year 1991.

20   SEC. 104. Of the funds appropriated or made avail-
21 able in this Act, the amount for fuel price increases shall
22 be allocated only to the fuel consumed in direct support
23 of Operation Desert Shield/Desert Storm.

24   SEC. 105. Any CHAMPUS (Civilian Health and
25 Medical Program of the Uniformed Services) medical pro-

HR 1282 RS

1515-10   0103

11

1 ~~vider may voluntarily waive the patient co-payment for~~

2 ~~medical services provided from August 2, 1990, until the~~

3 ~~termination of Operation Desert Shield/Desert Storm for~~

4 ~~dependents of active duty personnel: Provided, That the~~

5 ~~government's share of medical services is not increased~~

6 ~~during the specified time period.~~

7 ~~SEC. 106. Mitchel Field Health Care Facility in the~~

8 ~~State of New York shall only be funded from the Oper-~~

9 ~~ation and Maintenance, Navy, appropriation and shall not~~

10 ~~be funded or included within the congressionally imposed~~

11 ~~ceiling of the Uniformed Services Treatment Facility ac-~~

12 ~~count.~~

13   *SEC. 105. (a) All equipment, supplies, and other mate-*

14 *rials (including, to the maximum extent practicable, con-*

15 *struction equipment and construction materials described*

16 *in subsection (b)) of the United States that, after August*

17 *1, 1990, were transported to or procured by the United*

18 *States in the Middle East for the use of the Armed Forces*

19 *of the United States or the use of the armed forces of any*

20 *other member country of the multinational coalition par-*

21 *ticipating in Operation Desert Storm shall be removed from*

22 *the Middle East to the United States or to any United*

23 *States military installation outside the United States and*

24 *the Middle East as soon as practicable in conjunction with*

HR 1282 RS   *1515-11*   0104

12

1 *the removal of such forces of the Armed Forces of the United*

2 *States from the Middle East.*

3 *(b) The construction equipment and construction ma-*

4 *terials referred to in subsection (a) are construction equip-*

5 *ment and construction materials used in the construction*

6 *of military facilities for the Armed Forces of the United*

7 *States in the Middle East in connection with Operation*

8 *Desert Storm.*

9 *(c) Subsection (a) does not apply to any equipment,*

10 *supply, or material that—*

11 *(1) is to be transferred to a foreign government*

12 *and has negligible value, or*

13 *(2) is to remain under the control of United*

14 *States forces in the region, or*

15 *(3) is to be stored in the Middle East as*

16 *prepositioned equipment and material for the use of*

17 *the Armed Forces of the United States; or*

18 *(4) has been expended, depleted, or rendered un-*

19 *usable.*

20 *(d) The President shall attempt to obtain reimburse-*

21 *ment from the government of each country in the Middle*

22 *East for the cost to the United States of materials referred*

23 *to in subsection (a) that are not removed from that country*

24 *because of impracticality.*

HR 1282 RS   *1515-12*

0105

1   To equipment, supply, or material referred to in

2 subsection (a) or which was captured from Iraq by United

3 States forces in the context of Operation Desert Storm may

4 be transferred to the government or any entity of any for-

5 eign country in the Middle East unless the President first

6 notifies Congress of the proposed transfer and, after the date

7 on which Congress receives the notification, Congress enacts

8 a bill or joint resolution specifically authorizing the pro-

9 posed transfer.

10   (f) The President shall notify Congress of the proposed

11 storage of any equipment, supply, or material referred to

12 in subsection (a) in a prepositioned status referred to in

13 subsection (c)(3).

14   (g) The President shall report to the Committees on

15 Appropriations and Armed Services of the House and Sen-

16 ate sixty days after the enactment of this Act, on the quan-

17 tity, condition, value, disposition and manner of seizure of

18 all enemy equipment falling under the control or the posses-

19 sion of the United States, as well as all enemy equipment

20 falling under the control of allied forces, within the Desert

21 Storm theater of operations.

22   (h) For the purposes of this provision, the term "mate-

23 rial" shall include all lethal and non-lethal instruments of

24 war and their supporting elements, components and

25 subcomponents.

HR 1282 RS   1515-13

0106

14

1   SEC. 106. (a) Not later than 60 days after the date

2   of the enactment of this Act, the President shall submit to

3   Congress a report, in both classified and unclassified forms,

4   on the redeployment in the forces of the Armed Forces of

5   the United States that were deployed in the Persian Gulf

6   area in connection with Operation Desert Storm.

7   (b) The report shall contain the following information:

8   (1) A detailed specification of the costs of the re-

9   duction in such forces.

10   (2) The schedule for returning such forces to the

11 United States or other locations from which the forces

12 were deployed to the Persian Gulf area in connection

13 with Operation Desert Storm.

14   (3) The size and composition of any element of

15 the Armed Forces of the United States that will re-

16 main in the Persian Gulf area after fiscal year 1991.

17   (4) A detailed discussion of any arrangement for

18 a United States military presence that has been made

19 or is expected to be made to the government of any

20 country in the Middle East, including any such ar-

21 rangement that is expected to result from negotiations

22 between the United States and the government of such

23 a country.

24   (c) In this section, the term "Operation Desert Storm"

25 means Operation Desert Shield, Operation Desert Storm,

HR 1282 RS

1515 - 14

0107

15

1 *and any related successive operations of the Armed Forces*

2 *of the United States.*

3   *SEC. 107. None of the funds appropriated or otherwise*

4 *made available by this Act or any other provision of law*

5 *shall be available for sales, credits, or guarantees for defense*

6 *articles or defense services under the Arms Export Control*

7 *Act to any country that has made a commitment to contrib-*

8 *ute resources to defray any of the costs of Operation Desert*

9 *Storm and has not made such contributions.*

10   CHAPTER II

11   MILITARY CONSTRUCTION

12   (TRANSFER OF FUNDS)

13   MILITARY CONSTRUCTION, ARMY

14   For an additional amount for "Military Construction,

15 Army", $35,000,000, to remain available for obligation

16 until September 30, 1994.

17   CHAPTER III

18   DEPARTMENT OF TRANSPORTATION

19   (TRANSFER OF FUNDS)

20   COAST GUARD

21   OPERATING EXPENSES

22   For an additional amount for "Operating expenses",

23 $18,922,000.

HR 1282 RS

1515-15

0108

16

1   This Act may be cited as the "Operation Desert

2 Shield/Desert Storm Supplemental Appropriations Act,

3 1991".

Passed the House of Representatives March 7,
1991.

Attest: DONNALD K. ANDERSON,

Clerk.

Calendar No. 42

102d CONGRESS
1st SESSION

H. R. 1282

[Report No. 102-23]

AN ACT

Making supplemental appropriations and transfers
for "Operation Desert Shield/Desert Storm" for
the fiscal year ending September 30, 1991, and
for other purposes.

MARCH 11 (legislative day, FEBRUARY 6), 1991
Received; read twice and referred to the Committee on
Appropriations

MARCH 14 (legislative day, FEBRUARY 6), 1991
Reported with amendments

HR 1282 RS   1515-16

Calendar No. 42

| 102d Congress
1st Session | SENATE | Report
102–23 |

OPERATION DESERT SHIELD/DESERT STORM SUPPLEMENTAL APPROPRIATIONS BILL, 1991

March 14 (legislative day, February 6), 1991.—Ordered to be printed

Mr. Byrd from the Committee on Appropriations,
submitted the following

REPORT

[To accompany H.R. 1282]

The Committee on Appropriations, to which was referred the bill (H.R. 1282) making supplemental appropriations and transfers for "Operation Desert Shield/Desert Storm" for the fiscal year ending September 30, 1991, and for other purposes, reports the same to the Senate with various amendments, and with the recommendation that the bill be passed.

OPERATION DESERT SHIELD/DESERT STORM

A SPECIAL TRIBUTE TO THE HEROES OF OPERATION DESERT SHIELD AND OPERATION DESERT STORM

The Committee wishes to acknowledge the extraordinary accomplishments of the men and women of Operation Desert Shield/Desert Storm. Through their consummate skill, bravery, and sacrifice, the citizens of the United States and the allied coalition have realized a great victory over the forces of brutality and aggression. The prospect for peace in the Middle East is brighter today, because of what they have done. It is with pride and gratitude that we rejoice in the safe return of our troops.

COMMITTEE ACTION

OPERATION DESERT SHIELD/DESERT STORM BACKGROUND

On February 22, the President submitted a supplemental request to provide for the costs of Operation Desert Shield/Storm. Under

40-956 ==

2

the conditions established in the Omnibus Budget Reconciliation Act of 1990, Congress and the executive branch provided that the incremental costs of Desert Shield/Storm would be considered an emergency. As defined by that act, emergency requirements are not subject to the ceilings for discretionary spending under the budget summit agreement. Costs for such emergencies may be submitted as supplemental appropriations requests. In addition, to better account for the costs of the operation, the Congress created a special fund in the Treasury, the Defense Cooperation Account, in which contributions from individuals and foreign governments would accumulate to offset the cost of the Desert Shield/Storm operation. The Congress stipulated that funds in this account could be used after being specifically appropriated. The Fiscal Year 1991 Defense Appropriations Act provided that $1,000,000,000 of the amount contributed could be used to reimburse costs of incremental expenses for fuel, transportation, equipment maintenance, and purchases from funds in support of Operation Desert Shield/Storm. Since that time the Congress has not provided any additional obligations from the fund. These supplemental requests the use of these authorities to offset the costs of the Desert Shield/Storm operation.

SUPPLEMENTAL REQUEST

The President requested $15,000,000,000 in new appropriations and the authority to use this amount, along with any funds deposited in the Defense Cooperation Account, to transfer to Department of Defense programs for reimbursing costs associated with Operation Desert Shield/Storm. The request stated that funds were for incremental costs through March 31, along with other ancillary costs. The request, however, would not cut off the authority to use funds for expenses incurred after March 31. In addition, the budget request did not specify which programs would be funded, but provided only a notional description of the likely uses of funds. Further, no ceiling was established on how much funding could be expended for Desert Shield/Storm costs.

BUDGET ESTIMATES

The supplemental request divided its estimates for costs into an estimated $39,229,000,000 in incremental costs of Desert Shield/Storm for fiscal year 1991, and $6,430,400,000 for production surge and accelerated acquisition costs, $7,000,000,000 for the cost of postcombat phase down and $5,192,100,000 for the return of personnel and equipment to the United States or other operating locations. The request also estimated the daily cost of combat as between $150,000,000 and $1,650,000,000.

Administration witnesses testified to the Committee that $53,500,000,000 has been pledged by allied nations for deposit into the Defense Cooperation Account. As such, when the requested $15,000,000,000 in new budget authority is included, the supplemental actually seeks authority to spend up to $68,500,000,000. Witnesses testified that it was the administration's intention to use the Defense Cooperation Account to cover the costs of Desert Shield/Storm and to use U.S. funds to the extent these foreign con-

3

tributions were insufficient, and to meet cash-flow shortages that might occur, if the day-to-day requirements for funds exceeded the deposits into the Defense Cooperation Account. However, the administration did not propose specific language to require the use of Defense Cooperation Account funds prior to obligating any portion of the $15,000,000,000 in new budget authority. It did propose that any portion of the $15,000,000,000 remaining following Desert Shield/Storm operations would revert to the Treasury.

COMMITTEE RECOMMENDATIONS

The Committee recommends $15,000,000,000 in new budget authority to be appropriated to capitalize a new Persian Gulf Regional Defense Fund, as recommended by the House. The House provided that, in addition, amounts from the Defense Cooperation Account would be transferred to this fund for disbursement to specific Department of Defense appropriations. The Committee disagrees with the House action which would merge funding into a single account, but supports the delineation, where practicable, of the specific appropriations to which funding may be transferred. The Committee believes it is very important to differentiate between spending of new budget authority and funds from the Defense Cooperation Account.

The Committee supports the House intent to assure that the use of new budget authority would be allowed only to the extent that no funds were available in the Defense Cooperation Account and has clarified this restriction in bill language.

Both the House and the Committee recommendations would place a ceiling on the total amount which could be transferred under this new authority. The Committee recommends a ceiling of $42,625,822,000, this is $37,450,000 above the House allowance. In addition, the Committee would require that no funds could be transferred from the Persian Gulf Regional Defense Fund or the Defense Cooperation Account until at least 7 days following the notification of the Committees on Appropriations and Armed Services as to the requirements for and specific uses of any such funds. Senior administration officials testified before the Committee and gave specific assurances that the administration would abide by customary reprogramming procedures when preparing such transfers.

As recommended by the House, the Committee has included bill language which would require that, if a portion or all of the $15,000,000,000 is transferred and subsequent deposits are received in the Defense Cooperation Account, the deposits shall be used first to restore the $15,000,000,000 corpus of the Persian Gulf Regional Defense Fund. Moreover, as proposed by the administration, bill language would require that, if any funds remain in the Persian Gulf Regional Defense Fund following the Desert Shield/Storm operation, amounts up to $15,000,000,000 will revert to the Treasury. Any additional amounts would be maintained in the Defense Cooperation Account.

COMBAT COSTS

As submitted by the President, the supplemental did not provide a discrete estimate of the *total cost* for combat. Rather, it presented a range of estimates from an air war, assuming no combat losses, to a full land, sea, and air war with heavy losses. The House provided $6,300,000,000 to cover the cost of combat, an estimate based on the lowest cost factors provided by the administration which assumed only an air war with no combat losses. The Committee recommends $9,750,000,000, using a slightly higher estimate which recognizes combat losses during the air war, and noting that, although the ground war was relatively brief, certain combat losses did occur.

MLRS rockets.—The Committee directs the Department of Defense to provide an accounting of the number of MLRS rockets consumed between August 1990 and February 1991. The figures provided for rocket consumption should include not just those that were fired, but also those that were made unusable through shipment, handling, leakage, and other factors. The Committee also directs the Department to utilize such funds as are made available in this bill for combat costs to replace the MLRS rockets thus consumed during Operation Desert Shield and Desert Storm.

Hydra 70 rockets.—The Committee directs the Department of Defense to provide an accounting of the number of Hydra 70 rockets consumed between August 1990 and February 1991. The figures provided for rocket consumption should include not just those that were made unusable through shipment, handling, leakage, and other factors. The Committee also directs the Department to utilize such funds as are made available in this bill for combat costs to replace the Hydra 70 rockets thus consumed during Operations Desert Shield and Desert Storm.

Command and control consoles.—The Committee directs the Army to continue the procurement of command and control consoles from funds made available for combat costs within the Defense Cooperation Account.

Night vision devices.—The Committee directs the Department of the Navy to utilize such moneys as necessary from funds provided within this bill for combat costs to procure up to 14 sets of passive night vision equipment for Marine Corps helicopters in the Kuwait theater of operations.

Night flying operations will continue within the Kuwait theater of operations during the phasedown period. The procurement of additional passive night vision equipment will greatly enhance flight operations safety at night and during periods of reduced visibility.

ADDITIONAL RECOMMENDATIONS

Additional recommendations for the specific uses of funds transferred from the Defense Cooperation Account and from the Persian Gulf Regional Defense Fund are described by appropriation in the following pages.

CHAPTER I

DEPARTMENT OF DEFENSE—MILITARY

MILITARY PERSONNEL

The Committee recommends transfers of not to exceed $7,890,000,000 to fund additional military personnel expenses incurred as a result of Operation Desert Shield/Storm from October 1, 1990, through March 31, 1991. In addition, the fund would pay estimated personnel-related phase-down costs and the costs of returning personnel. Covered by these funds are such items as both voluntary and involuntary Reserve callups, imminent danger pay, added costs generated by the services' stop-loss policies, and other personnel-related expenses.

It should be noted that fuel costs associated with fuel price increases and included in the military personnel accounts have not been funded, because they are not considered to be incremental costs incurred because of Operation Desert Shield/Storm. Reductions have been made as follows: Army, −$15,000,000; Navy, −$5,000,000; Marine Corps, −$5,000,000; and Air Force, −$7,000,000.

The following table shows the Committee's recommendation by appropriation account:

[In millions of dollars]

Appropriation account	Oct. 1, 1990 Ex. 31, 1991	Phasedown	Return of personnel	Total	House allowance	Senate versus House
Military personnel, Army	2,052	2,450	307	4,819	4,864	−15
Military personnel, Navy	316	430	46	792	797	−5
Military personnel, Marine Corps	425	470	83	988	983	−5
Military personnel, Air Force	656	540	75	1,271	1,278	−7
Total	3,445	3,930	511	7,859	7,922	−32

MILITARY PERSONNEL, ARMY

1991 appropriation to date	$23,869,226,000
1991 supplemental estimate	
House allowance	4,863,700,000
Committee recommendation	4,849,000,000

The Committee recommends an appropriation of $4,849,000,000 for military personnel, Army, a decrease of $14,700,000 below the House allowance.

(5)

0112

Operation and maintenance, Army	16,393,750	...	-518,250
Operation and maintenance, Navy	3,009,500	2,331,000	-13,000
Operation and maintenance, Marine Corps	1,330,000	1,197,000	-1,054,000
Operation and maintenance, Air Force	4,080,000	3,026,000	-43,000
Operation and maintenance, Defense Agencies	236,000	173,000	-43,000
Operation and maintenance, Navy Reserve	16,000		-16,000
Operation and maintenance, Air National Guard	55,000		-55,000
Total	25,120,250	21,768,400	-3,351,850

The difference between the Committee's recommendations and those of the House for operation and maintenance appropriations results mostly from the changes described below.

FUEL PRICE INCREASE

The Department of Defense has requested funding to cover increased prices of the Department's planned (baseline) fiscal year 1991 purchases of fuel, other than fuel purchased for use by our forces in the Persian Gulf. Thus, our forces in the United States (and elsewhere) would receive funds from this supplemental appropriation to pay fuel costs even though they are not actively participating in Desert Shield/Storm activities. These costs cannot be considered incremental costs directly related to Operation Desert Shield/Storm. In its bill, the House directed that the amount for fuel price increases be allocated only to the fuel consumed in direct support of Operation Desert Shield/Storm, but made no reductions to the Department's request. Accordingly, the Committee recommends reducing the request by $1,247,000,000. Also, a general provision has been added that restricts the Department from obligating any funds appropriated in this supplemental for fuel costs other than those incremental costs directly associated with Desert Shield/Storm operations.

ASSISTANCE-IN-KIND

The supplemental request includes funding for such items as food, housing, construction equipment and vehicles. Some of the costs of these and other items have been borne by the allies in the form of material assistance-in-kind. In order to avoid double accounting of this in-kind support, the Committee recommends a reduction of $2,093,000,000 to the Department's request.

TIDEWATER, NORFOLK, VA

The House included an appropriation of $500,000 in operation and maintenance, Navy, to implement and staff an enhanced telephone system for the Tidewater Family Services Center. It also included $11,000,000 in operation and maintenance, Defense Agencies, for improvement in dependent medical care in the Tidewater area, including an automated health care provider appointment system. While these projects appear to be worthy of funding in an annual appropriation bill, neither of them is directly concerned

MILITARY PERSONNEL, NAVY

1991 appropriation to date	$19,065,967,000
1991 supplemental estimate	797,400,000
House allowance	792,000,000
Committee recommendation	

The Committee recommends an appropriation of $792,000,000 for military personnel, Navy, a decrease of $5,400,000 below the House allowance.

MILITARY PERSONNEL, MARINE CORPS

1991 appropriation to date	$5,891,502,000
1991 supplemental estimate	983,400,000
House allowance	978,000,000
Committee recommendation	

The Committee recommends an appropriation of $978,000,000 for military personnel, Marine Corps, a decrease of $5,400,000 below the House allowance.

MILITARY PERSONNEL, AIR FORCE

1991 appropriation to date	$19,738,572,000
1991 supplemental estimate	1,278,200,000
House allowance	1,271,000,000
Committee recommendation	

The Committee recommends an appropriation of $1,271,000,000 for military personnel, Air Force, a decrease of $7,200,000 below the House allowance.

TRANSFERS

The Committee provides the Secretary of Defense authority to transfer no more than $446,000,000 from personnel accounts of the Reserve components to active duty military personnel appropriations. These funds are available because of decreased Reserve components requirements caused by activation of units of the Reserves/National Guard. Funds to be transferred are available, as follows: Army Reserve, $178,000,000; Navy Reserve, $38,000,000; Marine Corps Reserve, $46,000,000; Air Force Reserve, $19,000,000; Army National Guard, $155,000,000; and Air National Guard, $15,000,000.

OPERATION AND MAINTENANCE

The Committee recommends transfers of up to $21,768,400,000 for operation and maintenance. These funds would cover actual and estimated expenses of Operation Desert Shield/Storm over the period October 1, 1990, to March 31, 1991, plus the estimated costs to phasedown activities and return personnel and equipment from the gulf region. The recommended amount is $3,351,850,000 less than the amount provided by the House.

A table showing the breakdown of funds by appropriation follows:

SUMMARY OF COMMITTEE ADJUSTMENTS

Committee adjustments to the House allowance are summarized in the following table:

Program	Committee adjustments
House allowance	$1,330,000,000
Fuel price increase	-8,000,000
Assistance-in-kind	-125,000,000
Total	1,197,000,000

OPERATION AND MAINTENANCE, AIR FORCE

1991 appropriation to date	$20,060,735,000
1991 supplemental estimate	
House allowance	4,080,000,000
Committee recommendation	3,026,000,000

The Committee recommends a supplemental appropriation of $3,026,000,000. This is $1,054,000,000 below the House level.

SUMMARY OF COMMITTEE ADJUSTMENTS

Committee adjustments to the House allowance are summarized in the following table:

Program	Committee adjustments
House allowance	$4,080,000,000
Fuel price increase	-675,000,000
Assistance-in-kind	-379,000,000
Total	3,026,000,000

Civil Reserve Air Fleet [CRAF].—The Committee believes that Operation Desert Storm has highlighted that the CRAF Program can be a cost-effective way to enhance readiness and deployability of U.S. troops. As we shift from a military posture which, since the end of World War II, has emphasized Europe, an essential ingredient of America's future global power projection must be the mobility of U.S.-based troops. The Committee is encouraged by the flexibility and recent success of the CRAF program and the fact that the program demonstrated its ability to respond to these changing needs. Therefore, the Committee requests the Secretary to continue the modification program and to develop further capacity within the fleet of convertible aircraft, to include wide body aircraft. The Committee notes that the Department is preparing an update of the congressionally mandated mobility study. In order to provide a basis for the Committee to make timely decisions on additional CRAF requirements, the Committee encourages the Department to expeditiously quantify the program requirement for airlift and to provide the Committee with its findings as directed so that funding for CRAF enhancement can be considered as early as fiscal year 1992.

OPERATION AND MAINTENANCE, DEFENSE AGENCIES

1991 appropriation to date	$8,448,957,000
1991 supplemental estimate	
House allowance	286,000,000
Committee recommendation	173,000,000

0114

---

with Operation Desert Shield/Storm and, in the Committee's view, ought not be included in this supplemental.

OPERATION AND MAINTENANCE, ARMY

1991 appropriation to date	$21,515,694,000
1991 supplemental estimate	
House allowance	16,393,750,000
Committee recommendation	14,981,400,000

The Committee recommends a supplemental appropriation of $14,981,400,000. This is $1,412,350,000 below the House level.

SUMMARY OF COMMITTEE ADJUSTMENTS

Committee adjustments to the House allowance are summarized in the following table:

Program	Committee adjustments
House allowance	$16,393,750,000
Fuel price increase	-101,000,000
Assistance-in-kind	-1,311,000,000
Memorial Day celebration	-350,000
Total	14,981,400,000

The Committee has not included funding of $350,000 for the 1991 Memorial Day celebration. The Committee believes our nation should honor our Armed Forces who served with such distinction and bravery in Operation Desert Shield/Storm. Funding for honors ceremonies and military band performances has already been provided in the annual Defense appropriations bill.

OPERATION AND MAINTENANCE, NAVY

1991 appropriation to date	$23,161,647,000
1991 supplemental estimate	
House allowance	3,009,500,000
Committee recommendation	2,391,000,000

The Committee recommends a supplemental appropriation of $2,391,000,000. This is $618,500,000 below the House level.

SUMMARY OF COMMITTEE ADJUSTMENTS

Committee adjustments to the House allowance are summarized in the following table:

Program	Committee adjustments
House allowance	$3,009,500,000
Fuel price increase	-367,000,000
Assistance-in-kind	-251,000,000
Tidewater, Norfolk, VA	-500,000
Total	2,391,000,000

OPERATION AND MAINTENANCE, MARINE CORPS

1991 appropriation to date	$1,882,200,000
1991 supplemental estimate	
House allowance	1,330,000,000
Committee recommendation	1,197,000,000

The Committee recommends a supplemental appropriation of $1,197,000,000. This is $133,000,000 below the House level.

The Committee recommends a supplemental appropriation of $173,000,000. This is $63,000,000 below the House level.

SUMMARY OF COMMITTEE ADJUSTMENTS

Committee adjustments to the House allowance are summarized in the following table:

Program	Committee adjustments
House allowance	$236,000,000
Fuel price increase	−25,000,000
Assistance-in-kind	−27,000,000
Tidewater, Norfolk, VA	−11,000,000
Total	173,000,000

OPERATION AND MAINTENANCE, NAVY RESERVE

1991 appropriation to date	$998,000,000
1991 supplemental estimate	16,000,000
House allowance	
Committee recommendation	

The Committee recommends no supplemental appropriation. This is $16,000,000 below the House level

SUMMARY OF COMMITTEE ADJUSTMENTS

Committee adjustments to the House allowance are summarized in the following table:

Program	Committee adjustments
House allowances	$16,000,000
Fuel price increase	−16,000,000
Total	

OPERATION AND MAINTENANCE, AIR NATIONAL GUARD

1991 appropriation to date	$2,247,200,000
1991 supplemental estimate	55,000,000
House allowance	
Committee recommendation	

The Committee recommends no supplemental appropriation. This is $55,000,000 below the House level.

SUMMARY OF COMMITTEE ADJUSTMENTS

Committee adjustments to the House allowance are summarized in the following table:

Program	Committee adjustments
House allowance	$55,000,000
Fuel price increase	−55,000,000
Total	

PROCUREMENT

The administration's proposed Operation Desert Shield/Storm supplemental includes a request to obligate $6,414,600,000 within Defense procurement accounts. The requested procurement funding is to support ongoing United States military activities within the

151-5-22

Kuwait theater of operations and to provide funding to prevent production gaps for programs which had been directed by the Department to surge output.

The Committee is informed that this supplemental request for procurement funding is based upon the requirements of our forces in the gulf for continuous wartime operations through the end of the fiscal year. With upon the successful termination of the war during the past 2 weeks, this planning assumption is no longer valid.

Since the cessation of fighting on February 27, the Committee asked the Department of Defense for a revised estimate of its actual procurement needs relating to military activities in the Kuwait theater of operations. A revised estimate, submitted to the Committee on February 28, indicates a need for only $2,892,500,000 in procurement funding at this time. This revised list of procurement items is based upon actual consumption levels and inventory requirements. The Committee feels this is a more realistic assessment of the Department of Defense's supplemental procurement requirements and, therefore, recommends providing the authority to transfer funds up to this amount as outlined in the following table:

FISCAL YEAR 1991 DESERT SHIELD/STORM PROCUREMENT SUPPLEMENTAL

Appropriation	House allowance	Committee recommendation	Senate versus House
Aircraft procurement, Army	$7,100,000	$7,100,000	
Missile procurement, Army	311,900,000	311,900,000	
Procurement of weapons and tracked combat vehicles, Army	26,300,000	26,300,000	
Procurement of ammunition, Army	437,000,000	425,500,000	−11,200,000
Other procurement, Army	30,300,000	26,300,000	−4,000,000
Total, Army	812,600,000	797,400,000	−15,200,000
Aircraft procurement, Navy	15,000,000	15,000,000	
Weapons procurement, Navy	1,065,100,000	1,057,300,000	−7,800,000
Other procurement, Navy	34,600,000	34,600,000	
Procurement, Marine Corps	68,000,000	64,200,000	−3,800,000
Total, Navy	1,183,700,000	1,172,100,000	−11,600,000
Aircraft procurement, Air Force	101,200,000	101,200,000	
Missile procurement, Air Force	400,000,000	400,000,000	
Other procurement, Air Force	419,100,000	419,100,000	
Total, Air Force	920,300,000	920,300,000	
Procurement, Defense Agencies	2,700,000	2,700,000	
Total procurement	2,919,300,000	2,892,500,000	−26,800,000

AIRCRAFT PROCUREMENT, ARMY

1991 appropriation to date	$1,096,182,000
1991 supplemental estimate	7,100,000
House allowance	7,100,000
Committee recommendation	

0115

1515-73

COMMITTEE RECOMMENDED PROGRAM

The Committee recommends a supplemental appropriation of $7,100,000 for aircraft procurement, Army, the same as recommended by the House. The following table details the Committee's recommendations as compared to the House allowance:

[Dollar/ammo amounts in thousands]

Appropriation/line item	House allowance		Committee recommendation		Senate versus House	
	Quantity	Amount	Quantity	Amount	Quantity	Amount
Aircraft procurement, Army: CH-47 mod		$7,100		$7,100		

MISSILE PROCUREMENT, ARMY

1991 appropriation to date		$2,218,422,000
1991 supplemental estimate		
House allowance		311,900,000
Committee recommendation		311,900,000

COMMITTEE RECOMMENDED PROGRAM

The Committee recommends a supplemental appropriation of $311,900,000 for missile procurement, Army, the same as recommended by the House. The following table details the Committee's recommendations as compared to the House allowance:

[Dollar/ammo amounts in thousands]

Appropriation/line item	House allowance		Committee recommendation		Senate versus House	
	Quantity	Amount	Quantity	Amount	Quantity	Amount
Missile procurement, Army:						
Patriot		$100,000	158	$100,000		
Patriot (reprogramming source)	158	114,000		114,000		
ATACMS	87	50,000	87	50,080		
Hellfire	1,063	42,400	1,063	42,450		
TOW	208	5,500	208	5,500		
Total		311,900		311,900		

PROCUREMENT OF WEAPONS AND TRACKED COMBAT VEHICLES, ARMY

1991 appropriation to date		$2,172,021,000
1991 supplemental estimate		
House allowance		26,300,000
Committee recommendation		26,300,000

COMMITTEE RECOMMENDED PROGRAM

The Committee recommends a supplemental appropriation of $26,300,000 for procurement of weapons and tracked combat vehicles, Army, the same as recommended by the House. The following

table details the Committee's recommendations as compared to the House allowance:

[Dollar/ammo amounts in thousands]

Appropriation/line item	House allowance		Committee recommendation		Senate versus House	
	Quantity	Amount	Quantity	Amount	Quantity	Amount
Procurement of weapons and tracked combat vehicles, Army M-1 tankmods		$26,300		$26,300		

PROCUREMENT OF AMMUNITION, ARMY

1991 appropriation to date		$1,367,549,000
1991 supplemental estimate		437,000,000
House allowance		425,900,000
Committee recommendation		

COMMITTEE RECOMMENDED PROGRAM

The Committee recommends a supplemental appropriation of $425,800,000 for procurement of ammunition, Army, $11,200,000 below the House allowance. The following table details the Committee's recommendations as compared to the House allowance:

[Dollar/ammo amounts in thousands]

Appropriation/line item	House allowance		Committee recommendation		Senate versus House	
	Quantity	Amount	Quantity	Amount	Quantity	Amount
Procurement of ammunition, Army:						
Cartridge, 25 mm, APFSDS-T, M-919	240	$25,700	240	$25,700		
Cartridge, 25 mm, APDS-T, M-791	3,400	41,400	1,400	41,400		
Cartridge, 25 mm, AP training, M-910	1,191	23,800	1,191	23,800		
Cartridge, 25 mm, HEI-T M-792	3,000	20,000	1,000	20,000		
Cartridge, tank, 105 mm, APFSDS-T M-900A1	8	16,000	8	16,000		
Cartridge, tank, 120 mm, APFSDS-T M-E29A1	52	83,100	52	83,100		
Cartridge, tank, 120 mm, HEAT-MP-T M-830	30	50,000	30	50,000		
Cartridge, tank, 120 mm, TP-T M-831	27	26,000	27	26,000		
Cartridge, tank, 120 mm, IPSDS-T M-865	30	22,000	30	22,000		
Projectile, artillery, 155 mm, HE, M-107	118	22,500	59	11,300	-59	-$11,200
Projectile, artillery, 155 mm, HE, RAP M-549	53	41,000	53	41,000		
Projectile, artillery, 155 mm, ADAM	7	36,000	7	36,000		
Projectile, artillery, 155 mm, illuminating M-485	18	4,500	18	4,330		
Projectile, charge, 155 mm, red bag, M-119	125	20,000	125	20,000		
Total		437,000		425,800		-11,200

OTHER PROCUREMENT, ARMY

1991 appropriation to date		$2,451,057,000
1991 supplemental estimate		30,300,000
House allowance		26,300,000
Committee recommendation		

0116

COMMITTEE RECOMMENDED PROGRAM

The Committee recommends a supplemental appropriation of $20,300,000 for other procurement, Army, $4,000,000 below the House allowance. The following table details the Committee's recommendations as compared to the House allowance:

[Dollar/Amounts amounts in thousands]

Appropriation/line item	House allowance		Committee recommendation		Senate versus House	
	Quantity	Amount	Quantity	Amount	Quantity	Amount
Other procurement, Army:						
Classified program		$15,000		$15,000		
Counterfire equipment		11,300		11,300		
Command-control consoles	15	4,000			-15	-$4,000
Total		30,300		26,300		-4,000

AIRCRAFT PROCUREMENT, NAVY

1991 appropriation to date	$7,810,452,000
1991 supplemental estimate	
House allowance	16,000,000
Committee recommendation	16,000,000

COMMITTEE RECOMMENDED PROGRAM

The Committee recommends a supplemental appropriation of $16,000,000 for aircraft procurement, Navy, the same as recommended by the House. The following table details the Committee's recommendations as compared to the House allowance:

[Dollar/Amounts amounts in thousands]

Appropriation/line item	House allowance		Committee recommendation		Senate versus House	
	Quantity	Amount	Quantity	Amount	Quantity	Amount
Aircraft procurement, Navy: Spare and repair parts		$16,000		$16,000		

WEAPONS PROCUREMENT, NAVY

1991 appropriation to date	$5,825,171,000
1991 supplemental estimate	
House allowance	1,065,100,000
Committee recommendation	1,057,300,000

COMMITTEE RECOMMENDED PROGRAM

The Committee recommends a supplemental appropriation of $1,057,300,000 for weapons procurement, Navy, $7,800,000 below the allowance of the House. The following table details the Committee's recommendations as compared to the House allowance:

[Dollar/Amounts amounts in thousands]

Appropriation/line item	House allowance		Committee recommendation		Senate versus House	
	Quantity	Amount	Quantity	Amount	Quantity	Amount
Weapons procurement:						
Tomahawk	290	$377,000	290	$377,000		
HARM	2,033	437,000	2,033	437,000		
SLAM	8	7,800			-8	-$7,800
MK-83 1,000 pound general purpose bomb	6	40,400	6	40,400		
2.75 inch rocket illuminating warhead	1	500	1	500		
Cartridge, 20 mm, SAFEI, PGU-28	150	1,200	150	1,200		
Cartridge, 25 mm, PGU-25	30	700	30	700		
Cartridge, 25 mm, API, PGU-28	45	900	45	900		
MK-83 1,000 pound practice bomb	27	32,500	27	32,500		
CBU-78 gator	5	12,400	5	12,400		
FMU-140 proximity fuze for rockeye	29	138,200	29	138,200		
Tomer land kits for rockeye	12	500	12	500		
MK-83 laser guided bomb kit	8	16,000	8	16,000		
Total		1,065,100		1,057,300		-7,800

Tomahawk.—The Committee recommends $377,000,000 for the procurement of at least 290 Tomahawk missiles. This is the same amount as the House allowance.

It is the Committee's understanding that the Navy plans to continue its existing prime contractor dual-sourcing acquisition strategy for the additional Tomahawks to be procured with these funds. The Committee has also been informed that the Navy plans to release a new request for proposal [RFP] for Government-furnished Tomahawk engines, even though these engines are now made by only one producer. All qualified contractors will have the opportunity to fully compete for these additional engines and the Navy will make an award based upon the best interest of the U.S. Government.

The Committee supports the Navy's proposed acquisition plan to acquire the additional 290 Tomahawk missiles.

OTHER PROCUREMENT, NAVY

1991 appropriation to date	$5,627,160,000
1991 supplemental estimate	
House allowance	34,600,000
Committee recommendation	34,600,000

COMMITTEE RECOMMENDED PROGRAM

The Committee recommends a supplemental appropriation of $34,600,000 for other procurement, Navy, the same as recommended by the House. The following table details the Committee's recommendations as compared to the House allowance:

17

ommended by the House. The following table details the Committee's recommendations as compared to the House allowance:

[Dollar amounts in thousands]

Appropriation/line item	House allowance		Committee recommendation		Senate versus House	
	Quantity	Amount	Quantity	Amount	Quantity	Amount
Aircraft procurement, Air Force:						
Spare and repair parts		$68,300		$68,300		
War consumables		15,200		15,200		
Classified programs		17,700		17,700		
Total		101,200		101,200		

MISSILE PROCUREMENT, AIR FORCE ... $5,813,532,000

1991 appropriation to date	
1991 supplemental estimate	
House allowance	400,000,000
Committee recommendation	400,000,000

COMMITTEE RECOMMENDED PROGRAM

The Committee recommends a supplemental appropriation of $400,000,000 for missile procurement, Air Force, the same as recommended by the House. The following table details the Committee's recommendations as compared to the House allowance:

[Dollar amounts in thousands]

Appropriation/line item	House allowance		Committee recommendation		Senate versus House	
	Quantity	Amount	Quantity	Amount	Quantity	Amount
Missile procurement, Air Force:						
Maverick	5,000	$370,000	5,000	$370,000		
Classified program		30,000		30,000		
Total		400,000		400,000		

OTHER PROCUREMENT, AIR FORCE ... $7,503,356,000

1991 appropriation to date	
1991 supplemental estimate	
House allowance	419,100,000
Committee recommendation	419,100,000

COMMITTEE RECOMMENDED PROGRAM

The Committee recommends a supplemental appropriation of $419,100,000 for other procurement, Air Force, the same as recommended by the House. The following table details the Committee's recommendations as compared to the House allowance:

0118

16

[Dollar amounts in thousands]

Appropriation/line item	House allowance		Committee recommendation		Senate versus House	
	Quantity	Amount	Quantity	Amount	Quantity	Amount
Other procurement, Navy:						
R-144 chaff cartridge	500	$1,000	500	$1,000		
MJU-22 Infrared decoy flare	10	1,400	10	1,400		
MJU-27 Infrared decoy flare	18	1,400	18	1,400		
CXU-83	500	800	500	800		
EXU chaff		800		800		
Special purpose support system	1,500	4,100	1,500	4,100		
Spare and repair parts		16,200		16,200		
		8,700		8,700		
Total		34,600		34,600		

PROCUREMENT, MARINE CORPS ... $719,141,000

1991 appropriation to date	
1991 supplemental estimate	68,000,000
House allowance	64,200,000
Committee recommendation	

COMMITTEE RECOMMENDED PROGRAM

The Committee recommends a supplemental appropriation of $64,200,000 for procurement, Marine Corps, $3,800,000 below the House allowance. The following table details the Committee's recommendations as compared to the House allowance:

[Dollar amounts in thousands]

Appropriation/line item	House allowance		Committee recommendation		Senate versus House	
	Quantity	Amount	Quantity	Amount	Quantity	Amount
Procurement, Marine Corps:						
UAV 2A	323	$3,800	323	$3,800	-329	-$3,800
Cartridge mortar, 81 mm, HE/RAD	73	18,700	73	18,700		
Smoke mortar, 81 mm, smoke	32	8,200	32	8,200		
Cartridge mortar, 81 mm, illuminating	58	13,100	58	13,100		
Propellant charge, 8 inch, red bag	18	4,200	18	4,200		
Spare and repair parts		20,000		20,000		
Total		68,000		64,200		-3,800

AIRCRAFT PROCUREMENT, AIR FORCE ... $9,541,455,000

1991 appropriation to date	
1991 supplemental estimate	101,200,000
House allowance	101,200,000
Committee recommendation	

COMMITTEE RECOMMENDED PROGRAM

The Committee recommends a supplemental appropriation of $101,200,000 for aircraft procurement, Air Force, the same as rec-

19

was better able to meet most of the needs of both services. It was determined that continuation of two separate programs was un-needed and unaffordable.

On January 10, 1991, OSD informed Congress that the Defense Department was creating a joint program to combine both projects. At that time, it was stated that the Marines' surf zone clearance was the top airborne countermine requirement.

Since then, several events have occurred which support an alternative course of action. First, close examination of the proposed program indicates much of it appears to continue the Marine Corps candidate airborne mine detection and surveillance [AMDAS] project under the joint program rubric.

Second, Operations Desert Shield and Desert Storm have increased Navy interest in developing the other candidate, the Magic lantern system, as a near-term capability.

Third, the Persian Gulf experience has prompted a new review of Navy/Marine longer term mine warfare requirements with a view to better identifying requirements and priorities.

Accordingly, the Committee directs the release of $9,200,000 of withheld fiscal year 1991 funds to complete development of two Magic lantern prototypes.

REVOLVING AND MANAGEMENT FUNDS

The Committee recommends $271,000,000 for revolving and management funds, the same total funding level as provided by the House, but realigns the funds to the appropriate account as requested by the Department of Defense.

ARMY STOCK FUND

1991 appropriation to date	$376,520,000
1991 supplemental estimate	57,000,000
House allowance	214,000,000
Committee recommendation	

AIR FORCE STOCK FUND

1991 appropriation to date	$1,152,110,000
1991 supplemental estimate	
House allowance	214,000,000
Committee recommendation	57,000,000

GENERAL PROVISIONS

FUEL PRICE INCREASE

The Committee recommends including a House provision, section 104, which states that of the funds appropriated or made available in this act, the amount for fuel shall be allocated only to the fuel consumed in direct support of Operation Desert Shield/Desert Storm.

WAIVER OF CHAMPUS COPAYMENTS

The Committee has deleted section 105 from this bill, dealing with waiver of CHAMPUS copayments, and believes that this

0113

18

[Dollar/items amounts in thousands]

Appropriation/line item	House allowance Quantity	Amount	Committee recommendation Quantity	Amount	Senate versus House Quantity	Amount
Other procured, Air Force:						
Cartridge, impulse, ARD-863		$350	375	$350		
CBU-89 gator	1.2	41,400	1.2	41,400		
GBU-15 Electro-optic guided glide bomb	.1	45,600	.1	45,600		
GBU-24 laser guided bomb kit	1.2	102,000	1.2	102,000		
GBU-27 laser guided bomb kit	.3	68,000	.8	68,000		
CBU-87 combined effects munition	9	108,000	9	108,000		
MK-13 1,000 pound bomb (area denial)	.9	14,600	.9	14,600		
FMU-139 fuze electric	154	5,200	154	5,200		
ALA-17 infrared decoy flare	36	9,500	36	9,500		
ALA-7 infrared decoy flare	20	700	20	700		
M-206 infrared decoy flare	100	1,500	100	1,500		
Long range dispenser		200		200		
MJU-10 infrared decoy flare	2	100	2	100		
Pallets		15,000		15,000		
Kits		6,500		6,500		
Total		419,100		419,100		

PROCUREMENT, DEFENSE AGENCIES

1991 appropriation to date	$2,354,646,000
1991 supplemental estimate	
House allowance	2,700,000
Committee recommendation	2,700,000

COMMITTEE RECOMMENDED PROGRAM

The Committee recommends a supplemental appropriation of $2,700,000 for procurement, Defense Agencies, the same as recommended by the House. The following table details the Committee's recommendations as compared to the House allowance:

[Dollar/items amounts in thousands]

Appropriation/line item	House allowance Quantity	Amount	Committee recommendation Quantity	Amount	Senate versus House Quantity	Amount
Procurement, Defense Agencies: SOF communications equipments		$2,700		$2,700		

RESEARCH, DEVELOPMENT, TEST AND EVALUATION

RESEARCH, DEVELOPMENT, TEST AND EVALUATION, NAVY

Magic lantern/USN-USMC mine warfare.—To eliminate wasteful, costly duplication, Congress in its fiscal year 1991 military spending measure required the Office of the Secretary of Defense [OSD] to choose between two proposed, laser-based systems for meeting the mine warfare needs of the Navy and the Marine Corps. The conferees directed the selection of one system which

matter should be addressed in the military benefits authorization bill.

MITCHEL FIELD DEPENDENT MEDICAL CARE

The House included a provision (section 106) mandating that the Mitchel Field Health Care Facility in New York must be funded from the operation and maintenance, Navy, appropriation and that it is not to be included in or funded under the "Uniformed services treatment facility" account. The Department of Defense is working to provide a solution to this problem that will allow the Mitchel Field Health Care Facility to remain open and, therefore, the Committee does not recommend its inclusion. In addition, funding for the Mitchel Field facility is not directly related to Operation Desert Shield/Storm. The Committee, therefore, has recommended deletion of this provision.

DISPOSITION OF UNITED STATES AND CAPTURED MILITARY EQUIPMENT

The amount, range, and value of U.S. equipment transferred to the Middle East theater in connection with Operation Desert Shield/Storm since last August is enormous, and the Committee wishes to ensure that every effort is made to return all usable equipment, supplies, and materiel with more than negligible value back to the United States, or to other locations to be used in the future by U.S. forces. The Committee recognizes that it is not feasible to return some items of value, such as those associated with permanent military construction, and also that it may be desirable to preposition some equipment and supplies in the Middle East theater as a contingency for possible future use by U.S. forces.

Therefore, the Committee provides in section 105 that all equipment, supplies, or materiel that the administration wishes to sell, give, or otherwise transfer to any foreign nation or non-U.S. entity may only be done with the formal approval of the Congress after a request has been made by the administration.

The Committee does not object to the concept of prepositioned equipment and supplies, but only if those items remain the property of the United States and for the exclusive use of U.S. forces. The Committee requires that the administration notify the Congress and provide a report detailing the specific prepositioning contemplated or accomplished.

A special situation has arisen given the vast quantities of war materiel captured by U.S. forces from Iraq in the context of the war. The Committee wishes to take action now to begin an effective policy to reduce the practice of arms sales and weapons buildup in the region, so as to lessen the opportunities for future aggression by nation states in the region. The Committee does not object to the destruction of such equipment, but in the event that the administration wishes to transfer or sell any of it to other nations or entities, it must first seek and secure the formal approval of the Congress.

The Committee understands that the amounts requested by the administration for winddown costs were based on the best estimates available during a time of great uncertainty as to the course of the conflict. Because hostilities now have ceased, the Department of Defense should be better able to judge what those costs will be. Section 105 calls on the President to submit a report to the Congress with a schedule for the withdrawal of troops from the theater and details of the costs associated with that withdrawal.

The Committee is concerned that all U.S. forces deployed to the Persian Gulf region as a result of the Iraqi aggression in August 1990, be returned home to the United States or their permanent duty stations elsewhere. While the return of our forces is reasonably expected to take several months, the long-term presence of U.S. forces in the Persian Gulf region should not be planned without the full concurrence of the Congress. The Committee is concerned that such a long-term presence amounts to a costly new commitment by the United States. Therefore, the report requires an accounting of any forces that the administration contemplates will remain in the region beyond October 1, 1991.

Further, the required report will include a detailed discussion of any arrangements, made or contemplated, to provide a continuing military presence in the region. Such a discussion is critical in laying the foundation for a congressional consensus on the U.S. role in the region, a consensus which will be absolutely essential if the administration plans to commit the United States to a costly new overseas military presence.

ALLIED CONTRIBUTIONS

While the United States, Great Britain, Saudi Arabia, and the forces of many other nations carried the day as an international military coalition, the extensive planning and commitment by the United States of manpower, logistics and raw military power was clearly the determining factor. Other nations, in addition to Kuwait, particularly the oil-producing states of the Persian Gulf threatened by the aggressive actions of Saddam Hussein, and nations heavily dependent on gulf oil but politically unable to contribute military forces, have promised financial and other resources to help defray the enormous costs borne by the United States. By and large, the resources that have been promised appear adequate to defray the so-called incremental costs of the war, costs which, in reality, represent only the icing of a cake composed of over one-half million American servicemen and base costs in excess of $100,000,000,000 carried exclusively by the American taxpayer.

Allied commitments to date, primarily by Saudi Arabia, Kuwait, Japan, Germany, and others to defray expenses through the end of this month amount to $53,545,000,000, of which less than one-half, $17,903,000,000, has been received. If all commitments made had been redeemed, the Committee would not have found it necessary to authorize $15,000,000,000 in additional U.S. taxpayers dollars. The Committee regards the $15,000,000,000 as necessary only in the event that allied promises are not in fact redeemed.

0120

The Committee understands the administration is considering the sale of sophisticated American weapons to some of the countries which have pledged aid but not yet fully delivered on their pledges. It does not feel that it is proper for such arms sales to be submitted to the Congress for its approval until the full amount of the money promised has been delivered, since if the promisor nation has money to buy arms from us, it can first use that money to fulfill its pledge to help defray some of our costs. Therefore, the Committee has included a provision in this measure (sec. 107) which prohibits any arms sale to any nation which has not yet contributed the amount which it pledged.

Furthermore, the Committee expresses its disappointment at the reluctance of the United Arab Emirates to commit appropriate levels of resources to help defray American costs. The UAE is a country on the Arabian peninsula America directly protected against the threats of Saddam Hussein, and is a cash-rich oil-producer. The administration attempted to secure a pledge of over $7,000,000,000 from the UAE, a sum well within that nation's means at this time, but the UAE has only agreed to pledge some $3,000,000,000, of which it still owes $1,000,000,000. The administration has testified before this Committee that a further commitment from the UAE is under discussion with that nation. The Committee encourages the administration to withhold submitting any request to the Congress to sell arms to the UAE until that nation agrees to contribute an amount more reflective of its geographical location and its ability to pay.

CHAPTER II

DEPARTMENT OF DEFENSE

MILITARY CONSTRUCTION

The Committee recommends $35,000,000 to replenish funds previously reprogrammed to support Operation Desert Shield. The amount provided is to be applied toward planning and design expenses in support of Desert Shield/Storm and to restore those projects originally deferred to finance the reprogramming actions.

CHAPTER III

DEPARTMENT OF TRANSPORTATION

COAST GUARD

OPERATING EXPENSES

The Committee recommends $18,922,000 for the incremental costs borne by the Coast Guard in support of Operations Desert Shield/Storm. This is the same as the amount provided by the House and $570 more than the President's request. These funds are provided by transfer from the "Defense cooperation" account. Coast Guard support of Operations Desert Shield/Storm has taken many forms including the inspecting of the Ready Reserve Fleet, supervising the loading of hazardous materials and ammunition, providing waterside security in United States, Saudi, and Bahraini ports,

and the boarding of merchant vessels in the gulf region to ensure compliance with the international trade embargo against Iraq. Many of these missions have been complemented by the efforts of Coast Guard reservists as part of the first involuntary call-up of the Coast Guard Reserves. The Committee wishes to praise the enthusiastic and skilled contributions of these reservists in this, the fiftieth anniversary year of the Coast Guard Reserves.

The Coast Guard also has lead responsibility for the President's interagency task force charged with assessing the catastrophic oil-spill in the Persian Gulf. This activity has resulted in the deployment of HU-25 *Falcon* jets equipped with AIREYE spill tracking radar as well as the deployment of numerous specially trained Coast Guard personnel. The Committee wishes to note that the administration has yet to request funding for these activities. Thus, no funds have been provided to support this mission at this time.

BUDGETARY IMPACT OF BILL

PREPARED BY THE CONGRESSIONAL BUDGET OFFICE PURSUANT TO SEC. 308(a), PUBLIC LAW 93-344, AS AMENDED

[In millions of dollars]

	Budget authority		Outlays	
	Committee allocation	Amount of bill	Committee allocation	Amount of bill
Comparison of amounts in the bill with the Committee allocation to its subcommittees of amounts in the First Concurrent Resolution for 1991	NA	42,526	NA	31,414
Projection of outlays associated with budget authority recommended in the bill:				
1991				31,414
1992				6,597
1993				2,557
1994				1,038
1995 and future year				514
Financial assistance to State and local governments for 1991	NA		NA	

	Direct loans	Loan guarantees
Credit authority estimates, fiscal year 1991		

NOTE: Pursuant to section 251(a)(2)(C)(i)(II) of the Budget Enforcement Act of 1990 (title XIII of the Omnibus Budget Reconciliation Act of 1990), these levels are not scored against the Committee's allocations.

NA: Not applicable.

COMPARATIVE STATEMENT OF NEW BUDGET (OBLIGATIONAL) AUTHORITY ESTIMATES AND AMOUNTS RECOMMENDED IN THE BILL

House Doc.	Department or activity	Budget estimates	House bill	Senate Committee recommendation	Senate Committee recommendation compared with (+ or −)	
					Budget estimates	House bill
	FISCAL YEAR 1991 DESERT SHIELD/DESERT STORM SUPPLEMENTAL					
	CHAPTER I					
	DEPARTMENT OF DEFENSE—MILITARY					
102–43	Persian Gulf regional defense fund	$15,000,000,000	$15,000,000,000	$15,000,000,000		
	MILITARY PERSONNEL					
	(BY TRANSFER FROM THE DEFENSE COOPERATION ACCOUNT)					
	Military personnel, Army		(4,863,700,000)	(4,849,000,000)	(+$4,849,000,000)	(−$14,700,000)
	Military personnel, Navy		(797,400,000)	(792,000,000)	(+792,000,000)	(−5,400,000)
	Military personnel, Marine Corps		(983,400,000)	(978,000,000)	(+978,000,000)	(−5,400,000)
	Military personnel, Air Force		(1,278,200,000)	(1,271,000,000)	(+1,271,000,000)	(−7,200,000)
	Total, Military personnel		(7,922,700,000)	(7,890,000,000)	(+7,890,000,000)	(−82,700,000)
	OPERATION AND MAINTENANCE					
	(BY TRANSFER FROM THE DEFENSE COOPERATION ACCOUNT)					
	Operation and maintenance, Army		(16,393,750,000)	(14,981,400,000)	(+14,981,400,000)	(−1,412,350,000)
	Operation and maintenance, Navy		(3,009,500,000)	(2,391,000,000)	(+2,391,000,000)	(−618,500,000)
	Operation and maintenance, Marine Corps		(1,380,000,000)	(1,197,000,000)	(+1,197,000,000)	(−183,000,000)
	Operation and maintenance, Air Force		(4,080,000,000)	(3,026,000,000)	(+3,026,000,000)	(−1,054,000,000)
	Operation and maintenance, Defense Agencies		(236,000,000)	(173,000,000)	(+173,000,000)	(−63,000,000)
	Operation and maintenance, Navy Reserve		(16,000,000)			(−16,000,000)
	Operation and maintenance, Air National Guard		(55,000,000)			(−55,000,000)
	Total, Operation and maintenance		(25,120,250,000)	(21,768,400,000)	(+21,768,400,000)	(−3,351,850,000)
	PROCUREMENT					
	(BY TRANSFER FROM THE DEFENSE COOPERATION ACCOUNT)					
	Aircraft procurement, Army		(7,100,000)	(7,100,000)	(+7,100,000)	
	Missile procurement, Army		(311,900,000)	(311,900,0000)	(+311,900,000)	
	Procurement of weapons and tracked combat vehicles, Army		(26,300,000)	(26,300,000)	(+26,300,000)	
	Procurement of ammunition, Army		(437,000,000)	(425,800,000)	(+425,800,000)	(−11,200,000)
	Other procurement, Army		(30,300,000)	(26,300,000)	(+26,300,000)	(−4,000,000)
	Aircraft procurement, Navy		(16,000,000)	(16,000,000)	(+16,000,000)	
	Weapons procurement, Navy		(1,065,100,000)	(1,057,300,000)	(+1,057,300,000)	(−7,800,000)
	Other procurement, Navy		(34,600,000)	(34,600,000)	(+34,600,000)	
	Procurement, Marine Corps		(68,000,000)	(64,200,000)	(+64,200,000)	(−3,800,000)
	Aircraft procurement, Air Force		(101,200,000)	(101,200,000)	(+101,200,000)	
	Missile procurement, Air Force		(400,000,000)	(400,000,000)	(+400,000,000)	
	Other procurement, Air Force		(419,100,000)	(419,100,000)	(+419,100,000)	
	Procurement, Defense Agencies		(2,700,000)	(2,700,000)	(+2,700,000)	
	Total, Procurement		(2,919,300,000)	(2,892,500,000)	(+2,892,500,000)	(−26,800,000)
	RESEARCH, DEVELOPMENT, TEST AND EVALUATION					
	(BY TRANSFER FROM THE DEFENSE COOPERATION ACCOUNT)					
	Research, development, test and evaluation, Army		(1,200,000)			(−1,200,000)
	REVOLVING AND MANAGEMENT FUNDS					
	(BY TRANSFER FROM THE DEFENSE COOPERATION ACCOUNT)					
	Army stock fund		(57,000,000)	(214,000,000)	(+214,000,000)	(+157,000,000)
	Air Force stock fund		(214,000,000)	(57,000,000)	(+57,000,000)	(−157,000,000)
	Total, revolving and management funds		(271,000,000)	(271,000,000)	(+271,000,000)	
	OTHER DEPARTMENT OF DEFENSE APPROPRIATIONS					
	(BY TRANSFER FROM THE DEFENSE COOPERATION ACCOUNT)					
	Combat operations		(6,300,000,000)	(9,750,000,000)	(+9,750,000,000)	(+3,450,000,000)
	Total, chapter I:					
	New budget (obligational) authority	15,000,000,000	15,000,000,000	15,000,000,000		
	(By transfer from the Defense Cooperation Account)		(42,534,450,000)	(42,571,900,000)	(+42,571,900,000)	(+37,450,000)

24

1515-29   0122

COMPARATIVE STATEMENT OF NEW BUDGET (OBLIGATIONAL) AUTHORITY ESTIMATES AND AMOUNTS
RECOMMENDED IN THE BILL—Continued

House Doc.	Department or activity	Budget estimates	House bill	Senate Committee recommendation	Senate Committee recommendation compared with (+ or −)	
					Budget estimates	House bill
	CHAPTER II					
	DEPARTMENT OF DEFENSE—MILITARY					
	(BY TRANSFER FROM THE DEFENSE COOPERATION ACCOUNT)					
	Military construction, Army..........		(85,000,000)	(85,000,000)	(+85,000,000)	....
	CHAPTER III					
	DEPARTMENT OF TRANSPORTATION					
	COAST GUARD					
	(BY TRANSFER FROM THE DEFENSE COOPERATION ACCOUNT)					
102–43	Operating expenses	(18,921,430)	(18,922,000)	(18,922,000)	(+570)	....
	Grand total:					
	New budget (obligational) authority...............	15,000,000,000	15,000,000,000	15,000,000,000	....	
	(By transfer from the Defense Cooperation Account)...............	(18,921,430)	(42,588,872,000)	(42,625,822,000)	(+42,606,900,570)	(+37,450,000)

O

USW (下)- 0933
수신 장관 (미주, 시안, 충동일, 기정)
발신 주이대사
제목 걸프전쟁 추가지불 법안 (11매)

IB

Union Calendar No. 8

102D CONGRESS
1ST SESSION

H. R. 1282

[Report No. 102–10]

Making supplemental appropriations and transfers for "Operation Desert Shield/Desert Storm" for the fiscal year ending September 30, 1991, and for other purposes.

IN THE HOUSE OF REPRESENTATIVES

MARCH 5, 1991

Mr. WHITTEN, from the Committee on Appropriations, reported the following bill; which was committed to the Committee of the Whole House on the State of the Union and ordered to be printed

---

A BILL

Making supplemental appropriations and transfers for "Operation Desert Shield/Desert Storm" for the fiscal year ending September 30, 1991, and for other purposes.

1 　　*Be it enacted by the Senate and House of Representa-*

2 *tives of the United States of America in Congress assembled,*

3 That the following sums are appropriated, out of any

4 money in the Treasury not otherwise appropriated, to pro-

5 vide supplemental appropriations for the fiscal year end-

6 ing September 30, 1991, and for other purposes, namely:

0124

2

1 PERSIAN GULF REGIONAL DEFENSE FUND

2   (INCLUDING TRANSFER OF FUNDS)

3   For incremental costs of the Department of Defense

4 and the Department of Transportation(associated with op-

5 erations in and around the Persian Gulf as part of oper-

6 ations currently known as Operation Desert Shield (in-

7 cluding Operation Desert Storm),)$15,000,000,000 is ap-

8 propriated to the Persian Gulf Regional Defense Fund,

9 (which is hereby established in the Treasury of the United

10 States,)and in addition such sums as necessary are appro-

11 priated to such Fund by transfer from current and future

12 balances in the Defense Cooperation Account,) such sums

13 so appropriated to the Persian Gulf Regional Defense

14 Fund to be available only for transfer in a total amount

15 not to exceed $42,588,372,000 to the following chapters

16 and accounts in not to exceed the following amounts:

17   CHAPTER I

18   DEPARTMENT OF DEFENSE—MILITARY

19   MILITARY PERSONNEL

20   (TRANSFER OF FUNDS)

21   MILITARY PERSONNEL, ARMY

22   For an additional amount for "Military Personnel,

23 Army", $4,863,700,000.

0933-2

HR 1282 RH

3

1   MILITARY PERSONNEL, NAVY

2   For an additional amount for "Military Personnel,

3 Navy", $797,400,000.

4   MILITARY PERSONNEL, MARINE CORPS

5   For an additional amount for "Military Personnel,

6 Marine Corps", $983,400,000.

7   MILITARY PERSONNEL, AIR FORCE

8   For an additional amount for "Military Personnel,

9 Air Force", $1,278,200,000.

10   OPERATION AND MAINTENANCE

11   (TRANSFER OF FUNDS)

12   OPERATION AND MAINTENANCE, ARMY

13   For an additional amount for "Operation and Main-

14 tenance, Army", $16,393,750,000, of which $350,000

15 shall be available only for the 1991 Memorial Day Celebra-

16 tion.

17   OPERATION AND MAINTENANCE, NAVY

18   For an additional amount for "Operation and Main-

19 tenance, Navy", $3,009,500,000.

20   OPERATION AND MAINTENANCE, MARINE CORPS

21   For an additional amount for "Operation and Main-

22 tenance, Marine Corps", $1,330,000,000.

23   OPERATION AND MAINTENANCE, AIR FORCE

24   For an additional amount for "Operation and Main-

25 tenance, Air Force", $4,080,000,000.

HR 1282 RH   0933-3

                                          0126

4

1   OPERATION AND MAINTENANCE, DEFENSE AGENCIES

2   For an additional amount for "Operation and Main-

3   tenance, Defense Agencies", $236,000,000.

4   OPERATION AND MAINTENANCE, NAVY RESERVE

5   For an additional amount for "Operation and Main-

6   tenance, Navy Reserve", $16,000,000.

7   OPERATION AND MAINTENANCE, AIR NATIONAL GUARD

8   For an additional amount for "Operation and Main-

9   tenance, Air National Guard", $55,000,000.

10   PROCUREMENT

11   (TRANSFER OF FUNDS)

12   AIRCRAFT PROCUREMENT, ARMY

13   For an additional amount for "Aircraft procurement,

14 Army", $7,100,000.

15   MISSILE PROCUREMENT, ARMY

16   For an additional amount for "Missile procurement,

17 Army", $311,900,000.

18   PROCUREMENT OF WEAPONS AND TRACKED COMBAT

19   VEHICLES, ARMY

20   For an additional amount for "Procurement of weap-

21 ons and tracked combat vehicles, Army", $26,300,000.

22   PROCUREMENT OF AMMUNITION, ARMY

23   For an additional amount for "Procurement of am-

24 munition, Army", $437,000,000.

HR 1282 RH   0933-K   0127

5

1　OTHER PROCUREMENT, ARMY

2　For an additional amount for "Other procurement,

3　Army", $30,300,000.

4　AIRCRAFT PROCUREMENT, NAVY

5　For an additional amount for "Aircraft procurement,

6　Navy", $16,000,000.

7　WEAPONS PROCUREMENT, NAVY

8　For an additional amount for "Weapons procure-

9　ment, Navy", $1,065,100,000.

10　OTHER PROCUREMENT, NAVY

11　For an additional amount for "Other procurement,

12　Navy", $34,600,000.

13　PROCUREMENT, MARINE CORPS

14　For an additional amount for "Procurement, Marine

15　Corps", $68,000,000.

16　AIRCRAFT PROCUREMENT, AIR FORCE

17　For an additional amount for "Aircraft procurement,

18　Air Force", $101,200,000.

19　MISSILE PROCUREMENT, AIR FORCE

20　For an additional amount for "Missile procurement,

21　Air Force", $400,000,000.

22　OTHER PROCUREMENT, AIR FORCE

23　For an additional amount for "Other procurement,

24　Air Force", $419,100,000.

O933-5

0128

HR 1282 RH

6

1   PROCUREMENT, DEFENSE AGENCIES

2   For an additional amount for "Procurement, Defense

3 Agencies", $2,700,000.

4   RESEARCH, DEVELOPMENT, TEST AND

5   EVALUATION

6   (TRANSFER OF FUNDS)

7 RESEARCH, DEVELOPMENT, TEST AND EVALUATION,

8   ARMY

9   For an additional amount for "Research, Develop-

10 ment, Test and Evaluation, Army", $1,200,000.

11   REVOLVING AND MANAGEMENT FUNDS

12   (TRANSFER OF FUNDS)

13   ARMY STOCK FUND

14   For an additional amount for "Army Stock Fund",

15 $57,000,000.

16   AIR FORCE STOCK FUND

17   For an additional amount for "Air Force Stock

18 Fund", $214,000,000.

19 COMBAT COSTS OF OPERATION DESERT

20   SHIELD/DESERT STORM

21   (TRANSFER OF FUNDS)

22   For expenses, not otherwise provided for, necessary

23 to finance the estimated partial costs of combat and other

24 related costs of Operation Desert Shield/Desert Storm in

25 the following additional amounts: for Operation and main-

HR 1282 RH   0933-6   0129

7

1 tenance, $5,000,000,000;   for   Procurement,

2 $1,300,000,000; In all: $6,300,000,000.

3   GENERAL PROVISIONS

4   (INCLUDING TRANSFER OF FUNDS)

5   SEC. 101. (a) In administering the Persian Gulf Re-

6 gional Defense Fund, the Secretary of Defense shall use

7 the corpus of the Fund only to the extent that amounts

8 transferred to the Fund from the Defense Cooperation Ac-

9 count established under section 2608 of title 10, United

10 States Code, are not currently available.

11   (b) If the balance of the corpus of the Persian Gulf

12 Regional Defense Fund is less than $15,000,000,000, the

13 Secretary shall transfer amounts from the Defense Co-

14 operation Account to the Persian Gulf Regional Defense

15 Fund, to the extent that amounts are available in that

16 Account, to restore the balance in the corpus of the Fund

17 to $15,000,000,000.

18   (c) For purposes of this section, the term "corpus of

19 the Fund" means the amount of $15,000,000,000 appro-

20 priated by this Act to the Persian Gulf Regional Defense

21 Fund from the general fund of the Treasury, as such

22 amount is restored from time to time by transfers from

23 the Defense Cooperation Account.

C933-7

0130

HR 1282 RH

8

1 (INCLUDING TRANSFER OF FUNDS)

2   SEC. 102. (a) The authority provided in this Act to

3 transfer funds from the Persian Gulf Regional Defense

4 Fund is in addition to any other transfer authority con-

5 tained in this or any other Act making appropriations for

6 the Department of Defense for fiscal year 1991.

7   (b) Amounts transferred from the Persian Gulf Re-

8 gional Defense Fund shall be merged with and be available

9 for the same purposes and the same time period as the

10 appropriations to which transferred.

11   (c) Amounts appropriated to the Persian Gulf Re-

12 gional Defense Fund shall remain available until trans-

13 ferred.

14   (d)(1) Upon payment of all incremental costs associ-

15 ated with the purpose for which the Persian Gulf Regional

16 Defense Fund is established, the Fund shall be termi-

17 nated.

18   (2) If the balance in the Fund at the time of the ter-

19 mination is $15,000,000,000 or less, the balance shall re-

20 vert to the general fund of the Treasury. If the balance

21 in the Fund at the time of the termination is in excess

22 of $15,000,000,000, the amount of $15,000,000,000 shall

23 revert to the general fund of the Treasury and the remain-

24 ing amount shall revert to the Defense Cooperation Ac-

25 count.

1282 RH   0933 d

9

1   (TRANSFER OF FUNDS)

2   SEC. 103. (a) For the purpose of adjusting amounts

3   (appropriated to the Department of Defense for fiscal year

4   1991) to reflect changes in expenses due to the order(to

5   active duty (other than for training) of members of the

6   National Guard and Reserves in connection with oper-

7   ations in and around the Persian Gulf (as part of oper-

8   ations currently known as Operation Desert Shield (in-

9   cluding Operation Desert Storm),) the Secretary of De-

10 fense may during fiscal year 1991 transfer not to exceed

11 $446,000,000 (among the fiscal year 1991 Military Per-

12 sonnel appropriation accounts) of the Department of De-

13 fense.

14   (b) Amounts transferred under subsection (a) shall

15 be merged with and be available for the same purposes

16 and the same time period as the appropriations to which

17 transferred.

18   (c) A transfer of funds under subsection (a) is subject

19 to regular congressional reprogramming notification re-

20 quirements.

21   (d) The transfer authority in subsection (a) is in ad-

22 dition to any other transfer authority contained in this or

23 any other Act making appropriations for the Department

24 of Defense for fiscal year 1991.

HR 1282 RH   0933 - P   0132

10

1   SEC. 104. Of the funds appropriated or made avail-

2 able in this Act, the amount for fuel price increases shall

3 be allocated only to the fuel consumed in direct support

4 of Operation Desert Shield/Desert Storm.

5   SEC. 105. Any CHAMPUS (Civilian Health and

6 Medical Program of the Uniformed Services) medical pro-

7 vider may voluntarily waive the patient co-payment for

8 medical services provided from August 2, 1990, until the

9 termination of Operation Desert Shield/Desert Storm for

10 dependents of active duty personnel: *Provided*, That the

11 government's share of medical services is not increased

12 during the specified time period.

13   SEC. 106. Mitchel Field Health Care Facility in the

14 State of New York shall only be funded from the Oper-

15 ation and Maintenance, Navy, appropriation and shall not

16 be funded or included within the congressionally imposed

17 ceiling of the Uniformed Services Treatment Facility ac-

18 count.

19   CHAPTER II

20   MILITARY CONSTRUCTION

21   (TRANSFER OF FUNDS)

22   MILITARY CONSTRUCTION, ARMY

23   For an additional amount for "Military Construction,

24 Army", $35,000,000, to remain available for obligation

25 until September 30, 1994.

11

1 CHAPTER III

2 DEPARTMENT OF TRANSPORTATION

3 (TRANSFER OF FUNDS)

4 COAST GUARD

5 OPERATING EXPENSES

6 For an additional amount for "Operating expenses",

7 $18,922,000.

8 This Act may be cited as the "Operation Desert

9 Shield/Desert Storm Supplemental Appropriations Act,

10 1991".

HR 1282 RH   0933-1/   0134

외 무 부

판리
번호 91-756

종 별 : 지 급

번 호 : USW-1289

수 신 : 장관(미북,미안,중동일,기정)

일 시 : 91 0320 1633

발 신 : 주 미 대사

제 목 : 걸프전비 추가 지출법안

연:WUS-1117(1),1285(2)

1. 당관 조태열 서기관은 금 3.20 오전 표제법안 하원통과시 연호(1) 결의안을 발의한바 있는 JIM CHAPMAN 하원의원의 보좌관 KAREN TROUTMAN 을 접촉, 걸프전비 기여금 기약속분을 이행키 않는 국가에 대한 제재조치 관련 의회 동향을 탐문한바, 요지 아래 보고함.

가. CHAPMAN 의원의 연호 결의안 발의는 이문제에 대한 하원내 전반적 분위기를 반영, 관련국가에 대한 적절한 경고문안 채택이 필요하다는 판단에서 이루어진것이며, 구체적인 조치를 염두에 둔것은 아니었음. 동결의안 통과시에도 별다른 논쟁이나 필요조치의 구체적 내용에 관한 논의는 없었으며, 구두 표결(VOICE VOTE)로 통과되었음.

나. 동하원 결의안과는 달리, 작일 상원을 통과한 법안은 관련국에 대한 무기 수출 금지등 구체적 조치 내용을 포함하고 있는바, 양법안에 차이가 있는 부분은 세출위 양원 합동회의를 통해 조정이 이루어질것이나, 현재로서는 별다른 움직임이 없어 결과를 예측할수는 없음.(자신이 아는한 CHAPMAN 의원도 이문제와관련, 특별한 구상은 없는것 같다고 부언)

다. 하원 결의안이 법적 구속력이 없는 SENSE OF CONGRESS RESOLUTION 인데반해, 상원 통과 법안은 관련 문안이 법안의 일반 규정으로 삽입된 구속력 있는 조항인바, 양원 합동심의 과정에서 어떠한 형태로 조정될 것인지를 문의한데 대해, 이문제에 대해서도 아직은 판단하기 어렵다면서 진전사항이 있으면 알려주겠다고만 답변함.

2. 한편, 금일 오후 당관을 방문한 WOLFF 전 하원의원은 향후 이문제와 관련, 의회내 상당한 논란이 예상된다면서 의회 분위기로는 무역제재등의 조치도 논의될수 있을 것으로 본다고 언급함.

미주국 안기부	장관	차관	1차보	2차보	미주국	중아국	외연원	총리실

PAGE 1

91.03.21   09:50
외신 2과 통제관 CH
0135

3. 이와관련, 금일자 W.P 지는 상기 상원의 조치는 독일이 기약속분 삭감을위해 내주중 대표단을 미국에 파견할 것이라는 보도의 와중에서 나온것이며, 행정부 고위관리의 말을 인용, 미국은 신속한 종전에도 불구, 기약속 기여금 전액을 제공받길 기대하고 있다고 보도함. 또한, 미연방예산국은 성명을 통해 동상원 조치는 불필요하고 부적절한 (UNNECESSARY AND INAPPROPRIATE)것이라고 논평하고, 외국 기여금 제공이 지연되고 있는것은 미 행정부의 전비산출이 늦어진데에도 일부 원인이 있다고 해명함.(관련 기사 사본 별전 FAX 송부)

4. 동건 관련 의회동향 수시 탐문 보고예정임.

첨부 USW(F)-939

(대사 현홍주-국장)

예고:91.12.31 까지

검토필 (1 ℓ (. 6 . 5 .) 신

원 본

외 무 부

종 별 : 지급

번 호 : USW-1336

일 시 : 91 0322 1501

수 신 : 장관(미북)미안,중동일,기정)

발 신 : 주 미 대사

제 목 : 걸프전비 추가 지출법안

연:USW-1289

1. 상. 하 양원 세출위는 작 3.21. 저녁 늦게까지 표제법안 관련 합동심의를 진행, 문안조정 작업을 완료한바, 금일 오전 연호 기약속 공여분 미이행국에 대한 무기금수 관련 수정안을 발의한 BYRD 상원의원실을 접촉, 확인한바에 의하면 동 수정안은 별다른 반대 없이 조정법안에 포함되었다함.(동 수정안 별전 FAX 송부)

2. 상. 하 양원은 금일 각각 본회의를 개최, 동 세출위 합동회의 결과 보고서 (CONFERENCE REPORT)를 기초로 표제 법안에 관한 토의를 가질 예정인바, 내주부터 양원이 부활절 휴회에들어감에 비추어 금일중 토의를 완료, 법안을 통과시킬 것으로 보임.(본회의 투표 결과 추보 예정)

3. 한편, 당관이 확인한바에 의하면, 표제 법안과는 별도로 걸프전비 추가 지출을 위한 수권법안 (AUTHORIZATION BILL:HR 1175, S 725)심의시 BRYANT 하원의원(D-TX)의 발의로 별도 수정안이 제출되었는바, 동수정안은 재정공여국이 6 개월내 기약속분을 이행하지 않을 경우 기여금 전액 제공시까지 해당국에 주둔하고 있는 미군기지등 미국방부에 고용된 해당국민의 임금지불을 보류(WITHOLD)한다는것을 골자로하고 있음.(동 수정안 별전 FAX 송부)

동수정안은 작일 양원 세출위 합동심의시 동 수권법안에 포함되었다하는바, 수정안 내용이 아국에 직접적 영향을 미칠 사항이므로 동 수권법안에 대한 양원 본회의 심의동향등을 계속 파악, 보고예정임. 첨부:USW(F)-969

(대사 현홍주-국장)

예고:91.12.31 까지

검토필 (1 6.   )

미주국	장관	차관	1차보	2차보	미주국	중아국	청와대	안기부

PAGE 1

주 미 대 사 관

번호 : USW(F) - 969

수신 : 장 관 (미북, 미안, 중동1, 기정)

발신 : 주미대사

제무 : 걸프전비 추가지출법안 (첨부물 2매)

Byrd 수정안

Sec. 109. None of the funds appropriated or otherwise made available by this Act or any other provision of law shall be available for sales, credits, or guarantees for defense articles or defense services under the Arms Export Control Act to any country that has made a commitment to contribute resources to defray any of the costs of Operation Desert Storm and that has not fulfilled its commitments.

Sec. 110. The establishment of the Persian Gulf Regional Defense Fund by this Act and the establishment of a working capital account pursuant to title I of the Persian Gulf Conflict Supplemental Authorization and Personnel Benefits Act of 1991 shall be treated for all purposes as establishment of the same account in the Treasury.

, and on page 10, delete lines 1, 2, 3 and 4 of the House of Representatives engrossed bill, H.R. 1282, and insert in lieu thereof the following:

"Sec. 104. None of the funds appropriated to the Persian Gulf Regional Defense Fund shall be used for fuel price increases.".

969-1

BRYANT556

MARCH 12, 1991

AMENDMENT TO H.R. 1175, AS REPORTED

OFFERED BY MR. BRYANT OF TEXAS

At the end of title I (page ___, after line ___), insert the following new section:

1 SEC. 109. WITHHOLDING OF PAYMENTS TO INDIRECT-HIRE CIVILIAN

2 PERSONNEL OF NONPAYING PLEDGING NATIONS.

3 (a) GENERAL RULE.--Effective as of the end of the six-

4 month period beginning on the date of the enactment of this

5 Act, the Secretary of Defense shall withhold payments to any

6 nonpaying pledging nation that would otherwise be paid as

7 reimbursements for expenses of indirect-hire civilian

8 personnel of the Department of Defense in that nation.

9 (b) NONPAYING PLEDGING NATION DEFINED.--For purposes of

10 this section, the term ``nonpaying pledging nation'' means a

11 foreign nation that has pledged to the United States that it

12 will make contributions to assist the United States in

13 defraying the incremental costs of Operation Desert Shield

14 and which has not paid to the United States the full amount

15 so pledged.

16 (c) RELEASE OF WITHHELD AMOUNTS.--When a nation affected

17 by subsection (a) has paid to the United States the full

18 amount pledged, the Secretary of Defense shall release the

19 amounts withheld from payment pursuant to subsection (a).

969-2 (END)

외 무 부

원 본

종 별 : 지 급

번 호 : USW-1337

일 시 : 91 0322 1501

수 신 : 장관(미북)미안,중동일,기정)

발 신 : 주 미 대 사

제 목 : 걸프전비 추가 지출법안

연:USW-1336

연호 BYRD 수정안 및 BRYANT 수정안 관련, 당관 조태열 서기관이 금 3.22 오전 일본 대사관 KAWAI 1 등서기관을 접촉, 일측의 관찰 내용을 탐문한바, 요지 아래 보고함.

1. BYRD 수정안은 사우디와 UAE 를 대상으로한것이므로, 일본이나 한국에는 별다른 영향이 없을 것으로 보며, 따라서 일측으로서는 큰 관심을 두고 있지 않음. 동수정안에 대해 미행정부는 반대 입장을 취하고 있는바, 이문제에 FREE HAND 를 유지하고자하는 미행정부의 기본 입장을 반영하는것임.

2. 일본으로서는 오히려 BRYANT 수정안에 우려를 갖고 있는바, 동수정안은 미군이 주둔하고 있는 일본과 한국에 직접적 영향을 미치는것으로서 기약속분의 조속 제공을 촉구하기 위한 압력의 일환으로 제안되었다고 판단됨.

3. BRYANT 수정안에 대한 미행정부의 반응은 확인치 못하였으며 최종 채택 전망도 분명치 않음.

(대사 현홍주-국장)

예고:91.12.31 까지

미주국	장관	차관	1차보	2차보	미주국	중아국	청와대	안기부

PAGE 1

91.03.23   05:58

외신 2과 통제관 CF

0140

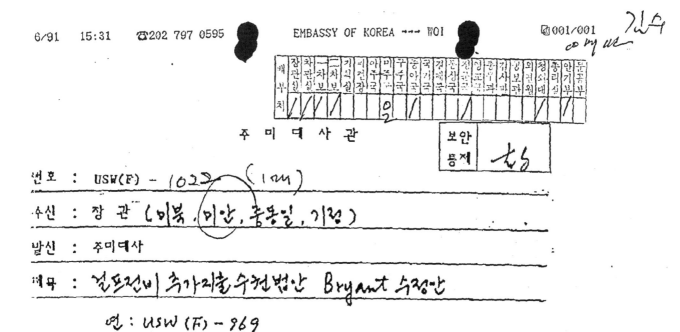

주 미 대 사 관

번호 : USW(F) - 1022 (1매)

수신 : 장 관 (미북, 미안, 중동일, 기협)

발신 : 주미대사

제목 : 걸프전비 추가지출 수정법안 Bryant 수정안

연 : USW (F) - 969

최종 심의과정에서 아래 (d)항 추가

SEC. 608. WITHHOLDING OF PAYMENTS TO INDI-RECT-HIRE CIVILIAN PERSONNEL OF NONPAYING PLEDGING NATIONS.

(a) GENERAL RULE.—Effective as of the end of the six-month period beginning on the date of the enactment of this Act, the Secretary of Defense shall withhold payments to any nonpaying pledging nation that would otherwise be paid as reimbursements for expenses of indirect-hire civilian personnel of the Department of Defense in that nation.

(b) NONPAYING PLEDGING NATION DEFINED.—For purposes of this section, the term "nonpaying pledging nation" means a foreign nation that has pledged to the United States that it will make contributions to assist the United States in defraying the incremental costs of Operation Desert Shield and which has not paid to the United States the full amount so pledged.

(c) RELEASE OF WITHHELD AMOUNTS.—When a nation affected by subsection (a) has paid to the United States the full amount pledged, the Secretary of Defense shall release the amounts withheld from payment pursuant to subsection (a).

(d) WAIVER AUTHORITY.—The Secretary of Defense may waive the requirement in subsection (a) upon certification to Congress that the waiver is required in the national security interests of the United States.

0141

관리
번호 91-191

외 무 부

종 별 : 지 급

번 호 : USW-1341   일 시 : 91 0322 1626

수 신 : 장관(미북,미안,중동일,기정)

발 신 : 주 미 대사

제 목 : 걸프전비 추가 지출 법안

연 WUS-1336

1. 표제 법안은 금 3.22 개최된 연호 상. 하원 본회의에서 각각 구두 표결(VOICE VOTE)로 통과 되었음.

2. 동 법안은 대통령의 서명으로발효 하게되는바, 행정부의 입장등 관련 동향 추보 예정임.

(대사 현홍주 -국장)

91.12.31 까지

대고문에의거 일반문서로
재분류 1991. 12. 31 서명

검 토 필 (1991.6.

미주국	1차보	2차보	미주국	중아국	청와대	안기부

외 무 부

종 별 : 지 급

번 호 : USW-1355　　　　　　　　　　일 시 : 91 0322 1841

수 신 : 장관(미북,미안,중동일,기정)

발 신 : 주 미대사

제 목 : 걸프 전비 추가 지출 수권 법안

　　연 USW-1336

　　1. 표제 수권 법안은 금일 양원 합동 비공식 회의에서 재심의를 거쳐 정식 통과되었음.

　　2. 당관이 확인한바에 의하면, 연호 BRYANT 수정안은 국무장관이 국가 안보를 위해 필요하다고 판단될 경우에는 임금을 지불할수 있다는 취지의 단서 조항이 추가 되어 통과되었다함. 동 최종문안 입수하는대로 FAX 송부 예정임.

　　3. 한편, 금일 양원 본회의에서 통과된 연호 지출법안에는 3.7 하원을 통과한 CHAPMAN 결의안(4.15 까지 약속분 미납국에 대한 제재 조치 결의안)은 삭제된바, 이는 작일 저녁 양원 세출위 합동심의에서 조정된결과임.

　　4. 상기 BRYANT 수정안에 대한 행정부(백악관 국방성등)의 입장은 계속 파악 보고 예정임.

　　(대사 현홍주-국장)

　　91.12.31 까지

검 토 필 (19

미주국	1차보	2차보	미주국	중아국	청와대	안기부

報 告 事 項

報 告 畢

1991. 3. 23.
美 洲 局
北 美 課(18)

題 目 : 美 議會, 걸프戰 關聯 追加 歲出 法案 調整

上.下 兩院 歲出委는 3.21(목) 걸프전 追加 支出 法案 關聯 合同審議를 통해 3.19. 上院 通過 旣約束 供與分 未 履行國에 대한 武器禁輸 關聯 修正案을 포함 키로 確定하였으며, Bryant 下院議員(民主, TX) 發議로 友邦國 寄與 約束額의 早期 執行을 促求하는 別途 修正案이 包含되었는 바, 관련사항 아래 報告 드립니다.

---

1. Bryant 修正案

○ 財政 供與國이 6個月內 旣約束分을 履行치 않을 경우, 寄與金 全額 執行時 까지 該當國 駐屯 美軍基地內 美 國防部가 고용한 該當 國民의 賃金 支拂을 保留한다는 것을 골자로 함.

* 駐韓美軍 고용 韓國人 勤勞者 人件費는 年間 約 4億弗이며 91年度부터 我側이 4,300万弗을 負擔中임.

○ 美軍 駐屯中인 日本과 韓國에 대해 旣約束分 早速 執行 促求를 위한 壓力의 一環으로 提案된 것으로 判斷됨.
  - 美 行政府 立場 및 最終 採擇 展望은 尙今 不確實

양고재	91년 3월 23일	담당	과장	심의관	국장	차관보	차관	장관

0144

2. Byrd 修正案

   ○ 3.19. 上院審議時 Byrd 上院議員(民主, WVa) 發議로 旣約束 供與分 未 履行國에
     대한 武器禁輸를 규정하고 있음.

     - 上.下院 兩院 歲出委 合同審議時 修正없이 通過
     - 美 行政府는 分明한 反對意思 表明中
     - 사우디 및 UAE를 대상으로 한 것이며 韓國 및 日本에는 별무 영향 豫想

                                          - 끝 -

報 告 事 項

1991. 3. 23.
美 洲 局
北 美 課(18)

題 目 : 美 議會, 걸프戰 關聯 追加 歲出 法案 調整

上.下 兩院 歲出委는 3.21(목) 걸프전 追加 支出 法案 關聯 合同審議를 통해 3.19. 上院 通過 旣約束 供與分 未 履行國에 대한 武器禁輸 關聯 修正案을 포함키로 確定하였으며, Bryant 下院議員(民主, TX) 發議로 友邦國 寄與 約束額의 早期 執行을 促求하는 別途 修正案이 包含되었는 바, 관련사항 아래 報告 드립니다.

---

1. Bryant 修正案

º 財政 供與國이 6個月內 旣約束分을 履行치 않을 경우, 寄與金 全額 執行時 까지 該當國 駐屯 美軍基地內 美 國防部가 고용한 該當 國民의 賃金 支拂을 保留한다는 것을 골자로 함.

* 駐韓美軍 고용 韓國人 勤勞者 人件費는 年間 約 4億弗이며 91年度부터 我側이 4,300万弗을 負擔中임.

º 美軍 駐屯中인 日本과 韓國에 대해 旣約束分 早速 執行 促求를 위한 壓力의 一環으로 提案된 것으로 判斷됨.
   - 同 修正案의 最終 採擇 展望은 不確實

0146

2. Byrd 修正案

° 3.19. 上院審議時 Byrd 上院議員(民主, WVa) 發議로 旣約束 供與分 未 履行國에
대한 武器禁輸를 규정하고 있음.

- 上.下院 兩院 歲出委 合同審議時 修正없이 通過

- 美 行政府는 分明한 反對意思 表明中

- 사우디 및 UAE를 대상으로 한 것이며 韓國 및 日本에는 별무 영향 豫想

- 끝 -

0147

배부처	장관실	차관실	一차보	二차보	기획실장	외전국	아주국	미주국	구주국	중아국	국제국	경제국	통상국	정산국	영교과	종교과	기사과	정보과	외신과	청와대	총리실	안기부	문공부
	/	/	/					의		/		/			/		/		/			/	/

주 미 대 사 관

보안통제 : 上

번호 : USW(F) - 1022 (1대)

수신 : 장관 (미북, 미안, 중동일, 기정)

발신 : 주미대사

제목 : 걸프전비 추가지출 수권법안 Bryant 수정안

연 : USW (F) - 969

최종 심의과정에서 아래 (d)항 추가

SEC. 608. WITHHOLDING OF PAYMENTS TO INDIRECT-HIRE CIVILIAN PERSONNEL OF NONPAYING PLEDGING NATIONS.

(a) GENERAL RULE.—Effective as of the end of the six-month period beginning on the date of the enactment of this Act, the Secretary of Defense shall withhold payments to any nonpaying pledging nation that would otherwise be paid as reimbursements for expenses of indirect-hire civilian personnel of the Department of Defense in that nation.

(b) NONPAYING PLEDGING NATION DEFINED.—For purposes of this section, the term "nonpaying pledging nation" means a foreign nation that has pledged to the United States that it will make contributions to assist the United States in defraying the incremental costs of Operation Desert Shield and which has not paid to the United States the full amount so pledged.

(c) RELEASE OF WITHHELD AMOUNTS.— When a nation affected by subsection (a) has paid to the United States the full amount pledged, the Secretary of Defense shall release the amounts withheld from payment pursuant to subsection (a).

(d) WAIVER AUTHORITY.—The Secretary of Defense may waive the requirement in subsection (a) upon certification to Congress that the waiver is required in the national security interests of the United States.

0148

외 무 부

원 본

종 별 : 지 급

번 호 : USW-1651

일 시 : 91 0408 1807

수 신 : 장관(미북,미안,중동일,기정,국방부)

발 신 : 주 미 대사

제 목 : 걸프전비 지원금 관련 하원 군사위 보고서

대:WUS-1076

연:USW(F)-1142

1. 하원 군사위는 금 4.8. 우방국들의 걸프전비 지원현황에 관한 ASPIN 위원장 (D-WIS) 명의 평가보고서(SHARING THE BURDEN OF THE PERSIAN GULF: ARE THE ALLIES PAYING THEIR FAIR SHARE)를 작성, 배포하였는바, 아국에 관하여는 1.30. 2 억 8 천만불의 추가지원 약속 사실을 언급하고, 4.1. 현재 1 억 3 천 8 백만불(3.28. 현금 지원액 6 천만 포함)을 제공, 기약속분 3 억 8 천 5 백만불의 35 퍼센트를 이행하였다고 밝힘. 동 수치는 연호 미국방부 보고서를 기초로 작성된 것으로 보이는바, 아측 수치와 6 백만불의 차이가 생긴것은 대호 대미수송 지원액(3 천 4 백만불) 에 대한 양측의 산출 기준 차이에서 오는 오차인것으로 판단됨.

2. 동 보고서는 우방국의 전비 지원이 미국의 지속적인 압력의 결과로 이루어진 것이라고 언급하고, 특히 일본의 소극적 자세(RELUCTANT CONTRIBUTOR DESPITE ITS WEAALTH)와 UAE 의 지원액 규모에 대해 비판적 논평을 한반면, 아국에 대하여는 지원규모와 이행현황에 대한 사실 보고 위차로 기술하고 있으며, 사우디에 대하여는 지원액 규모 및 이락의 쿠웨이트 침공직후 다국적군 지원을 위한 신속한 정치적 결정을 내린 사실등을 호의적으로 평가하고 있음.

일본에 대하여는 91 년 지원 약속액 90 억불중 90 퍼센트만이 미국이 제공된다는 사실과 달러화가 아닌 엔화로 지불됨으로써 실질적 지원액이 76 억불에 불과할것이라는 점(엔화의 대달러화 강세가 그 이유) 에 대해 특별한 불만을 표시함.

3. 한편, 동 보고서는 미국이 현재까지 우방국으로 부터 지원받은 액수는 기약속분의 60 퍼센트에 해당한다고 밝히고, 미국의 걸프전기 지출액중 75 퍼센트 정도를 우방국이 부담한다면, 공평한 전비 분담이 될것이나, 문제는 지원액수보다는

미주국 국방부	장관	차관	1차보	2차보	미주국	중아국	청와대	안기부

PAGE 1

91.04.09 07:51

외신 2과 통제관 BW

0149

기약속분 이행을 여하히 확보하느냐에 있다고 결론을 맺고, 이행 촉구를 위한 지속적 압력이 필요(KEEP UP THE HEAT)하다고 언급함.

    4. 상기 보고서 전문 별전 팩스 송부함(USW(F)-1235)

    (대사 현홍주- 국장)

    91.12.31. 일반

검토필 (1 `91.6.P.)안

번호 : USN(F)-1235
수신 : 장관 (미북.미안.충동일.기정.국방부)
발신 : 주미대사
제목 : 걸프전비 지원금 관련 위선군사위 보고서 (12매) (첨부물)

REPORT ON ALLIED CONTRIBUTIONS TO PERSIAN GULF WAR EFFORT RELEASED BY HOUSE ARMED SERVICES COMMITTEE CHAIRMAN LES ASPIN (D-W APRIL 8, 1991 (TEXT)

Sharing the Burden of the Persian Gulf:
Are the Allies Paying Their Fair Share?
A Report by
Rep. Les Aspin, Chairman
House Armed Services Committee
April 8, 1991

Introduction

Last November, I issued a report on burdensharing that graded our allies on their contributions -- both financial and military -- to the common cause in the Gulf crisis.[1] I warned then that the richer states should expect an American backlash if they were seen clutching their wallets while American men and women were fighting and losing their lives in the war with Iraq. In fact, it was only a matter of days after hostilities began that the pledges to support the U.S. military operation jumped from about $10 billion to about $53 billion (see Table A).

Concerns remained, however. Both houses of Congress passed legislation urging foreign governments to deliver on their commitments promptly, calling for appropriate action if they failed to do so, and requiring the Administration to report to Congress on the details of the contributions.

Obviously, financial contributions to offset the U.S. war costs are only part of the burdensharing picture, but because the Congress is now engaged in making difficult decisions on paying such U.S. costs, this second report on burdensharing will concentrate on the allied financial contributions to the United States. We will examine the cost of the war to the United States, whether the allied contributions represent a fair share of that cost, and whether the allies are making good on their pledges.

In this paper, I will present a concise overview of the issue and then offer a more detailed, country-by-country account of allied burdensharing.

What Are the Costs of the war?

The full cost of the war is not yet known. The fighting is over, but large numbers of our military forces remain in the Kuwait Theater of Operations. The attempt to deal with the costs of the war has begun in earnest, however.

In its FY 1991 supplemental defense authorization request, the Administration asked Congress for $15 billion to meet the costs of the war. This is in addition to

1226-1

0151

the $2 billion Congress provided in the Desert Shield supplemental appropriation at the end of last year. In his testimony before the House Armed Services Committee last month, the Defense Department Comptroller, Sean O'Keefe, said:

> This $15 billion in new budget authority, plus the $53.5 billion pledged by our allies, could prove sufficient to cover all our Desert Shield/Storm incremental costs. But it will be a while before we know that. More new budget authority might be needed. On the other hand, we may not need the full $15 billion.

Defense Department estimates so far are controversial. Some argue that the Defense Department is underestimating U.S. costs by not taking fully into account such matters as additional veterans benefits in the years ahead, replacement of weapons and equipment expended or worn down in the war, and additional expenses of non-defense agencies of the government.

Others, like the U.S. Comptroller General, express concern that the Defense Department might be overstating the costs of the war by including higher fuel costs paid for operations outside the Middle East and the purchase of large amounts of spare parts not consumed in the war.

There are those who have attempted their own calculations. Based on Defense Department materials submitted with the FY 1991 supplemental request, the Defense Budget Project, a private organization, estimates total U.S. incremental war costs are likely to be about $47.5 billion. The Congressional Budget Office has estimated such costs at about $45 billion, including the costs of bringing U.S. troops and equipment home. There is some concern, therefore, that allied contributions will be in excess of incremental U.S. war costs.

Is the Aggregate Allied Contribution to the War Fair?

The fairness of the total allied contribution to the U.S. will, of course, be determined by its relationship to the final Desert Shield/Storm cost. According to current Defense Department figures, the allied pledges to the war effort will cover about 75 percent of estimated U.S. costs for the operation. This calculation assumes that the total war cost will not exceed the sum of the $15 billion requested in this year's defense supplemental, the $2 billion appropriated last year, and the allied pledges.

There is a minor difficulty with the Defense Department's figures concerning Japan. Mr. O'Keefe's sum of $53.5 billion for allied contributions includes the full 1991 Japanese pledge of $9 billion. But, Tokyo does not intend the full amount for the United States. The Japanese told U.S. Secretary of State James Baker III when they made the pledge in late January that most but not all of the money would be slated for the United States, with the remainder going to other military participants in the coalition. Japanese Government officials said that about 90 percent of the pledge (roughly $8.1 billion) was pledged to the U.S. Treasury. Fortunately, however, the United Arab Emirates recently increased its pledge by $1 billion, bringing allied pledges to a total of more than $53.6 billion and maintaining Mr. O'Keefe's calculation of the allied offset at about 75 percent of U.S. incremental costs.

These calculations so far beg the question of what is a fair percentage for the aggregate allied contribution to the incremental costs of the war with Iraq.

The United States had its own vital interests in the Persian Gulf and the only military capable of executing Desert Storm. The U.S. contribution was appropriate in comprising three-fourths of the troops of Desert Storm as well as incurring some costs. By the same token, our allies should also participate and pay for the cost of the war in a way commensurate with their ability and their stake in its outcome. So

/235-2

the figure we should aim for in allied financial contribution should not be 100 percent of U.S. costs, but nevertheless something very significant.

There is no precise formula by which this right number can be fixed. The current working figure of about 75 percent from U.S. allies seems an appropriate level for aggregate allied contributions.

A country-by-country analysis of financial contributions and judgments on whether they individually constitute fair shares of the burden are found in the annex.

Are the Checks in the Mail?

Apparently many of them are; and several big ones from the donors causing the most concern. The U.S. Treasury received $5.78 billion from Japan on March 27, bringing receipts from Tokyo to roughly 75 percent of the Japanese pledge. Japanese officials say the remainder of their pledge has actually been disbursed to the Gulf Cooperation Council's Gulf Peace Cooperation Fund and will be transferred to the U.S. Treasury very shortly.

In the second half of March, the German Government deposited another $3.28 billion in the U.S. Treasury. That brought German contributions to more than 97 percent of the amount Bonn has pledged to the U.S. war effort.

With its March contributions, the United Arab Emirates also hit the 75 percent mark, having delivered just over $3 billion of its $4 billion pledge. Kuwaiti deposits are nearing the halfway point and large Kuwaiti deposits are arriving on a regular basis. Saudi Arabia is credited with just over 40 percent of its total pledge, and updated accounting for continuing in-kind contributions will soon bring that country considerably closer to fulfilling its commitment. Korea is credited with about 35 percent of the $385 million it has pledged.

In sum, as of April 1, the United States has received almost 60 percent of the total allied pledges of cash and in-kind contributions to offset U.S. war costs (see Table A). Administration officials have stated before the House Armed Services Committee that the remainder of the pledges will be delivered soon and additional contributions are arriving regularly.

Conclusion

If the full pledges are received, and I believe the bulk of them will be, and if they are adequate to offset 75 percent of the U.S. costs for the war as is now estimated, do they represent a fair share of the burden? The answer to that is yes. If the contributions of our allies offset at least 75 percent of our costs, that will be an adequate contribution.

The problem would be not so much with the aggregate amount pledged, however, but rather with the amount of browbeating required to obtain it. Gathering pledges was like pulling teeth. The United States had to publicly deploy cabinet officials on fund-raising tours to embarrass major powers into contributing to an operation that was clearly in their own vital interests. We should make no mistake about this: It was pressure from the United States that prompted many of the pledges and it will take pressure from the United States to make sure we collect. We have to keep up the heat.

In addition, for reasons made clear in the country-by-country analysis below, two of our allies deserve special criticism.

1235—3

0153

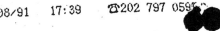

Japan was a reluctant contributor despite its wealth, and when we read the fine print, we discovered there was less to the pledge of $9 billion than met the eye.

First, Japan intends only about 90 percent of its $9 billion 1991 pledge for the United States. The widespread initial impression was that the entire amount was intended to defray U.S. war costs.

Second, Japan is fudging on even that pledge with its currency dealings. While other allies are making good their pledges in dollars, Japan is delivering its pledge in yen. That benefits Japan because the dollar has strengthened against the yen since the pledge was made. And the Japanese aren't increasing the number of yen in their contribution to compensate. At the time the pledge was made, it was worth about $8.42 billion to the United States. Now, the same number of yen is worth $7.6 billion, and that's all the Japanese say they're contributing.

The United Arab Emirates also deserve American criticism. The UAE has a higher GNP than Kuwait and higher per capita income than either Kuwait or Saudi Arabia, it is unscathed from the war, and it did not make a huge, costly military commitment to the conflict. Yet, it pledged only $1 billion for 1990 and only $2 billion for 1991 before being shamed into adding an additional $1 billion. The UAE should agree to pick up a share of the Saudi and Kuwaiti pledges.

If it delivers on all its pledges, and I believe it will, Saudi Arabia will get a pat on the back from most Americans. It not only committed to almost $17 billion in assistance to U.S. military operations, it made the prompt political decision after the Iraqi invasion of Kuwait to request help from multinational forces and provide them the facilities and support needed to reverse that aggression.

There was a controversy over what was happening to the windfall profits Saudi Arabia received as a result of increases in oil prices. Some said they were being pocketed, but the Saudi Embassy in Washington denied it, saying the profits were being spent. Our independent investigation showed two things. First, the Saudis did not appear to be spending as much as the embassy said. But second, and most important, it appears that the Saudis will spend their windfall profits and more on the war.

TABLE A
PLEDGES TO THE U.S. IN SUPPORT OF DESERT SHIELD/STORM
(as of April 1, 1991, dollars in millions)

	First Pledge	Second Pledge	Total	Cash Received	Value of In-Kind Received a/	Total Received
Saudi Arabia	3,339	13,500 b/	16,839	4,536	2,388	6,924
Kuwait	2,506	13,500	16,006	7,000	16	7,016
United Arab Emirates	1,000	3,000	4,000	2,870	179	3,049
Japan	1,740 c/	8,100 d/	9,840	6,646 e/	633	7,279
Germany	1,072	5,500	6,572	5,772	629	6,401
Korea	80 f/	305	385	110	28	138
Other g/	3	n/a	3	0	3	3
TOTAL	9,740	43,905	53,645	26,934	3,876	30,810

Value of Commitment to US

1235-4

NOTE: Does not include pledges or contributions to other countries in support of the multinational Gulf effort.

---

a/   As of March 19, 1991. Understated as figure does not include in-kind material currently in the pipeline.

b/   The Saudis have made an open-ended commitment to provide host nation support (HNS). The Saudi HNS pledge includes no-cost food, fuel, water, facilities, and local transportation for all U.S. forces in Saudi Arabia and surrounding waters. For calendar 1990, the Saudi pledge has been estimated at $3.339 billion. The Saudi pledge of $13.5 billion is for the first three months of calendar 1991.

c/   The original Japanese pledge to the multinational forces included $1,740 billion to the United States and $260 million to other coalition forces.

d/   This figure reflects the estimate by Japanese Government officials that 90 percent or more of the $9 billion pledged by the Japanese Government in January 1991 to the coalition military effort is intended for the United States, with the remainder going to other coalition forces.

e/   Includes the $5.78 billion received on March 27, 1991.

f/   Originally reported as a pledge of $95 million for calendar 1990 and $25 million for calendar 1991. The State Department has suggested that only 84 percent, or $80 million, of the calendar 1990 pledge was for the United States.

g/   Represents the contributions of Denmark ($1.0 million), Bahrain ($1.2 million), Oman ($600 thousand), and Qatar ($200 thousand).

ANNEX

COUNTRY-BY-COUNTRY ANALYSIS

Japan

Total Pledge to the United States

Japan's January pledge of about $8.1 billion is in addition to the $1.74 billion it pledged to the United States last year, bringing the total Japanese commitment to the United States to about $9.84 billion. As of April 1, Japan was credited with delivery to the United States of $7.279 billion, following the deposit on March 27 of the yen equivalent of $5.78 billion. Japanese officials tell me the remainder of the pledge has been deposited in the Gulf Peace Cooperation Fund and is to be transferred to the U.S. Treasury in the very near future.

The Japanese are quick to point out that their Gulf-related burdensharing contributions are supplemented by their commitments to offset major portions of U.S. expenses involved in maintaining U.S. troops in Japan. The Government of Japan recently signed a new Host Nation Support Agreement with the United States in which Tokyo agreed to increase substantially its share of those U.S. costs. Over the five years covered by the agreement, Japan will increase its share from its current 40 percent to more than 50 percent. Excluding the pay and allowances for U.S. military personnel in Japan, the Japanese payments will come to roughly 73 percent of total U.S. costs. The White House announcement on the new agreement called it "by far the most generous host nation support program that we have anywhere in the world."

1235-5

0155

The New Pledge and Deliveries

However, even if Japanese pledges for the Iraq war come in on schedule, there will be a couple of problems with the new receipts.

The first problem is that the January Japanese pledge was not intended solely for the United States, despite the popular perception to the contrary. When Tokyo made the commitment to Secretary Baker, Japanese officials told him that most, but not all, of the assistance would go to the United States. They indicated to me that about 90 percent or more would end up in our treasury. So, from the beginning, the United States was slated for roughly $8.1 billion of the new $9 billion Japanese pledge to the coalition military effort.

The second problem will cause more concern. In late January, when Tokyo made the commitment to provide $9 billion worth of assistance to offset coalition military costs, the currency exchange rate stood at 130 yen per dollar. The Japanese Government asked its Parliament to approve an expenditure in yen equivalent to $9 billion at that rate (1 trillion, 170 billion yen). That request was approved, and funds in that amount are being disbursed. In the two months since the commitment was made, however, the dollar has strengthened against the yen and at the current exchange rate of about 139 yen; per dollar, the Japanese pledge of $9 billion is valued at about $8.42 billion, and the 90 percent U.S. cut of that would be about $7.6 billion.

Japan is the only contributor that has tied its contribution clearly to the original exchange rate and is disbursing its pledge in native currency. The other countries are delivering their pledges in dollars and appear to be intent on providing the full dollar amount pledged. The Japanese will receive another round of American criticism if the popular perception of a $9 billion pledge crashes up against a $7.6 billion delivery.

Political-Economic Context and the Strings Attached

The Japanese Government has called for one-year increases in taxes on oil, business and cigarettes to fund the pledge of $9 billion for the multinational military effort in the Gulf. The tax hike is drawing domestic criticism but will be manageable within Japan's robust economy. That economy is the second largest in the world -- larger than those of Britain, France and Italy combined. The core of the Japanese economy is a manufacturing sector that imports about 90 percent of the oil it burns -- about 70 percent from the Gulf.

The Japanese constitution, imposed by the United States following World War II, bars the threat or use of force as a means of settling international disputes. Consequently, despite its economic capacity, its stakes in the Gulf and its competent, well-equipped and sizable armed force (250,000 active personnel -- only about 55,000 fewer than Britain), Japan committed no military forces to the crisis, and has attached strings to its financial contributions.

Domestic concerns stemming from this constitutional constraint have resulted in Japan's insistence that the money it contributes be limited to non-military uses. The U.S. State Department has given Tokyo assurances that this issue will not lead to a "practical problem," saying that anticipated U.S. logistic needs exceed the amount of the Japanese pledges.

Overall Assessment

The problem is not so much with the size of the Japanese pledges -- more than $9.8 billion. The problems have involved the amount of arm twisting required to extract the pledges, slow delivery on the pledges, payments in yen valued at dollar levels lower than those originally pledged, and the strings attached.

1235-6

0156

Germany

The New Pledge

On January 31, Bonn announced a new commitment of $5.5 billion to "be made available to the Government of the United States of America as Germany's contribution toward the costs of American operations in the Gulf region for the first three months of 1991." According to the German Government's spokesman, the entire amount is to be in the form of _cash_ transfers.

Total Pledge to the United States

Combined with the 1990 pledge to the United States of about $1.1 billion, the 1991 pledge brings Bonn's total to roughly $6.6 billion. Most of the 1990 pledge was in the form of in-kind assistance. It was to include 60 special reconnaissance vehicles designed to detect the presence of radiation, or chemical or biological weapons on the battlefield valued at $130 million. Much of the other equipment pledged to the United States was reportedly surplus from the now-dissolved East German Army. This is in effect a no-cost item for Germany, which does not want the equipment. The only East German equipment that was to be transferred to the U.S. military was equipment the U.S. military identified as useful.

The Political Context

The German constitution, written at the conclusion of World War II with a lot of international attention, contains constraints that many Germans argue prohibit deployment of German forces outside the NATO region -- a limitation the Federal Republic has honored throughout the post-war period. But this constitutional bar is not as explicit as Japan's; some have even questioned if it might be simply a convenient crutch when Germans don't really want to do more. Unlike the case with the Japanese, however, these German political constraints did not result in any strings being attached to the funds being transferred to the United States.

The Economic Context

The German economy is one of the world's strongest and has continued to grow at a healthy rate. Germany is the world's leading exporter.

The German financial agenda, however, is admittedly crowded. The economic burdens of last fall's reunification are substantial. The cost of the reconstruction of what was East Germany will be imposing; just converting East German to West German currency was a considerable drain. Bonn has also pledged more than $8 billion to the Soviet Union in ways intended to facilitate the prompt departure of Soviet troops from Germany.

Overall Assessment

Germany has been a staunch NATO ally and instrumental in the recent historic achievements in Europe. It continues to contribute to stability and reconstruction in Central Europe in ways that seriously strain its treasury. It is experiencing some constraints, stemming from its unique history, on fuller participation in the international community.

Still, Germany is an economic superpower and has one of the world's finest armed forces. It has the capacity to do more and to fulfil its pledges promptly. As of April 1 in fact, Germany was credited with delivery of about $6.4 billion -- more than 97 percent of its pledge to the United States.

Bonn should also proceed with some urgency to resolve its constitutional difficulties regarding deployment of military forces. On balance, Chancellor Kohl was

1235-7

0157

correct when he summarized his country's performance, "...we are not fully assuming our responsibility" in the Gulf crisis.

Saudi Arabia

The New Pledge

On January 26, Secretary of State Baker announced that Saudi Arabia had just pledged an additional $13.5 billion for the first three months of 1991 to help defray the cost of U.S. operations in the Gulf. It is unclear at this time how much of this amount will come in cash transfers and how much will be in what is called in-kind support such as facilities, trucks, petroleum and the like, but it is intended solely for the United States.

Total Pledge to the United States

Last year, the Saudi Government pledged to provide coalition forces deployed in that country with basic supplies. In November, it signed an agreement with the United States, for example, to provide fuel, lubricants, fresh food, local transportation, water and other goods and services required by U.S. forces in country. The value of such assistance pledged by the Saudis in 1990 is estimated at about $3.3 billion which, combined with the 1991 pledge of $13.5 billion, sets the total Saudi pledge at about $16.8 billion. As of April 1, the Saudis are credited with delivery of almost $7 billion, but that figure will climb quickly as U.S. accounting catches up with additional in-kind assistance provided and more checks arrive from Riyadh, as they have been doing regularly.

The "Windfall Profits" Issue

The relevant question regarding Saudi contributions is simple: Is the Saudi regime devoting all of its "windfall" oil profits to this crisis? Saudi Ambassador Prince Bandar recently wrote stating that the Saudi government had not only spent all its 1990 windfall profits but dipped into its reserves to finance this operation.

After reviewing the embassy's numbers and other data available from public and private sources, it can be concluded that Saudi Arabia has not spent quite as much as the embassy reports, but will nonetheless probably spend all of its windfall profit and more on this operation before it is over. A conclusive, bottom-line number cannot be given at this time because it is not known a) when this operation will end and hence what it will cost, or b) how much the Saudi windfall profit will be since oil prices are fluctuating so wildly.

The embassy calculations cover the August-December 1990 period. For those months, the Saudis report they obtained windfall profits of about $13 billion and spent $25 billion on the confrontation. My estimate is that the Saudis obtained windfall profits in 1990 of $13 billion to $15 billion and actually spent about $10 billion. The Saudis, however, committed themselves to spend additional sums this year -- and oil prices so far this year have been much lower than last fall. As a result, it is reasonable to conclude that Saudi Arabia will spend all of its windfall profits -- and more -- before this crisis is over.

Table B lists the chief components of Saudi Arabia's expenditures as of April 1st on behalf of this confrontation. The following numbered paragraphs conform to the numbered lines in Table B.

1235-8

0158

Table B
ESTIMATED SAUDI OUTLAYS
(In Millions of Dollars)

		CY90 Embassy	Aspin	1st Qtr 91
	Military Support to Allies			
1	United States	3000	1714	1500
2	Others	--	400	400
3	Economic Aid to Frontline States	3650	3000	1400
	Increased Saudi Military Spending			
4	Purchases form U.S.	7600	815	576
5	Purchases from Others	5000	536	380
6	Domestic	1700	1700	1020
7	Expenses to Raise Oil Output	4000	500	300
8	Aid for Refugees	--	500	--
	TOTAL	24950	9165	5576

1   **Military support for the United States:** The embassy letter lists the volume of support for U.S. Operation Desert Shield at $3 billion during calendar year 1990. In November, the United States and Saudi Arabia signed an agreement under which Riyadh agreed to supply the United States fuel, lubricants, fresh food, local transportation, water and other goods and services required by the U.S. forces within Saudi Arabia. The Ambassador has said these items will be supplied under a receipted system so that a full accounting can be made. In addition, the Saudi government agreed to reimburse the United States for its expenses in these categories before the signing of the agreement. For example, immediately after arriving in Saudi Arabia in August, the U.S. military signed contracts for water supply and also leased trucks and buses. The Saudis have now reimbursed the United States for that. The Pentagon reported in mid-January that it had been reimbursed $760 million in cash and supplied goods in-kind valued at $854 million through December 31. That makes a total of $1,614 million. Another $100 million has been added here on the assumption that receipts will continue to trickle in for awhile. The embassy letter stated that "recently" oil provided free to coalition military forces in the kingdom was "running over two million barrels a day." Defense Department fuel officials, however, have informed the committee that free fuel supplied by Saudi Arabia to American military forces in Saudi Arabia and surrounding waters averaged 150,000 barrels a day during Desert Shield, a significant difference of several orders of magnitude. After Desert Storm began, the Saudi in-kind contribution rose to around 450,000 barrels a day, they report.

2   **Military support for the other coalition partners:** The embassy included nothing for Saudi aid to the Egyptian, Syrian and other coalition forces located in Saudi Arabia. At the very least, the Saudi government is supplying considerable transport and logistics support for the allies. It is reported from some sources that the Saudis are picking up an even bigger share of the costs of supporting some of the smaller allied presences. No firm dollar figures are available. These costs are estimated in this paper at $400 million. Because these costs were almost entirely confined to the last quarter of 1990, the assumption is that the same costs apply for the first quarter of 1991.

1235 - 9

0159

3   Aid to frontline states: Saudi Arabia is making payments to a number of states hard hit by the economic disruption of the confrontation. Some of the payments might even be crudely called the purchase of mercenary forces. Be that as it may, the costs of this aid are legitimately attributable to the confrontation. These are economic aid payments that are separate and distinct from the direct support to military forces present in Saudi Arabia, addressed in Line #2. The embassy prices the 1990 costs at $3.65 billion. Evidence has been located of 1990 payments to a half dozen countries totaling $3 billion with commitments as of now for another $1.4 billion in the coming months. As this is being written, there are unconfirmed reports of yet another payment to one of these countries totaling $1 billion over an unknown time frame.

4   Increased Saudi military purchases from the United States: The embassy cites $7.6 billion. This is a classic example of mixing commitments with actual payments. After the invasion of Kuwait, Saudi Arabia made two emergency weapons procurements from the United States, one for $2.2 billion and the second for $7.6 billion. The embassy cites $7.6 billion as the Saudi expenditure for emergency weapons. It is not clear why the first emergency procurement is excluded. Defense Department records, however, show that during 1990 Saudi Arabia actually paid $815 million for those emergency purchases. The rest was committed and will largely be paid out over 1991. But only $815 million was paid in 1990 and should be counted as an offset to windfall profits made in 1990.

5   Increased military purchases from other countries: It is not clear what these purchases are. The embassy says the total comes to $5 billion. With no detail available, it is assumed that this figure also applies to contracts rather than actual outlays. That being the case, the same rate of payout as to the United States in Line #4 is assumed, resulting in $536 million as 1990 expenditures for arms from other countries.

6   Increased domestic military expenditures: This is the cost of forming new units, more intensive training and a greater tempo of operations. Again, we cannot know the precise figure. The figure cited by the embassy of $1.7 billion is reasonable, so it is adopted. For future outlays, the same rate as in 1990 has been assumed ~ $340 million per month.

7   Expenses to boost oil output: Another element is the sum the Saudis had to spend to raise their oil output from about 5.5 million barrels a day to 8.5 million. The increased output was a key contributor to the lowering of oil prices after the initial post-invasion surge. By November, increased production in Saudi Arabia and other countries had completely erased the deficit caused by the shut-in of Iraqi and Kuwaiti production. The embassy cited a figure of $4 billion for the costs to boost Saudi output. A Saudi Finance Ministry official in December put the investment at $5 billion. Both the Finance and Foreign Ministries have a political interest in using large numbers. Oil industry sources, however, told "Petroleum Industry Weekly" in December that the additional production had cost $2.5 billion. It is significant, however, that Saudi Arabia had already decided before the confrontation to boost its production capacity and had announced a multi-year investment plan for doing so. To that end, Fluor Corp. won a contract valued within the industry at from $2 billion to $5 billion. That contract was announced the last week of June, five weeks before the Iraqi Invasion of Kuwait. I therefore consider it an investment made during Operation Desert Shield that would have been made anyhow and should not be charged against Desert Shield. The expansion was speeded up, and some costs planned for 1991 or 1992 may have been expended in 1990. But that is still not a legitimate Desert Shield cost. The only legitimate costs attributable to the confrontation would be additional costs for overtime or insurance or special pays to attract workers to a crisis location or premiums paid to get orders fulfilled expeditiously and the like. For example, a 15 percent crisis raise was awarded all Saudi Aramco employees in October for the duration. Based on Aramco advertising, it would appear that much of what the firm has done to expand production has been

1235-10

0160

to hire more maintenance people to demothball existing facilities and to enable Saudi Arabia to get more out of its existing equipment. For example, a Saudi Aramco spokesman told "Oil Daily" (Nov 5) that if all shut-in facilities were brought on-line, total production could reach 9.6 million barrels a day. Industry sources do not report seeing a lot of new contracts being issued. It is difficult to put a dollar figure against Desert Shield for this, but, somewhat arbitrarily, the figure is set at $500 million, which a very liberal sum. It is only fair to note that Saudi efforts to rapidly and significantly boost oil output contributed mightily to the rapid fall in the price of oil last autumn. In other words, the Saudi windfall profit is much less than it would have been had not the Saudi government taken action to pump more oil onto international markets.

8   Aid for refugee care: The embassy's letter does not claim any Saudi costs for the care of refugees that flooded out of Kuwait after the Iraqi invasion. The Saudis launched a major effort to care for them, and this is certainly a cost of the confrontation. Based on a variety of reports, $500 million seems reasonable for refugee expenditures during 1990.

Income: The embassy's letter places revenues over and above those anticipated for 1990 at $13 billion. The term "windfall profits" is most often used. Defining that term is difficult, however. Is it the sum over and above what Saudi Arabia anticipated at the start of the year, as cited by the embassy? Is it the amount Saudi Arabia received over and above $18 a barrel, the OPEC price target for the first half of 1990? Is it the amount received over $21 a barrel, the OPEC target for the second half of the year? The base is a matter of choice, not objective judgment. As the ambassador notes in his letter, calculating the revenues over and above that base is complicated by the variety of different prices for different qualities of oil and different contract arrangements. Curiously, a number of different analyses using different bases and different assumptions for sales prices have come up with an estimated Saudi windfall of $13 billion to $15 billion. Others have produced much higher figures, but as the ambassador notes, they commonly fail the rules of logic by assuming that all oil revenues -- not just those above a certain baseline -- comprise the windfall or by projecting August's price spike out into the future. Given the subjectivity of the base price, it is reasonable to assume that Saudi Arabia's windfall profits total about $13 billion to $15 billion.

Deficit: Many news reports have made reference to the fact that Saudi Arabia ran a deficit of several billion dollars in 1990. That is frequently cited as evidence that the Saudi government made no "profit" out of the confrontation. It should be noted, however, that the Saudi government has run a deficit of several billion in each of the last few years since the price of oil dropped precipitously in 1986.

Overall Assessment

In light of the vital role it has played from the beginning as host nation for the coalition forces, along with its recently increased financial pledge and indications of its military resolve, we believe Saudi Arabia is now contributing to our common cause in a way that is commensurate with its capabilities, assuming all financial pledges are fulfilled.

Kuwait

Secretary Baker announced on January 26 that Kuwait had pledged an additional $13.5 billion for the first three months of 1991 to help defray U.S. costs for the Gulf operation. Last year, Kuwait pledged $2.5 billion to U.S. military efforts. All the money pledged in 1990 has been received in the U.S. Treasury. Payments on the 1991 pledge are beginning to come in regularly at the rate of $1 billion per week.

1235-11

0161

Kuwait suffered a brutal invasion, tragic loss of life, and tremendous destruction and plundering at the hands of the Iraqis. The reconstruction of Kuwait and the revitalization of its economy will be a huge financial drain on the Kuwaiti treasury, but the Kuwaiti Government is still managing to deliver on its pledges to the United States.

United Arab Emirates (UAE)

The UAE generally gets very little attention in these discussions about burdensharing. It should get more. The UAE has pledged -- and is well on its way toward paying -- $4 billion toward the costs of Operation Desert Shield/Storm. That makes the UAE the fifth principal contributor after Saudi Arabia, Kuwait, Japan and Germany. On the surface that sounds adequate. But is it?

o The UAE is an oil giant with a small population. Through the late 1980's, its GNP was greater than Kuwait's -- $23.3 billion versus $20.5 billion; and its per capita GNP was $11,680 -- compared to $10,500 for Kuwait and $4,720 for Saudi Arabia.[2] With increased oil production and higher prices during this crisis, the UAE also enjoyed additional profits of probably several billion dollars.

o Furthermore, the UAE had a great interest in our protection. In Saddam Hussein's buildup toward the invasion of Kuwait in July 1990, he focused his anger and rhetoric not only on Kuwait but also on the UAE for exceeding its OPEC oil production quota -- the reason for the UAE's immense wealth.

o Finally, the UAE emerged unscathed from this war. Unlike Kuwait, it does not face an immense burden of repair and reconstruction. Unlike Saudi Arabia, it did not make a huge and costly military commitment to the confrontation with Iraq.

For all these reasons, we -- and the Kuwaitis and Saudis -- have a right to expect the UAE to pay more. While the United States probably will not require any added payments to cover a reasonable share of our costs, the UAE ought to be dunned to pick up a share of the Saudi and Kuwaiti pledges, which are collectively more than eight times greater than the current UAE pledge.

South Korea

On January 30, the Republic of Korea announced an additional pledge of $280 million to the Gulf military effort, "especially for the U.S. forces." $170 million of this amount is to consist of military supplies and equipment; the other $110 million is to be in cash and transport services. It is difficult to determine exactly how much of its contribution Seoul intends for the United States, but combined with last year's pledge, our estimate is a total of $385 million to offset U.S. costs. As of April 1, Korea was credited with deliveries to the United States of $138 million, following a deposit of $60 million on March 28.

# # # #

---

[2] Central Intelligence Agency, The World Factbook 1990, Washington, D.C.

1235-12

0162

報 告 事 項

1991. 4. 9.
美 洲 局
北 美 課(27)

題 目 : 友邦國의 걸프戰費 支援金 執行關聯 美 下院 軍事委 報告書

美 下院 軍事委는 Les Aspin(民主, IS) 委員長 名義로 '걸프戰費 分擔 :
友邦國들은 그들의 정당한 몫을 부담하고 있는가 ?' 제하 友邦國들의 걸프 戰費
支援 現況 評價 報告書를 作成, 配布하였는 바, 同 要旨 아래 報告드립니다.

---

1. 槪 要

○ 우방국의 전비 지원금 집행은 미국의 지속적 압력의 결과로 이루어진
  것이라 전제함.

○ 한국에 대해서는 지원규모와 집행 현황에 대한 사실 보고 위주로 기술함.
  - 4.1.현재 한국 정부는 대미 기여 약속액 3억8천5백만불중 35%인
    1억3천8백만불을 집행(3.28. 송금 6천만불 포함)

○ 일본의 소극적 지원 자세와 UAE의 지원액 규모에 대해 비판적 논평을 함.
  - 일본의 경우 91년 추가지원 약속액 90억불중 90% 만 미측에 제공하고
    $화가 아닌 ¥화 기준으로 집행, 실질적 대미 추가지원액은 76억불에
    불과(5억불의 환차액 발생)하다며 노골적 불만을 표시
  - U.A.E.의 경우 GNP 규모에 비해 40억불 기여 약속은 매우 미흡함을 지적
    · 사우디 및 쿠웨이트의 부담 경감을 위한 U.A.E.의 추가기여 촉구
    · 90년도 기여 약속액 10억불, 91년도 20억불 기여을 약속하였으나
      기여액수가 적다는 비판여론에 못이겨 10억불 추가 부담

0163

o 사우디에 대해서는 사태 초기 이래 적극적 지원 태도, 특히 미군에 대한
  원활한 군수 지원 및 전비 지원을 평가함.

o 우방국의 기여 약속액 규모보다는 기약속분의 이행 확보가 중요하므로
  지속적 압력행사 필요성 강조

2. 友邦國의 對美 寄與 約束額/執行額 現況

(단위 : 백만불)

구분\n지원\n국명	약 속 액			집 행 액		
	1차 지원\n약속액	2차 지원\n약속액	소 계	현 금\n수 령	현물,수송\n지원집행	총수령액
사 우 디	3,339	13,500	16,839	4,536	2,338	6,924
쿠웨이트	2,506	13,500	16,006	7,000	16	7,016
U A E	1,000	3,000	4,000	2,870	179	3,049
일 본	1,740	8,100	9,840	6,646	633	7,279
독 일	1,072	5,500	6,572	5,772	629	6,401
한 국	80	305	385	110	28	138
기 타	3	0	3	0	3	3
계	9,740	43,905	53,645	26,934	3,876	30,810

3. 國別 執行現況

가. 일 본

o 최근 미.일간 체결된 주일미군 지원 협정으로 주둔비 부담률이 40%에서
  50%이상으로 증대(미군 인건비 제외시 73%에 육박), 일측의 걸프전 기여액은
  주일미군 주둔비 부담 증대로 보완되고 있음을 지적하고 있음.

0164

o 91.1. 2차 지원 재원 확보를 위한 국회심의시(130¥/$ 환율 적용, 1,700억¥ 예산 확보)와 91.3.27. 집행시 환율(139¥/$) 변동으로 5억8천만불의 환차손이 발생함.

 - 대외 기여액 집행에 있어 자국환을 적용한 유일 국가로서 비판 받아 마땅하다는 지적

나. 독 일

o 1억3천만불 상당의 방사능, 생.화학무기 탐지 차량 60대를 포함, 1차 지원 약속액의 대부분은 현물 지원 형태임.

o 기타 지원 장비 대부분은 동독군 사용 장비로 미군 사용은 불능

다. 사우디 아라비아

o 사우디 주둔 미군에 33억불 상당의 연료, 윤활유, 식량, 현지교통 및 식수를 제공(4.1.현재 70억불을 집행)

o 사우디측은 90년도 원유 가격 상승으로 인한 횡재성 소득(Windfall Profit) 전액을 사막의 폭풍 작전에 투입하였음을 주장함.

라. 쿠웨이트

o 90년도 약속액 25억불 전액 집행

o 91년도 약속액은 매주 10억불씩 구분 송금

마. U.A.E.

o U.A.E. 정부는 기본적으로 걸프 전비의 분담에 대해 미온적이며, 더이상의 기여가 필요함.

- 끝 -

0165

報 告 事 項

報 告 畢

1991. 4. 9.
美 洲 局
北 美 課(27)

題 目 : 友邦國의 걸프戰費 支援金 執行關聯 美 下院 軍事委 報告書

美 下院 軍事委는 Les Aspin(民主, IS) 委員長 名義로 '걸프戰費 分擔 :
友邦國들은 그들의 정당한 몫을 부담하고 있는가 ?' 제하 友邦國들의 걸프 戰費
支援 現況 評價 報告書를 作成, 配布하었는 바, 同 要旨 아래 報告드립니다.

---

1. 槪 要

ㅇ 우방국의 전비 지원금 집행은 미국의 지속적 압력의 결과로 이루어진
   것이라 전제함.

ㅇ 한국에 대해서는 지원규모와 집행 현황에 대한 사실 보고 위주로 기술함.
   - 4.1.현재 한국 정부는 대미 기여 약속액 3억8천5백만불중 35%인
     1억3천8백만불을 집행(3.28. 송금 6천만불 포함)

ㅇ 일본의 소극적 지원 자세와 UAE의 지원액 규모에 대해 비판적 논평을 함.
   - 일본의 경우 91년 추가지원 약속액 90억불중 90% 만 미측에 제공하고
     $화가 아닌 ¥화 기준으로 집행, 실질적 대미 추가지원액은 76억불에
     불과(5억불의 환차액 발생)하다며 노골적 불만을 표시
   - U.A.E.의 경우 GNP 규모에 비해 40억불 기여 약속은 매우 미흡함을 지적
     · 사우디 및 쿠웨이트의 부담 경감을 위한 U.A.E.의 추가기여 촉구
     · 90년도 기여 약속액 10억불, 91년도 20억불 기여을 약속하였으나
       기여액수가 적다는 비판여론에 못이겨 10억불 추가 부담

0166

o 사우디에 대해서는 사태 초기 이래 적극적 지원 태도, 특히 미군에 대한 원활한 군수 지원 및 전비 지원을 평가함.

o 우방국의 기여 약속액 규모보다는 기약속분의 이행 확보가 중요하므로 지속적 압력행사 필요성 강조

2. 友邦國의 對美 寄與 約束額/執行額 現況

(단위 : 백만불)

구분 지원 국명	약 속 액			집 행 액		
	1차 지원 약속액	2차 지원 약속액	소 계	현 금 수 령	현물,수송 지원집행	총수령액
사 우 디	3,339	13,500	16,839	4,536	2,338	6,924
쿠웨이트	2,506	13,500	16,006	7,000	16	7,016
U A E	1,000	3,000	4,000	2,870	179	3,049
일 본	1,740	8,100	9,840	6,646	633	7,279
독 일	1,072	5,500	6,572	5,772	629	6,401
한 국	80	305	385	110	28	138
기 타	3	0	3	0	3	3
계	9,740	43,905	53,645	26,934	3,876	30,810

3. 國別 執行現況

가. 일 본

o 최근 미.일간 체결된 주일미군 지원 협정으로 주둔비 부담률이 40%에서 50%이상으로 증대(미군 인건비 제외시 73%에 육박), 일측의 걸프전 기여액은 주일미군 주둔비 부담 증대로 보완되고 있음을 지적하고 있음.

0167

○ 91.1. 2차 지원 재원 확보를 위한 국회심의시(130¥/$ 환율 적용, 1,700억¥ 예산 확보)와 91.3.27. 집행시 환율(139¥/$) 변동으로 5억8천만불의 환차손이 발생함.

   - 대외 기여액 집행에 있어 자국환을 적용한 유일 국가로서 비판 받아 마땅하다는 지적

나. 독 일

○ 1억3천만불 상당의 방사능, 생.화학무기 탐지 차량 60대를 포함, 1차 지원 약속액의 대부분은 현물 지원 형태임.

○ 기타 지원 장비 대부분은 동독군 사용 장비로 미군 사용은 불능

다. 사우디 아라비아

○ 사우디 주둔 미군에 33억불 상당의 연료, 윤활유, 식량, 현지교통 및 식수를 제공(4.1.현재 70억불을 집행)

○ 사우디측은 90년도 원유 가격 상승으로 인한 횡재성 소득(Windfall Profit) 전액을 사막의 폭풍 작전에 부입하였음을 주장함.

라. 쿠웨이트

○ 90년도 약속액 25억불 전액 집행

○ 91년도 약속액은 매주 10억불씩 구분 송금

마. U.A.E.

○ U.A.E. 정부는 기본적으로 걸프 전비의 분담에 대해 미온적이며, 더이상의 기여가 필요함.

- 끝 -

0168

걸프戰費 分擔 :

友邦國들은 그들의 正當한 몫을 負擔하고 있는가 ?

(걸프戰 關聯 美 下院 軍事委 報告書)

91.4.8.

美 下院 軍事委 委員長

레스 아스핀(民主, 위스콘신)

0169

　　지난 11월 本人은 걸프사태 관련 공동의 목표를 위한 美 友邦國들의 財政的 軍事的 寄與度를 분류한 防衛費 分擔 報告書를 발간한 바 있음. 동 報告書를 통해 本人은 美軍 兵士들이 목숨을 잃고 이라크와 戰爭을 치루고 있을때 부유한 友邦國들은 그들의 지갑을 틀어 잠그려하는 것으로 보여질 경우, 美國民의 批判을 감수하여야 할 것이라는 事實을 警告한 바도 있음.

　　사실상 戰爭 勃發以後 美國의 軍事作戰을 지원한다는 기여 약속액은 순식간에 100億弗에서 約 530億弗로 急增 하였음.

　　그러나 우려는 계속되고 있음. 上.下 兩院은 友邦國들로 하여금 그들의 寄與 約束額을 조속히 집행토록 권유하고, 만일 그렇지 않을 경우 適切한 措置를 行政府가 취하도록 하며, 行政府로 하여금 友邦國 寄與 約束額 執行 상세 현황을 議會에 報告토록하는 法案을 通過시킨 바 있음.

　　이 報告書에는 同 問題에 관한 개관과 함께 상세한 友邦國 國別 戰費 負擔 現況을 제시코자 함.

0170

걸프戰 戰費

걸프戰의 總 經費는 아직 알 수 없음. 戰爭은 끝났으나 美軍의 상당수가
쿠웨이트 隣近 作戰 地域에 殘留中임. 그러나 전비 계산을 위한 성실한 작업은
이미 개시되었음. 1991 會計年度中 行政府가 議會에 요청한 추가 국방세출
要請額은 150億弗이었음. 동 금액은 지난해 말 「沙漠의 防牌」 作戰을 위해
議會가 承認한 20억불에 추가하여 승인한 것임. 지난 3월 Sean O'Keefe 국방부
豫算局長은 下院 軍事委 證言에서 다음과 같이 밝힘.

「새로이 議會에 承認을 要請한 150億弗과 友邦國이 寄與를 約束한 535億弗로
  沙漠의 防牌 및 沙漠의 暴風 作戰으로 인한 추가 예산 소요를 충족할 수 있을
  것임. 새로운 追加 豫算 承認이 필요할 수도 있을 것임. 한편 150億弗 全額이
  소진되지 않을 수도 있을 것임.」

美 國防部側의 이러한 예상에 대해서는 아직 논란의 여지가 있음. 일부
人士는 國防部側 계산이 참전 용사들에 대한 앞으로의 受惠 費用, 戰爭中 使用된
武器, 裝備의 交替 費用 및 國防部 이외의 각 기관들의 追加 費用等을 충분히
감안치 않고 있다고 主張함.

0171

監査院長을 비롯한 또다른 인사들은 國防部側의 計算이 中東地域 以外에서의 作戰에 사용된 유류대금 및 戰爭에 사용되지 않은 장비의 部品 代金等이 포함되어 있어 戰費를 과도하게 늘려잡고 있다는 우려를 표명하고 있음.

이와는 별도로 걸프戰費를 獨自的으로 計算하고 있는 기관들이 있음. 防衛 豫算 計劃(Defense Budget Project)이라는 사설기관은, 1991년도 追加歲出 要請과 관련 國防部가 제출한 자료를 기초로 산정한 追加 걸프戰費는 약 475 億弗이라 주장하고 있음. 議會 예산실은 걸프지역 배치 美軍과 裝備의 本國 送還 費用을 包含 약 450억불로 전비를 추정하고 있음. 이에 따라 友邦國 寄與 約束額이 이와 같은 기관들의 推定 戰費를 훨씬 상회하고 있어 우려가 발생하고 있음.

0172

友邦國 寄與 約束額의 公正性 問題

美國에 대한 友邦國들의 기여 약속액 총액의 공정성 문제는 「沙漠의 防牌/暴風 作戰」의 最終 戰費 總額과의 상관관계하에 판단될 것임. 현재 國防部側 推定 資料에 따르면, 友邦國들의 寄與 約束額이 美側 推定 戰費의 75%를 충당할 것으로 나타나고 있음. 同 計算은 推定 戰費 總額이 91년도 追加 歲出 承認額 150億弗, 90년도 승인액 20억불, 友邦國 寄與 約束額 535억불 총 705억불을 넘지 않으리라는 判斷을 基礎로 하고 있음.

日本側의 寄與 約束額과 관련, 국방부측 계산에 있어 약간의 문제점이 있음. O'Keefe 國防部 豫算局長이 제시한 友邦國 寄與 約束額 535억불에는 日本이 91년도 追加 寄與를 약속한 90억불이 포함되어 있음. 그러나 日本側은 90億弗 全額이 美國에 대한 지원이 아니라 主張하고 있음. 日本側은 지난 1월 追加 支援 發表時 동 기여액중 일부는 餘他 多國籍軍 派遣國을 위한 支援임을 베이커 國務長官에 통보하였음. 즉, 日本 政府 官吏는 기여 약속액 90억불중 90%인 약 81억불만이 美國에 대한 支援이라 밝혔음.

그러나 다행스럽게도 U.A.E.가 10億弗을 追加로 寄與를 約束하여, 우방국 寄與 約束額 總額은 536億弗이 됨으로써, O'Keefe 局長이 주장한 우방국 기여 約束額으로 戰費의 75%를 충당할 수 있을 것이라는 計算이 계속 맞을 수 있게 되었음.

0173

이러한 計算들은 이라크와의 戰爭을 위한 追加 費用中 友邦國 寄與 約束
額의 공정한 비율과 관련한 問題들을 提示하고 있음.

　　美國은 걸프地域에 死活的 이해가 걸려 있으며, 「沙漠의 暴風 作戰」을
軍事的으로 수행할 능력도 있음. 美國의 寄與分은 일부 전비부담과 「沙漠의
暴風 作戰」兵力의 3/4 파병등 적절한 기여였음. 같은 기준으로 우리의
友邦國들은 兵力을 派遣하거나, 國力과 戰爭의 결과에 따른 이해 정도에 상응한
財政的 寄與를 해야 했던 것임. 그러므로 美國이 目標로 하고 있는 友邦國들의
財政的 寄與分은 戰費의 100%는 아니나 상당한 부분임.

　　同 比率을 정하는 명확하게 정해진 方式은 없음. 現在 推進中인 友邦國
寄與 75%라는 比率은 적절한 수준인 것으로 보여짐.

　　各國別 財政的 寄與가 적절한 분담인지 여부에 대한 分析 및 判斷은 부록에
收錄되어 있음.

0174

友邦國 寄與 執行現況

友邦國 寄與 約束額 대부분, 특히 高額 寄與國 몇몇 國家들의 執行은 많은 우려를 낳게하고 있음. 日本 政府는 3.27. 美 國庫에 57억 8천만불을 송금함으로써 日本側 寄與 約束額의 약 75%를 집행하였음. 日本側 관리는 나머지 기여 約束額은 걸프 協力 委員會 걸프지역 평화 협력 기금을 통해 執行될 것이며 美 國庫에 조만간 入金될 것이라 밝히고 있음.

3월하순 獨逸 政府는 약 32억 8천만불을 美 國庫에 送金하였음. 이로써 獨逸側 約束額의 執行率은 97%에 이르게 되었음.

지난 3월 U.A.E.는 40億 寄與 約束額中 30억불을 상회하는 집행을 함으로써 75%를 약간 넘는 執行率을 보이고 있음. 쿠웨이트 政府도 약 50%이상의 집행율을 보이고 있으며 定期的으로 나머지 寄與 約束額을 執行하고 있음. 사우디 정부는 약 40%를 上廻하는 執行率을 보이고 있으며 現物 支援을 계속하고 있으므로 조만간 寄與 約束額 全額을 거의 집행할 수 있을 것으로 보임. 韓國은 3億8千 500万弗의 寄與 約束額中 35% 정도의 집행율을 보이고 있음.

4월1일 현재 美國은 友邦國 기여 약속액의 약60%정도의 現金 또는 現物支援을 수령함.(별첨도표 참조) 行政府 관리들은 하원 군사위 증언을 통해 友邦國 寄與約束 額中 未 執行分들이 곧 집행될 것이며 정기적으로 이를 수령하고 있다고 밝히고 있음.

0175

結　論

　　友邦國들이 寄與 約束額 全額을 집행하리라 확신하고 있으며, 全額을 受領
할 경우 또한 同 金額이 현재 추정하고 있는 戰費의 75%를 충당할 경우, 이것은
공정한 戰費 分擔일 것인가 ? 이 질문에 대한 對答은 "그렇다"임.
友邦國 寄與額이 戰費의 75%를 충당할 경우, 同 寄與額은 適切한 寄與일 것임.

　　問題는 寄與 約束額 總額과 관련된 문제가 아니라, 同 履行을 위해 威脅
행사의 정도와 관련된 문제일 것임. 寄與 約束을 이끌어 내는 作業은 이를
빼는 作業과도 유사함. 美國은 友邦國 자신의 사활적 이해가 걸려 있는 作戰
에의 寄與를 끌어내기 위해 閣僚로 하여금 主要 友邦國을 巡訪, 公開的으로 募金
旅行을 하도록 하였음. 많은 寄與 約束額의 신속한 모금을 위해 美側이 壓力을
행사하였듯이, 분명히 이를 收金하기 위해서도 美國이 계속 압력을 행사하는
일을 늦춰서는 안되며 우리는 계속 이 趨勢를 維持해야 할 것임.

　　또한 添附한 各國別 分析에서 나타난 이유들로 인해 友邦國中 日本, U.A.E.
等 2개국은 특별한 非難을 받아도 무방할 것임.

0176

日本은 經濟力에도 불구 매우 미온적 供與國이며 90억불 공여 약속의 이행 方式을 綿密히 分析해 보면 이에 모자라는 기여를 이행하고 있음.

첫째 日本은 91년도 寄與 約束額 90억불중 90%만이 美國에 대한 支援임. 初期에 널리 알려진 바로는 90억불 전액이 美軍 戰費에 充當될 것이라는 인상을 준 바 있었음.

둘째로 日本은 위와같은 90%의 對美 寄與 決定에서 한걸음 더 나아가 換率 問題로 또다른 문제를 둘러대고 있음. 다른 友邦國들은 달러화로 그들의 寄與 分을 執行하고 있는 반면, 日本側은 연화로 그들의 寄與 約束額을 執行하고 있음. 寄與 約束이 發表된 以後 달러화의 연화에 대한 강세 기조 지속으로 日本側은 利得을 보고 있음. 또한 日本側은 同 換差損을 補塡하기 위해 연화 寄與額을 追加 시키지 않고 있음. 寄與 約束이 이루어진 시점에서의 對美 支援 約束額은 84億2千万弗이었으나 현재는 76億弗로 減少되었으나, 日本側은 同 金額만이 대미 支援額이라 主張하고 있음.

U.A.E. 도 美側의 非難을 받아 마땅함. U.A.E.의 GNP는 쿠웨이트를 능가하며 일인당 GNP 에 있어서는 사우디, 쿠웨이트를 능가하고 있으며, 戰爭으로 인한 直接 被害도 없었으며, 걸프戰에 軍事的으로 큰 寄與도 제공치 않았음. 그럼에도 불구하고 U.A.E.는 90年度 10億弗, 91年度에 20億弗만을 寄與 約束 하였으며, 적은 寄與로 인해 창피를 당한후 10億弗을 追加로 寄與키로 함.

0177

U.A.E.는 사우디나 쿠웨이트에 버금가는 寄與를 約束하는데 동의해야 할 것임.

友邦國들의 寄與 約束額은 全額 執行될 것이라 확신하며, 동 경우 대부분의 美國民들로부터 격려와 感謝를 받을 만한 友邦國은 사우디임. 사우디 政府는 170億弗에 달하는 財政支援을 約束 하였을뿐 아니라, 이라크의 쿠웨이트 侵攻 直後 多國籍軍 派遣 要請과 함께 多國籍軍이 侵略을 격퇴하는데 필요한 支援과 設備를 提供하는 정치적 결단을 신속히 하였음.

사우디側의 油價 급등으로 인한 수익 증가와 관련 논란의 여지는 있음. 一部 人士들은 사우디側이 이를 着服했다고 主張하고 있으나 駐美 사우디 大使館側은 同 追加 수익은 전비로 지출하였다고 上記 主張을 否認하고 있음. 議會側의 獨自的 調査에 따르면, 사우디 政府는 大使館側 主張처럼 많은 額數를 支出치는 않았으나 더욱 중요한 점은 사우디 政府가 戰後 諸般問題들을 위해 동 수익을 앞으로도 계속 支出할 것이라는 사실임.

0178

友邦國의 對美 寄與 約束額/執行額 現況

(4.1.현재, 단위 : 백만불)

구분 지원 국명	약 속 액			집 행 액		
	1차 지원 약 속 액	2차 지원 약 속 액	소 계	현 금 수 령	현물,수송 지원집행	총수령액
사 우 디	3,339	13,500	16,839	4,536	2,338	6,924
쿠웨이트	2,506	13,500	16,006	7,000	16	7,016
U A E	1,000	3,000	4,000	2,870	179	3,049
일 본	1,740	8,100	9,840	6,646	633	7,279
독 일	1,072	5,500	6,572	5,772	629	6,401
한 국	80	305	385	110	28	138
기 타	3	0	3	0	3	3
계	9,740	43,905	53,645	26,934	3,876	30,810

0179

附　錄 (國別 執行現況)

1. 日　本

ㅇ 日本의 對美支援額은 1次 支援 約束額 17억 4천만불, 2次 支援 約束額 81億弗, 總 98億 4千万弗임.

   - 3.27. 57억 8천만불 送金으로 4.1.현재 72억 7,900만불 執行

   - 日本 政府는 잔여 금액을 걸프 平和 基金에 전달필 주장

ㅇ 最近 美.日間 締結된 駐日美軍 支援 協定으로 駐屯費 부담률이 40%에서 50%이상으로 증대(美軍 人件費 제외시 73%에 육박)

ㅇ 91.1. 2차 支援 財源 確保를 위한 國會審議時(130¥/$ 換率 適用, 1,700億¥ 豫算 確保)와 91.3.27. 執行時 換率(139¥/$) 變動으로 5억 8천만불의 換差損이 發生함.

   - 對美 支援額은 同 金額의 90%인 76억불로 축소

   - 對外 寄與額 執行에 있어 자국환을 적용한 유일 國家로서 批判 받아 마땅하다는 指摘

ㅇ 油類, 담배에 대한 消費稅率 增加로 財源을 確保함.

0180

2. 獨 逸

o 獨逸의 對美 寄與額은 1차 지원 約束額 11억불, 2차 지원 約束額 55億弗 總 66億弗임.

o 1차 支援 約束額의 대부분은 現物 支援 形態이며, 1억3천만불 상당의 放射能, 生.化學武器 探知 車輛 60대 포함.

o 其他 支援 裝備 대부분은 동독군 사용 장비로 美軍 使用은 不能

o 4.1.現在 64억불을 執行 97% 집행률을 보임.

3. 사우디 아라비아

o 사우디 政府의 寄與 約束額은 1차 支援 約束額 33억불, 2차 支援 約束額 135억불 총 168억불임.

o 사우디 駐屯 美軍에 33억불 상당의 燃料, 潤滑油, 食糧, 現地交通 및 食水를 提供(4.1.현재 70억불을 執行)

o 사우디측은 90년도 原油 價格 上昇으로 인한 횡재성 所得(Windfall Profit) 全額을 沙漠의 暴風 作戰에 投入하였음을 주장함.

o 戰時 주류국으로서 사우디의 積極的 役割을 평가함.

0181

4. 쿠웨이트

   ○ 쿠웨이트의 對美 寄與額은 1차 支援 約束額 25억불과 2차 支援 約束額
     135억불, 총 160억불임.

   ○ 90년도 約束額 25억불 全額 執行

   ○ 91년도 約束額은 매주 10억불씩 區分 送金

5. U.A.E.

   ○ U.A.E. 政府는 기본적으로 걸프 戰費의 分擔에 대해 微溫的이며,
     더이상의 寄與가 必要함.

   ○ 90년도 寄與 約束額 10억불, 91년도 20억불 寄與를 約束하였으나
     寄與 額數가 적다는 비판 여론에 못이겨 10억불 追加 負擔

   ○ 쿠웨이트 보다 적은 人口를 保有하면서도 GNP가 더 많은 U.A.E.가
     40億弗 정도만을 寄與 約束한 것은 매우 未洽함을 指摘
     - 사우디 및 쿠웨이트의 負擔 輕減을 위한 追加 寄與 促求

0182

외 무 부

종 별 : 지 급

번 호 : USW-1725   일 시 : 91 0411 1936

수 신 : 장관(동구일,중동일,미북,미안,기정,국방부)

발 신 : 주 미 대사

제 목 : 하원 외무위 청문회(걸프전후 소련의 대중동 정책)

1. 하원 외무위 군비통제, 국제안보 및 과학소위 (위원장:HAMILTON 의원)는4.11 걸프전후 소련의 대중동 정책에 관한 청문회를 개최한바, 동청문회에 출석한 MARK KATZ 죠지메이슨 대 교수의 증언 요지 아래 보고함.

가. 중동지역에서의 소련의 영향력

0 소련이 과거 중동에서 강력한 영향력을 행사할수 있었던 것은 강경 아랍국에 대한 소련의 지원과 온건 아랍국이 대미 관계 에서 소련 카드를 이용할수 있었기 때문임.

0 그러나, 이제는 소련이 대미 또는 대서방 관계를 희생하면서 까지 중동에서의 영향력을 추구할수 없는 상황이되었음. 고르바쵸프가 걸프지상전 개시직전 시도했던 평화외교공세를 중도에 포기한 사실이 이를 입장함. 더우기, 동 조치가고르바쵸프가 보수세력과 연합하기 시작한 이후에 이루어졌다는 사실은 소련내보수.강경세력 조차 중동에서 미국에 반대하기 보다는 협력하는것이 더 낫다고판단했기 때문일것임.

따라서, 아랍국들이 이용할 소련 카드는 더이상 없게되었으며, 또한 이지역에서 소련의 주요 역할을 유도할 실익도 없게 되었음.

나. 향후 소련의 대중동정책

0 중.장기적 관점에서 소련이 이지역에서 미국에 도전하는 세력으로 다시 영향력 행사를 추구하게될 가능성(개혁정책의 성공적 완료, 보수세력의 재집권, 소련내 회교 공화국의 분리운동 방지를 위한 대아랍 적극지원 필요성등)도 전혀 배제할수는 없으나, 이경우에도 과거와 갑은 팽창정책이나 대서방 경쟁정책 보다는 미국, 서방 및 아랍부국들과의 협력관계를 통해 중동에서의 이익을 추구하게될것임.

2. 상기 증언에 이어 진행된 질의 답변 내용중 주요 사항은 아래와갑음.

가. 소련의 대중동 무기수출 정책(BERMAN 의원 질의)

구주국	장관	차관	1차보	2차보	미주국	미주국	중아국	외연원
청와대	안기부	국방부						

PAGE 1   91.04.12   09:45

0 이지역에서 효율적 군비통제가 이루어지기 위해서는 다자적 접근방법이 필요하다는 견해에 대해, BERMAN 의원은 이문제가 미행정부의 정책과제에 포함조차 되어 있지 않다는데 문제가 있다고 지적하고, HAMILTON 의원과 FASCELL 의원이 최근 부시 대통령앞 서한을 통해 다자적 합의 추구와 함께 미국의 일방적 대중동 무기수출 금지 조치를 촉구한것도 그러한 이유때문이라고 말함.

0 이에 대해 KATZ 는 미.소 양국이 군부 및 군수업계 이해관계로 인해 대중동 무기 수출을 중단하는데 어려움이 있을것이며, 그일례로 소련 군부가 고르바쵸프 승인 없이 시리아에 무기수출을 해왔다고 말함. 동인은 이와관련, 소련내부보수세력은 고르바쵸프의 군비통제 정책에 반대하는 이유로 미국의 무기 수출 정책을 이용하고 있으며, 만약 미국이 이문제에 진지한 자세로 임한다는것이 확인된다면 소련도 이지역에서 다자적인 군비통제 노력에 동참할수 있을 것이라고 부언함.

0 동인은 중동지역 개별국가에 대한 소련의 무기 수출 현황에 대하여는 아래와같이 말함.

- 소련은 최근 시리아와 20 억불 규모의 무기 수출계약을 체결했으며, 대이락 무기 수출은 중단했으나, 소련측이 모두 철수했다고 주장하는 군사고문단은 약간 남아 있을지도 모름.

- 최근 소련이 이집트에 군사장비 부품을 수출하고 있다는 정보를 들었으며, 동정보가 사실이라면 이는 이집트의 대소 부채상환을 25 년간 연기해준 소련의 최근 조치와 더불어 양국관계 개선에 기여하게될것임.

- 소련이 이란과 국경을 접하고 있다는 사실과 소련내 회교도에 대한 이란의 영향력 및 경제적 기대 이익등으로 인해 소련내 개혁, 보수세력 공히 이란과의 관계개선을 원하고 있으며, 밝혀지지는 않고 있으나 현재 소련은 이란에도 무기를 수출하고 있음.

나. 중동평화 협상에서 소련의 역할 (HAMILTON 의원 질의)

0 아랍권에 대한 소련의 영향력이 감소되기는 하였으나, 아직 완전히 사라진것은 아님. 최근 이스라엘의 대소관계 개선움직임은 중동평화 협상에 기여할수 있는 요소라고 봄.

0 미국은 아랍권에 대해 소련이 이지역에서 미국과 경쟁하고 있지 않으며, 따라서 이들이 더이상 미.소 양국의 경쟁관계를 이용할수없다는 점을 인식시킬 필요가 있으며, 그러한 이유에서도 소련을 중동평화 협상에 참여시켜야 함.

PAGE 2

0184

0 소련은 유엔의 걸프전 종전 결의안을 준수할것이나, 이지역에서 계속 영향력 행사 (STAY IN THE BALL GAME)를 원하고 있으므로 후세인의 존속 여부에 상관없이 이락과의 관계 정상화를 시도할 것임.

3. 상기 증언문 파편송부함.

(대사 현홍주-국장)

예고:91..6.30 까지

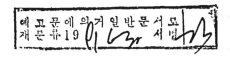

외　무　부

종　별 : 지급

번　호 : USW-1726　　　　　　　　　　일　시 : 91 0411 1936

수　신 : 장관(미북,미안, 기정)사본:국방부

발　신 : 주미대사

제　목 : 상원군사위 청문회(미 군사전략 관련)

1. 상원 군사위(위원장:SAM NUNN)는 금 4.11. FY 92/93 국방 수권예산 요청안과 관련 미 군사전략에 관한 청문회를 개최한바, 동 청문회에 출석한 WOLFOWITZ 국방차관 및 DAVID JEREMIAH 합참차장의 아국관련 증언 요지를 아래 보고함(증언문 해당부분 별전 팩스 참조)

　　가. WOLFOWITZ 국방 차관

　　O 걸프 사태 과정에서 동맹국을 비롯한 외국의 미국에 대한 경비 지원은 역사적으로 전례가 없는 것으로서 90 년중 동맹국이 DERSERT SHIELD 소요경비의 80퍼센트 이상으로 부담했으며, 91 년중 발생한 걸프전 추가 경비는 동맹국 기여금에서 대부분 충당하게 될것임.

　　O 동맹국들의 능력 증강에따라 미군의 감축과 역할 재조정이 가능하게 되었으며, 특히 한국과 일본의 방위능력 증대로 아시아 지역에서 15,250 명의 미군을감축 계획인바, 이는 미국이 군비를 축소해 나가면서도 전세계적 책임을 감당해 나갈수 있도록하는 중요한 요인이 되고 있음.

　　나. JEREMIAH 합참 차장

　　O 태평양 지역은 미국에게 점점 중요한 지역으로 부상하고 있으며, 경제발전을 거듭하고 있는 동북아 및 태평양 연안국과의 통상, 정치, 군사 유대 유지가미국에 있어 매우 중요함.

7 대 군사 강국이 자리하고 있는 동지역에서 침략 억지력을 계속 유지하고 동맹국에 대한 방위의지 천명을 위해 태평양 지역 에서의 미군배치가 긴요하며, 이는 군사동맹국 뿐 아니라 동지역 전체의 안정에도 유익함.

　　O 한국의 군사능력 증대에 따라 미지상군의 감축이 가능할 것으로 보이나, 보다 소규모의 부대는 계속 유지해 나갈것임. 주한 미공군력도 감축될것이나, 북한의

미주국	장관	차관	1차보	2차보	미주국	청와대	안기부	국방부

모험주의에 대비하여 한반도에서의 미군 개입은 계속 필요함.

ㅇ 동지역 주둔 미군에 대한 우방국의 방위 비 분담 능력 제고에 따라 동지역에서의 미군 주둔 경비는 계속 감소할것으로 기대됨.

2. 이어 진행된 질의 응답에서 WARNER 의원이 미국의 방위예산 감축에 따라우방국에 대한 방위분담 증대 압력을 강화해 나갈 필요성을 질문한데 대해, WOLFOWITZ 차관은 우방국은 물론 기타 국가로부터 걸프전 지원 확보를 위해 대통령을 비롯한 행정부가 기울인 노력에도 나타나듯이 우방국에 대한 방위분담 압력을 계속해 나가고 있다고 답변함.

3. 증언문 전문은 파편 송부함.

(대사 현홍주- 국장)

91.6.30. 까지

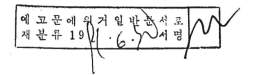

주 미 대 사 관

미국(의) 700- 792   1991. 4. 12.

수신 : 장 관
참조 : 구주국장, 중동아프리카국장, 미주국장
제목 : 하원 외무위 청문회 (걸프전후 소련의 대중동 정책)

        연 : USW - 1725

        연호 표제 청문회에 출석한 Mark Katz 죠지 메이슨대 고수의 증언문을
별첨 송부합니다.

        첨부 : 상기 증언문.   끝.

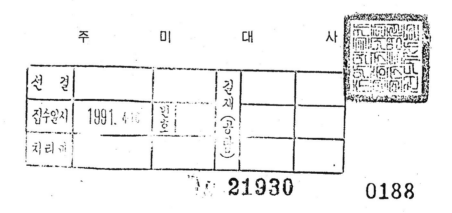

주 미 대 사

선 결			결재 (공란)		
접수일시	1991. 4.	관			
처리과					

21930   0188

Does Moscow Still Matter in the Middle East?

Mark N. Katz

Department of Public Affairs
George Mason University
Fairfax, VA   22030-4444

Statement Prepared for the
Subcommittee on Europe and the Middle East
Committee on Foreign Affairs
U.S. House of Representitives
April 11, 1991

0189

Does Moscow Still Matter in the Middle East?

Mark N. Katz

The Gulf War destroyed more than just Saddam Hussein's military might. It also marked the virtual end of Soviet influence in the Middle East, at least in the short-run.

Soviet cooperation with the U.S. and other governments was, of course, crucial for authorizing the use of force against Iraq by the UN Security Council. The task of driving Iraq out of Kuwait would have been vastly more complicated without Soviet help. Moscow, though, is no longer willing to pursue a Middle East policy which Washington considers objectionable.

This was shown by Gorbachev's futile diplomacy to prevent the launching of the ground war against Iraq. He issued two peace proposals which called for Iraq to be exempted first from all and then from some UN sanctions if Baghdad agreed to withdraw from Kuwait. But once it became clear that the United States and its Coalition allies were going to proceed with the ground war, Gorbachev backed down and supported Coalition demands for Iraq to abide by all Security Council resolutions.

What is especially noteworthy about Moscow's quick abandonment of these diplomatic initiatives which the Bush Administration found objectionable was that this did not take

1

0190

place when the reformers were still in the ascendant in Moscow. Instead, this occurred after Gorbachev had shifted considerably to the right, most of his top reformist advisers had resigned, and the hard-liners had become increasingly influential. Despite their rhetoric, even Soviet conservatives saw that their interests were better served through cooperating with Washington in the Middle East rather than opposing it.

This is because the primary goal for Gorbachev and the conservatives is to keep the Soviet Union intact. Except for the ultra-right wing fringe, the conservatives recognize that Moscow desperately needs the West's money and good will if they are to have a chance at preventing the breakup of the USSR.

Soviet conservatives would prefer to keep Iraq as an ally, or perhaps more accurately, as a paying customer for Soviet weapons. They know, however, that Iraqi arms purchases could not make up for Western trade, aid, and investment which Moscow would lose through resuming its alliance with Baghdad now.

The same logic holds for Soviet foreign policy toward the Arab-Israeli conflict. While Moscow actively worked to disrupt American-sponsored peace proposals in the past, the Soviet government no longer has an interest in doing so. Gorbachev and his conservative supporters need Western friendship too much to risk losing it through opposing America in the Middle East now.

Gorbachev, though, still hopes to retain Soviet influence in the Middle East. Soviet spokesmen have already stated that an overall settlement of the Gulf conflict should take Soviet

2

interests into account. But if Moscow cannot afford to pursue a foreign policy in the Middle East in opposition to American foreign policy, then the Soviets cannot realistically hope to gain or even retain much influence in the region.

The reason Moscow previously enjoyed such strong influence in radical Arab states was because the Soviet Union provided them with support in both retaining power and pursuing anti-American foreign policies. Even the conservative Arab states could gain America's attention through playing the "Soviet card": they would threaten to turn to Moscow unless Washington pursued policies more to their liking.

Now, however, there is no Soviet card for the Arabs to play since Moscow is unwilling to seriously oppose America in the Middle East. But since this is the case, the Arabs have no interest in allowing Moscow to play a large role in the region.

For if it will not vigorously oppose American support for Israel, Moscow has nothing else to offer the Arabs. The USSR obviously cannot provide economic assistance. In fact, Moscow has begun to receive aid from the rich Arab states and hopes to persuade them to give even more. After the poor showing of Iraqi-owned Soviet weaponry in this last war, the Arabs are unlikely to buy Soviet weapons even if they are cheaper. All Moscow can offer is rhetorical support for Arab causes. But as the Arabs know, that is not worth much.

Gorbachev would like to see the USSR have good relations with the West while at the same time being an influential power

3

0192

in the Middle East. However, he cannot have both these things.
Soviet influence in the Middle East can only be obtained at the
price of poor relations with the U.S. But as long as Gorbachev
or any other Soviet leader is unwilling to pay this price, the
USSR simply cannot be an influential power in the region.

If the Soviets are unlikely to play an influential role in
the Middle East in the short-run, will they play one in the long-
run? This is only likely if at some point in the future Moscow
is again willing to pursue a competitive policy in the region
despite American and Western opposition to it. Such a situation
is likely to arise only after some larger change affecting
international relations generally.

Predicting what this change might be or its probability of
occurrence lies more in the realm of speculation than analysis.
Nevertheless, as the past few years have shown, unexpected events
can and do occur in international relations. The possibility of
unexpected scenarios occurring in the future, then, must clearly
be considered.

What scenarios would result in Moscow aggressively
reasserting its influence in the Middle East in defiance of
America? There are several possibilities.

One scenario under which this could happen would be the
sudden decline of American power and influence as a result of
severe economic depression. If America were less able to offer
Moscow political and economic benefits as well as to deter Soviet
expansionism, then Moscow would be highly likely to resume its

4

0193

quest for influence in the Middle East. The savings and loan and
banking crises notwithstanding, this scenario appears highly
unlikely.

Another scenario which could lead to the resumption of
aggressive Soviet behavior in the Middle East would be the rapid
and successful completion of Gorbachev's economic reform efforts.
If the Soviet economy became completely modernized, Moscow may
decide that it can afford to lose Western good will through
competing with the U.S. for influence in the Middle East and
elsewhere. Whether Moscow would actually behave this way if the
USSR possessed a modernized economy is unclear. It is highly
unlikely, however, that Gorbachev or any other Soviet leader will
succeed in implementing perestroika for many years, if at all.
Moscow, then, is not likely to be able to afford the loss of
Western good will which would occur if it resumed its
expansionism in the Third World.

Of course, the unreformed Soviet leadership before Gorbachev
pursued expansionism in the Middle East and the Third World
despite its negative effect on relations with America and the
West. A third scenario would be the return to power of a
similarly unreformed leadership. Even if this occurred, however,
an unreformed Soviet regime in the future would not enjoy the
same advantages that the Brezhnev regime did in the 1970s. A
conservative Soviet leadership will find its energies absorbed by
continued ethnic unrest in the USSR and an ever-deteriorating
economy indefinitely. Even if it had poor relations with the

5

0194

West, a conservative Soviet leadership in the future would probably be unwilling and perhaps unable to divert much effort away from its domestic problems to attempts at expanding its influence in the Middle East which Moscow could not sustain in the face of American and Western opposition.

A fourth scenario which could lead to the expansion of Soviet influence in the Middle East would be the rise of Marxism-Leninism in the region. Marxism, though, has had relatively limited appeal in the Middle East even at the height of Soviet power and prestige. Now that so many countries have renounced Marxism and this ideology has come under heavy criticism for its economic failings and other problems in the USSR itself, it is doubtful that Marxism will suddenly become popular in the Middle East. Some other revolutionary ideology, such as Islamic fundamentalism or radical nationalism, may become increasingly popular in the region. Soviet interests will not be enhanced, however, if this revolutionary ideology infects the Muslim republics of the USSR. Moscow may then be desperately seeking American and Western support against these revolutionary forces stemming from the Middle East.

A fifth, and more likely, scenario is the prospect that Moscow will face growing unrest in the Muslim republics of the Soviet Union. Either a reformist or a conservative Soviet leadership may conclude that Moscow must strongly support the Arabs against Israel in order to retain the loyalty of its Muslim citizens. If keeping the Soviet Union intact is the most

6

0195

important goal for the Soviet leadership (as it apparently is for Gorbachev), Moscow may conclude that risking the loss of American and Western support is a necessary cost which must be incurred if Soviet Muslims insist upon vigorous Soviet support for the Arabs as their price for remaining part of the USSR.

Of course, Soviet Muslims might not be persuaded to remain in the USSR even if Moscow heavily supports the Arab cause; their own growing nationalism may result in their seeking to secede from the USSR anyway. Ironically, if the Muslim republics did secede from the USSR, they would be too poor and weak to strengthen the Arabs against Israel. And Russia without the Muslim republics would not find it necessary to militantly support the Arab cause in order to appease the relatively small Muslim population remaining within its shrunken borders.

Finally, a Russia shorn of the non-Russian republics will be a great power, but not a superpower. Its energies are likely to be fully occupied with modernizing its economy and worrying about the probably unstable new countries on its periphery. Moscow may seek American and Western sympathy or even help in dealing with these new security threats. It is not likely to antagonize the U.S. by competing with it for influence in the Middle East--which will be a relatively distant region from a smaller Russia.

Even in the long-run, then, it seems unlikely that the Soviet Union or Russia will be in a position to pursue an expansionist or even a competitive policy vis-a-vis the West in the Middle East. This does not mean that Moscow will no longer

7

0196

have any interests in the region. As before, Moscow will seek to
preserve its access to the Mediterranean Sea and to the shortest
sea line of communication between western Russia and Vladivostok,
which runs through the Suez Canal, Red Sea, Bab al-Mandab, and
Indian and Pacific Oceans. But instead of pursuing these and
other interests competitively with the U.S., Moscow will probably
seek them through cooperation with America, the West, and the
wealthy Arab states. Moscow is likely to try to assuage their
fears that Russia's presence in the region will threaten them
since Moscow will not want them to retaliate by reducing their
economic relations with the USSR or aiding Muslim opposition
forces within the USSR. Moscow may increasingly seek to
cooperate with the oil producing states of the region to raise
the price of oil. But this is a normal form of economic
competition which even some of our NATO allies engage in.

The Middle East will undoubtedly present many serious
challenges to American foreign policy in the short-run as well as
the long-run. Competition with the Soviets for influence in the
region, however, is not likely to be one of them.

8

0197

외 무 부

관리번호 91-989

종 별 :

번 호 : USW-1804   일 시 : 91 0416 1807

수 신 : 장관(미북, 미안, 중동일, 기정, 국방부)

발 신 : 주 미 대사

제 목 : 걸프전비 추가 지출 법안

   연:USW-1341,1355

   1. 연호 걸프전비 추가지출을 위한 수권법안(HR 1175, S 725) 및 동 지출법안 (HR 1281, HR 1282)은 부시 대통령이 각각 4.6 및 4.10 서명함으로써 발효 되었음.

   2. 동 법안에 포함된 BRYANT 수정안과 BYRD 수정안에 대한 국무부 실무진의 의견을 탐문한바 , BRYANT 수정안은 법안심의 과정에서 연호 단서 조항(국가안보 관련 예외 인정) 이 추가되었고, BYRD 수정안도 문안이 완화 (무기 금수 대상국을 기여금 미납국에서 약속분 미이행국으로 수정) 되어 행정부로서는 별다른 제약을 느끼지 않아도 될 만큼 자체에 LOOPHOLE 이 크다고 판단하고 있으며, 따라서 크게 신경쓰지 않아도 될것이라는 반응을 보였음.

   (대사 현홍주- 국장)

   91.12.31. 까지

검토필 (1.91.6.30.)

미주국 국방부	장관	차관	1차보	2차보	미주국	중아국	청와대	안기부

PAGE 1   91.04.17   08:06

외신 2과 통제관 BW

0198

외 무 부

종 별 : 긴 급

번 호 : USW-1999

일 시 : 91 0425 1858

수 신 : 장관(미북)

발 신 : 주 미 대사

제 목 : 걸프전비 추정액

대:WUS-1754

연:(1)USW-1285, (2) USW(F)-1235

1. 대호 관련사항 아래 보고함.

가. 걸프전비 추정액

0 미행정부는 걸프전비와관련, 지금까지 어떠한 추정액도 공식 발표한바 없음. 다만 91 년도 추가 세출예산 150 억불과 우방국 기여금 535 억불을 합칠경우전비 충당이 가능할 것이라는 일반적인 견해를 표명한바 있을뿐임. (연호 (2)참조)

조기종전으로 인한 잔액발생 가능성에 대하여는 백악관을 포함한 미행정부 관리들은 아직 잔류중인 병력유지 비용과 손실 또는 파괴된 군장비 보전 비용을 합할 경우 600-650 억불은 될것이므로, 우방국 기여금에서 남는 돈은 없을 것이라는 입장을 취하고 있음.

0 연호 91 년도 추가 세출 예산법안에 언급된 426 억불은 의회가 승인한 지출한도액일뿐이며 동액수가 걸프전비 총 추정액을 의미하는것은 아님. 연호 (2) 하원 군사위 보고서 (2 페이지)에도 우방국 기여금 535 억불은 걸프전비 총 추정액의 75 % 정도를 커버할것이라고 언급되어 있는바, 이를 역산할 경우 전비 총 추정액은 713 억불 규모에 달한다는 계산이 가능함.

0 미의회는 90 년말 DESERT SHIELD OPERATION 을 위해 이미 30 억불(자체예산 20 억불 PLUS 우방국 기여금 10 억불)의 추가 세출 예산을 승인한바 있으므로이를 포함할 경우 지금까지 지출 승인된 총전비는 456 억불임.

나. 걸프전비 관련자료

0 91 년 추가세출 예산법안의 426 억불은 상기한바와같이 승인된 지출한도액에 불과하므로, 동법안 (HR1282)에는 자체예산 150 억불의 상세 내역만 명기되어

미주국   장관   차관   1차보   2차보   중아국   청와대   안기부

PAGE 1

있을뿐이며 426 억불의 내역은 포함되어 있지 않음.(법안 및 관련 보고서 별전 FAX 송부)

　　O 미국방부의 전비 추정액 관련 자료는 상기한대로 아직 외부에 배포된것이없으며 금 4.25. 당관이 미국방부 담당관을 접촉, 확인한바에 의하면 4.29(월)의회에 관련 보고서를 제출키로 되어 있으나 그때까지는 여하한 경우에도 외부에 공개할수 없다함. 동자료는 가능한 4.29 중 입수, FAX 편 송부 예정이니 양지바람.

　　O BOWSHER GAO 원장이 걸프전비 관련 WSJ 지에 기고문을 계재한바는 없으며, 다만,3.25. 자 동지 관련기사에 동원장의 발언을 인용 , 보도한것이 있을 뿐임. 동기사 FAX 편 별송함.

　　2. 동건 관련 별도 상세 자료가 입수될 경우 FAX 편 송부하겠음.(대사 현홍주-국장)

　　예고 91.12.31 까지

1991. 12. 31 애 예고문에
의거 일반문서로 재 분규됨.
㊞

외 무 부

종 별 : 긴 급

번 호 : USW-2030

일 시 : 91 0429 1707

수 신 : 장관(미북)

발 신 : 주 미 대사

제 목 : 걸프전비 추정액

조서기관
(김서기관)

연:USW-1999

연호 미 국방부의 대의회 보고서 및 BOWSHER GAO 원장의 2.27. 하원 예산위청문회 증언문을 팩스편 별송함.

첨부:USW(F)-1565

(대사 현홍주- 국장)

예고:91.12.31. 까지

검 토 필 (1991. 6.30)

주 미 대 사 관

번호 : USV(F) - 1565

수신 : 장관(미붕)

발신 : 주미대사

제목 : 겅도전비 추가액 완료라도 (3월04)

보안
봉재

미축법북기 대시체보라시 (4.27자) 및 Bowsher GAO
원장의 하원예산기 청문회 증인문 (2.27자)은 별첨
송부함.

UNITED STATES COSTS IN THE PERSIAN GULF CONFLICT AND
FOREIGN CONTRIBUTIONS TO OFFSET SUCH COSTS

Report #2: April 27, 1991

Section 401 of P.L. 102-25 requires a series of reports on
incremental costs associated with Operation Desert Storm and on
foreign contributions to offset such costs. This is the second of
such reports. As required by Section 401 of P.L. 102-25, it covers
costs incurred during January and February 1991 and contributions made
during January, February and March 1991. The first report, dated
April 20th, concerned the costs and contributions for the period
beginning August 1, 1990, and ending on December 31, 1990.

Costs

The costs covered in this and subsequent reports are full
incremental costs of Operation Desert Storm. These are additional
costs resulting directly from the Persian Gulf crisis (i.e., costs
that would not otherwise have been incurred). It should be noted that
only a portion of full incremental costs are included in Defense
supplemental appropriations. These portions are costs that require
financing in fiscal year 1991 and that are exempt from statutory
Defense budget ceilings. Not included in fiscal year 1991
supplemental appropriations are items of full incremental costs such
as August - September 1990 costs and costs covered by in-kind
contributions from allies.

Table 1 summarizes preliminary estimates of Department of Defense
full incremental costs associated with Operation Desert Storm from
August 1, 1990, through February 28, 1991. The cost information is
shown by the cost and financing categories specified in Section 401 of
P.L. 102-25. Tables 2-9 provide more detailed information by cost
category. Costs shown in this report were developed by the Department
of Defense and are based on the most recent data available.

Through February 1991, costs of about $32 billion were reported
by the Department of Defense. Although the combat phase was over by
the end of February, the costs reported so far are preliminary. These
costs do not include such items as the total cost of equipment repair,
rehabilitation, and maintenance caused by the high operating rates and
combat use during this period. They also do not include the costs of
phasedown of operations and the return home of the deployed forces.
Further, certain long-term benefit and disability costs have not been
reflected in the estimates. These costs will be reported in later
reports. The costs through February plus the other costs not yet
reported are expected to result in total incremental costs of $60
billion or more.

Incremental Coast Guard costs of $11.4 million were incurred
during this reporting period, with cumulative costs of $17.9 million
through February to support military operations in the Persian Gulf.

Contributions

Section 401 of P.L. 102-25 requires that this report include the
amount of each country's contribution during the period covered by the

1565-2   0203

report, as well as the cumulative total of such contributions. Cash
and in-kind contributions pledged and received are to be specified.

Tables 10 and 11 list foreign contributions pledged in 1990 and
1991, respectively, and amounts received in January, February and
March. Cash and in-kind contributions are separately specified.

As of April 25, 1991, foreign countries contributed $8.0 billion
of the $9.7 billion pledged in calendar year 1990, and $28.1 billion
of the $44.8 billion pledged in calendar year 1991. Of the total
$36.1 billion received, $31.3 billion was in cash and $4.8 billion was
in-kind assistance (including food, fuel, water, building materials,
transportation, and support equipment). Table 12 provides further
detail on in-kind contributions.

Table 13 summarizes the current status of commitments and
contributions received for the period August 1, 1990, through
April 25, 1991.

Future Reports

As required by Section 401 of P.L. 102-25, the next report will
be submitted by May 15th. In accord with the legal requirement, it
will cover incremental costs associated with Operation Desert Storm
that were incurred in March 1991, and foreign contributions for April
1991. Subsequent reports will be submitted by the 15th day of each
month, as required, and will revise preliminary reports to reflect
additional costs as they are estimated or re-estimated.

List of Tables

Table 1 -   Summary, Incremental Costs Associated with Operation Desert Storm
Table 2 -   Airlift, Incremental Costs Associated with Operation Desert Storm
Table 3 -   Sealift, Incremental Costs Associated with Operation Desert Storm
Table 4 -   Personnel, Incremental Costs Associated with Operation Desert Storm
Table 5 -   Personnel Support, Incremental Costs Associated with Operation Desert Storm
Table 6 -   Operating Support, Incremental Costs Associated with Operation Desert Storm
Table 7 -   Fuel, Incremental Costs Associated with Operation Desert Storm
Table 8 -   Procurement, Incremental Costs Associated with Operation Desert Storm
Table 9 -   Military Construction, Incremental Costs Associated with Operation Desert Storm
Table 10 - Foreign Contributions Pledged in 1990 to Offset U.S. Costs
Table 11 - Foreign Contributions Pledged in 1991 to Offset U.S. Costs
Table 12 - Description of In-kind Assistance Received to Offset U.S. Costs as of March 31, 1991
Table 13 - Foreign Contributions Pledged in 1990 and 1991 to Offset U.S. Costs

-2-

0204

Table 1

SUMMARY 1/

INCREMENTAL COSTS ASSOCIATED WITH OPERATION DESERT STORM
Incurred by the Department of Defense
From August 1, 1990 Through February 28, 1991
($ in millions)
Preliminary Estimates

	FY 1990	FY 1991			Partial and Preliminary Aug 1990 – Feb 1991
	Aug – Sep	Oct – Dec	This period Jan – Feb	Total through Feb	
(1) Airlift	425	412	571	783	1,208
(2) Sealift	234	658	1,413	2,101	2,335
(3) Personnel	268	1,192	1,381	2,574	2,842
(4) Personnel Support	364	2,112	2,028	4,140	4,504
(5) Operating Support	1,241	3,721	5,245	8,966	10,205
(6) Fuel	578	932	1,537	2,459	3,048
(7) Procurement	129	719	6,180	6,899	7,028
(8) Military Construction	47	126	229	355	402
Total	3,287	9,902	18,385	28,287	31,574 2/
Nonrecurring costs Included above 3/	373	845	8,560	9,405	9,778
Costs offset by:					
In-kind contributions	225	1,032	2,818	3,850	3,875
Realignment 4/	928	379	1,814	2,193	3,119

1/ Data was compiled by OMB. Source of cost data — Department of Defense.

2/ Although the combat phase was over by the end of February, the costs reported so far are preliminary.
These costs do not include such items as the total cost of equipment repair, rehabilitation, and
maintenance caused by the high operating rates and combat use during this period. They also do not
include the costs of phasedown of operations and the return home of the deployed forces. Further,
certain long-term benefit and disability costs have not been reflected in the estimates. Those costs will
be reported in later reports. The costs through February plus the other costs not yet reported are
expected to result in total incremental costs of $60 billion or more.

3/ Nonrecurring costs include investment costs associated with procurement and Military Construction,
as well as other one-time costs such as the activation of the Ready Reserve Force ships.

4/ This includes the realignment, reprogramming, or transfer of funds appropriated for activities
unrelated to the Persian Gulf conflict.

-3-

0205

Table 2

AIRLIFT

INCREMENTAL COSTS ASSOCIATED WITH OPERATION DESERT STORM
Incurred by the Department of Defense
From August 1, 1990 Through February 28, 1991
($ in millions)
Preliminary Estimates

| | FY 1990 | FY 1991 | | | Partial and Preliminary Aug 1990 - Feb 1991 |
| | | | This period | Total | |
	Aug - Sep	Oct - Dec	Jan - Feb	through Feb	
Airlift					
Army	207	141	88	229	436
Navy	85	71	194	265	350
Air Force	127	195	84	279	406
Defense Logistics Agency		3		3	3
Defense Intelligence Agency		0	0	0	0 1/
Special Operations Command	6	2	5	7	13
Total	425	412	371	783	1,208

Nonrecurring costs included above	0	0	72	72	72
Costs offset by:					
In-kind contributions	2	27	23	50	52
Realignment 2/	0	0	0	0	0

1/ Costs are less than $500 thousand.
2/ This includes the realignment, reprogramming, or transfer of funds appropriated for activities unrelated to the Persian Gulf conflict.

This category includes costs related to the transportation by air of personnel, equipment and supplies.

At the height of operations, 127 planes landed daily in the desert in Southwest Asia, averaging one arrival every eleven minutes. Over 8,500 missions were flown in this period, involving both the Military Air Command and civilian air carriers. These missions carried over 190,000 people and 223,000 short tons of equipment to the region.

-4-

0206

Table 3

SEALIFT

INCREMENTAL COSTS ASSOCIATED WITH OPERATION DESERT STORM
Incurred by the Department of Defense
From August 1, 1990 Through February 28, 1991
($ in millions)
Preliminary Estimates

	FY 1990	FY 1991		Total	Partial and Preliminary Aug 1990 – Feb 1991
			This period		
	Aug – Sep	Oct – Dec	Jan – Feb	through Feb	
Sealift					
Army	123	542	344	986	1,109
Navy	99	33	968	1,001	1,100
Air Force	11	13	95	107	118
Defense Logistics Agency		1	4	5	5
Special Operations Command	2		2	2	4
Total	234	588	1,413	2,101	2,335

Nonrecurring costs included above	57	0	981	981	1,038
Costs offset by:					
In-kind contributions	1	24	38	62	63
Realignment 1/	0	11	7	18	18

1/ This includes the realignment, reprogramming, or transfer of funds appropriated for activities unrelated to the Persian Gulf conflict.

This category includes costs related to the transportation by sea of personnel, equipment and supplies.

A total of 93 ships were activated or chartered during this period. Of the these ships, 24 were Ready Reserve Force ships, which completed 22 trips. During this period, 900,000 short tons of dry cargo and 2.4 million tons of refined petroleum products were shipped to the Gulf region in 89 trips.

-8-

/565-6

Table 4

PERSONNEL

INCREMENTAL COSTS ASSOCIATED WITH OPERATION DESERT STORM
Incurred by the Department of Defense
From August 1, 1990 Through February 28, 1991
($ in millions)
Preliminary Estimates

	FY 1990	FY 1991		Total	Partial and Preliminary Aug 1990 – Feb 1991
	Aug – Sep	Oct – Dec	This period Jan – Feb	through Feb	
Personnel					
Army	178	836	981	1,817	1,994
Navy	22	199	133	332	354
Air Force	70	157	268	425	494
Total	268	1,192	1,381	2,574	2,842

Nonrecurring costs included above	0	0	0	0	0
Costs offset by:					
In-kind contributions	0	0	0	0	0
Realignment 1/	28	54	95	150	178

1/ This includes the realignment, reprogramming, or transfer of funds appropriated for activities unrelated to the Persian Gulf conflict.

This category includes pay and allowances of members of the reserve components of the Armed Forces called or ordered to active duty and the increased pay and allowances of members of the regular components of the Armed Forces incurred because of deployment in connection with Operation Desert Storm.

By the end of February, over 200,000 Reservists had been called to active duty and over 500,000 people were in theater.

-6-

1565-7

0208

Table 5

PERSONNEL SUPPORT

INCREMENTAL COSTS ASSOCIATED WITH OPERATION DESERT STORM
Incurred by the Department of Defense
From August 1, 1990 Through February 28, 1991
($ in millions)
Preliminary Estimates

	FY 1990	FY 1991			Partial and Preliminary Aug 1990 – Feb 1991
	Aug – Sep	Oct – Dec	This period Jan – Feb	Total through Feb	
Personnel Support					
Army	209	1,748	1,452	3,200	3,409
Navy	104	251	420	671	775
Air Force	36	100	142	241	278
Defense Intelligence Agency	2	2	5	6	8
Defense Logistics Agency	12	7	7	13	25
Defense Mapping Agency		3	0	3	3
Special Operations Command	2	1	3	4	6
Office of the Secretary of Defense	-	1	0	1	1
Total	364	2,112	2,028	4,140	4,504

Nonrecurring costs included above	8	0	1,098	1,098	1,106
Costs offset by:					
In-kind contributions	33	351	601	952	985
Realignment 1/	19	113	40	153	172

1/ This includes the realignment, reprogramming, or transfer of funds appropriated for activities unrelated to the Persian Gulf conflict.

This category includes subsistence, uniforms and medical costs.

Subsistence costs of $1.5 billion were the bulk of costs incurred in this period. Most of the remaining were Reserve activation costs of about $950 million.

-7-

1565 -A

0209

Table 8

OPERATING SUPPORT

INCREMENTAL COSTS ASSOCIATED WITH OPERATION DESERT STORM
Incurred by the Department of Defense
From August 1, 1990 Through February 28, 1991
($ in millions)
Preliminary Estimates

	FY 1990	FY 1991			Partial and Preliminary Aug 1990 – Feb 1991
	Aug – Sep	Oct – Dec	This period Jan – Feb	Total through Feb	
Operating Support					
Army	666	2,676	5,874	8,550	7,414
Navy	223	538	845	1,383	1,608
Air Force	130	268	683	951	1,092
Defense Intelligence Agency			1	1	1
Special Operations Command	15	7	10	17	32
Defense Communications Agency		0	1	1	1
Defense Logistics Agency		9		9	9
Defense Mapping Agency	9	23	18	41	50
Office of the Secretary of Defense		1	2	3	3
Total	1,241	3,721	5,245	8,966	10,206

Nonrecurring costs included above	133	0	0	0	133
Costs offset by:					
In-kind contributions	169	417	1,058	1,475	1,644
Realignment 1/	691	105	175	280	971

1/ This includes the realignment, reprogramming, or transfer of funds appropriated for activities unrelated to the Persian Gulf conflict.

This category includes equipment support costs, costs associated with increased operational tempo, spare parts, stock fund purchases, communications, and equipment maintenance.

Costs of almost $4.6 billion were incurred as a result of combat operations and the larger force in theater. Accrued costs of equipment maintenance and the reconstitution of equipment for Navy construction and cargo handling battalions are also included within the costs for this period.

-8-

165-9

0210

Table 7

FUEL

INCREMENTAL COSTS ASSOCIATED WITH OPERATION DESERT STORM
Incurred by the Department of Defense
From August 1, 1990 Through February 28, 1991
($ in millions)
Preliminary Estimates

	FY 1990	FY 1991			Partial and Preliminary Aug 1990 –
			This period	Total	
	Aug – Sep	Oct – Dec	Jan – Feb	through Feb	Feb 1991
Fuel					
Army	10	80	31	110	120
Navy	19	193	621	814	833
Air Force	90	658	881	1,539	1,629
Special Operations Command		3	2	8	8
Defense Logistics Agency	480			0	480
Total	579	932	1,537	2,469	3,048

Nonrecurring costs included above	0	0	0	0	0
Costs offset by:					
In-kind contributions	21	91	617	708	729
Realignment 1/	13	0	0	0	13

1/ This includes the realignment, reprogramming, or transfer of funds appropriated for activities unrelated to the Persian Gulf conflict.

This category includes the additional fuel required for higher operating tempo and for airlift and sealift transportation of personnel and equipment as well as for the higher prices for fuel during the period.

The additional fuel used in combat operations accounted for slightly over $1 billion of the costs in this period. The balance was for higher prices paid for fuel.

-9-

1585 –10

0211

Table 6

PROCUREMENT

INCREMENTAL COSTS ASSOCIATED WITH OPERATION DESERT STORM
Incurred by the Department of Defense
From August 1, 1990 Through February 28, 1991
($ in millions)
Preliminary Estimates

	FY 1990	FY 1991			Partial and Preliminary Aug 1990 - Feb 1991
	Aug - Sep	Oct - Dec	This period Jan - Feb	Total through Feb	
Procurement					
Army	49	447	827	1,273	1,222
Navy	47	187	2,047	2,293	2,281
Air Force	32	81	8,192	8,273	3,305
Defense Intelligence Agency	1	1	1	1	2
Defense Communications Agency		0	0	0	0 1/
Special Operations Command			88	88	88
Defense Mapping Agency			1	1	1
Office of the Secretary of Defense		3	18	19	19
Total	129	719	6,180	6,899	7,028

Nonrecurring costs included above	129	719	6,180	6,899	7,028
Costs offset by:					
In-kind contributions	0	0	57	57	57
Realignment 2/	128	95	1,497	1,592	1,721

1/ Costs are less than $500 thousand.
2/ This includes the realignment, reprogramming, or transfer of funds appropriated for activities unrelated to the Persian Gulf conflict.

This category includes ammunition, weapon systems improvements and upgrades, and equipment purchases.

These figures reflect the value of major end item losses, to include: 27 Army aircraft, 11 Bradley Fighting Vehicles, nine M1A1 Abrams tanks, and various other wheeled and tracked vehicles (at a cost of nearly $200 million); 23 Navy and Marine Corps aircraft, six tanks, and seven armored vehicles (at a cost of more than $570 million); and 21 Air Force aircraft (at a cost of more than $450 million). These estimates are based on the current cost, if the system is still in production or the last procurement, if out of production. Additionally, approximately $1.1 billion was used to augment munitions stocks and to procure specialized equipment, such as chemical defense equipment, missile modifications and aircraft modifications, to facilitate operations in Southwest Asia. Incremental costs of munitions totaled approximately $3.8 billion.

-10-

1565 -11

0212

Table 9

MILITARY CONSTRUCTION

INCREMENTAL COSTS ASSOCIATED WITH OPERATION DESERT STORM
Incurred by the Department of Defense
From August 1, 1990 Through February 28, 1991
($ in millions)
Preliminary Estimates

	FY 1990	FY 1991			Partial and Preliminary Aug 1990 - Feb 1991
	Aug - Sep	Oct - Dec	This period Jan - Feb	Total through Feb	
Military Construction					
Army	31	126	228	353	384
Navy				0	0
Air Force	16		2	2	18
Total	47	126	229	355	402

Nonrecurring costs included above	47	126	229	355	402
Costs offset by:					
In-kind contributions	0	121	225	346	346
Realignment 1/	47	0	0	0	47

1/ This includes the realignment, reprogramming, or transfer of funds appropriated for activities unrelated to the Persian Gulf conflict.

This category includes the cost of constructing temporary billets for troops, and administrative and supply and maintenance facilities.

Projects included cantonment areas and associated services such as electricity, water and sewers. Detention facilities for enemy POW's were also provided during the period.

-11-

1565 - 12

0213

Table 10

FOREIGN CONTRIBUTIONS PLEDGED IN 1990 TO OFFSET U.S. COSTS 1/
($ in millions)

	Commitments			Receipts in Jan., Feb. and Mar.			Receipts through April 25, 1991			Future Receipts
	Cash	In-kind	Total	Cash	In-kind	Total	Cash	In-kind	Total	
GCC STATES	5,861	984	6,845	446	13	459	4,256	984	5,240	1,605
SAUDI ARABIA	2,474	855	3,339	126	11	137	886	855	1,751	1,588 2/
KUWAIT	2,500	5	2,505			0	2,500	8	2,508	0
UAE	887	113	1,000	320	2	322	870	113	983	17 3/
GERMANY 4/	260	812	1,072		716	716	272	782	1,054	18 5/
JAPAN 4/	961	779	1,740	533	449	982	961	655	1,616	124 6/
KOREA	50	30	80		19	19	50	30	80	0
BAHRAIN		1	1			0		1	1	0
OMAN/QATAR		1	1			0		1	1	0
DENMARK		1	1			0		1	1	0
TOTAL	7,132	2,608	9,740	979	1,197	2,176	5,539	2,454	7,993	1,747

1/ Data was compiled by OMB. Sources of data: commitments — Defense, State, and Treasury; cash received — Treasury; receipts and value of in-kind assistance -- Defense.

2/ This is reimbursement for enroute transportation through December for the second deployment and for U.S. in-theater expenses for food, building materials, fuel, and support. Bills for reimbursement have been forwarded to Saudi Arabia.

3/ This is undergoing a final accounting.

4/ 1990 cash contributions were for transportation and associated costs.

5/ It is anticipated that this commitment will prove to have been fully met, though final accounting is not yet available.

6/ Resolution of balance is under discussion.

-12-

0214

Table 11

FOREIGN CONTRIBUTIONS PLEDGED IN 1991 TO OFFSET U.S. COSTS 1/
($ in millions)

	Commitments 2/			Receipts in Jan., Feb., and Mar.			Receipts through April 25, 1991			Future Receipts
	Cash	In-kind	Total	Cash	In-kind	Total	Cash	In-kind	Total	
GCC STATES	27,713	2,287	30,000	10,150	2,287	12,437	12,400	2,287	14,687	15,313
SAUDI ARABIA	11,306	2,194	13,500	3,650	2,194	5,844	3,650	2,194	5,844	7,656
KUWAIT	13,485	15	13,500	4,500	15	4,515	5,750	15	5,765	5,735
UAE	2,922	78	3,000	2,000	78	2,078	2,000	78	2,078	922
GERMANY	5,500	0	5,500	5,500	0	5,500	5,500	0	5,500	0
JAPAN	9,000	0	9,000	5,780	0	5,780	7,832	0	7,832	1,168
KOREA	291	14	305	60	14	74	60	14	74	231
DENMARK	0	6	6		6	6		6	6	0
OTHER	4	2	6		2	2	4	2	6	0
TOTAL	42,508	2,309	44,817	21,490	2,309	23,799	25,796	2,309	28,105	16,712

1/ Data was compiled by OMB. Sources of data: commitments — Defense, State, and Treasury; cash received — Treasury; receipts and value of in-kind assistance — Defense.

2/ 1991 commitments in most instances did not distinguish between cash and in-kind. The commitment shown above reflects actual in-kind assistance received.

-13-

0215

Table 12

DESCRIPTION OF IN-KIND ASSISTANCE RECEIVED
TO OFFSET U.S. COSTS AS OF MARCH 31, 1991
($ in millions)

	Calendar Year 1990	Calendar Year 1991
SAUDI ARABIA .... Host nation support including food, fuel, housing, building materials, transportation and port handling services.	865	2,194
KUWAIT .... Transportation	8	18
UNITED ARAB EMIRATES .... Fuel, food and water, security services, construction equipment and civilian labor.	113	76
GERMANY .... Vehicles including cargo trucks, water trailers, buses and ambulances; generators; radios; portable showers; protective masks, and chemical sensing vehicles	782	0
JAPAN .... Construction and engineering support, vehicles, electronic data processing, telephone services, medical equipment, and transportation.	655	0
KOREA .... Transportation	30	14
BAHRAIN .... Medical supplies, food and water	1	6
OMAN/QATAR .... Oil, telephones, food and water	1	0
DENMARK .... Transportation	1	0
OTHER .... Transportation		2
TOTAL	2,454	2,309

-14-

/565-15

0216

Table 13

FOREIGN CONTRIBUTIONS PLEDGED IN 1990 AND 1991 TO OFFSET U.S. COSTS
COMMITMENTS AND RECEIPTS THROUGH APRIL 25, 1991 1/
($ In millions)

	Commitments			Receipts 2/			Future Receipts
	1990	1991	Total	Cash	In-kind	Total	
GCC STATES	5,845	50,000	55,845	15,556	3,271	18,827	16,918
SAUDI ARABIA	3,339	13,500	16,839	4,558	3,059	7,595	9,244
KUWAIT	2,506	13,500	16,006	9,250	21	9,271	6,735
UAE	1,000	3,000	4,000	2,870	191	3,061	939
GERMANY	1,072	5,500	6,572	5,772	782	6,554	18 3/
JAPAN	1,740	9,000	10,740	8,793	655	9,448	1,292
KOREA	80	305	385	110	44	154	231
OTHER	3	12	15	4	11	15	0
TOTAL	9,740	44,817	54,557	31,335	4,763	36,098	18,460

1/ Data was compiled by OMB. Sources of data: commitments -- Defense, State, and Treasury; cash received -- Treasury; receipts and value of in-kind assistance -- Defense.

2/ Cash receipts are as of April 25, 1991. In-kind assistance is as of March 31, 1991.

3/ It is anticipated that this commitment will prove to have been fully met, though final accounting is not yet available.

-15-

/565-16

0217

United States General Accounting Office

GAO

Testimony

For Release
on Delivery
Expected at
9:30 a.m.
Wednesday
Feb. 27, 1991

The Administration's Proposal for Financing
Operations Desert Shield and Desert Storm

Statement of
Charles A. Bowsher, Comptroller General
of the United States

Before the
Committee on Budget
United States House of Representatives

I appreciate the opportunity to testify today before this
Committee on the Administration's proposal for financing
Operations Desert Shield and Desert Storm and on the
Administration's estimate of the operations' cost. We began
assessing the cost of the operation and our allies contributions
at the request of the Chairman of the House Committee on Armed
Services. On January 4, 1991, I testified before this Committee[1]
on the uncertainties of cost estimates of Operation Desert
Shield. A few days ago we received the Administration's
proposal, and we have begun analyzing its contents. We intend to
continue our work on the issues raised today and will provide
further reporting to the Armed Services Committee as our work
progresses.

SUMMARY

There are three major points I would like to stress today,
Mr. Chairman. First, the cost of Operation Desert Storm must be
financed to assure that our troops in the Gulf receive all the
support they need. Second, we believe that rather than providing
an "open checkbook" to fund the war, Congress should provide
needed money only through periodic supplemental appropriations.
Third, funds to prosecute the war should come first from the
money pledged by our allies. Money from the American taxpayers

---

[1]Statement of Charles A. Bowsher before the Committee on Budget,
House of Representatives (GAO/T-NSIAD-91-3)

0219

should be appropriated only to the extent that it is needed to supplement allied pledges.

My statement today will elaborate on these major points.

The cost of Operations Desert Shield and Desert Storm will be considerable. As I testified before this Committee in January, the total U.S. cost of Operation Desert Shield without any hostilities could exceed $130 billion in fiscal year 1991, assuming the forces now in place remain there throughout the fiscal year. This cost consisted of three components. One was the baseline cost of the U.S. forces committed to Desert Shield, which is already provided for in the fiscal year 1991 budget. We estimated the cost of paying, equipping, and maintaining these forces to be nearly $100 billion in fiscal year 1991. These funds would be expended whether the troops were in the Middle East or elsewhere. However, as a result of the Gulf crisis these costs are higher than planned because the crisis postponed the reduction of about 100,000 troops directed by the 1991 Defense Authorization Act. A second component was the incremental cost of mounting the operation, including deploying the troops, calling up the reserves, and providing the required additional support for the forces. Estimates of this cost for more than 400,000 troops were in the $30 billion range for fiscal year 1991. The third component involved other related costs, such as debt forgiveness for Egypt and humanitarian assistance. We

2

1365-19

0220

estimated this cost to be about $7 billion. With the armed
conflict now in progress, the cost will be higher, although it is
not possible to estimate the final cost because of critical
unknowns such as the duration and intensity of fighting.

Separate from the Operations' cost, there is a need to finance it
to assure that our troops in the Gulf receive all the support
they need to fight the war. My testimony today addresses this
financing requirement. To finance the incremental cost of
Operations Desert Shield and Desert Storm, the Administration has
made a supplemental proposal that calls for establishing a
working capital type account, rather than the traditional
approach in which the Department of Defense (DOD) requests and
the Congress appropriates funds by functional account, such as
military personnel, operations and maintenance, and procurement.
Under the working capital proposal, DOD, through the Office of
Management and Budget, would have direct access to, and spending
discretion over, the funds without further congressional
oversight or review. The working capital account would be funded
by an initial $15 billion appropriation and up to $50 billion in
transfers of allied contributions from the Defense Cooperation
Account.

This approach appears inconsistent with Congress' intent to
maintain funding control over allied contributions when it
established the Defense Cooperation Account. Under the existing

3

_/565-20_

0221

law, funds in this account may be used for such defense programs
and activities as are authorized and appropriated by the
Congress, including defraying the cost of Desert Shield and
Desert Storm. The Administration's proposed approach also
appears similar to the Administration's proposal for funding the
Resolution Trust Corporation. As I stated in testimony before
the House Banking Committee[2] last week, providing the Corporation
with an "open checkbook" would effectively eliminate controls
over its obligational authority written into the existing law. I
believe in the case of the Resolution Trust Corporation, as I do
in the case of the Defense Cooperation Account, that it is
important to retain the budget and appropriation control
mechanisms already in place and functioning. Moreover, if the
Administration's approach were adopted, it would be much more
difficult for Congress to be sure that the allies' contributions
were not used to fund aspects of defense subject to the three-
year limitations of the budget agreement.

To date the allies have pledged $53.5 billion in cash and in-kind
contributions to support U.S. Desert Shield and Desert Storm
operations. About $12.2 billion has been received in cash and
deposited in the Defense Cooperation Account. Another estimated

---

[2]Statement of Charles A. Bowsher before the Committee on Banking,
Finance, and Urban Affairs, House of Representatives
(GAO/T-GGD-91-7)

4

0222

$2.7 billion has been received in the form of in-kind
contributions, such as fuel and food.

I testified in January that there are many uncertainties in
estimating the incremental cost of Desert Shield and Desert Storm
and that Congress should provide periodic supplemental funding
until actual costs become clearer. We believe that many
uncertainties still exist today and we have some concerns
regarding the costs estimates provided with the supplemental
proposal. Specifically, the estimate (1) includes higher fuel
costs that DOD is paying for operations outside the Middle East,
(2) overstates costs that are being incurred because it does not
take into account rebates and credits that are being accrued
within DOD that will reduce actual outlays, and (3) does not
fully reflect substantial savings resulting from free fuel and
other in-kind contributions. Moreover, based on past GAO work,
we have found that it is generally difficult to obtain good
actual cost data because DOD lacks effective cost accounting
systems.

For these reasons we continue to believe that Congress should
provide periodic supplemental funding through the traditional
supplemental appropriations process. We further believe that an
initial supplemental appropriation of $17 billion based on the
actual and estimated Desert Shield and Desert Storm obligations
would support current operations through March 31, 1991,
including operations and pressing procurement needs. The

5

1565 —22

0223

Congress could then provide further appropriations quarterly as
actual experience clarifies spending requirements.

The first increment of supplemental funding should be provided by
appropriating the $11 billion balance now in the Defense
Cooperation Account together with additional funds from that
account as they become available, not to exceed the $17 billion
we believe to be required through March 31. This would eliminate
the need for immediate U.S. funding beyond the over $100 billion
already appropriated for the baseline cost of the U.S. forces in
the Middle East.

Subsequent quarterly supplemental appropriations should be
enacted in response to specific requests from DOD (as approved by
the Office of Management and Budget and the President) and should
draw first on accumulating balances in the Defense Cooperation
Account. Only if Desert Storm funding requirements exceed
anticipated contributions in the Defense Cooperation Account
should additional U.S. funds be appropriated.

To assure to the extent possible that proper accountability and
control are maintained, appropriations to finance Desert Shield
and Desert Storm should take the normal form and be specified as
to account, purpose, and period of availability. Upon the
conclusion of hostilities, there should be a full accounting for

6

/f6f -23

0224

and audit of the expenditure of all the funds that have been
appropriated, including those from the Defense Cooperation
Account.

DESCRIPTION OF THE ADMINISTRATION'S REQUEST

The funding mechanism the Administration is requesting consists
of two basic elements. One element is the establishment of a
Desert Shield Working Capital Account, which would be funded
initially by $15 billion in new budget authority provided by the
U.S. Government and would subsequently be replenished by foreign
contributions as funds become available from the Defense
Cooperation Account. The funds in this account would be used to
maintain a continuity of payment for the funding requirements of
Desert Shield and Desert Storm. The other element is the
authority to transfer additional funds from the Defense
Cooperation Account to reimburse defense appropriation accounts
depleted by the incremental costs of Desert Shield and Desert
Storm.

The Administration's request is not a traditional appropriations
request for authority to obligate specified amounts of money in
specific appropriations accounts, such as military personnel and
operations and maintenance. This request would instead provide
as much as about $26 billion immediately (the sum of the $15
billion in new budget authority plus approximately $11 billion in

7

db5-24

foreign contributions deposited in the Defense Cooperation Account). As additional foreign contributions are deposited in the Defense Cooperation Account, the Administration's proposal would make them available as well. Currently, the Administration estimates that foreign contributions committed to the Operations but not yet received total about $39 billion, which when added to the funds now in the Defense Cooperation Account plus the additional $15 billion requested by the Administration totals about $65 billion. To the extent the sum of the $15 billion and the funds deposited in the Defense Cooperation Account are not sufficient to cover the Operations' cost, the Administration plans to seek additional funds from Congress or additional contributions.

The Administration's request would give the Secretary of Defense, with the approval of the Office of Management and Budget, the authority to transfer funds from the Defense Cooperation Account without further Congressional action and to use these funds as it deemed necessary to cover the incremental costs of the Operations. The proposal provides less Congressional control than the existing mechanism for accessing funds from the Defense Cooperation Account, which the Congress established October 1, 1990, under Public Law 101-403. The 1990 act authorized the Secretary of Defense to accept contributions of money and property. Cash contributions and the proceeds from the sale of property are deposited in the Account. Funds in this Account may

8

0226

be used for such defense programs and activities as are
authorized and appropriated by Congress, including to defray the
costs of Desert Shield and now Desert Storm. In the 1991 Defense
Appropriation Act the Congress appropriated $1 billion for
transfer from the Account to operations and maintenance
appropriations of DOD for the purpose of reimbursing incremental
expenditures made for fuel, transportation, equipment
maintenance, and purchases from stock. The Administration's
request would significantly diminish the Congressional role
established in October 1990.

STATUS OF ALLIED CONTRIBUTIONS

Since the Iraqi invasion of Kuwait and the outbreak of
hostilities, 46 countries have pledged or contributed some type
of support for the Persian Gulf crisis. These pledges and
contributions include deployment of military forces to the Gulf
region; cash donations to the U.S. Treasury; in-kind support to
U.S. forces in Saudi Arabia and other Gulf states; and economic
assistance to countries affected by the U.N. economic embargo
against Iraq. Some countries have provided other types of
support, such as basing and overflight rights and military
assistance to countries affected by the hostilities.

9

165-26

Military Contributions

Currently, 31 countries have sent ground, air or naval forces, or
support units to the Gulf region to participate in the
multinational force supporting Desert Shield, Desert Storm and
maritime enforcement of the economic embargo. Since the outbreak
of hostilities in mid-January 1991, allied forces have
participated in combat and combat support missions during the air
campaign against Iraq.

Cash Contributions and In-Kind Support to the United States

Major contributors of cash and in-kind support to the United
States include Saudi Arabia, Kuwait, United Arab Emirates, Japan,
Germany, and Korea. As of February 1991, these countries pledged
a total of $53.5 billion. These pledges were to cover the costs
of Operation Desert Shield and Desert Storm from August 1990
through March 1991.

As of February 20, 1991, Saudi Arabia, Kuwait, United Arab
Emirates, Japan, Germany, and Korea contributed about $12.2
billion in direct cash contributions to the Defense Cooperation
Account. Of this amount, Japan and Germany contributed about
$3.3 billion and asked that these funds and any of their
subsequent cash donations be used to cover expenses related to
transporting U.S. troops, equipment, and materials to the Gulf

10

0228

region. The other countries did not place any conditions on the
use of their contributions.

In-kind contributions include food, fuel, water, transportation,
material, and facilities. Major contributors included Saudi
Arabia, United Arab Emirates, Kuwait, Japan, Germany, and Korea.
As of February 20, 1991, DOD has reported receipts through
January 1991 of in-kind support valued at about $2.7 billion. We
have not had the opportunity to evaluate the basis for these
reported levels; however, we intend to visit the Central Command
in the near future to review in-kind reporting procedures.
The breakdown of pledges and contributions is as follows

11

Allied Pledges and Contributions of Cash and In-Kind Support to the United States
(U.S. $ Millions)

Country	Pledges[a] 1990	1991	Total	Contributions Cash (2/20/91)	In-Kind (1/31/91)	Total
Saudi Arabia	3,339	13,500	16,839	4,457	1,566	6,023
Kuwait	2,506	13,500	16,006	3,500	10	3,510
United Arab Emirates	1,000	2,000	3,000	870	140	1,010
Germany	1,072	5,500	6,572	2,432	531	2,963
Japan	1,740	9,000	10,740	866	457	1,323
Korea	80	305	385	50	21	71
Other[b]	3	0	3	0	3	3
Total	9,740	43,805	53,545	12,175	2,728	14,903

[a]1990 pledges are for August 1990 through December 1990 and 1991 pledges are for January 1991 through March 1991.

[b]Includes Oman, Qatar, Bahrain and Denmark.

As the above table indicates, total allied pledges are about $53.5 billion compared with total contributions of about $14.9 billion. Thus, about $38.6 billion is due in total future receipts. Of the $9.7 billion pledged for 1990 costs, about $5.8 billion had been contributed as of December 31, 1990. As of February 20, 1991, these contributions increased to about $7.3 billion. The remaining $2.4 billion includes about $1.7 billion that DOD intends to bill Saudi Arabia in the near future for reimbursement of in-kind support and enroute transportation expenses for the second deployment of U.S. forces; about $19 million in cash recently requested from the United Arab Emirates and $700 million from Germany, Japan, and Korea for in-kind

〃65-2P

0230

support. According to DOD officials, the outstanding in-kind
support reflects goods and services that have been ordered and
will be delivered soon.

Economic Assistance to Frontline States and Other Countries

In addition to cash and in-kind support, the European Commission
and 24 countries have pledged economic assistance to Turkey,
Jordan and Egypt, referred to as frontline states, and other
countries affected by the economic embargo against Iraq. This
support includes concessional loans, import financing grants and
project assistance. As of February 1991, these pledges totaled
about $14.7 billion for the period of August 1990 through December
1991, and contributions totaled about $6.7 billion.

13

165-30

0231

The status of pledges and contributions is as follows

Economic Assistance to Frontline States (FLS) and other Countries
As of 2/19/91 (U.S. $ Millions)

Donor	Pledge to FLS	Contribution to FLS	Pledge to Other States	Contribution to Other States	Total Pledges	Total Contribution
Gulf States						
Saudi Arabia	2,848	1,788	1,503	1,203	4,351	2,991
Kuwait	2,500	855	1,184	763	3,684	1,618
United Arab Emirates	1,000	587	418	418	1,418	1,005
European Commission						
EC Budget	805	78	0	0	805	78
Bilateral						
Belgium	33	7	0	0	33	7
Denmark	30	10	0	0	30	10
France	200	0	30	0	230	0
Germany	1,190	360	144	0	1334	360
Ireland	6	0	0	0	6	0
Italy	150	37	9	0	159	37
Luxembourg	4	1	0	0	4	1
Netherlands	63	45	0	0	63	45
Portugal	1	0	0	0	1	0
Spain	36	9	0	0	36	9
United Kingdom	5	5	0	0	5	5
Other European Countries/ Australia						
Australia	14	3	0	0	14	3
Austria	11	1	0	0	11	1
Finland	15	13	0	0	15	13
Iceland	3	2	0	0	3	2
Norway	32	14	21	21	53	35
Sweden	52	21	0	0	52	21
Switzerland	109	9	0	0	109	9
Japan	2,120	445	0	0	2,120	445
Canada	66	17	0	0	66	17
Korea	83	5	17	2	100	7
Total	11,375	4,311	3,326	2,407	14,701	6,718

14

けた-31

0232

<u>Other Types of Contributions</u>

In addition to military, economic, and in-kind support, our allies
have contributed with other means. For example, Germany has
deployed a fighter squadron to Turkey and ships to the Eastern and
Central Mediterranean Sea, and pledged about $2.7 billion in
military assistance to Turkey, Israel, and the United Kingdom.
Further, Japan has sent oil booms to Saudi Arabia to assist in
counteracting the Gulf oil slick. In addition, our NATO allies
and certain Gulf countries have granted basing and transit rights.

<u>UNCERTAINTIES AND CONCERNS REGARDING ADMINISTRATION
COST ESTIMATES SUGGESTS PERIODIC SUPPLEMENTAL FUNDING</u>

We have several concerns about the cost estimates provided with
the supplemental proposal. Specifically, the estimate (1)
includes higher fuel costs that DOD is paying for operations
outside the Middle East; (2) overstates costs that are being
incurred because it does not take into account rebates and
credits that are being accrued within DOD that will reduce actual
outlays; and (3) fails to fully reflect substantial savings
resulting from free fuel and other in-kind contributions.

DOD also includes in its cost estimate the purchase of large
amounts of supplies such as spare parts to support the deployment
and military action. To the extent these supplies are not

15

_15┟-32_

consumed during the Operations, they could meet DOD inventory requirements for some time to come. This could reduce future defense budgets by the value of any excess inventory.

Fuel Costs

DOD includes in its estimate for all of fiscal year 1991 $2.8 billion to cover the higher price all of DOD is paying for fuel for its operations throughout the world. In DOD's view, higher fuel prices are a Desert Shield cost because fuel costs rose as a result of Iraqi aggression, which lead to the deployment of military forces to the Gulf. As we testified in January, we do not believe that these fuel costs should be included in a supplemental appropriation for Desert Shield. The Omnibus Budget Reconciliation Act of 1990, which provides that the incremental costs for Operation Desert Shield are to be treated as emergency funding requirements, defines such costs as those associated with increased operations in the Middle East. DOD's need to pay higher overall fuel costs is no different than any other federal agency's.

In addition, the drop in oil prices over the past few months should alleviate some of DOD's need for funding in this area. The Defense Stock Fund continues to charge the services $44.10 per barrel of refined fuel. However, the fund is currently paying only about $37 a barrel. If this pattern continues throughout the

16

165-33

0234

balance of the fiscal year, the Stock Fund will likely make a profit which could be rebated to the services.

Rebates

The issue of rebates and credits arises in several areas. We are concerned that these be accurately accounted for so that DOD does not receive some future windfall. For example, the Navy and the Marine Corps obligate funds for fuel they receive in the Persian Gulf. Most of this fuel was provided free by Saudi Arabia and other Gulf states to some part of DOD, usually the Army or the Air Force. If, for example, an Air Force tanker fuels up Navy planes, the Air Force charges the Navy for that fuel--even though the Air Force received it free. That obligation will at some point have to be undone, or if paid, rebated to the Navy. Until that point, however, the costs of Desert Shield and Desert Storm are overstated.

As I testified in January, the Military Airlift Command (MAC) could show an operating profit when it closes its books on fiscal year 1991. MAC is also receiving some free fuel as well as donated airlift support normally provided by MAC aircraft. However, MAC bills the services for any transportation it provides as though it were paying for all the costs - regardless of whether any are received free. According to MAC officials, they will rebate to the services any operating profits resulting

17

/t$lf - ℋℒ

from its operations, including those attributable to donated fuel
and airlift, and other factors, such as recapturing more fixed
costs than they incur[3]. The magnitude of any operating profit,
however, will not be known until the end of the fiscal year.
Our concern is that DOD will receive appropriations to cover
expenses that should not really exist.

Assistance In-kind

DOD's cost estimates do not reflect the savings from the likely
receipt of assistance in-kind throughout the fiscal year. As of
February 20, 1991, DOD had reported receipts of about $2.7 billion
of in-kind support from October 1990 through January 1991;
however, it has not adjusted its estimates to reflect any offset
of direct costs for this support or expected future support. Our
estimate for future receipts through the end of fiscal year 1991

---

[3]MAC develops its tariffs based on its estimates of costs it will
incur, including an amount to recapture fixed costs. The fixed
costs are spread over its approved flying hours, 450,000 in the
1991 budget. To the extent MAC bills more than its approved
flying hours, it will be recovering an amount in excess of its
fixed costs. MAC officials advised us that they may end the year
having flown twice their approved flying hours. Actual billed
hours will of course not be known until the end of the fiscal
year.

18

is about $3.7 billion based on about $700 million due from Japan,
Germany, and Korea from their 1990 pledges, and a projected amount
of $3 billion from Saudi Arabia for its 1991 pledge[4].

ALTERNATIVE TO ADMINISTRATION PROPOSAL

Given the uncertainties and concerns regarding the Operations'
cost estimates, we believe a traditional supplemental
appropriation would be more advisable than the Administration's
working capital proposal. Such an appropriation would be
emergency funding not subject to the defense spending limits
contained in the Omnibus Budget Reconciliation Act of 1990. We
estimate that an appropriation of $17 billion would be required
to cover the anticipated funding requirements of the Operation
from October 1, 1990, through March 31, 1991, the first half of
fiscal year 1991. Our estimate is based on first quarter fiscal
year 1991 obligations of $5.8 billion for deployment and
subsistence reported by DOD minus the higher price DOD is paying
for fuel worldwide; GAO's estimate of second quarter obligations
based on DOD's projection of operating tempo; and the cost of
accelerated acquisitions needed for use in the Gulf this fiscal
year. The Congress could then provide further appropriations

---

[4]Pledges for 1991 from Japan, Germany, and Korea consist of cash
contributions, and Saudi Arabia's pledge is for cash and in-kind
support. Because Saudi Arabia provides in-kind support on an
ongoing basis, we projected the amount for the remainder of the
fiscal year based on the value of support provided in December
1990.

19

0237

quarterly as actual experience clarifies spending requirements.
This funding should be provided by appropriating the $11 billion
in the Defense Cooperation Account and additional funds from that
account as they become available, not to exceed the $17 billion we
believe to be required through March 31. This funding plan would
eliminate the need for immediate U.S. funding beyond the over $100
billion already appropriated by Congress for the base costs of
our forces in the Middle East.

CONCLUSION

We need to assure that our troops in the Gulf receive all the
support they need to fight the war. The Administration, rather
than requesting a specific funding level to pursue the war, has
asked Congress to establish a unique funding mechanism with
little Congressional control. The obvious alternative to this
funding mechanism is the traditional appropriations process. We
believe that a $17 billion appropriation, which should be drawn
from funds deposited in the Defense Cooperation Account, would be
required to cover the anticipated funding requirements of the
Operations for the first half of fiscal year 1991. Congress,
however, should place limits on its use. Specifically, we believe
that Congress should make clear that incremental costs do not
include the higher fuel costs DOD is incurring outside the Middle
East. We further believe that upon the conclusion of hostilities
there should be a full accounting of the expenditure of funds and

20

0238

the assets consumed to assure appropriate disposition of all funds
and assets made available for the Operations.

- - - -

Mr. Chairman, this concludes my statement. I would be happy to
respond to any questions.

21

1f65-38

0239

정 리 보 존 문 서 목 록					
기록물종류	일반공문서철	등록번호	2012090508	등록일자	2012-09-17
분류번호	772	국가코드	US/XF	보존기간	영구
명 칭	걸프사태 : 미국 의회 동향, 1990-91. 전5권				
생 산 과	북미1과	생산년도	1990~1991	담당그룹	
권 차 명	V.5 1991.5-8월				
내용목차	* 걸프사태 관련 미국 의회에서의 각종 논의, 법안, 결의안, 청문회 개최 동향 등				

0001

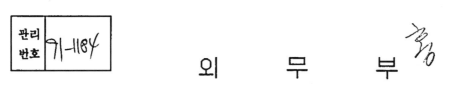

관리	91-1184

원 본

외 무 부

종   별 :

번   호 : USW-2327   일   시 : 91 0514 1657

수   신 : 장 관(미북,미안,중동일,기정,경기원,재무부)

발   신 : 주 미국 대사

제   목 : 우방국의 걸프전비 지원 관련 하원 청문회

연:USW-2299

1. 하원 외무위(위원장:FASCELL 의원)는 금 5.14. MULFORD 재무부 차관
및MCALLISTER 국무부 경제차관보를 출석시킨 가운데, 표제 청문회를 개최 하였는바,
동 청문회 증언문 및 관련자료를 팩스편 별송함.

2. 상기 청문회시 MCALLISTER 차관보는 아국이 국제적 책임(GLOBAL
RESPONSIBILITIES)을 인식, 걸프전비를 지원하였다고 말하고, 3억 8천 5백만불의
약속액중 1억 5천만불을 이행하였다고 밝혔을뿐, 질의 응답 과정에서도 아국 관련
언급 사항은 없었음.

3. 걸프전비 총 추정액 에 관한 FASCELL 위원장의 질의에 대해 MULFORD 차관은
아직 확실한 추정액은 알수없으나, 국방부와 OMB 에의하면 600-700억불 가량이
될것이라고 답변함. MCALLISTER 차관보는 행정부가 우방국의 기여금을 조속확보하기
위해 사우디,쿠웨이트,일본 및 걸프 재정공여국 그룹을 중심으로 계속 노력중이며,
금년중에는 전액 이행될것으로 믿는다고 말함.끝.

(대사 현홍주-국장)

예고:91.12.31. 까지

검토필 (1 91.6.50.

일반문서로 재분류(19 1.12.31.)

미주국 경기원	장관 재무부	차관	1차보	2차보	미주국	중아국	청와대	안기부

PAGE 1   91.05.15   09:09

외신 2과 통제관 BS

0002

STATEMENT BY
DAVID C. MULFORD
UNDER SECRETARY
FOR INTERNATIONAL AFFAIRS
U.S. DEPARTMENT OF THE TREASURY
BEFORE THE
COMMITTEE ON FOREIGN AFFAIRS
U.S. HOUSE OF REPRESENTATIVES
May 14, 1991

Mr. Chairman and members of the Committee, I appreciate the opportunity to comment on the Treasury Department's role in encouraging and facilitating burden sharing for a positive resolution to the Gulf crisis. As recent events have underscored, the solidarity of the international community has been crucial in reaching the objectives of dislodging the Iraqi military from Kuwait, restoring the legitimate government of that country, and laying the groundwork for greater regional stability in the future.

The financial support from our allies has sharply reduced the budgetary cost to the American people of our efforts. This is an important objective of the U.S. government. We have been successful in generating strong financial support -- both in the level of commitments and the pace of disbursements to date.

The Treasury Department has been most directly responsible for burden sharing related to securing exceptional economic assistance for those countries most seriously affected by the crisis. We have been accomplishing this through the Gulf Crisis Financial Coordination Group. We have had considerable success in this area and I would like to go into some detail on this Group.

The other aspect of Treasury involvement in burden sharing concerns foreign contributions for Operations Desert Shield and Desert Storm. The Treasury Department has played an active part -- along with the Defense Department, the State Department, NSC, and OMB -- in interagency efforts to maximize such contributions.

Treasury has also used the regular G-7 Finance Ministers' Meetings and other international fora to attain USG objectives on the economic and military aspects of burden sharing.

Gulf Crisis Financial Coordination Group

The Gulf Crisis Financial Coordination Group's (GCFCG) contributions on the economic front have been an important element in the coalition strategy to achieve a satisfactory resolution to the crisis. Key economies in the region, such as Egypt, Turkey, and Jordan, were particularly hard hit by Saddam Hussein's attack on Kuwait and the imposition by the U.N. of economic sanctions against Iraq. To complement the military and diplomatic leadership of the United States, President Bush

0003

1822-1

announced on September 25 the creation of the Gulf Crisis
Financial Coordination Group to: 1) maintain and support
effective implementation of U.N. economic sanctions against Iraq;
2) demonstrate international resolve in mobilizing financial
assistance for the front line states; and, 3) establish an
informal coordination process to secure appropriate
responsibility-sharing among creditors and donors for those
countries hardest hit by the crisis.

The Coordination Group has met five times, most recently in
Luxembourg on March 11. There is also a working level group that
meets on a more regular basis. The meetings are chaired by the
Treasury Department with the State Department as deputy chair.
Participants include 26 countries, the European Commission, and
the Gulf Cooperation Council. Representatives of the
International Monetary Fund and the World Bank also attend to
provide technical and analytical support.

The Coordination Group assists in quantifying the
exceptional financial needs of those countries most seriously
affected by the crisis, generating international resources to
meet these needs, and encouraging the creditors and donors to
direct these resources appropriately to the individual countries.
These resources are provided through traditional bilateral
channels among donors and recipients. The Group does not pool or
centralize resources for further distribution.

To date the Coordination Group has secured $16.1 billion in
commitments for the period August 1990 through end-1991. Of this
amount, $11.7 billion has been pledged to the front line states
of Egypt, Turkey, and Jordan. Commitments have come from: the
Gulf States ($9.8 billion); the European Community and its member
states ($3.2 billion); Japan ($2.6 billion); and other creditors
($500 million). Close to two-thirds of the assistance for which
terms have been determined are being made available in the form
of cash or in-kind grants. Moreover, $8.9 billion of the total
commitments have already been disbursed, $6 billion of which has
gone to Egypt, Turkey, and Jordan. Donors have indicated that
substantial additional disbursements will be made in the coming
months.

Role of the International Financial Institutions

The international financial institutions are also playing an
important role. In response to suggestions made by President
Bush and Treasury Secretary Brady at the Annual Meetings of the
World Bank and IMF last fall, these institutions took rapid and
concrete action to adapt their lending procedures and policies to
permit them to counter more effectively the economic effects of
the crisis on a broad range of countries.

Specifically, an oil import element has been incorporated
into the IMF's Compensatory and Contingency Financing Facility
(CCFF), traditionally used to compensate member countries for
external shocks which reduce their foreign exchange earnings.

182-2   0004

New potential financing is estimated at up to $5 billion,
depending on recipient countries having satisfactory energy
policies and an IMF program.

For its part, the World Bank estimates that its commitments
to countries seriously affected by the crisis will increase by
$4 billion over a two year period. Priority is being given to
helping countries develop and promptly implement adjustment
policies to strengthen their economies over the longer run. As
part of this effort, the Bank plans to increase its concessional
lending to lower middle-income countries. Increased World Bank
and IDA lending can be accommodated with the Bank's current
financial resources. The Bank is in the middle of a capital
increase approved in 1988 and, therefore, has resources
sufficient to meet these increased demands.

In sum, we have had substantial success in meeting the
objectives of providing extraordinary economic assistance through
the Coordination Group and the international financial
institutions. Remarkably broad cooperation has been demonstrated
in commitments to, and enforcement of, U.N. sanctions against
Iraq. Our ability to provide economic support to key countries
in their efforts to enforce the sanctions contributed to the
fulfillment of the U.N. mandates for Iraq to withdraw from Kuwait
and has helped to prepare the basis for greater future stability
in the region.

Developing a Post-War Economic Framework

Clearly, we need to move from the short-term crisis
management efforts of the past nine months to a more
comprehensive, farther-reaching approach to post-war regional
economic growth and development. At its meeting in Luxembourg,
the Coordination Group began to discuss future multilateral
arrangements for coordinating assistance and promoting long-term
development in the region. At the Group's request, the World
Bank and IMF are examining these and other regional economic
issues. We look forward to discussing these issues with the
Group in the near future.

Our view is that any future multilateral arrangement should
meet several criteria:

   o   It must make the best possible use of resources already
        available, both within and outside of the region to
        ensure appropriate burden sharing.

   o   It must ensure an appropriately central role for
        countries of the region.

   o   And it must address the need for sound policies, as
        well as financing to meet the residual impact of war
        and longer-term regional integration and economic
        development.

0005

Indeed, during Secretary Brady's recent trip to the Middle
East, senior officials of the GCC states confirmed that they
would establish a program to support regional development. They
are particularly concerned that such financing incorporate
economic reform measures and attach importance to supporting the
program activities of the World Bank and IMF.

We believe that an effective approach supporting long term
development in the Middle East would be one that is closely
associated with the World Bank and the IMF. This could be
through the establishment of a fund, facility, or subsidiary,
within the World Bank, supported by or coordinated with the IMF.
We look forward to working closely with countries in the Middle
East and elsewhere during the months ahead in order to develop
the precise elements of a global strategy to support long term
development in the region.

Contributions to Operations Desert Shield and Desert Storm

As I mentioned earlier, Treasury's role in generating
foreign contributions for Operations Desert Shield and Desert
Storm has been in its participation in interagency consultations
and contacts with foreign officials. In September 1990, Treasury
Secretary Brady visited several of our allies in Europe and Asia
to discuss financial and economic support for U.S. military
actions in the Gulf and for those economies severely affected by
the crisis, particularly through their support for the U.N.
sanctions. At the same time, Secretary of State Baker traveled
to Europe and several Gulf states with a similar message. These
meetings accomplished much in confirming the support of our major
allies and in producing initial substantial commitments of
military and economic assistance.

As noted in the Administration's recent reports to Congress,
these approaches and subsequent contacts resulted in 1990
commitments of $9.7 billion by our allies for incremental costs
incurred by Operation Desert Shield. Additional commitments for
the first four months of 1991 have reached $44.8 billion. Thus,
commitments for Operations Desert Shield and Desert Storm through
April total over $54.5 billion.

Let me close by addressing the technical aspect of
Treasury's role in this issue. The Treasury Department's system
of accounts is normally the initial recipient of all governmental
receipts, including, foreign cash contributions for U.S. military
activities during Operations Desert Shield and Desert Storm.
Under a law passed last year, the Defense Cooperation Account has
been established at the Treasury to receive monetary
contributions and proceeds for Operations Desert Shield and
Desert Storm. Using the same interagency consultation process
mentioned earlier, we actively coordinate with the Department of
Defense, State, and OMB to ensure that those monies received from
foreign contributors are credited against their commitments to
the United States for 1990 and for 1991.

184-4

0006

TESTIMONY BY

EUGENE J. MCALLISTER

ASSISTANT SECRETARY OF STATE

FOR ECONOMIC AND BUSINESS AFFAIRS

BEFORE THE

HOUSE FOREIGN AFFAIRS COMMITTEE

TUESDAY, MAY 14, 1991

MR. CHAIRMAN, MEMBERS OF THE COMMITTEE, THANK YOU FOR THE

OPPORTUNITY TO TESTIFY TODAY ON GULF RESPONSIBILITY SHARING

EFFORTS.   LAST SEPTEMBER WE EMBARKED ON A VERY IMPORTANT AND

HISTORIC EFFORT.   SECRETARIES BAKER AND BRADY TRAVELED TO THE

MIDDLE EAST, EUROPE AND ASIA TO ENCOURAGE OUR PARTNERS TO

CONTRIBUTE TO THE EFFORT TO LIBERATE KUWAIT BY HELPING OFFSET

THE ENORMOUS INCREMENTAL COSTS OF THE U.S. MILITARY PRESENCE

AND ASSISTING THOSE COUNTRIES CRITICAL TO THE SANCTIONS EFFORT.

IN MY TESTIMONY, I WOULD LIKE TO STRESS THREE POINTS: (1) THE

EXTRAORDINARY LEVELS OF RESPONSIBILITY SHARING THAT HAVE BEEN

ACHIEVED, BOTH MILITARY AND ECONOMIC; (2) THE VIGOROUS NATURE

OF U.S. EFFORTS TO ASSURE TIMELY PAYMENTS; AND (3) TO EMPHASIZE

OUR CONFIDENCE THAT ALL COMMITMENTS WILL BE HONORED.

/ハ~5 .   0007

-2-

<u>THE SCOPE OF RESPONSIBILITY SHARING</u>

THE UNPROVOKED AGGRESSION OF SADDAM HUSSEIN AND THE GULF WAR
ELICITED AN EXTRAORDINARY RESPONSE FROM THE INTERNATIONAL
COMMUNITY: 14 U.N. RESOLUTIONS RANGING FROM CONDEMNING THE
IRAQI INVASION TO PERMITTING THE USE OF ALL NECESSARY MEANS TO
END IRAQI OCCUPATION OF KUWAIT; A SANCTIONS REGIME THAT WAS THE
MOST COMPREHENSIVE AND EFFECTIVE IN MODERN HISTORY; AND THE
FORMATION OF A MILITARY COALITION OF 29 COUNTRIES.

ONE OF THE MOST REMARKABLE ELEMENTS OF THE CRISIS WAS THE
UNPRECEDENTED RESPONSIBILITY SHARING EFFORT:

o   OVER $70 BILLION IN TOTAL FINANCIAL CONTRIBUTIONS WAS
     RAISED. THIS $70 BILLION IN EXTRAORDINARY SPENDING IS
     GREATER THAN THE GDP OF A NUMBER OF COUNTRIES, INCLUDING
     GREECE, PORTUGAL AND YUGOSLAVIA.

o   IN THE SPHERE OF ECONOMIC ASSISTANCE, 26 COUNTRIES HAVE
     COMMITTED $16 BILLION IN 1990 AND 1991 MAINLY FOR THOSE
     "FRONT LINE" STATES CRITICAL TO THE SANCTIONS REGIME,
     NOTABLY EGYPT AND TURKEY. THIS EFFORT HAS BEEN COORDINATED
     THROUGH THE U.S. LED GULF CRISIS FINANCIAL COORDINATION
     GROUP.

182-6   0008

-3-

o   IN MILITARY RESPONSIBILITY SHARING, OUR PARTNERS HAVE
    COMMITTED $54.6 BILLION TO THE U.S.:

    -- $9.7 BILLION IN 1990, OR 73 PERCENT OF THE $13.2 BILLION
       IN 1990 INCREMENTAL COSTS; AND

    -- $44.8 BILLION FOR 1991 INCREMENTAL MILITARY COSTS.

o   IN ADDITION, CONTRIBUTORS TO RESPONSIBILITY SHARING HAVE
    ASSISTED OUR MILITARY PARTNERS. GERMANY, FOR INSTANCE,
    PROVIDED $822 MILLION TO THE U.K., AND JAPAN PROVIDED $330
    MILLION TO THE UK. GULF STATES -- KUWAIT, SAUDI ARABIA,
    AND THE UAE -- HAVE PROVIDED $6 BILLION TO SUPPORT OUR
    MILITARY PARTNERS.

BEFORE TURNING TO OUR EFFORTS TO ENSURE TIMELY PAYMENTS, LET ME
BRIEFLY HIGHLIGHT THE CONTRIBUTIONS OF SEVERAL KEY COUNTRIES:

    -- KUWAIT: IN ADDITION TO $16 BILLION PLEDGED TO OFFSET
       OUR MILITARY COSTS, KUWAIT ALSO PLEDGED $3.7 BILLION FOR
       ECONOMIC SUPPORT TO ASSIST THE STATES DIRECTLY AFFECTED
       BY THE CRISIS AND A FURTHER $1.3 BILLION TO HELP OFFSET
       THE UK'S MILITARY COSTS.

/822-7   0009

-4-

-- SAUDI ARABIA: THE SAUDIS OF COURSE COMMITTED THEIR
   ENTIRE ARMED FORCES TO DESERT SHIELD/STORM, BUT THEY
   ALSO PLEDGED:

   -- $16.8 BILLION FOR US DESERT SHIELD/STORM;
   -- $4.7 BILLION FOR ECONOMIC ASSISTANCE THROUGH THE
      GCFCG; AND
   -- $3.4 BILLION FOR OTHER MILITARY FORCES.

-- GERMANY: THE FEDERAL REPUBLIC STRONGLY SUPPORTED THE
   COALITION EFFORTS. ITS BROAD SUPPORT INCLUDED:

   -- $6.6 BILLION FOR US DESERT SHIELD/STORM;
   -- $1.3 BILLION FOR ECONOMIC ASSISTANCE THROUGH THE
      GCFCG;
   -- $822 MILLION FOR U.K. DESERT SHIELD/STORM:
   -- SUPPORT FOR TURKEY, INCLUDING $1 BILLION IN FINANCIAL
      ASSISTANCE, DEPLOYMENT OF TROOPS, AIRCRAFT AND AIR
      DEFENSE BATTERIES TO TURKEY; AND
   -- SUPPORT FOR ISRAEL, INCLUDING PATRIOT MISSILES AND
      OTHER ASSISTANCE VALUED AT $1 BILLION.

-- JAPAN: THE GOVERNMENT OF JAPAN PLEDGED OVER $13 BILLION
   FOR THE GULF EFFORT, THE LARGEST FINANCIAL CONTRIBUTION
   OUTSIDE THE GULF STATES:

1822-8

0010

-5-

-- $11 BILLION FOR COALITION MILITARY PARTNERS; AND

-- $2.6 BILLION FOR ECONOMIC ASSISTANCE THROUGH GULF
   CRISIS FINANCIAL COORDINATION GROUP.

-- UAE: THE UAE PLEDGED:

-- $4 BILLION FOR U.S. DESERT SHIELD/STORM;

-- $1.4 BILLION IN ECONOMIC ASSISTANCE THROUGH GULF
   CRISIS FINANCIAL COORDINATION GROUP; AND

-- $1 BILLION FOR EUROPEAN ALLIES WHO PARTICIPATED IN
   DESERT STORM.

EFFORTS TO ENSURE TIMELY PAYMENTS

LET ME BRIEFLY REVIEW THE STATUS OF COMMITMENTS AND
DISBURSEMENTS:

-- GERMANY HAS DISBURSED ALL OF ITS DESERT SHIELD/STORM
   COMMITMENTS. GERMANY'S STRONG COMMITMENT TO
   RESPONSIBILITY SHARING WAS DEMONSTRATED BY ITS VERY
   RAPID DISBURSEMENTS OF MILITARY FINANCING IN SUPPORT OF
   DESERT SHIELD AND DESERT STORM. IN LATE JANUARY
   CHANCELLOR KOHL COMMITTED $5.5 BILLION FOR DESERT
   STORM. TWO MONTHS LATER, ALL OF THAT COMMITTED FUNDING
   HAD BEEN DEPOSITED IN THE DEFENSE COOPERATION ACCOUNT.

182-9   0011

-6-

-- THE UNITED ARAB EMIRATES HAS DISBURSED NEARLY ALL OF ITS
   $4 BILLION 1990 AND 1991 DESERT SHIELD/STORM COMMITMENTS
   AND ALL OF ITS GULF CRISIS FINANCIAL COORDINATION GROUP
   ECONOMIC ASSISTANCE COMMITMENTS.

-- SAUDI ARABIA HAS DISBURSED THE BULK OF ITS 1990 DESERT
   SHIELD COMMITMENTS PARTICULARLY WITH REGARD TO ITS CASH
   COMMITMENTS; THE U.S. GOVERNMENT HAS TRANSMITTED OUR
   1990 TRANSPORTATION AND IN-THEATER EXPENSES, WHICH ARE
   BEING JOINTLY REVIEWED. FOR 1991, THE SAUDIS HAVE
   DISBURSED NEARLY HALF OF THEIR $13.5 BILLION COMMITMENT.
   WITH REGARD TO ECONOMIC ASSISTANCE, THE SAUDIS HAVE
   DISBURSED 78 PERCENT OF THEIR $4.7 BILLION GULF CRISIS
   FINANCIAL COORDINATION GROUP COMMITMENTS.

-- KUWAIT HAS MET ALL OF ITS 1990 DESERT SHIELD COMMITMENTS
   AND 50 PERCENT OF ITS 1991 DESERT SHIELD/STORM
   COMMITMENTS. KUWAIT ALSO HAS DISBURSED NEARLY HALF OF
   ITS $3.7 BILLION GULF CRISIS FINANCIAL COORDINATION
   GROUP COMMITMENTS.

-- JAPAN HAS DISBURSED $9.4 BILLION TO THE U.S. IN DESERT
   SHIELD/STORM COMMITMENTS. WE ARE CONTINUING TO DISCUSS
   WITH JAPAN HOW IT CAN CONTRIBUTE TOWARDS OUR ON-GOING
   MILITARY COSTS ASSOCIATED WITH THE CRISIS.

182-10   0012

-7-

-- KOREA, IN RECOGNITION OF ITS GLOBAL RESPONSIBILITIES
   ALSO CONTRIBUTED FINANCIALLY TO OFFSET OUR COSTS AND HAS
   DISBURSED $154 MILLION OF ITS $385 MILLION DESERT
   SHIELD/STORM COMMITMENTS.

THE BUSH ADMINISTRATION IS VERY VIGOROUSLY CONVEYING TO OUR
PARTNERS OUR DESIRE TO ACHIEVE RAPID DISBURSEMENTS OF THE
REMAINING COMMITMENTS:

WE ARE FOCUSING ON SAUDI ARABIA, KUWAIT, JAPAN, AND THE GULF
CRISIS FINANCIAL COORDINATION GROUP.

WE ARE RAISING THE NEED FOR RAPID DISBURSEMENTS THROUGH ALL
AVAILABLE CHANNELS, INCLUDING THE DEPARTMENT OF DEFENSE,
DIPLOMATIC CHANNELS -- OUR AMBASSADOR ABROAD -- SECRETARY
BAKER, AND EVEN THE PRESIDENT. THESE INTERVENTIONS ARE SHOWING
RESULTS:

-- THE SAUDI GOVERNMENT FOR INSTANCE HAS STATED IT WILL
   COMPLETE ITS DESERT STORM COMMITMENT THROUGH TWO PAYMENTS,
   THE FIRST COMING AT THE END OF MAY; THE SECOND AT THE END
   OF JUNE.

-- THE KUWAITI GOVERNMENT HAS MADE SIX DISBURSEMENTS, EACH OF
   AT LEAST $1 BILLION, SINCE THE DESERT STORM PLEDGE WAS MADE

/82-11   0013

-8-

IN LATE JANUARY. WE EXPECT THE KUWAITIS TO CONTINUE TO
MAKE REGULAR PAYMENTS UNTIL ITS PLEDGE IS FULLY MET.

--- WE EXPECT A COMPLETE DISBURSEMENT OF KOREA'S COMMITMENT BY
THE END OF JUNE AFTER THE KOREAN LEGISLATIVE PROCESS IS
COMPLETED.

CONFIDENCE IN COMPLETE PAYMENT

MR. CHAIRMAN, PLEASE BE ASSURED THAT RECEIVING THE FINAL
PAYMENTS REMAINS A TOP PRIORITY OF THE ADMINISTRATION. WE
RECOGNIZE ITS IMPORTANCE TO THE CONGRESS, AND OUR PARTNERS DO
AS WELL.

182-12

0014

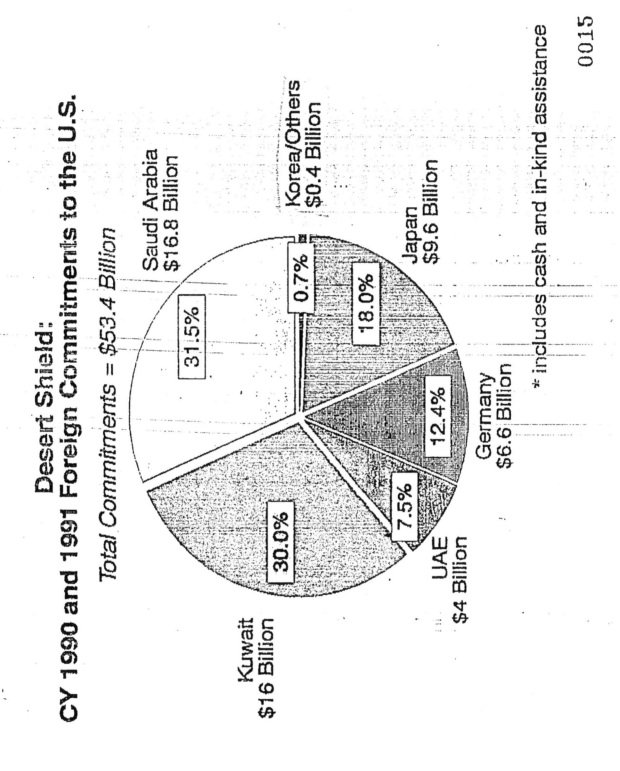

Desert Shield:
CY 1990 and 1991 Foreign Commitments to the U.S.

Total Commitments = $53.4 Billion

Saudi Arabia $16.8 Billion — 31.5%

Kuwait $16 Billion — 30.0%

UAE $4 Billion — 7.5%

Germany $6.6 Billion — 12.4%

Japan $9.6 Billion — 18.0%

Korea/Others $0.4 Billion — 0.7%

* includes cash and in-kind assistance

Desert Shield:
CY 1990 and 1991 Foreign Commitments to the U.S.

Total Receipts = $36.1 Billion

Saudi Arabia
$7.60 Billion

Korea/Others
$.17 Billion

Japan
$9.45 Billion

Kuwait
$9.27 Billion

UAE
$3.06 Billion

Germany
$6.55 Billion

21.14%

0.05%

26.29%

25.79%

8.51%

18.22%

* includes cash and in-kind assistance

0016

CONTRIBUTIONS
TO THE UNITED STATES FOR DESERT SHIELD AND DESERT STORM
(In billions of dollars)

	Pledges for Cash and In-Kind Assistance (Estimates) [1]			Contributions Received [2]		
	First Pledge	Second Pledge	Total	Cash	In-Kind [3]	Total
Saudi Arabia	3.3	13.5	16.8	4.54	3.06	7.60
Kuwait	2.5	13.5	16.0	9.25	0.02	9.27
UAE	1.0	3.0	4.0	2.87	0.19	3.06
Japan [4]	1.7	7.8 - 9.0	9.6 - 10.7	8.79	0.65	9.45
Germany	1.1	5.5	6.6	5.77	0.78	6.55
Korea	0.1	0.3	0.4	0.11	0.04	0.15
Other [5]	0.0	0.0	0.0	0.00	0.01	0.02
Total:	9.7	43.6 - 44.8	53.4 - 54.5	31.34	4.76	$6.10

1. Sources: OMB, DoD, Embassy Officials

2. In-kind is as of March 31, 1991; cash is as of April 26, 1991. Details may not add to totals due to rounding. (Sources: DoD and Daily Treasury Statements)

3. According to OMB Director Darman, total in-kind assistance is not expected to exceed about $5 billion to $6 billion.

4. The lower range is consistent with the Japanese estimate of their pledge; the upper range is consistent with the Administration's estimate of the Japanese pledge.

   Japan states its contribution of 1.17 trillion yen fulfilled its second pledge to the United States and the multinational forces. This was originally valued at $9 billion, but the dollar strengthened relative to the yen before the funds were deposited in the Defense Cooperation Account. This exchange rate loss (about $500 million), combined with a $700 million contribution to the multinational forces, decreased the contribution to the United States to about $7.8 billion.

   The Administration states that the second pledge was solely to the United States, and the pledge was $9 billion, regardless of currency fluctuations.

5. Other pledges total less than $100 million

Kent R. Christensen
226-2840
05/01/91

184 -15

0017

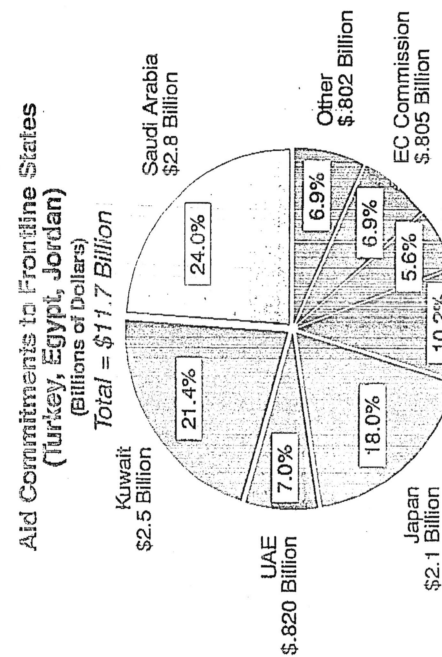

Aid Commitments to Frontline States
(Turkey, Egypt, Jordan)
(Billions of Dollars)
Total = $11.7 Billion

Saudi Arabia
$2.8 Billion

Kuwait
$2.5 Billion

UAE
$.820 Billion

Japan
$2.1 Billion

Germany
$1.195 Billion

Italy
$.650 Billion

EC Commission
$.805 Billion

Other
$.802 Billion

24.0%
21.4%
7.0%
18.0%
10.2%
5.6%
6.9%
6.9%

* DOES NOT INCLUDE TOTAL COMMITMENTS OF $4.393 BILLION TO BANGLADESH, DJIBOUTI, LEBANON, MOROCCO, PAKISTAN, SOMALIA, AND SYRIA

91 — (81)

0018

Table 1

GULF CRISIS FINANCIAL ASSISTANCE *
COMMITMENTS FOR 1990-91
DISBURSEMENTS THROUGH 5/1/91
(US$ Millions)

Creditor	Egypt/Turkey/Jordan Commitments	Disbursements	Other States 1/ Commitments	Disbursements	TOTAL Commitments	Disbursements
GULF STATES	6168	3863	3636	2845	9804	6708
Saudi Arabia	2918	2188	1833	1463	4681	3651
Kuwait	2500	855	1184	763	3684	1618
	1020	820	619	619	1499	1430
EC	3039	1225	177	1	3216	1226
	605	623	0	0	405	625
	2234	601	177	1	2411	602
	200	0	30	0	230	0
Germany	1195	462	137	0	1332	462
	650	37	9	0	659	37
Other EC 2/	189	102	1	1	190	103
	2126	803	481	0	2607	803
OTHERS	413	112	99	62	512	174
	95	19	17	2	115	21
	24	7	82	60	106	67
...land 3/	120	16	0	0	120	16
	171	70	0	0	171	70
TOTAL COMMITMENTS	11746	6003	4393	2908	16139	8911

All commitments and disbursements are bilateral economic assistance and do not include contributions to the multinational force.
Totals may not equal sum of components due to rounding. Based on data submitted to the Gulf Crisis Financial Coordination Group.
1/ Bangladesh, Djibouti, Lebanon, Morocco, Pakistan, Somalia, and Syria.
2/ Other EC includes Belgium, Denmark, Ireland, Luxembourg, Netherlands, Portugal, Spain, and the U.K.
3/ includes Austria, Canada, Finland, Iceland, and Sweden.
05/14/91

0013

TABLE A

GULF CRISIS FINANCIAL ASSISTANCE *

($ Billions -- as of 5/1/91)

Donor/Creditor	Commitments
GULF STATES	9.8
EUROPEAN COMMUNITY	3.2
JAPAN	2.6
OTHER	0.5
TOTAL	16.1

* Includes all commitments to date for extraordinary economic assistance in 1990 and 1991. Does not include contributions to the multinational force, existing bilateral assistance, or funds made available by the IMF and World Bank.

TABLE B

GULF CRISIS FINANCIAL ASSISTANCE *

(\$ Billions -- as of 5/1/91)

Creditor	Total Commitments	1990-91 Commitments		
		Egypt/Turkey/Jordan	Humanitarian**	Other States
GULF STATES	9.8	6.2	0.0	3.6
EUROPEAN COMMUNITY	3.2	2.3	0.7	0.2
	2.6	2.0	0.1	0.5
	0.5	0.3	0.1	0.1
	16.1	10.8	0.9	4.4

Includes all commitments to date for extraordinary economic assistance in 1990 and 1991.
Does not include contributions to the multinational force, existing bilateral assistance, or funds made available by the IMF and World Bank.
Includes both unallocated commitments and multilateral humanitarian assistance.

1991-20 (EA/b)

0022

TABLE C

GULF CRISIS FINANCIAL ASSISTANCE *

($ Billions -- as of 5/1/91)

Donor/Creditor	Commitments	Disbursements
GULF STATES	9.8	6.7
EUROPEAN COMMUNITY	3.2	1.2
JAPAN	2.6	0.8
OTHER	0.5	0.2
TOTAL	16.1	8.9

* Includes all commitments to date for extraordinary economic assistance in 1990 and 1991.
Does not include contributions to the multinational force, existing bilateral
assistance, or funds made available by the IMF and World Bank.

외 무 부

종 별 :

번 호 : USW-2395   일 시 : 91 0516 1901

수 신 : 장 관(미붕,미안,중동일,기정,경기원,재무부)

발 신 : 주 미국 대사

제 목 : 우방국의 걸프전비 지원 관련 하원 청문회

연:USW-2327

1. 하원 예산위(위원장 :PANETTA 의원)는 5.15. O'KEEFE 국방부 회계국장과 HECKLINGER 국무부 경제담당 부차관보등을 증인으로 출석시킨 가운데 표제 청문회를 개최하였는바, 아국관련 사항은 현재까지의 기여금 납부현황 (현금 1 억 1천만불, 물자지원 5 천 3 백만불)에 대한 설명과 국회 입법절차가 완료되는 6 월말까지 전액 이행될것이라는 기대표명 이외에는 특별한 언급이 없었음.

2. 걸프전비 총 추정액 관련 O'KEEFE 국장은 아래 경비가 아직 산정되지 않아 확실한 추정액을 알수 없으나 대략 600 억불 이상이 될것으로 본다고 증언함.

0 장비 철수 비용 및 이에 필요한 인건비

0 참전 용사에 대한 특별수당등 지원금

0 군장비 손실액 및 보전, 수리 비용

0 향후 지역 안보체제 수립에 대비한 비축용으로 걸프지역에 남겨둔 물자 가치등

3. O'KEEFE 국장은 또한 90-91 년간 우방국이 약속한 지원금 총액은 546 억불 이며, 5.13. 현재 371억불이 납입되었다고 밝히고, 이중 현금지원은 320 억불 이며 물자지원액 (4.30 현재)은 71억불이라고 증언함.

4. 상기 관련 증언문 파편 송부 예정임.끝.

(대사 현홍주-국장)

예고:91.12.31.까지

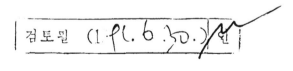

검토필 (1.91.6.30.)

일반문서로 재분류(1991.12.31.)

| 미주국 | 장관 | 차관 | 1차보 | 2차보 | 미주국 | 중아국 | 청와대 | 안기부 |
| 경기원 | 재무부 | | | | | | | |

PAGE 1   91.05.17   09:00

외신 2과 통제관 BS

0023

THE WHITE HOUSE, WASHINGTON, DC REGULAR BRIEFING   BRIEFER: MARLIN
FITZWATER   THURSDAY, MAY 16, 1991

MR. FITZWATER: I don't know. Here the -- personnel says they
don't know. I'm sorry, Deborah?

Q   As of now probably Saudi Arabia and Kuwait both have paid
only about half of what they promised to toward the Gulf War. Are
we dissatisfied about the speed of payment and what are we doing to
speed it up?

MR. FITZWATER: I don't have the exact numbers here but I think
they have paid more than half. As I understood they were much
closer to 75 percent and we were satisfied. We felt it was
progressing well. There was a suggestion a few days ago that by --
I am not sure where it came from, here, I guess, or in the Congress
or someplace -- that we accept oil instead of cash. We would prefer
to have the cash but we are nevertheless satisfied that the payments
are going according to plan and that they will indeed make their
entire commitment.

주　미　대　사　관

미국(의) 700-1116   1991. 5. 17.

수신 : 장　관
참조 : 미주국장, 중동아프리카국장
제목 : 걸프전비 관련 하원 예산위 청문회

　　　　연 : USW - 2395

　　　　연호 표제 청문회 증언문 3부를 별첨 송부합니다.

첨부 : 상기자료.　　　　　끝.

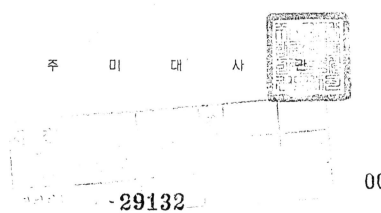

0025

-29132

U.S. HOUSE OF REPRESENTATIVES

COMMITTEE ON THE BUDGET

MEETING

NOTICE

214 House Annex No. 1
Washington, D.C. 20515
(202) 226-7200

LEON E. PANETTA, CHAIRMAN

*** FULL COMMITTEE HEARING ***

Wednesday, May 15, 1991

9:00 a.m.

210 Cannon House Office Building

TOPIC: Update on the Budget Costs of Desert Shield/Desert Storm

WITNESSES

9:00 a.m.   PANEL: The Honorable Sean O'Keefe
                            Comptroller
                            Department of Defense

                            Mr. Richard Hecklinger
                            Principal Deputy Assistant Secretary for
                            Economic and Business Affairs
                            Department of State

10:30 a.m.   Mr. Frank C. Conahan
                 Assistant Comptroller General
                 National Security and International Affairs Division
                 General Accounting Office

0026

STATEMENT OF
THE COMPTROLLER OF THE
DEPARTMENT OF DEFENSE

SEAN O'KEEFE

BEFORE THE

HOUSE BUDGET COMMITTEE

IN CONNECTION WITH

DESERT SHIELD/DESERT STORM
COSTS AND CONTRIBUTIONS

MAY 15, 1991

0027

STATEMENT OF THE HONORABLE SEAN O'KEEFE
COMPTROLLER OF THE DEPARTMENT OF DEFENSE
IN CONNECTION WITH DESERT SHIELD/STORM COSTS AND CONTRIBUTIONS
HOUSE BUDGET COMMITTEE
MAY 15, 1991

Mr. Chairman, members of the Committee, I am happy to be here to help update you on the costs and contributions for Operation Desert Shield/Desert Storm.

GULF-RELATED U.S. COSTS AND ALLIED CONTRIBUTIONS

When I last appeared before this committee on February 27, coalition forces were in the final hours of a stunning victory in the Gulf War. That success reflected an effective sharing of responsibility by a diverse international coalition. Nearly 50 nations contributed to the coalition's military effort, and about 35 sent personnel to the area of operations. Our allies committed about 245,000 troops and 650 fixed-wing aircraft, 1300 tanks, and 64 warships.

Allied contributions also have been helping to cover the heavy U.S. costs for the Gulf operation. The Administration is keeping Congress informed on the status of those contributions, and on its Desert Shield/Storm costs, through monthly "Schumer/Panetta" reports on United States Costs in the Persian Gulf Conflict and Foreign Contributions to Offset Such Costs, as required by Section 401 of the supplemental authorization act.

The first of these cost reports, dated April 20, estimated incremental U.S. costs for August through December 1990 to be $13.2 billion. Our latest report, dated May 15, estimates incremental U.S. costs for August 1990 through March 31, 1991, to be $36.1 billion. The costs reported so far are partial and preliminary. They do not include such items as total costs of equipment repair, rehabilitation, and maintenance caused by high operating rates and combat stress. They also do not include the total costs of phasedown of operations and return of deployed forces. Further, certain long-term benefit and disability costs have not been reflected in the estimates. Costs through March, plus costs not yet reported, are expected to result in total incremental costs of $60 billion or more.

These U.S. costs will be covered by a combination of (1) cash and in-kind contributions from our allies, (2) the realignment, reprogramming, or transfer of defense funds appropriated for activities unrelated to the Gulf conflict, and (3) potentially, the Persian Gulf Regional Defense Fund, established by Congress in the supplemental appropriations bill enacted on March 22, 1991.

0028

Allied contribution commitments for 1990 and 1991 total
$54.6 billion. As of May 13 we had received $37.1 billion: $32
billion in allied cash contributions, through May 13; and $5.1
billion of in-kind assistance, through April 30. The
Administration continues to be confident that America's
coalition partners will fulfill their commitments for offsetting
U.S. gulf-related costs.

RETIRING U.S. DESERT SHIELD/STORM COSTS

With the Congress's passage of the FY 1991 Desert
Shield/Storm supplemental appropriations, we are making steady
progress in retiring our Gulf-related costs. The supplemental
established the Persian Gulf Regional Defense Fund with $15
billion of new budget authority. It also provided for the
transfer to Department of Defense (DoD) appropriation accounts
of current and future balances in the Defense Cooperation
Account, the total of the transfers not to exceed $42.6 billion.

Section 101 of the supplemental appropriations mandates that
DoD draw on the Regional Defense Fund only to the extent that
amounts from the Cooperation Account are not available. It
further requires that, if the Fund balance is less than $15
billion, DoD shall transfer to it amounts from the Cooperation
Account to the extent that Account monies are available to
restore the Fund balance to $15 billion.

The supplemental allows transfers from either the
Cooperation Account or the Regional Defense Fund 7 days after
notification to Congress. On April 10, the Department notified
Congress of its intention to transfer to various DoD accounts a
total of up to $28.1 billion from the Cooperation Account and
$3.7 billion from the Regional Defense Fund. Following our
notification, we proceeded with transfers from the Cooperation
Account totalling $27.1 billion through the end of April. As
required by Section 106 of the FY 1991 supplemental
authorization act, details of these transfers were reported (on
May 6) to the congressional defense committees. To date, no
transfers have been made from the Regional Defense Fund.

Our transfers in April ended up falling short of the
ceilings we projected in our April 10 notification. The primary
reason is that the pace of our transfers is being determined by
the pace of our refinement and validation of the cost data
submitted by the military services and defense agencies. We
will retire our Gulf-related costs as fast as we prudently can,
but only as requirements are firmly established. Moreover, we
seek to avoid any transfers from the direct U.S. appropriations
in the Persian Gulf Regional Defense Fund unless absolutely
necessary.

2

0029

GULF COSTS NOT YET FULLY REPORTED

It is important to note the types of costs that are not yet reflected in the estimates we have reported so far.

One is the cost incident to removing from the Gulf theater the equipment we plan to remove. This task is proving to be slower and more involved than some may have expected. Loading ships and planes takes longer than unloading, even without the added requirement of thoroughly cleaning and inspecting everything.

A related unknown are costs for the U.S. personnel required to support the equipment removal and for other tasks. It is uncertain how many personnel will be needed. As of May 14, 128,000 U.S. military personnel were in the CENTCOM area of responsibility (as distinguished from European Command's area in eastern Turkey and northern Iraq.) Over 413,000 troops have redeployed from the Gulf--which is over 76 percent of the total force there during the war.

Also not yet fully reported are certain special pay, benefits, and veterans costs--a number of which are funded in the FY 1991 supplemental. The dollar amounts of these are relatively low, but they strongly reflect our nation's gratitude to its uniformed men and women and their families.

Regarding investment, our reported costs already include an estimate for most losses of major end items (aircraft, tanks, etc.). However, decisions on replacing those major losses have not yet been completed. Additionally, there is still a great deal of assessment going on to determine the actual consumption of or degree of damage to support equipment, munitions, and other items. Much of this is being done at the deployment ports. We also are analyzing the magnitude of the wear and tear on major equipment to determine what refurbishment may be necessary. So it will be a while before we know all the repairs, rehabilitation, or restocking that will be required as a result of Gulf operations.

Other costs not yet fully reported include the value of material left in the Gulf area as pre-positioned stockpiles for our new regional security arrangements. The extent of these costs, if any, will be based on agreements that are currently being negotiated.

DoD is continuing to match the Gulf costs that are accumulating with the amounts appropriated for various DoD accounts, to determine the need for redistributing among the accounts or the need for an increase in budget authority through another supplemental request. Since the cost picture is still quite uncertain, I cannot project when such a request will be made.

3

0030

CLOSING

As discussed above and in our various reports, we are moving steadily, but carefully toward retiring our Desert Shield/Storm costs. We look forward to continued cooperation with Congress for completing this demanding task.

(The attached charts show Gulf-related costs and contributions.)

4

0031

DESERT SHIELD/DESERT STORM
Major Foreign Contributions
(U.S. $ Million)

Contributor	Commitments 1/	Receipts		
		Cash 2/	In-Kind 2/	Total
Saudi Arabia	16,839	4,536	3,407	7,943
Kuwait	16,006	9,250	24	9,274
UAE	4,000	3,570	197	3,767
Japan	10,740	8,792	637	9,429
Germany	6,572	5,772	782	6,554
Korea	385	110	53	163
Others	20	4	16	20
Total	**54,562**	**32,034**	**5,116**	**37,150**

1/ Commitments do not include pledges to other countries.

2/ Cash received as of May 13; In-Kind as of April 30,1991.

0032

INCREMENTAL DoD COSTS
FOR OPERATION DESERT SHIELD/DESERT STORM
($ in Million)

Category	FY 1990 Total	FY 1991 Oct-Dec	FY 1991 Jan-Mar	FY 1991 Total	Grand Total
Airlift	425	412	810	1,222	1,647
Sealift	234	688	1,911	2,599	2,833
Personnel	268	1,192	2,344	3,536	3,804
Personnel Support	364	2,112	2,675	4,787	5,151
Operating Support	1,241	3,721	6,596	10,317	11,558
Fuel	579	932	1,908	2,840	3,419
Procurement/RDT&E	129	719	6,410	7,129	7,258
Military Construction	47	126	271	397	444
Grand Total	**3,287**	**9,902**	**22,926**	**32,828**	**36,115**

0033

United States General Accounting Office

GAO

Testimony

For Release
on Delivery
Expected at
9:00 a.m. EDT
Wednesday
May 15, 1991

Cost of Operation Desert Shield and Desert
Storm and Allied Contributions

Statement of
Frank C. Conahan, Assistant Comptroller General
National Security and International Affairs
Division

Before the
Committee on Budget
House of Representatives

0034

GAO/T-NSIAD-91-34

GAO Form 160 (12/87)

I appreciate the opportunity to testify today before this
Committee on the cost of Operations Desert Shield and Desert
Storm and allied contributions to help defray this cost. At the
outset, I would like to emphasize that the Office of Management
and Budget (OMB) reports on the incremental costs of the
Operations. We have reported on both incremental and total costs
and now estimate that total costs could exceed $100 billion. Our
allies have pledged about $54.6 billion or about half of the
total cost. Having said that, I will present our views on the
Administration's most recent cost estimates, the differences
between estimated costs and funding requirements, and the extent
to which taxpayer financing will be required.

In summary, we believe that, for the most part, OMB's and the
Department of Defense's (DOD) estimated cost through May 1991 is
reasonable, but we believe that the estimate of future costs is
unsupported and appears high. More importantly, we believe that
incremental funding requirements will be substantially less than
OMB's cost estimate, and that fiscal year 1991 incremental
funding needs can be fully financed through allied contributions
to the Defense Cooperation Account.

COST ESTIMATE CONCERNS

As you know, OMB, as required by the Persian Gulf Conflict
Supplemental Authorization and Personnel Benefits Act, is
providing monthly reports on the incremental costs of Operation
Desert Storm[1]. OMB's latest report, dated April 27, 1991, lists
incremental costs of $31.6 billion, including combat costs, from
the inception of the operation in August 1990 through February
1991. OMB's report states that additional costs will include the
phasedown of operations; redeployment of forces; equipment

---

[1]These reports include the cost of Operation Desert Shield as
well. I shall refer to Operations Desert Shield and Desert
Storm as the operation for the balance of this statement.

1

refurbishment, that is, repair, rehabilitation, and maintenance, caused by high operating rates and combat use during the war; and long-term benefit and disability costs. OMB reports that the costs reported through February 1991 plus these additional costs are expected to result in total incremental costs of $60 billion or more.

DOD estimates the cost for a three month post-combat period and redeployment will total about $12.2 billion. The remaining cost of at least $16.2 billion ($60 billion minus $43.8 billion, the sum of reported costs through February of $31.6 billion and estimated phasedown and redeployment costs of $12.2 billion) is primarily due to the cost of equipment refurbishment.

We have not had the opportunity to fully evaluate the $31.6 billion in incremental cost OMB reported through February, but we have seen no evidence to dispute the bulk of this cost estimate. One concern we do have involves the inclusion of the higher fuel prices DOD is paying for non-operation related activities worldwide, which total about $1.6 billion for the period reported. We do not believe higher fuel prices to be a cost of the operation. A second concern we have is that the estimate may also reflect higher-than-actual costs charged by DOD's revolving fund accounts. Because of the increased volume of services provided, revolving fund operations, such as air and sea transportation and depot maintenance, might have charged users higher-than-actual costs. As we testified in February, the revolving funds may ultimately rebate or credit the overcharges back to the using services. This would reduce the services' fiscal year 1992 budget needs.

We also have not had an opportunity to evaluate DOD's $12.2 billion estimate for the three month post-combat period and redeployment, but have seen no evidence to dispute it. We

2

0036

understand that OMB will report a March cost estimate of $4.6 billion.

The residual $16.2 billion for additional costs is unsupported. DOD has not yet developed an estimate for the majority of these costs. In addition, the residual cost appears high because some funds are already available for equipment refurbishment. Specifically, DOD's fiscal year 1991 budget includes $8.4 billion for depot maintenance. Depot maintenance programs fund the overhaul, repair, and maintenance of aircraft, missiles, ships, combat vehicles, and other equipment, including the overhaul and repair of engines and other exchangeable component parts. While this budget is for all of DOD, given the large volume of equipment deployed to the Persian Gulf, it is reasonable to assume that a portion of these funds would have been available for refurbishing this equipment. Furthermore, DOD's post-combat phasedown cost estimate includes $600 million for all equipment to be inspected and fully repaired using in-theater spare parts. Consequently, while the final cost of equipment repair and maintenance remains unknown at this time, we believe the incremental cost could be less than $16.2 billion.

Finally, although there may be additional costs, there may also be reductions in future budget needs because of the buildup of inventories that were not needed as a result of the war's short duration.

Overall we believe that the cost of the operation could total more than $100 billion if you include the approximately $50 billion we estimate it cost the United States to raise, equip, and maintain the force that was deployed and as much as $10 billion in other costs, including $7 billion in debt forgiveness for Egypt.

3

0037

INCREMENTAL COSTS VS INCREMENTAL FUNDING REQUIREMENTS

An important distinction needs to be made between costs and
funding needs. Funding requirements represent outlays that the
United States will ultimately be required to make, either from
funds contributed by the allies or from the new budget authority
provided by the Congress. The $43.8 billion in incremental costs
reported by OMB and DOD for operations and redeployment includes
$31.6 billion for operations through February 1991 and $12.2
billion in post-combat phasedown and redeployment costs. The
$43.8 billion in incremental costs for operations and
redeployment includes actual expenditures, the value of
assistance-in-kind, and anticipated expenditures for which DOD
has not actually obligated funds. Anticipated expenditures
include such items as the replacement of equipment destroyed in
the war, the deactivation of Ready Reserve Fleet ships, and the
restocking of maritime prepositioned ships. Some anticipated
expenditures may never translate into obligations because DOD may
choose not to make certain expenditures.

On the basis of our review of DOD's data on obligations and costs
and of OMB's reports, we believe that incremental funding
requirements for fiscal year 1991 for the operation will be about
$33 billion. There are three reasons for the difference between
our funding estimate and OMB's higher cost estimate, which
involve costs incurred in fiscal year 1990, the treatment of
assistance-in-kind, and other costs that may not require funding.

One reason is that OMB's report includes fiscal year 1990 costs
of $3.3 billion, which have already been funded. A second reason
is that OMB is using cost estimates rather than actual costs.
Using DOD's obligations data as a measure of actual costs
suggests such costs are considerably lower than OMB's reported
costs. For example, DOD reported obligations for the first
quarter of fiscal year 1991 of $5.8 billion for the operation

4

0038

while OMB reported estimated costs of $9.9 billion. This is a difference of $4.1 billion. Obligations data are not yet available for January and February 1991, but DOD officials have advised us that obligations will be substantially lower than OMB's reported costs for January and February.

OMB's reported cost estimate of $9.9 billion is in part higher than obligations because costs include the value of assistance-in-kind provided by our allies, which do not require DOD to obligate funds since they are received free. In the first quarter of fiscal year 1991, OMB reported assistance-in-kind of $1 billion. This accounts for about one-fourth of the $4.1 billion difference between first quarter obligations and costs. We have been attempting to correlate obligations and reported costs to better understand the balance of the disparity between the two; however, to date DOD has not provided us with a reconciliation.

The third reason that obligations are lower than costs is that anticipated expenditures, which are included in OMB's reports, do not result in DOD's immediately obligating funds and may never result in the obligation of funds. For example, in its April 27 report, OMB reported procurement costs of $6.9 billion for the first five months of fiscal year 1991. This amount included $1.2 billion to reflect the value of major equipment destroyed during the conflict. However, because equipment losses were limited and the administration's current budget proposal includes a substantial reduction in the armed forces over the next several years, it may be unnecessary to replace destroyed equipment.

We believe that the reporting of anticipated expenditures, including combat losses, accounts for the substantial disparity between reported procurement costs and DOD's supplemental funding estimate. DOD originally estimated procurement needs of $6.4 billion in fiscal year 1991, but it revised this figure down to

5

0039

$2.9 billion following the war's rapid conclusion. DOD's revised estimate is $4 billion less than OMB's reported cost, which suggests that many of the reported costs are anticipated expenditures that may never result in the obligation of funds.

Draw on New Appropriations Not Needed

To provide funding for the operation, Congress appropriated $15 billion to a newly established Persian Gulf Regional Defense Fund and authorized the transfer of funds in the Defense Cooperation Account to various DOD appropriations accounts. As of May 13, 1991, our allies had contributed about $32 billion to the Defense Cooperation Account and are expected to contribute an additional $15.3 billion, for a total of $47.3 billion.

On the basis of our estimated funding needs of $33 billion for operations through February 1991 and post-combat phasedown and redeployment and an as yet undetermined amount of the $16.2 billion in equipment refurbishment and other costs, which I described earlier, we believe that allied contributions will be sufficient to meet the incremental funding requirements for the operation. It will therefore not be necessary to draw funds from the $15 billion in new appropriations provided by Congress.

STATUS OF ALLIED CONTRIBUTIONS

Since the Iraqi invasion of Kuwait, 38 countries have contributed support for the Persian Gulf crisis. These contributions include the deployment of military forces to the Gulf region, cash payments to the U.S. Treasury, in-kind support to U.S. forces in Saudi Arabia and other Gulf states, and economic assistance to countries affected by the United Nations economic embargo against Iraq. Some countries have also provided other support, such as basing and overflight rights, military assistance to countries affected by the hostilities, and assistance to Kurdish refugees.

6

0040

Military Contributions

Allied military contributions have included the deployment of
ground, air, naval or support forces to participate in the
multinational force supporting Desert Shield, Desert Storm and the
maritime enforcement of the economic embargo. These forces,
representing 31 countries, participated in combat and combat
support missions during the military campaign against Iraq, and
some remain to assist U.S. forces in enforcing the cease-fire
agreement.

Cash Contributions and In-Kind Support to the United States

Major contributors of cash and in-kind support to the United
States include Saudi Arabia, Kuwait, the United Arab Emirates,
Japan, Germany, and Korea. As of May 1991, these countries had
pledged about $54.6 billion to offset U.S. costs. According to
State and DOD officials, no additional pledges are anticipated.

As of May 13, 1991, Saudi Arabia, Kuwait, the United Arab
Emirates, Germany, Japan, and Korea had contributed about $32
billion in cash to the Defense Cooperation Account. Of this
amount, Japan and Germany specified that the cash they had
contributed toward their 1990 pledges was to be expended to
transport U.S. troops, equipment, and materials to the Gulf
region. Japan also requested that the cash contributions under
its 1991 pledge be used for logistics related expenses.

In-kind contributions include food, fuel, water, transportation,
material, and facilities. Major contributors include Saudi
Arabia, the United Arab Emirates, Kuwait, Japan, Germany and
Korea. As part of its 1990 pledge, Japan specified that its in-
kind airlift and sealift support be used to transport cargo other
than weapons, ammunition, or personnel. The other countries did
not place conditions on the use of in-kind support.

7

0041

As of May 13, 1991, DOD had reported receipts of in-kind support, through April 1991, valued at about $5.1 billion. Because the U.S. Central Command and the U.S. Transportation Command, which are responsible for determining the value of in-kind support, did not always have access to data on actual expenditures, this value may differ from the cost incurred by the contributor. For example, Central Command officials determined the value of food supplied to U.S. troops in Saudi Arabia based on the amount paid to contractors under U.S. contracts before the Saudi government assumed responsibility for the contracts in November 1990. The actual amount paid by the Saudi government is unknown.

The breakdown of pledges and contributions is shown as follows:

Allied Pledges and Contributions for Cash and In-Kind Support to the United States
(U.S. dollars in millions)

	Pledges			Contributions			Balance Remaining	Percent of Pledge Met
	1990	1991	Total	Cash (5/13/91)	In-Kind (4/30/91)	Total		
Saudi Arabia	3,339	13,500	16,839	4,536	3,407	7,943	8,896	47
Kuwait	2,506	13,500	16,006	9,250	24	9,274	6,732	58
United Arab Emirates	1,000	3,000	4,000	3,570	197	3,767	233	94
Japan	1,740	9,000[a]	10,740	8,792[b]	637	9,429	1,311	88
Germany	1,072	5,500	6,572	5,772[c]	782	6,554	18	99
Korea	80	305	385	110	53	163	222	42
Other[d]	3	12	15	4	16	20	0	100
Total	9,740	44,817	54,557	32,034	5,116	37,150	17,412	68

[a]Pledge amount is under discussion. Japanese government states that the pledge is $8.3 billion (now $7.8 billion due to decline in yen). U.S. government believes the amount is $9 billion.
[b]Includes $961 million to be expended for transportation costs.
[c]Includes $272 million to be expended for transportation costs.
[d]Includes Oman, Qatar, Bahrain and Denmark.

The table shows that total contributions are about $37.2 billion compared to pledges of about $54.6 billion. Of the remaining $17.4 billion, a total of about $15.3 billion is expected to be

8

0042

in cash payments from Saudi Arabia, Kuwait, United Arab Emirates, Japan and Korea and the remaining $2.1 billion in in-kind support from Saudi Arabia, Germany and Korea.

Economic Assistance to Frontline States and Other Countries

In addition to cash and in-kind support, the European Commission and 24 countries pledged economic assistance to Turkey, Jordan, and Egypt, referred to as "frontline states," and to other countries affected by the economic embargo against Iraq. This support includes import financing and project assistance grants, and concessional loans. As of May 1, 1991, these pledges were about $16.1 billion for 1990 and 1991, and contributions were about $8.9 billion.

9

0043

The status of pledges and contributions is shown as follows:

Economic Assistance to Frontline States and Other Countries
As of 5/1/91 (U.S. dollars in millions)

Donor	Frontline States		Other Countries[a]		Total	
	Pledge	Contribution	Pledge	Contribution	Pledge	Contribution
GULF STATES	6,168	3,863	3,636	2,845	9,804	6,708
Saudi Arabia	2,848	2,188	1,833	1,463	4,681	3,651
Kuwait	2,500	855	1,184	763	3,684	1,618
United Arab Emirates	820	820	619	619	1,439	1,439
EUROPEAN COMMISSION	3,039	1,225	177	1	3,216	1,226
Budget	805	624	0	0	805	624
Bilateral	2,234	601	177	1	2,411	602
France	200	0	30	0	230	0
Germany	1,195	462	137	0	1,332	462
Italy	650	37	9	0	659	37
Other[b]	189	102	1	1	190	103
JAPAN	2,126	803	481	0	2,607	803
OTHERS	413	112	99	62	512	174
Korea	98	19	17	2	115	21
Norway	24	7	82	60	106	67
Switzerland	120	16	0	0	120	16
Other[c]	171	70	0	0	171	70
Total	11,748	6,003	4,393	2,908	16,139	8,911

[a] Bangladesh, Djbouti, Lebanon, Morocco, Pakistan, Somalia, and Syria
[b] Belgium, Denmark, Ireland, Luxembourg, Netherlands, Portugal, Spain and United Kingdom
[c] Australia, Austria, Canada, Finland, Iceland, and Sweden

Other Types of Contributions

In addition to military, economic and in-kind support, our allies have contributed in other means. For example, Germany deployed a fighter squadron to Turkey and ships to the eastern and central Mediterranean Sea, and pledged about $2.7 billion in military assistance to Turkey, Israel, and the United Kingdom. Further, Japan sent oil booms to Saudi Arabia to assist in counteracting the Gulf oil slick. In addition, our NATO allies and certain

10

0044

Gulf countries have granted basing and transit rights and several
countries are providing assistance to Kurdish refugees.

- - - -

Mr. Chairman, this concludes my statement. I would be happy to
respond to questions at this time.

(396754)

11

Testimony by
Richard Hecklinger
Principal Deputy Assistant Secretary of State
for Economic and Business Affairs
Before the
House Budget Committee
Wednesday, May 15, 1991

Mr. Chairman, Members of the Committee, thank you for the opportunity to appear once again before your Committee. My statement today will update information I provided on February 27. I would like to cover both the military and economic dimensions of responsibility sharing in the Gulf Crisis.

Military Responsibility Sharing

Desert Shield and Desert Storm were truly coalition efforts. Militarily and financially, the sharing of responsibility was remarkable, the largest in scope since the Second World War.

Twenty-eight nations joined the United States in contributing military forces to the coalition confronting Iraq. Six other nations provided hospital, logistic and other support personnel. These 28 countries provided:

-- 245,000 troops;
-- 650 fixed-wing combat aircraft;
-- 2,600 armored vehicles, including 1,300 tanks; and,
-- 64 warships.

Six nations have made commitments totalling $54.6 billion to offset a substantial portion of U.S. military costs: $9.7 billion for CY-90, and $44.8 billion for CY-91. The $9.7 billion committed for CY-90 will cover 73 percent of our revised cost estimate for that year. Though it is still too soon to make firm predictions, foreign contributions for CY-91 could well exceed that percentage.

So far we have received over $36 billion, or over two-thirds of the commitments. This is an impressive achievement, especially as the bulk of the commitments were made in late January.

The Administration is making a strong effort to obtain the remaining one-third of the pledged amounts. In bilateral discussions with our partners, we continue to underscore the importance of rapid disbursement.

The major contributors are also making sizable contributions to cover the military costs of other members of the coalition: Saudi Arabia, Kuwait, Germany, Japan and the UAE have pledged about $9 billion in assistance to other coalition members.

Economic Support for States Affected by the Crisis (Through the GCFCG)

On the economic side, 26 countries joined together in the Gulf Crisis Financial Coordination Group (GCFCG), chaired by the United States, to provide exceptional assistance to the countries most severely affected by the crisis.

As of May 10, 1991, the Group has mobilized $11.7 billion in commitments to the "Front Line States" (Egypt, Jordan and Turkey) for the period September 1990 - December 1991, of which $6.0 billion has been disbursed. The GCFCG members have also committed another $4.4 billion in exceptional assistance to other affected states, of which $2.9 billion has been disbursed. The Administration continues to press GCFCG members to disburse their pledges as soon as possible.

0046

Summary of Commitments

I believe that it would be useful to provide a summary of total assistance pledged by the five major contributors:

1. **Saudi Arabia:** The Saudis committed their entire armed forces to Desert Shield/Storm. They also pledged about $25 billion in financial and in-kind assistance. This includes:

    -- $16.8 billion for U.S. Desert Shield/Storm;
    -- $4.7 billion for economic assistance reported through the Gulf Crisis Financial Coordination Group; and
    -- $3.4 billion for other military forces.

2. **Kuwait:** In addition to $16 billion pledged to offset our military costs, Kuwait also pledged $3.7 billion for economic support to assist states affected by the crisis and a further $1.3 billion to help offset the U.K.'s military costs. This totals approximately $21 billion.

3. **Japan:** The Government of Japan pledged over $13 billion for the Gulf effort, the largest financial contribution outside the Gulf states. This includes:

    -- $11 billion for coalition military partners; and
    -- $2.6 billion for economic assistance reported through the Gulf Crisis Financial Coordination Group.

4. **Germany:** The Federal Republic of Germany has pledged about $11 billion in military and economic support. This includes:

    -- $6.6 billion for U.S. Desert Shield/Storm;
    -- $1.3 billion for economic assistance reported through the Gulf Crisis Financial Coordination Group;
    -- $822 million for U.K. Desert Shield/Storm;
    -- support for Turkey, including $1 billion in financial assistance, deployment of troops, aircraft and air defense batteries to Turkey; and
    -- support for Israel, including Patriot missiles and other assistance valued at $1 billion.

5. **United Arab Emirates:** The UAE pledged over $6 billion. This includes:

    -- $4 billion for U.S. Desert Shield/Storm;
    -- $1.4 billion in economic assistance reported through the Gulf Crisis Financial Coordination Group; and,
    -- $1 billion for European allies who participated in Desert Storm.

Summary of Disbursements

I'd also like to briefly review the status of disbursements:

1. **Saudi Arabia** has disbursed the bulk of its 1990 Desert Shield commitments particularly with regard to its cash commitments; the U.S. Government has transmitted our remaining 1990 transportation and in-theater expenses, which are being jointly reviewed. For 1991, the Saudis have disbursed nearly half of their $13.5 billion commitment and intend complete disbursement through payments at the end of May and June. With regard to economic assistance, the Saudis have disbursed 78 percent of their $4.7 billion Gulf Crisis Financial Coordination Group commitments.

2. **Kuwait** has met all of its 1990 Desert Shield commitments and 50 percent of its 1991 Desert Shield/Storm commitments. It has made six disbursements of over

0047

$1 billion toward its 1991 commitment. We expect that it will continue to make periodic payments until its $13.5 billion pledge is fully met. Kuwait also has disbursed nearly half of its $3.7 billion Gulf Crisis Financial Coordination Group commitments.

3. **Japan** has disbursed $9.4 billion to the U.S. in Desert Shield/Storm commitments. We are continuing to discuss with Japan how it can contribute towards our on-going military costs associated with the crisis. Japan has disbursed about $800 million of its Gulf Crisis Financial Coordination Group commitment.

4. **Germany** has disbursed all of its Desert Shield/Storm commitments. Germany's strong commitment to responsibility sharing was demonstrated by its very rapid disbursements of military financing in support of Desert Shield and Desert Storm. In late January Chancellor Kohl committed $5.5 billion for Desert Storm. Two months later, all of that amount had been deposited in the Defense Cooperation Account. Germany has disbursed $462 million of its Gulf Crisis Financial Coordination Group commitments.

5. The **United Arab Emirates** has disbursed nearly all of its $4 billion 1990 and 1991 Desert Shield/Storm commitments and all of its Gulf Crisis Financial Coordination Group economic assistance commitments.

6. **Korea**, in recognition of its global responsibilities, also contributed financially to offset our costs and has disbursed $154 million of its $385 million Desert Shield/Storm commitments. We expect a complete disbursement of Korea's commitment by the end of June after the Korean legislative process is completed.

The Administration is actively engaged in making sure that all the pledges made by our partners are rapidly disbursed. We believe the progress we have made to date is considerable. We are confident that the outstanding amounts will be disbursed soon.

Thank you, Mr. Chairman.

0048

주 미 대 사 관

미국(의) 700- 1509   1991. 7. 23.
수신 : 장 관
참조 : 중동아프리카국장, 미주국장, 국제기구조약국장
제목 : 이락의 유엔 결의안 준수 문제 관련 미의회 청문회 증언문

　　　　7.18. 미하원 구주.중동 소위(위원장 : Hamilton 의원)와 인권 국제기구
소위 (위원장 : Yatron 의원) 궁등 주최로 개최된 표제 청문회에 출석한 Thomas
Pickering 주유엔 미국대사 및 John R. Bolton 국무부 국제기구담당 차관보의
증언문을 별첨 숭부하니 참고하시기 바랍니다.

첨부 : 상기 증언문 2부.　　　　끝.

주 　　　　미 　　　　대

선 결			결재(공람)		
접수일시	1991. 1. 31	편호			
처리과	43106				

0049

Committee on Foreign Affairs
U.S. House of Representatives
Washington, DC 20515

July 12, 1991

<table>
<tr><td>Subcommittee on Europe and the
  Middle East
Hon. Lee Hamilton, Chairman</td><td>Subcommittee on Human Rights
  and International Organizations
Hon. Gus Yatron, Chairman</td></tr>
</table>

TO: **MEMBERS OF THE COMMITTEE ON FOREIGN AFFAIRS**

You are cordially invited to attend the following joint **OPEN MEETING** of the Subcommittee on Europe and the Middle East and the Subcommittee on Human Rights and International Organizations:

DATE: Thursday, July 18, 1991

TIME: 9:00 a.m.

PLACE: Room 2172 Rayburn House Office Building

SUBJECT: U.N. ROLE IN THE PERSIAN GULF AND IRAQI COMPLIANCE WITH U.N. RESOLUTIONS

WITNESSES: The Honorable Thomas R. Pickering
              U.S. Ambassador to the United Nations
              Department of State

              The Honorable John R. Bolton
              Assistant Secretary
              Bureau for International Organization Affairs
              Department of State

John J. Brady, Jr.
Chief of Staff

0050

STATEMENT OF AMBASSADOR THOMAS R. PICKERING
US PERMANENT REPRESENTATIVE TO THE UNITED NATIONS

before the

HOUSE OF REPRESENTATIVES FOREIGN AFFAIRS COMMITTEE

SUBCOMMITTEE ON HUMAN RIGHTS AND
INTERNATIONAL ORGANIZATIONS

and

SUBCOMMITTEE ON EUROPE
AND THE MIDDLE EAST

JULY 18, 1991

Chairman Yatron, Chairman Hamilton, Members of the Committees, I welcome this opportunity to address the Committees this morning and to report on the implementation of the major elements of the ceasefire agreement, Security Council resolution 687, reached last March between Iraq and the countries cooperating with Kuwait.

As you know, SC 687 represents a comprehensive program designed to assure Iraq's fulfillment of all resolutions occasioned by its invasion of Kuwait and to strengthen the basis for peace and security in the northern Persian Gulf. Its central provisions cover the following critical areas:

- elimination of nuclear, chemical, and biological weapons and weapons related activities, and of ballistic missiles;

- guidelines for the control of future arms sales to Iraq;

- modifications to and maintenance of the sanctions (embargoes) on Iraqi exports and imports;

- demarcation of the Iraq-Kuwait border;

- return of Kuwait and third country nationals;

- return of stolen Kuwaiti and other property;

- establishment of a compensation fund for direct loss or damage as a result of Iraqi aggression;

- creation of a demilitarized zone between Iraq and Kuwait and of a UN observer force to patrol it;

- and a commitment by Iraq that it will not in the future carry out or support acts of terrorism or terrorist organizations.

0051

Chairmen Yatron and Hamilton let me begin my remarks by offering the observation that our experience with the implementation of the ceasefire resolution has been sharply mixed. On the one hand, we have been very pleased with the effectiveness and professionalism with which the United Nations, its specialized agencies and the IAEA have embraced the many complicated and novel challenges required for implementation of resolution 687. But at the same time we have been repeatedly frustrated, and in the case of its nuclear program, dismayed, by a pattern of Iraqi behaviour ranging from delaying tactics in some areas - such as repatriation of people and property - to grave and outright violations of the ceasefire agreement in the area of Iraq's nuclear activities. Dealing effectively with Iraq's malfeasance has now become a central preoccupation of our efforts at the UN and of US foriegn policy itself. Let me therefore open my remarks with a summary of our concerns regarding Iraqi statements and actions in the nuclear area.

Iraqi Nuclear Activities

To ensure against the reemergence of an Iraqi nuclear threat to its neighbors and the region at large, the Security Council, acting through resolution 687, unconditionally bound Iraq:

- not to acquire or develop nuclear weapons or weapons usable material, or any subsystems, components, or any research, development support or manufacturing facilities;

- to disclose the locations, types and amounts of all the above items;

- to place all of its nuclear weapons usable material under the exclusive control, for custody and removal, of the IAEA;

- to accept urgent on-site inspections and the destruction, removal or rendering harmless of all items specified above;

- and to accept a plan for the future ongiong monitoring and verification of its compliance with these provisions.

Violations

- As Committee members are aware, we know now that Iraq has systematically violated every applicable injunction or prohibition I just listed. This is not the occasion to present an exhaustive record of Iraq's violations but let me try to summarize:

0052

- <u>Iraq has not fully disclosed its uranium enrichment and nuclear weapons capabilties</u>. Despite numerous letters and lists Iraq has not provided an accurate accounting of its nuclear activities. In our view Iraq's last such letters, the 29 page communication of July 7 and subsequent addenda are still incomplete. To take one example, Iraq failed to notify the UN of a major enrichment facility and still insists that it is a plant with a peaceful purpose.

- <u>Iraq has obstructed inspection efforts</u>. Baghdad repeatedly violated the May 6 agreement between the United Nations and the Government of Iraq, which detailed the rights, privileges, and immunities of the Special Commision and IAEA representatives. On June 23 and 25 at the Abu Gharaib site, and on June 28 at the Fallujah site, inspectors were denied access and the opportunity to photograph suspected nuclear areas, objects and related activities. Efforts were made to confiscate cameras, to intimidate by means of small arms fire and to deny urgent medical care to a team member. At both sites, objects to which inspectors sought access were removed before inspectors were permitted access. I should add that photographic evidence has led the IAEA to conclude that the removed material was clearly related to previously undeclared uranium enrichment activities. The Iraqis, realizing that their attempts at concealment have failed, have now admitted being engaged in a massive covert enrichment program.

- <u>High level team not satisfied</u>. A senior UN delegation was sent to Baghdad to exact commitments that would ensure immediate and unimpeded access to the objects sought on June 28. Iraq failed to give such commitments,

- <u>Iraq has denied the right to use air transport</u>. Notwithstanding their commitments to the contrary, Iraq has prevented inspection teams from using aircraft to support inspections, handicapping the teams' ability to conduct genuine challenge inspections outside the Baghdad area;

- <u>Iraq now admits having a secret program for uranium enrichment</u>. In its letter of July 7, Iraq acknowledged that it maintained an unsafeguarded, covert uranium enrichment program, involving three different processes for enriching uranium: electron magnetic isotopic separation (EMIS); ultra-centrifuge; and a chemical process. At the same time it has admitted producing no more than half a kilo of enriched uranium. The non-admission and continuation of this secret program, and the unilateral destruction of elements of the program violates Iraq's obligations under 687 as well as its safeguards responsibilities under the Nuclear Non-Proliferation Treaty and associated IAEA safeguards agreements. Inspection team members describe the EMIS program as "excellent quality, comparable in scope to the Manhattan Project" and estimate the total cost at $5 - $10 billion.

- **We believe Iraq sought nuclear weapons**. Iraq maintains that its extensive secret nuclear program was for peaceful purposes only. We and the IAEA disagree. As IAEA experts explained to the Security Council, the Iraqi's multi-billion dollar electro-magnetic enrichment program (EMIS), makes no sense as a peaceful program aimed at nuclear power development. As an IAEA expert later commented, powering a nuclear reactor by enriched uranium produced by this method would consume five times the energy which the reactor would create.

Next Steps

The foregoing list suggests, at a minimum, that Saddam has not gotten the message. He does not yet realize that the United Nations Security Council, and the United States in particular are "deadly serious", as President Bush said a week ago . But we are.

As an earnest of our seriousness we have joined with the other Permanent members of the Security Council to make the following unconditional demands upon Iraq:

1. That it provide by July 25, the full, final and complete disclosure required by resolution 687.

2. That it allow the Special Commission (UNSCOM), the IAEA and their inspection teams unhindered use of Iraqi airspace for insepction, transportation, logistics and surveillance purposes on terms they themselves shall establish.

3. That it allow UNSCOM, IAEA and their inspection teams immediate unconditional and unrestricted access to anything they wish to inspect.

4. That it cease movement immediately of any material or equipment related to its nuclear, chemical, biological or ballistic missile programs wihtout notification to and consent of UNSCOM.

5. That it immediately make available to IAEA, UNSCOM and their inspection teams any items to which they were previously denied access.

6. That it provide or facilitate immediately any transportation, medical and logistical support requested by UNSCOM, IAEA or their inspection teams.

7. That it respond fully, completely and promptly to any questions or requests from UNSCOM, IAEA, and their inspection teams.

Iraq must not miscalculate a second time. Its pattern of reckless defiance of the expressed will of the international community is intolerable. The United States, together with the other members of the Security Council are determined that it will not be allowed to continue.

Other Weapons of Mass Destruction

In addition to its intensive work in the nuclear area, the Special Commission has conducted numerous inspections and some destruction of other Iraqi weapons of mass destruction. In the case of ballistic missiles for example, a total of 61 have been inspected and destroyed, along with a quantity of launchers, related equipment, and production capacity. While this number represents all of Iraq's declared surviving missiles, our best estimates suggest a much larger number remain unaccounted for. UNSCOM 's inspections of designated suspected sites will therefore continue.

As you know, Iraq has denied that it manufactured or possesses biological weapons. Here again we have reason to believe this is false. UNSCOM will commence shortly inspections of sites it designates in order to test the Iraqi claim.

The chemical weapons effort is now fairly far along. UNSCOM has inspected one of 12 declared sites, confirmed the presence of hundreds of tons of previously declared bulk agent (nerve and blister) and thousands of filled munitions, including missile warheads, bombs and rockets. Its overall finding is that Iraq's chemical arsenal is subject to widespread leaking and overpressure and is generally in a highly unstable condition. UNSCOM is now preparing a destruction plan which will require bringing existing mobile and transportable disposal facilities from other countries to a central location in Iraq where the bulk agent and munitions will be brought for destruction.

UNSCOM Budget

The activities of UNSCOM not related to disposal work or longterm verification are expected to cost in excess of $35 million for 1991 alone. The removal and destruction of chemical and nuclear weapons related materials will cost many times this amount although a reasonably reliable estimate cannot be made until a destruction regime for chemical weapons -- the most problematic element -- is developed. However, projections on the order of $100 - $200 million have been made. These expenses are entirely due to the reckless and unlawful behavior of Iraq, hence the Security Council decided in resolution 699 that Iraq should bear the full costs of all activities carried out under the weapons of mass destruction section (c) of 687.

0055

This week, as requested by the Security Council, the Secretary General offered his recommendations for the most effective way of assuring payment. His report suggests an arrangement under which sanctions would be lifted for a limited period, under clearly defined conditions, to permit a supervised sale of oil or oil products. The proceeds of this sale would be deposited in a UN account and used to pay for the costs of carrying out the weapons of mass destruction section of resolution 687. While this or another arrangement chosen by the Security Council is being established, and in view of UNSCOM's need for immediate resources, resolution 699 encourages members to provide bridging assistance in cash and in kind. The US has already contributed $2 million dollars and a small number of vehicles, Japan has made a modest contribution and many other countries have provided in-kind support.

SANCTIONS

Directly related to the provisions on weapons of mass destruction are those dealing with the continuation of restrictions on exports to Iraq, and the prohibition on imports from Iraq. Regarding the former, you will recall that 687 eased the strictures of the then existing embargo by permitting the sale or supply of foodstuffs, with a notification to the Sanctions Committee. It also permitted sale or supply, on a "no objection" basis, of materials and supplies for "essential civilian needs" as identified in the March report of UN Under Secretary General Ahtisaari.

With the benefit of these changes, the Committee has, since March 22, received notifications of exporters' intentions to ship more than 2 million tons of foodstuffs to Iraq, or nearly one ton for every 9 Iraqis. This total does not include notifications to the Sanctions Committee in which actual amounts do not appear, nor does it include much of the food provided by coalition countries as part of Operation Provide Comfort. Using the "essential civilian needs" provision Iraq has also imported a wide variety of goods over a similar period, including fuel, generators, medicine and medical equipment, water pumps and water treatment systems, motor vehicles, temporary shelters, and so on.

While I'm on this subject let me say that the Sanctions Committee has routinely approved applications for provision of any equipment related to food production, water purification, sewage treatment, power generation or any other category integral to essential civilian needs which has been denied by the Sanctions Committee. Let me also add that a rapidly growing proportion of the above are commercial sales. This suggests that Baghdad has access to significant funds, notwithstanding official statements to the contrary.

0056

Finally, paragraph 21 of 687 provides for a Security Council review of Iraqi government policies and practices every 60 days to ascertain whether there should be a further lifting of restrictions on exports. The emphasis on "policies and practices" of the Iraqi government is intentionally broad so as to permit its application both to Iraqi fulfillment of 687 as well as to the government's treatment of its own population. At the first 60 day review, which took place last month, a majority of Council members believed Iraq's actions in both areas were unsatisfactory and the existing restrictions were maintained. In view of Iraq's violations and lack of good faith on nuclear weapons activities described a moment ago, we expect a similar result at the review coming up in August.

The 687 provision for exports from Iraq is very clear. It provides for the complete lifting of the embargo upon the satisfaction of two conditions : (1) fulfillment by Iraq of all its obligations under section (c) of 687, dealing with elimination of nuclear, chemical and biological weapons and ballistic missiles; and (2) approval by the Security Council of the Secretary General's proposals for dedicating a portion of the value of Iraqi petroleum exports to a compensation fund for the payment of claims against Iraq.

On May 20, the Security Council satisfied the second of these requirements by adopting, in resolution 692, the Secretary General's report proposing the establishment of a Compensation Fund and Commission. Unfortunately, Iraqi violations of 687's provisions on weapons of mass destruction, which I described a few moments ago, suggest that the first condition for renewed Iraqi exports is a very long way from being fulfilled.

You will recall that under paragraph 23 the ceasefire resolution also empowered the UN Sanctions Committee to approve exceptions to the prohibition on Iraqi exports when it can be shown that Iraq needs the additional revenue to meet essential civilian needs. This week the Committee received a report on conditions within Iraq prepared by the Secretary General's Executive Delegate Prince Sadruddin Aga Khan, as a consequence of which the Security Council may soon explore a measure permitting oil exports sufficient to generate resources to meet minimum humanitarian needs under full and complete United Nations control as suggested by Sadruddin Aga Khan.

I believe Assistant Secretary Bolton plans to address the Sadruddin report in some detail in his remarks, so I will focus on a related matter. Specifically, let me say that in the event the Security Council does adopt a paragraph 23 exception to sanctions to meet the legitimate humanitarian needs of the Iraqi population, we would want to protect two related concerns as well. First and foremost, we must continue to deny Saddam any

0057

external financial resources. This would necessitate a paragraph 23 regime that ensures total UN control over 100% of the proceeds of Iraqi oil sales and the purchases made with those proceeds. It must also impose strict monitoring to ensure equitable distribution of the food and humanitarian goods procured so that Saddam cannot continue his practice of diverting foodstuffs from the needy to his party and military loyalists. Second, we would be interested in developing a formula for allocating the revenues of Iraq's paragraph 23 sales among all the critical activities mandated by the ceasefire resolution for which Iraq is directly responsible, including the Special Commission budget.

Arms Embargo

Resolution 687 also called upon the Secretary General to develop guidelines for the reinforcement and continuation of the arms embargo against Iraq. Chemical, biological, and nuclear weapons weapons technology, and dual use technology, are permanently banned. Conventional weapons are also banned although with a provision for a review 4 months from the passage of 687 and regularly thereafter in the light of Iraqi compliance with 687 and regional progress towards arms control. In resolution 700, adopted on June 17, the Security Council accepted the Secretary General's proposed guidelines, requested member states to report within 45 days on measures taken to conform with them, and entrusted the Sanctions Committee with the task of monitoring compliance.

Compensation

Another central component of the ceasefire resolution was a provision calling for: a fund financed from Iraqi oil exports, to compensate those injured by Iraq's aggression; a settlement process to handle claims; and a Commission to manage the process and award payments. Last May, as required by 687, the Secretary General proposed a general plan for the organization and operation of the Governing Council which will administer the Fund as well as a specific number as the ceiling for the percentage of Iraqi exports of petroleum and petroleum products to be dedicated to the Fund.

The ceiling suggested by the Secretary General, 30%, was lower than the 50% favored by the United States which we believe is warranted by the need to assure rapid settlement of claims against Iraq, by the need to allow for windfall gains that could accompany a sharp increase in oil prices, and by the speed at which we believe Iraq could recover its oil production capability. Nevertheless, we could accept the 30% level so long as 30% is also the portion of oil export revenues actually dedicated to the Compensation Fund.

0058

While neither the Executive Secretary nor any of the Commissioners of the Fund have been appointed, we expect appointments shortly and are expressing our views regarding qualified candidates. The Geneva-based Governing Council will be holding its first session on July 23 which is scheduled to last for two weeks.

The Belgian member has been selected to serve as Council President. Regarding the agenda of this first session, one of our chief concerns is that the Council will treat settlement of claims by individuals as a priority and to that end will use this first meeting to adopt simple criteria for their submission.

Boundary Demarcation

Resolution 687 demanded that Iraq and Kuwait respect the inviolability of the boundary to which both agreed in 1963 and sought the assistance of the Secretary General for its demarcation. The first Geneva meetings of the demarcation commission set up by the Secretary General concluded July 12. After initial obstructionist tactics by the Iraqi delegate, the commission succeeded in deciding the western boundary of Kuwait and also made progress on the northern boundary. The off-shore border is slated to be on the agenda of the commission's August session. Once this phase is complete the commission will move to the actual physical emplacement of markers on a boundary line. This process, which is of course climate dependent, could start as early as September and is likely to rely to some extent on marker placement by helicopter in view of the continuing hazard of land mines.

Return of Kuwaiti and other Nationals

As you will recall, the ceasefire resolution reconfirms Iraq's responsibility, in cooperation with the ICRC, to repatriate and account for all Kuwaitis and third country nationals being held in Iraq. Over the past several months Iraq has been releasing these people in fairly small numbers on a more or less regular basis, but Iraq has not yet fulfilled its responsibilties under resolution 687. While the ICRC and Kuwait cannot state with absolute precision the number of Kuwaitis and third country nationals (claiming Kuwaiti residence) still held in Iraq, the best estimates are that there are as many as 1700 Kuwaitis and 1900 third country nationals from more than 20 states.

0053

Return of Property

The return of Kuwaiti property has moved at a slow and frustrating pace, explained in part by the disarray in Iraq itself but also in our view by delay tactics on the part of Baghdad. The sides appear to have agreed to carry out the transfers at Arar in western Saudi Arabia and have also agreed that the contents of the first property restitution shall be gold, coins and bank notes. Discussions concerning the second transfer are now proceeding and it appears that this will involve either military hardware, which Iraq says it has inventoried, or museum pieces. Unfortunately, the Iraqi government introduced a further complication by attempting to argue that the logistics of the transfer operation required the release of Iraqi fixed wing aircraft which were detained outside the country as required by Security Council decision. The Sanctions Committee has rejected this gambit and United Nations officials are now exploring alternative means for transporting the stolen property to the transfer point.

UNIKOM

One of the early successes made possible by the ceasefire resolution has been the establishment of the demilitarized zone between Iraq and Kuwait and an observer unit to patrol it. Established April 8th, under Security Council resolution 689, the United Nations Iraq-Kuwait Observation Mission (UNIKOM) drew participants from 32 countries. UNIKOM's original complement of more than 1400 personnel included 640 infantry temporarily assigned to provide security for the observer units until stability returned to the border area. UNIKOM's early success in restoring calm however, made possible the withdraw of the infantry companies ahead of schedule. The mine clearing activities of the observer force have also been progressing well, with the focus of UNIKOM's efforts now directed primarily to the southwestern sector where the borders of Iraq, Kuwait and Saudi Arabia meet. Violations of the DMZ are now minimal and typically involve nationals of Kuwait or Iraq who either lose their way or make use of the mine-cleared areas to traverse the border safely.

Terrorism

On June 11 Iraq presented letters to the Security Council President and the Secretary General in fulfillment of resolution 687's demand for an official Iraqi statement forswearing terrorism. While making the patently false assertion that Iraq has never pursued a policy favorable to international terrorism, the text does fulfill the requirements of this provision of 687 and conforms with recent General Assembly resolutions on the subject.

0060

Resolution 688 and Humanitarian Issues

The humanitarian situation in Iraq in general and Saddam's actions toward the Kurds and Shia in particular are matters of grave and immediate concern which are directly relevant to the subject of this hearing. However, as I noted earlier in my remarks these subjects are treated at length in the testimony you will shortly receive from Assistant Secretary Bolton, so with your permission I will omit humanitarian issues from my prepared remarks, although of course I will be happy to accept your questions.

Conclusion

In conclusion I want to return to the issue of Iraqi compliance because it is impossible to overstate the importance which the United States attaches to it. Iraq's failure to fulfill the provisions of 687, particularly relating to its weapons of mass destruction and its nuclear activities, are serious violations of the ceasefire that would directly imperil international peace and security in the area. Furthermore, non-compliance would unhinge the capacity of 687 to serve as a foundation stone for a new structure of peace and security in the region, one of the reasons we and so many others fought a painful and costly war. Finally it would have the transcendently poisonous effect of subverting the respect for international law so long sought and so dearly won. Let there be no mistake, defiance of the ceasefire cannot and will not be tolerated. Thank you.

0061

PREPARED STATEMENT OF JOHN R. BOLTON

ASSISTANT SECRETARY

INTERNATIONAL ORGANIZATION AFFAIRS

DEPARTMENT OF STATE

before the

HUMAN RIGHTS AND INTERNATIONAL ORGANIZATIONS SUBCOMMITTEE

and

EUROPE AND MIDDLE EAST SUBCOMMITTEE

of the

HOUSE FOREIGN AFFAIRS COMMITTEE

JULY 18, 1991

0062

Thank you, Mr. Chairman. I am pleased to have the opportunity to bring you and the other members of the Subcommittee up to date on the implementation of UN Security Council Resolution 687 and related matters.

In my last appearance here in April, I explained how the UN system would go about implementing this resolution which is the most far reaching and ambitious in scope of any adopted by the Security Council. At that point, because this resolution had only just been adopted, our discussion was mostly theoretical. Now, however, all aspects of the resolution including withdrawal of forces, interposition of the UN observers in UNIKOM, demarcation of the boundary, return of citizens, return of stolen assets, compensation, disclosure and destruction of nuclear, chemical and biological weapons of mass destruction as well as ballistic missiles with ranges in excess of 150 kilometers capable of delivering such weapons, have either totally or partially been implemented by the United Nations. Iraqi compliance, however, has been problematic, as you know, with regard to inspection of its nuclear program. The UN/IAEA task has been made extremely difficult by Saddam Hussein's continued intransigence and efforts to evade the requirements imposed on Iraq by the international community; I will discuss that later. As for the UN, I am pleased to be able to report the UN is performing completely up to specification, and enjoys the full confidence and support of the United States. We continue to believe that working with our partners in the UN Security Council and the international coalition under the framework of Resolution 687, as well as 688, is the most effective manner of holding Hussein in check and preventing his regime from continuing as a threat to Iraq's neighbors and to its own people.

Border Demarcation: The Border Commission was mandated under Resolution 687 to demarcate the international border between by Iraq and Kuwait, which was declared and guaranteed in UNSC Resolution 687. The Border Commission made its first trip to the border and began its first formal meeting in Geneva to discuss its findings on July 2. The methodology to be used in marking the western portion of the border, on the approximate location of the boundary in the vicinity of Safwan, and on further surveying and mapping were decided. Further surveying by a joint Sweden-New Zealand team will be carried out this fall. The next round of talks is scheduled for August 12. The Border Commission is comprised of representatives from Iraq and Kuwait and members from three neutral nations: Sweden, New Zealand, and Indonesia.

0064

UNIKOM: The UN Iraq-Kuwait Observer Mission is deployed and functioning smoothly. The armed infantry units which provided security for the Observers at the outset of their mission have been withdrawn and will not be replaced.

Return of missing Kuwaiti citizens: The International Committee of the Red Cross (ICRC) is working with Kuwait and Iraq to identify and repatriate Kuwaitis still being held in Iraq. We do not know the exact number of these persons.

Return of stolen property: UN Assistant Secretary General Foran is in the process of finalizing transfer of stolen gold, coins and banknotes from Iraq to Kuwait. He is working out transportation problems related to the return of the gold. Although Iraq is required to provide an inventory of looted cultural property, and facilitate its quick return to Kuwait, there has been little progress made on this aside from vague Iraqi assurances given to the UN.

Compensation: The Security Council has approved the Secretary General's proposal to establish a Compensation Commission. The Commission will be composed of a Governing Council (which is comprised of the 15 UNSC members) and experts who will establish mechanisms to compensate those who suffered losses and damages as a result of Iraq's illegal invasion and

0065

occupation of Kuwait. The Governing Council of the Commission
will establish the actual percentage of Iraq's eventual oil export
revenues to be made available for such compensation. The Security
Council, which must establish a ceiling for the percentage, has not
yet done so. The U.S. could support a ceiling lower than 50% as we
originally wanted, as long as the actual amount paid into the
Compensation Fund be set initially at 30%. We believe this will
leave Iraq ample funds to pay for its humanitarian and essential
civilian needs, particularly since Iraq is barred by Resolution 687
from the huge military expenditures it had made in the past.

The first meeting of the Compensation Fund's Governing
Council (made up of representatives from Security Council
members) will be held at the end of July. We hope the Governing
Council will focus at that meeting on its highest priority tasks: 1)
establishing procedures for the flow of contributions into the fund
and their use by the Commission, and 2) actions needed to begin
work on the most urgent claims.

Weapons of Mass Destruction: The Security Council is
actively discussing how to deal with Iraq's blatant deception
concerning its nuclear program, including its uranium enrichment
program. The Iraqis have tried to thwart the work of the IAEA and
the Special Commission established under

0066

Resolution 687 which is made up of experts from several countries. Iraq has lied to the UN and the IAEA about the existence of its uranium enrichment program and attempted to hide equipment related to that program from the IAEA/Special Commission inspection team. Iraq finally admitted it had a uranium enrichment program, but information it provided about that effort we believe contains significant omissions about its extent and nature. The Commission's chairman is a distinguished Swedish diplomat, Ambassador Rolf Ekeus, who has considerable expertise in arms control issues. Its deputy Chairman is an American, Dr. Robert Gallucci. The IAEA and the Special Commission are charged with working together to carry out the task of identifying and destroying or rendering harmless Iraq's nuclear-weapons related capabilities. The Special Commission has a similar task for Iraq's chemical and biological weapons-related capabilities, and its ballistic missiles.

In May, as required by Resolution 687, Iraq submitted to the UN a letter declaring all of its nuclear, chemical and biological weapons material and productions facilities. However, this letter, as proven by subsequent events, fell far short of reality. Given Iraq's demonstrated willingness to attempt to deceive the UN, we do not accept as complete or accurate Iraq's July 8 letter which, among other things admits

0067

to a considerable uranium enrichment program. This letter was submitted only after a Security Council directive to comply fully with UNSC Resolution 687 and the visit of high level UN and IAEA officials following Iraqi interference with inspections at two facilities (including movement of equipment the team had asked to inspect). We do not accept Iraqi "assurances" that the activities disclosed in the most recent letter were for "peaceful uses." As provided under the terms of Resolution 687, the Special Commission/IAEA are continuing their inspections program to monitor and verify the full disclosure and destruction of all of Iraq's weapons of mass destruction.

Iraq's deceptions concerning its nuclear related activities call into question its declarations concerning chemical and biological weapons. As for ballistic missiles, an inspection team has witnessed the destruction of 61 ballistic missiles which Iraq declared in its first letter to the UN. The team will continue its inspections of suspect sites until the Security Council is satisfied that all of Iraq's capability and existing ballistic missiles arsenal have been fully declared and destroyed or rendered harmless.

The role and performance of the IAEA/Special Commission in grappling with the thorny problem of disposing of

0068

Iraq's illicit nuclear capability has some positive implications for a stronger UN role in the issue of nuclear non-proliferation. What the international community learns from this experience may be applied if future aggressors attempt to develop nuclear weapons. It is an example of how the entire UN system needs to be involved in the international community's efforts to maintain international peace and stability.

Iraq's policies and practices: Under the terms of Resolution 687 the Security Council is to review Iraq's policies and practices every 60 days to determine if they warrant an easing of sanctions. The Security Council at the end of June undertook its first review and decided not to relax the sanctions regime. Subsequent events have born out the wisdom of that decision. Iraq has a request pending before the Sanctions Committee to be allowed to sell $1.5 billion of oil in order to pay for food, medicine and other humanitarian items. The Sanctions Committee has deferred consideration of that request pending a full disclosure from Iraq of its present foreign exchange holdings and other relevant financial information.

Sanctions: Iraq's violations of Resolution 687 regarding its nuclear program underscore the need to maintain

0069

the sanctions regime against Iraq. We have been keeping a close eye on reports of food shortages in Iraq, particularly among children and other vulnerable groups. As President Bush has repeatedly made clear, we are very sensitive to the plight of innocent civilians under Saddam Hussein's brutal regime, and the hardships it imposes on them.

Resolution 687 permits import of purchased or donated food, medicine and supplies for essential civilian needs. We understand that prices for certain commodities are very high and there are pockets of malnutrition. The summer grain harvest now underway could provide significant relief for a few months. There are reports that wider food shortages could be in the offing later this year.

To the extent that food is not getting to the Iraqi population most at risk, one major cause is the cynical manipulation of food stocks by Saddam Hussein's government. Last month the UN reported the diversion by Iraqi authorities of a World Food Program shipment intended for hungry children, and other genuinely needy groups. Instead the food was sent to Saddam's home town where there is not a pressing need. Saddam is diverting food to his loyalists in the Baathist party and to certain military units.

0070

A study on the needs of the Iraqi population by two Tufts University nutritionists commissioned by UNICEF concluded that although malnutrition was a problem in Iraq, particularly in the South, it was an endemic and long-standing one caused by Iraqi policies and methods of distributing food, rather than an actual shortfall of food supplies in the country as a whole.

On Monday, Prince Sadruddin Aga Khan the UN Executive Delegate submitted his report. It highlights pressing needs of Iraq's civilian population. The President has made it quite clear that there has never been any question of our willingness to feed vulnerable groups in Iraq. At the same time, Saddam Hussein has provided ample evidence of his willingness to exploit the good will of the international community and those who are genuinely concerned over the plight of innocent Iraqis. Food has been exempted from the sanctions régime since March 22. Medicine has never been subject to sanctions, and tons of medical supplies have flowed into Iraq before, during and after hostilities, thanks to the efforts of the International Committee of the Red Cross, UNICEF and other relief groups.

Iraq does possess foreign exchange that can be used for the purchase of imported commodities. Recently, the Iraqi government contracted to purchase 100,000 tons of grain from

Australia. The key requirement remains for the government of
Iraq to distribute these supplies equitably to those people who have
been identified in Sadruddin's report.

Additionally, the Sanctions Committee has notified
countries holding frozen Iraqi assets that Resolution 687 does not
require them to continue to do so and that they are free to release
such assets so that they may be used to purchase food, medicine
and other humanitarian materials as specified in 687. We are
aware of the amendment sponsored by Mr. Penny which would
release Iraq's assets held in the United States so that they could be
turned over to UNICEF and used to purchase humanitarian items
for Iraqi civilians. We oppose releasing Iraqi assets frozen in this
country at this time. There are many legitimate claims against
those resources by U.S. citizens, and sorting that out will be a
lengthy and difficult process. Finally, President Bush has made it
clear that he would not lift sanctions against Iraq while Saddam
Hussein was in power.

Given Saddam's demonstrated capacity and willingness
to turn international good will to his own sinister purposes, it is
clear that simply relaxing sanctions to allow the government of
Iraq to obtain humanitarian supplies will not alleviate the
suffering of those in need. Any mechanism

0072

developed to provide essential supplies to the people of Iraq must therefore include strict control and close monitoring. This in turn will require an extensive UN presence and Iraqi non-interference, so that supplies provided do not bolster Saddam's political control, and reach those targeted groups for whom they are intended.

The UN has responded effectively to the numerous humanitarian emergencies wrought through Saddam's savage policies directed at his own population. The UN Humanitarian Plan of Action issued on May 15 appeals for $449 million, including $65 million for the World Food Program. At a pledging conference held by the UN on June 12, I announced an additional U.S. contribution of $61.7 million for humanitarian relief in Iraq including $30.6 million for the WFP. This contribution brings the total U.S. humanitarian effort since January 1 to some $442 million, of which some $102.5 million has been provided through international organizations.

During his assessment mission last week, Sadruddin made it a priority to personally visit Southern Iraq where it had been reported thousands of Shiites were trapped in marshes surrounded by heavily armed Iraqi military forces. The Iraqi authorities managed to delay his inspection of this area until

0073

this military force had been withdrawn, but Sadruddin
nevertheless insisted that the UN be allowed to establish a food
distribution center with a detachment of UN guards. We hope this
UN presence near the marshes will provide a degree of assurance
to the population in Southern Iraq and allow them to return to
their homes permanently. We have reminded the Iraqis of their
obligations under Resolution 688 not to interfere with relief efforts
intended for this particularly vulnerable group of people.

The UN assumed responsibility for relief efforts in
Northern Iraq on June 7 after the major success of coalition relief
operations, and coalition forces have redeployed. UN
Humanitarian centers are located in Dohuk, Mosul, Zakhu,
Sulaymanieh, and Erbil. We estimate that some 400,000 returnees
have been assisted at these relief points.

As a confidence building measure, and to maintain a clear
international monitoring presence in Iraq, a UN guard force of 500
is being deployed throughout Iraq, near to population centers which
have been threatened by the Iraqi government. As of July 11, 271
of these guards have been deployed. The U.S. has contributed $5
million in cash and $1 million in kind to the force. The EC has
pledged to make up cash or personnel shortfalls.

0074

Throughout Iraq there are at present 642 international workers with the UN or private agencies supporting the UN. These staff, in addition to their regular duties, serve as witnesses and therefore help to deter further Iraqi depredations on civilians. We are fully aware, however, that neither these courageous individuals nor the UN guard force could cope with a determined Iraqi assault. To deal with that contingency we and the coalition will maintain an appropriate level of forces in the region. Saddam Hussein must know that the coalition is willing to respond militarily to Iraqi actions that disturb the peace.

An estimated 278,000 refugees from Iraq remain in Iran. The UN, working closely with the government of Iran and the Iranian Red Crescent, maintains an active presence. We are supporting the UN operation in Iran through our contributions to UN agencies.

In conclusion Mr. Chairman, let me reiterate our full confidence in the UN to carry out the complex and challenging

0075

requirements of Resolution 687. It is a job which requires the continuing full support of the international community, but when it has been successfully completed the entire UN system will have demonstrated a new found effectiveness. We hope to be able to build upon that success so that the UN can emerge a strengthened organization as it enters the next century.

0076

관리 번호	9-1687

외 무 부

종 별 : 긴 급

번 호 : USW-3786   일 시 : 91 0730 1840

수 신 : 장관(미일,미이,중동일,기정,국방부)

발 신 : 주 미 대사

제 목 : 걸프전 기여금 관련 하원 청문회

　　1. 하원 세입위(위원장:ROSTENKOWSKI 의원)는 명 7.31 오전 표제 청문회 (FOREIGN CONTRIBUTIONS TO GULF WAR COSTS)를 개최할 예정임.

　　2. 동 청문회에는 JOHN DINGELL (D-미시간), PETE STARK (D-캘리포니아), BYRON DORGAN (D-노스다코타)하원의원과 RICHARD DARMAN 연방예산국장이 증인으로 출석할 예정이며, MCALLISTER 국무부 경제차관보, HOLLIS MCLAUGHLIN 재무부 정책기획 차관보, SEAN O'KEEFE 국방부 회계감사관 및 FRANK CONAHAN GAO 감사관등이 패널리스트로 출석예정인바, 동청문회 내용 추보 하겠음.

　　(대사 현홍주-국장)

　　예고:91.12.31 까지

미주국	장관	차관	미주국	중아국	정와대	안기부	국방부

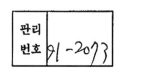

외　무　부

관리
번호 91-2073

종　별 : 지급

번　호 : USW-3822　　　　　　　　　　　일　시 : 91 0731 1959

수　신 : 장관(미일,미이),사본국방부장관

발　신 : 주 미대사

제　목 : 걸프전 전비 분담 관계 하원 청문회 개최

　　1. 금 7.31 하원 세입위 는 걸프전 전비 부담 현황및 의무 강제 이행을 위한 법령 제정 필요 여부 토의를 위한 청문회를 개최하였는바, 동 결과 아래 보고함.

　　가. 동 청문회는 강력한 의무 이행을 촉구하는 법안을 추진중인 DORGAN, STARK, DINGELL 의원이 증인으로 참석하여 주로 사우디와 쿠웨이트의 추가 부담 필요성 강조와 미.일 정상회담시 부시 대통령의 일본의 전비 부담 문제 종결 언급 경위를 추궁하였으며, 금번 BURDEN-SHARING 이 향후 우방국의 방위비 분담 증가의 모델이 되어야 될것을 강조하였는바, 특이 발언 내용 아래 임.

　　O BYRON DORGAN 의원(민주, ND)

　　-일본과 독일은 전체 전비의 25 프로와 15 프로씩을 부담토록 함으로서 현재보다 100 억불 부담 추가

　　-현금 보유고가 많은 사우디, 쿠웨이트등 중동 부국은 300 억불을 즉시 지불해야 하며, 미이행시 수입 제품에 관세 부과

　　-금번 협력 관계를 기초로 미국의 대외 군사 부담이 전면 조정되어야 하며, 일본의 경우 현행 방위비 부담률(주일 미군 주둔비 관련) 40 프로를 70 프로로 대폭 조정하고, 구주의 경우 현재 30 만명의 미군 주둔 수준을 15 만명선으로 축소

　　-독일 헌법 개정을 통해 유엔 평화 유지군 참여 촉구

　　-한국의 경우 위협적인 북한의 존재로 대폭적인 미군 삭감은 불가하다고 인정 되나, 대신 최근 대미 흑자 40 억불의 일부를 주한 미군 유지를 위해 사용하여야 할것이며, 한국측의 성의 있는 이행이 없는 경우 대폭적인 미군 주둔 삭감

　　O PETE STARK(민주, 캘리포니아)

　　-전비 부담 미이행국에 대해서는 걸프만 석유 의존 비율에 따라 수입 관세를 부과

　　나. 행정부측 증언 내용

미주국 국방부	차관	1차보	2차보	미주국	외정실	분석관	청와대	안기부

91.08.02　01:05

외신 2과 통제관 CF
0078

O DARMAN 예산 국장등 행정부측 증인들은 7.29 현재 각국 부담금 현황 및 일본의 지원액 조정 경위 설명을 마친후 금번 우방국들의 협조가 만족할만한것이었으며, 미수금의 확보에 대해서도 낙관적인 견해를 표명하면서 91 년 및 92 년 회계 년도 예산 확보 문제에 영향을 미치지 않을것이라고 답변하였음.

O 아울러 사우디와 쿠웨이트등 체납국에 대한 의무 확보 를 위한 TIME-TABLE 구상 계획은 없으며, 전후 경제 복구의 어려움을 안고 있는 양국의 입장을 고려, 다각적인 실무 교섭을 진행중이고 답변하였음.

다. 대아국 관련 업급

O MARTY RUSSO(민주-일리노이)의원은 질의 응답 과정에서 체납국인 한국에 대한 무기 수출 추진은 걸프전비 체납국에 대한 무기 수출 금지를 규정한 미공법 102-28(일명 BYRD 수정안)에 저촉된다고 언급하면서, 동법 109 조에 규정된 -FULLFILL COMMITMENTS- 에 대한 행정부의 해석을 문의하였음.

O 동 답변에서 MCALLISTER 국무부 경제 차관보는 동 규정은 약속액의 완불을 의미하지 않고 약속 이행의- 과정-으로 인식하고 있으며, 한국의 경우 의무 이행이 충실히 준수되고 있으므로 한국에 대한 무기 판매가 109 조에 반하는것으로 보지 않고 있다고 언급하고 부시 대통령도 F-16 기의 대한 판매가 적절한것으로 생각하고 있다고 답변하였음.

2. 당관 평가

가. 금번 청문회는 일차적으로 전체 체납금 78.9 억불의 96 프로를 차지하고 있는 사우디와 쿠웨이트에 대한 미수금 확보를 위한 영향력 행사와 일본에 대한 행정부의 보다 강력한 입장 고수 축구에 주안점이 있는것으로 보이나, 궁극적으로는 금번 우방국의 공동 전비 부담을 성공적인 MODEL 로 삼아 향후 주요 우방국에 대한 미국의 방위비 부담 비율을 상당한 수준으로 절감시키려는 구체적인 노력이 의회측에서 다각적으로 이루어질것으로 예상됨.

나. 아국 체납금 문제는 금번 청문회에서는 행정부측의 확고한 입장 표명으로 크게 문제시 되지는 않았으나, 사우디와 쿠웨이트의 체납금이 계속 지체될 경우 재론될 가능성이 있음.

3. 상기 증언문 및 제출 법안은 파편 송부 예정임.

(대사 현홍주-국장)

91.12.31 일반

PAGE 2

長 官 報 告 事 項

題 目 : 걸프戰費 執行關聯 美 議會 聽聞會

7.31(水) 美 下院歲出委는 友邦國의 걸프戰費 執行現況 및 未 執行額의
執行 加速化를 위한 法令制定 必要性 與否를 討議키 위해 聽聞會를 開催한
바, 同 結果를 아래 報告드립니다.

---

1. 聽聞會 開催 目的

ㅇ 걸프전 관련 우방국의 공동 전비부담을 성공사례로 삼아, 향후 주요
   우방국들의 방위비 부담 비율을 증가시키려는 미 의회측 노력의 일환임.
   - 우방국들의 걸프전비 기여 약속액 535억불중 체납금 78억9천만불의
     96%를 체납중인 사우디 및 쿠웨이트에 대한 약속이행 압력행사가
     주목적

2. 韓國關聯 論議內容

ㅇ Marty Russo(민주, IL)의원은 약속액 전액을 집행치 않은 한국에 대한
   무기수출은 Byrd 수정안에 저촉된다 언급하고 미 행정부의 견해를
   문의함.
   - McCallister 국무부 경제차관보는 한국의 경우 의무이행을 충실히
     준수하고 있으므로 버드 수정안 적용대상이 아니며, KFP 사업은
     적절한 것으로 생각한다는 점을 분명히 함.

0080

o   Dorgan 의원(민주, ND)은 한국의 경우, 북한 위협이 상존하고 있으므로
     대폭적인 주한미군의 감축은 불가하나 최근의 대미흑자 40억불의 일부를
     주한미군 유지를 위해 사용되어야 함을 주장함.

3.   美 行政府 答辯內容

o   7.29. 현재 우방국들의 걸프전비 집행관련 협조는 만족할 만한 수준임.
     - 체납금의 집행 계속에도 낙관적인 견해 표명

o   대표적 체납국인 사우디 및 쿠웨이트등의 전후 경제복구 노력에 따른
     어려움을 감안, 다각적인 실무교섭을 진행중임을 언급   - 끝 -

0081

주 미 대 사 관

미국(의) 700-1603   1991. 8. 2.
수신 : 장   관
참조 : 미주국장
제목 : 걸프전 전비 분담 관련 청문회 증언문

       연 : USW - 3822

       연호 걸프전 전비 분담 관계 하원 세입위 청문회 증언문 및 관련법안을
별첨 송부합니다.

       첨부 : 상기 증언문 및 법안 사본 각 1부.   끝.

                 주   미   대

0082

I

102D CONGRESS
1ST SESSION

H.R.317

To impose additional duties on the products of foreign countries if, and during such time as, such countries do not make sufficient contributions to the multinational military mobilization and operations being carried out in response to the invasion of Kuwait by Iraq.

IN THE HOUSE OF REPRESENTATIVES

JANUARY 3, 1991

Mr. DINGELL (for himself, Mr. FORD of Michigan, Mr. EVANS, Mr. MARKEY, Mr. FRANK of Massachusetts, Mr. STAGGERS, Mr. HAYES of Illinois, Mr. ESPY, Mr. BRYANT, Mr. BONIOR, Mr. CLEMENT, Mr. JONTZ, Mr. SANGMEISTER, and Mr. KANJORSKI) introduced the following bill; which was referred to the Committee on Ways and Means

---

A BILL

To impose additional duties on the products of foreign countries if, and during such time as, such countries do not make sufficient contributions to the multinational military mobilization and operations being carried out in response to the invasion of Kuwait by Iraq.

1   *Be it enacted by the Senate and House of Representa-*

2 *tives of the United States of America in Congress assembled,*

3 **SECTION 1. SHORT TITLE.**

4   This Act may be cited as the "Desert Shield Burden-

5 Sharing Act of 1991".

★

0083

1 **SEC. 2. DEFINITIONS.**

2   For purposes of this Act:

3   (1) The term "commensurate contribution"

4 means, in the case of a foreign country, that—

5   (A) such country is making a contribution

6 to the multinational military mobilization and

7 operations referred to in section 3; and

8   (B) such contribution is commensurate

9 with—

10   (i) the extent of the economic benefit

11 accruing to such country as a result of the

12 securing of supplies of Persian Gulf area

13 petroleum through such military mobiliza-

14 tion and operations, and

15   (ii) the ability of such country to con-

16 tribute, taking into account (in addition to

17 such other factors as the President consid-

18 ers relevant) the financial and economic

19 capabilities of the country and the balance

20 of trade of such country with the United

21 States.

22   (2) The term "entered" means entered, or with-

23 drawn from warehouse for consumption, in the cus-

24 toms territory of the United States.

25   (3) The term "foreign country" does not in-

26 clude any country that—

HR 317 IH1S

0084

1   (A) is party to a free trade area agreement

2   with the United States;

3   (B) is a beneficiary developing country

4   under title V of the Trade Act of 1974 (relating

5   to a generalized system of preferences); or

6   (C) is a beneficiary country under the Car-

7   ibbean Basin Economic Recovery Act.

8 **SEC. 3. PRESIDENTIAL DETERMINATIONS REGARDING**

9   **MULTINATIONAL CONTRIBUTIONS TO THE**

10   **MILITARY MOBILIZATION AND OPERATIONS**

11   **AGAINST IRAQI AGGRESSION.**

12   Within 60 days after the date of the enactment of

13 this Act, the President shall determine whether each for-

14 eign country is making a commensurate contribution to

15 the multinational military mobilization and operations

16 being carried out in and around the Arabian Peninsula

17 in response to the invasion of Kuwait by the armed forces

18 of Iraq on August 2, 1990.

19 **SEC. 4. ADDITIONAL DUTIES ON PRODUCTS OF COUNTRIES**

20   **DETERMINED NOT TO BE MAKING COMMEN-**

21   **SURATE CONTRIBUTIONS.**

22   (a) IMPOSITION OF ADDITIONAL DUTIES.—Subject

23 to subsection (b), the President shall, with respect to any

24 foreign country that is determined under section 3 not to

25 be making a commensurate contribution to the multi-

1 national military mobilization and operations referred to

2 in such section—

3   (1) apply to all of the dutiable products of that

4   country an additional duty at the rate of 20 percent

5   ad valorem or the specific rate equivalent; and

6   (2) apply to all duty-free products of that coun-

7   try a duty of 20 percent ad valorem.

8   (b) SPECIAL PROVISIONS.—(1) The duties imposed

9 under subsection (a) (1) and (2) on the products of a for-

10 eign country apply with respect to articles entered on or

11 after the 30th day after the date on which the determina-

12 tion under section 3 regarding such country is made.

13   (2) Duties may not be applied under subsection (a)

14 (1) or (2) on—

15   (A) articles that are duty-free; and

16   (B) the value of articles or contents of United

17   States origin that are exempt from duty;

18 under chapter 98 of the Tariff Schedule of the United

19 States.

20   (c) TERMINATION OF ADDITIONAL DUTIES.—The

21 duties imposed under subsection (a) (1) and (2) on the

22 products of any foreign country shall cease to apply effec-

23 tive with respect to articles entered on or after the date

24 on which—

HR 317 IH1S

1   (1) the President determines that such country

2   is making a commensurate contribution to the multi-

3   national military mobilization and operations re-

4   ferred to in section 3; or

5   (2) such military mobilization and operations

6   are terminated.

7 **SEC. 5. DISPOSITION OF ADDITIONAL DUTIES.**

8   (a) IN GENERAL.—There is established in the Treas-

9 ury of the United States a fund to be known as the Desert

10 Shield Reimbursement Fund which shall be available, sub-

11 ject to appropriation Acts, only for the reimbursement of

12 appropriations made to support the United States partici-

13 pation in the military mobilization and operations referred

14 to in section 3.

15   (b) DEPOSITS.—There shall be deposited into the

16 Fund established under subsection (a) all duties collected

17 pursuant to section 4.

18 **SEC. 6. REPORT.**

19   No later than the 180th day after the date of the

20 enactment of this Act, the President shall submit to the

21 Congress a report on the implementation of this Act, in-

22 cluding, with respect to each foreign country the products

23 of which are subject to duties imposed under section 4(a)

24 (1) and (2), the bases for the determination made under

1 section 3 regarding that country and the amounts col-

2 lected by reason of such duties.

O

0088

102D CONGRESS
1ST SESSION

H. J. RES. 292

Expressing the sense of Congress that the Republic of Hungary has embraced
democracy and renounced socialist rule.

IN THE HOUSE OF REPRESENTATIVES

JUNE 27, 1991

Mr. COX of California (for himself, Mr. THOMAS of Wyoming, Mr. WALKER,
Ms. ROS-LEHTINEN, Mr. DOOLITTLE, Mr. ROTH, Mr. IRELAND, Mr.
STEARNS, Mr. HANCOCK, Mr. BALLENGER, Mr. GINGRICH, Mr. KYL, Mr.
VANDER JAGT, Mr. ROHRABACHER, Mr. HORTON, Mr. PAYNE of Virgin-
ia, Mr. LENT, Mr. DUNCAN, Mr. MACHTLEY, Mr. PAXON Mr. DWYER of
New Jersey, Mr. KLUG, Mr. FROST, and Mr. DELAY) introduced the fol-
lowing joint resolution; which was referred to the Committee on Foreign
Affairs

Whereas Hungary—during its history of more than a thousand years—has enriched Western culture;

Whereas Hungary has displayed courage in preserving its integrity and defending its independence from foreign powers, including Nazi occupying forces;

Whereas the Soviet Union, contrary to its international obligations, occupied Hungarian territory in 1947, annihilat-
ed Hungarian sovereignty and arrested Hungary's attempts to rejoin the free world;

Whereas the Hungarian Communist party seized power and
created a one-party dictatorship by force in 1947-48—
with active Soviet intervention—by falsifying elections results, and by prosecuting and interning leading figures of
democratic parties;

0089

Whereas the Communist Party subverted Hungarian freedom through the use of fear and terror, the introduction of unprecedented measures of oppression, the taking of private property, and the denial of human rights—thus creating a Leninist-Stalinist dictatorship;

Whereas on October 23, 1956, the people of Hungary rose against this socialist dictatorship and illegal Soviet rule;

Whereas the revolution for freedom and independence was crushed by Soviet tanks in November 1956;

Whereas the military retaliation of the Soviet army and the collaborationist Kadar government murdered thousands of people, and caused 200,000 Hungarians to become refugees;

Whereas since 1968, economic reforms in Hungary have steadily opened greater freedom for private enterprise; and

Whereas the beginning of the 1970s brought the rebirth of the Hungarian democratic opposition;

Whereas mass demonstrations on March 15 and June 16, 1989, jointly organized by different opposition groups, have clearly illustrated the solidarity of the Hungarian people against socialist rule;

Whereas the joint efforts of the different democratic opposition groups have forced the Hungarian Communist Party to end its monopoly of power and to inaugurate Round Table discussions, which led to a peaceful transition to democracy and the dismantling of one-party rule in 1989;

Whereas at the Round Table discussions, the Communist Party agreed to hold free parliamentary elections, to disband its armed militia, and to amend the Constitution to provide for a pluralist democracy;

0090

HJ 292 IH

Whereas the overwhelming opposition of democratic forces
has effectively ended the Communist Party's attempts to
perpetuate its hold on power, and has succeeded in eliminating socialist hegemony;

Whereas on March 25 and April 8, 1990, free and fair parliamentary elections were held in Hungary, creating an au-
thentically representative democracy;

Whereas at the elections the opposition achieved a victory of
over 90 percent, while the successor of the former Communist party did not even reach the margin necessary to
obtain representation in the Parliament, becoming instead an insignificant and peripheral political factor;

Whereas by tearing down the Iron Curtain and by opening
its boundaries to East German fugitives, Hungary has
promoted the cause of freedom in other Eastern European countries;

Whereas Hungary reestablished diplomatic relations with the
State of Israel and is assisting Soviet Jews emigrate to
Israel;

Whereas the new Hungarian government has freed all political prisoners, and rehabilitated both the living and the
dead victims of socialist injustice and repression;

Whereas the Council of Europe already has accepted the Republic of Hungary in its midst as a genuinely democratic
country;

Whereas the new Hungarian government is fully committed
to the ideals of the free market, is in the process of
reprivatizing institutions of the free world; and

Whereas Hungary, in seeking to regain its sovereignty, has
agreed with the Soviet Union on the withdrawal of Soviet

0091

HJ 292 IH

troops from Hungarian territory, and has begun its withdrawal from the Warsaw pact: Now, therefore, be it

1   *Resolved,* That it is the sense of the United States
2   Congress to recognize—

3   (1) that the Republic of Hungary has made the
4   genuine and peaceful transition from an oppressive,
5   authoritarian, one-party socialist dictatorship to
6   Western democracy;

7   (2) that all political parties in the new, freely-
8   elected Hungarian parliament are fully dedicated to
9   the principles of human rights and free markets, and
10   the government of the Republic of Hungary fully de-
11   sires to integrate the country into the free world of
12   nations;

13   (3) that the Republic of Hungary has re-
14   nounced the hostile and confrontational military pos-
15   ture of the now-defunct Warsaw Pact; and

16   (4) that, based upon these findings, the United
17   States Congress declares that upon the final with-
18   drawal of Soviet troops from Hungarian territory,
19   scheduled for June 1991, Hungary will have re-
20   gained its freedom from outside domination and So-
21   viet influence, and shall no longer be considered a
22   socialist, one-party, non-market state, but a repre-
23   sentative democracy.

O   0092

HJ 292 IH

Testimony of
The Honorable John D. Dingell
on H.R. 317
"The Desert Shield Burden-Sharing Act"
before the
House Committee on Ways and Means
July 31, 1991

Thank you, Mr. Chairman, for inviting me to participate in this morning's proceedings to examine whether legislation is necessary to ensure that full payment is received from the nations who pledged financial contributions to support the multinational coalition during the Persian Gulf War. I would like to commend the Committee for taking the time to focus on an issue that I, and a number of my colleagues, consider to be a significant national concern.

One year ago this week Saddam Hussein shocked the world as he invaded Kuwait. Now, it appears that the Administration may be making concessions regarding the repayment of these obligations that are not in the national interest.

Last September I introduced H.R. 317, the Desert Shield Burden-Sharing Act. This legislation would allow the President to determine whether or not our international partners have made an equitable financial commitment to ensure allied success in the Persian Gulf War. If the President believes any nation has not paid its fair share given the benefits it received from our victory, he could impose a 20 percent ad valorem duty on any goods imported for sale in the United States.

As this Committee is well aware, the Dire Emergency Supplemental Appropriations Act expressed the sense of the Congress that financial contributions should be fulfilled, or payment arrangements made, by April 15, 1991. That deadline was not met. To prevent such disagreements from arising during future conflicts, the House in May approved a measure to authorize defense programs for Fiscal Year 1992, and included a provision to require the President to seek cost-sharing agreements so that our allies might contribute more equitably to the enormous cost of defending democracy.

0093

On July 15, the Office of Management and Budget (OMB) released its most recent report detailing both war costs and contributions promised and paid by foreign governments. OMB reports that the Department of Defense expects the incremental costs of Operation Desert Shield and Desert Storm to exceed $61 billion. While allied burden sharing commitments total over $54 billion, only $44 billion has been paid.

Mr. Chairman, the Administration's efforts to gather these international commitments are commendable, but these commitments are meaningless if left unfulfilled. Furthermore, I am disturbed by reports that the Administration has reexamined the commitment of the government of Japan, and decided unilaterally that Japan will not have to pay $668 million of its outstanding obligation. In fact, by forgiving this Japanese obligation, the OMB quotes the President as saying that, "any differences that might have existed...have been resolved." I would ask the following questions:

> What efforts is the Administration undertaking to ensure full payment of each nation's pledge to help pay the costs of the Persian Gulf War?

> What standard has the Administration used to determine whether each nation's pledge was commensurate with the benefits it received?

> How does the Administration plan to respond if a Nation fails to pay its pledge, or seeks to have that pledge reduced?

> Since the United States will receive almost $700 million less from Japan, who is the beneficiary?

> Under what authority can the Administration forgive a portion of any nation's pledge? Can such action take place without the consent of Congress?

While enactment of H.R. 317 will give the President the necessary tools to make certain that all war contributions are paid in full, Mr. Chairman, it does not explicitly prevent the President from using these commitments as bargaining chips in his conduct of foreign policy. I suspect that additional language may be needed to ensure that no games are played with these commitments, which would be on the backs of our brave men and women who performed so brilliantly in Operation Desert Storm.

0094

Thank you, Mr. Chairman, for allowing me the opportunity to address the committee on this most important issue. I hope that this hearing will lead to the enactment of legislation that will assert the prerogatives of the Congress with regard to the collection and disposition of burden sharing funds.

0095

TESTIMONY OF
OF THE HONORABLE BYRON L. DORGAN
WAYS AND MEANS COMMITTEE
JULY 31, 1991

MR. CHAIRMAN:

I have requested time to testify on my bill H.J. Res 292, which would
require that our allies fairly share the mutual defense costs of the Persian
Gulf War. I raise this question before this committee because the legislation
authorizes the use of trade sanctions for wealthy allies which fail to pay a
reasonable share of the war's costs. I also do so because of the implications
for the federal budget and related revenue requirements.

I really want to underscore two points: first, we need to ensure that
America's allies complete their contributions to the cost of the Persian Gulf
War; second, that we recognize the overall success of that cost sharing effort
and apply it to the wider requirement for meaningful cost sharing agreements
with our allies for all mutual defense costs.

THE UNFINISHED BUSINESS OF THE PERSIAN GULF WAR.

My first point, then, is that I remain concerned that our allies have
paid up only $44.5 billion of the $54 billion which they have pledged,
according to OMB's recent report of July 12, 1991. We need to keep the heat on
until these accounts are settled. Let me review briefly the status of theses
accounts.

The Japanese and Germans have paid virtually all of their modest
commitments, which is as it should be. After all, these are the other two
economic superpowers of the world and our major trade competitors.

Given the most recent OMB estimated cost of the war at $61 billion,
these two wealthy allies with a much grater dependence on Persian Gulf oil
than ours, contributed only about 25% of the war's costs.

Let me point out that my bill would have required that Japan pay 25% of
the cost and Germany 15%. That in itself would have produced a return of about
$25 billion -- nearly $10 billion more than we now have received from these
allies. That would have been enough to cover the $7 billion in war costs which
allied pledges will not now erase.

Meanwhile the two main beneficiaries of the war, Kuwait and Saudi
Arabia, have each paid only about $12 billion of their respective pledges of
over $16 billion. Taken together, the payments shortfall from these two
nations amounts to almost $9 billion.

My bill also would have required some $30 billion in payments from
wealthy Arab states -- or about what Saudi Arabia and Kuwait have pledged. Now
I understand that both incurred substantial direct and indirect costs as a
result of the Iraqi invasion and the war itself. Nevertheless, both are very
wealthy nations. The Kuwaitis still have enormous cash reserves and the Saudis
are generating great income from increased oil production. I believe our
government should expect these two beneficiaries of U.S. military support to
pay promptly their remaining obligations.

If this does not occur, then Congress should consider the kind of
sanctions bill which Mr. Stark, Mr. Dingell, and myself have introduced.
Essentially, this would require that the president impose across-the-board
tariffs on the imported products of nations which have not paid their promised
share of Gulf War expenses.

We simply must insist that nations which benefitted handsomely from the
U.S. intervention in the Persian Gulf now make good on their financial
commitments. If that requires sanctions, so be it.

0096

FAVORABLE BUDGET IMPACT LIKELY

Assuming that we can collect the rest of the outstanding pledges, there is an important lesson to be learned about defense burden sharing from Operation Desert Storm. Our concerted diplomatic efforts produced widely-supported United Nations' resolutions and numerous bilateral agreements under which allies agreed to share the military requirements and financial costs of the Persian Gulf War. In other words, under the pressure of war and a universally-perceived threat to international law, we were able to get many allies to join in a military operation and to pledge billions of dollars to cover major costs of the war.

In contrast to our usual approach to mutual defense costs, in which the U.S. sends the troops and also picks up the tab, this campaign was different in the latter respect. The result is that most of the total cost of the Gulf War of $61 billion should be covered by allied in-kind and cash contributions. (Again, this assumes that we receive virtually all of the contributions pledged.) In other words, during the Persian Gulf War we have started to shape a New Financial Order to accompany the New World Order which the president has championed. We did so by undertaking intensive, comprehensive consultations with our chief allies. In effect, they participated in burdensharing or costsharing because we also stressed powersharing and decisionsharing.

The challenge before us is to translate this success into wider and more regular costsharing arrangements.

COSTSHARING IMPROVEMENTS NEEDED

Until recently, the annual share of U.S. defense costs attributable to Europe and Asia was thought to be between $100 and $150 billion. Naturally, we incurred this cost because we felt that there was a mutual security benefit in doing so. Nevertheless, it amounted to a substantial expenditure when measured against our rising national debt and our growing trade imbalances with both Europe and Asia. I remind my colleagues that our national debt has tripled in the last decade and that our trade deficit has increased from $43 billion to $123 billion between 1982 and 1989.

Some would say that the end of the Cold War also means the end of the burdensharing debate. The Persian Gulf War illustrates the contrary. But even on more traditional burdensharing issues, I would contend that there is as great a need for progress. Let me suggest several areas in which we need to exert our efforts to achieve budget savings. I'll touch upon the big picture and also make some suggestions about Europe and Asia.

Overseas bases and forces. We need to close some of the obsolete foreign bases even as we take similar steps at home. We operate 136 bases overseas and spend about $25-30 billion per year on direct overseas defense costs. I believe that we can achieve savings in overseas spending by keeping a moratorium on new construction of U.S. bases overseas. Nor should we let foreign governments hold us hostage to foreign aid contributions as the price we pay for defending their nations. If we can't reach sensible arrangements for bases and base rights, then we ought to make new deals.

NATO infrastructure spending. Last year we spent $233 million , compared with a budget request of $460 million. The FY 92 budget request is $379 million. I would recommend that we go no higher than last year's level and work at having Europeans absorb the full cost of such expenditures. The U.S. will still have to pay for whatever troops we assign to Europe and for those troops based in the U.S but designated for European contingencies and conflicts.

0097

The U.S. share for NATO infrastructure is nearly 28 percent. So we continue to shoulder a significant cost of activities which our Europeans allies could handle themselves. The U.S. share is actually .5 percent larger than it was in the early 1980's. The Europeans should do more. We should insist that they pay for the cost of environmental clean up at bases and that the U.S.receive compensation for the value of bases which close.

Similarly, we expect that U.S. troop levels will decline from some 300,000 to about 150,000 in the near future. Over time, that will help to reduce U.S. costs or to at least recycle much of the spending for European-oriented forces within the U.S. Even as that process goes forward, I would recommend that we ask our NATO allies to shoulder the cost of consolidating bases outside of Germany and refitting some bases as forward supply and staging areas for out-of-area NATO activities. This was done successfully in the Persian Gulf War and we ought to build upon that success for future contingencies.

Two other efforts can reinforce such a policy. One is to insist that the Soviet Union abide strictly by the terms of the Conventional Forces in Europe Treaty instead of trying to hide combat units under the guise of certain naval support forces. Treaty compliance will facilitate the withdrawal of U.S. forces from Europe. The other is to encourage Germany to amend or clarify its constitution so as to permit German participation in United Nations peacemaking and peacekeeping operations. This will reduce the burden on the U.S. to carry virtually the entire manpower burden of such peacemaking - operations as Desert Storm.

Host Nation Support in Asia. Japan is the other economic super power in the world. Yet we persist in making the only incremental changes in the trade and mutual defense arrangements which adversely affect our nation.

We have made some halting progress in getting Japan to shoulder a larger share of the Host Nation Support costs for stationing U.S. forces in Japan. My amendment to the 1990 DOD authorization bill called for enhanced consultations among our Pacific allies and a $2.5 billion increase in Japan's share of mutual defense costs.

A similar Bonior amendment to the FY 91 Defense bills mandated an increase of $4 billion in Japanese support payments to cover all Host Nation costs including the salaries of U.S. personnel. If these arrangements were not made, the U.S. would be obliged to reduce its troop presence in stages.

The administration negotiated a new agreement which would increase the Japanese share from about 40 percent to 50 percent over several years. My own view is that we should keep pressing for a 70 percent or greater contribution, as in the Dorgan and Bonior amendments, right away.

South Korea has also experienced enormous economic growth in recent years -- and a substantial bilateral trade surplus with the U.S. -- yet we continue to station troops there under essentially the same arrangements as existed twenty years ago. Repeated attempts to cut U.S. forces in South Korea have failed in the face of arguments that North Korea continues to pose a formidable security threat to South Korea -- and by extension to its allies.

However, even if we were only to make the modest U.S. force cuts of some 5,000 to 7,000 troops envisioned by Defense Secretary Cheney, why could we not expect the South Koreans to recycle some of the $4 billion trade surplus it enjoys with the U.S. in the form of a phased-in increase in Host Nation Support payments. Then, if negotiations to that end failed, we could exercise the stick of making larger U.S. troop cuts. I think that would be fair to both sides. This, too, could produce savings of a few billion or more when coupled with the Korean Government's pledge to absorb $1-3 billion for the cost of relocating our major base there.

0098

I would add that the American public continues to chafe at what it regards as inadequate contributions by our allies. A recent Harris Poll, for example, showed that 73 percent of the public felt that Japan got off without contributing a fair share for the Persian Gulf War. We simply can't fund the defense structure we need when lingering questions like this remain.

BURDENSHARING IMPROVEMENTS IN THE DOD AUTHORIZATION BILL

The bottom line here is that more appropriate cost sharing and powersharing arrangements could result in enormous savings. This could be achieved without eroding U.S. security or without placing an undue burden on our key allies. We must insist on dramatic improvements in our burdensharing agreements.

Fortunately, the House adopted my amendment to the Defense Authorization bill earlier this year which would require the president to negotiate cost sharing agreements with all of our military allies and to deposit contributions from those agreements in a U.S. Allies Mutual Payments Defense Account in the Pentagon. If implemented, this would bring about a very positive change in costsharing with our allies.

I am hopeful that the Senate will soon take a similar step in creating a New Financial Order to travel with the New World Order which we now see emerging.

Over time, I believe that responsible burdensharing or costsharing arrangements can help to curb the federal deficit by substantial amounts and also help to build a domestic consensus for defense spending which we really need.

Thank you, Mr. Chairman and colleagues. I would be pleased to respond to any questions you may have.

0099

Statement of Congressman Pete Stark
Committee on Ways and Means

July 31, 1991

Thank you, Mr. Chairman, for scheduling this hearing on the allies contributions to Operation Desert Storm/Shield. I appreciate having the opportunity to testify on this important issue.

For almost half a century the United States has played the world's policeman. We have spent trillions of dollars and lost countless numbers of lives protecting our allies in Europe and the Far East from military threats, real and imagined. Once upon a time this arrangement might have made some sense. But with the liberation of Eastern Europe and the reform in the Soviet Union, there is little rationale today for the U.S. to finance a military umbrella over countries like Germany and Japan. With the end of the cold war, we don't need and can't afford to spend $200 billion on more than 300,000 troops overseas. Not when we're experiencing a severe recession, huge federal budget deficits, and the prospect of closing military bases here at home. If our allies want us to keep troops overseas, then they should have to pay for the cost.

With the diminishing of the Soviet threat, the U.S. and our allies have two principle national security concerns today. With world trade flowing at $2 trillion annually, it is vital that certain narrow sea lanes are kept open for the safe passage of merchant fleet traffic. This is an important issue for the U.S. but much more critical for countries like Germany, Holland, Japan and South Korea, whose economies rely heavily on exports for growth. Our other major security need is to keep oil flowing freely from the Persian Gulf. Again, this is a greater concern to Europe and Japan which depend far more on imported oil than the U.S. does. While we buy less than 40 percent of our oil from abroad, Germany brings in 95 percent of its petroleum, and Japan is 100 percent dependent on imported oil. A cut-off in crude from the Middle East would hurt us, but would hurt our allies far more.

This latter issue relates directly to the focus of today's hearing. One year ago this Friday, Saddam Hussein launched his brutal invasion of Kuwait. For all the Administration's rhetoric about human rights violations, the only reason we intervened so quickly and decisively in the Gulf was to maintain the free flow of oil from the region. With Saddam holding Kuwait and threatening Saudi Arabia, he would have had effective control over forty percent of the

0100

world's proven reserves of petroleum, enough to freely manipulate the price of oil. Iraq would have had additional billions of petrodollars to finance the production of advanced military weapon systems, while higher oil prices would have slowed economic growth in the developed world and lead to stagnation among the poorer countries. The long-run answer to this concern is for the U.S. and the rest of the world to become much less dependent on oil and that should be a focus of our energy policy. But in the short term this crisis had to be addressed. And since it was a multi-national threat, it should have been a multi-national effort.

Since we were the ones who had hundreds of thousands of lives on the line, Europe and Japan should have been paying the cost of the efforts right from the start. After all, Operation Desert Shield/Storm was more in their interests than in ours. Instead, almost six months into the crisis, our allies had pledged little and actually contributed less. Much of what they had given was in the form of in-kind assistance, often of dubious value, such as Bonn contributing obsolete East German military equipment.

It was only after Congress reconvened in January and took steps to address this problem that the pledges started coming in from countries like Germany and Japan. On July 18, shortly after the war began, I introduced HR 587, legislation to impose an import surtax on countries not paying their fair share of the war's cost. The formula for the surtax was very simple: A country's contribution to the war was based on its use of oil from the Gulf--if it used a quarter of the Gulf's oil it should pay a quarter of the cost. To the extent it didn't pay its share, the shortfall would be made up in a surtax on that country's imports into the U.S. The surtax would be temporary, lasting only until the country's fair share of the cost was paid up.

This was not an ideal means of getting money from our allies, but it was our best available alternative. At around this same time, several of my colleagues introduced similar bills with the same intended purpose--to get the allies to pay up! Our legislation had the intended effect. Within the next few weeks, Germany pledged an additional $6 billion and Japan came up with $9 billion. These pledges along with about $40 billion from the Gulf states and a few million dollars more from South Korea covered most of the incremental costs of the war in the Gulf.

The next challenge was collecting the money. Once again, it took steady arm-twisting and vigilance from Washington, but by the end of March Germany had paid almost all of its total and Japanese had contributed about 75 percent of theirs. Several pitfalls remained with the Japanese, such as restrictions on what we could spend their money on, and questions about their pledge was in yen or dollars. In the end, these issues were resolved, for the most part on our terms. As of this week, we have collected essentially all of what Germany and Japan had promised us. South Korea is still about $130 million short--a

0101

small fraction of the total contribution but a large percentage of their pledge. The Koreans wish to give the rest of their money as in-kind assistance and the issue apparently is exactly what form that assistance will take. We're still awaiting almost $12 billion from the Gulf states, but that money appears to be moving steadily through the pipeline.

Overall, the good news is that, with lots of noise and pressure from Congress, the U.S. has now collected more than $46 billion in contributions from the allies, more than $40 billion of which was in cash. We eventually anticipate collecting almost $53 billion altogether, against an approximate cost of the war of $61 billion. This is a good departure from the traditional burden-sharing arrangements between the U.S. and our allies. The bad news was that the $61 billion counts only the incremental costs of the war--the U.S. is still spending perhaps another $200 billion annually to maintain our huge permanent troop and base presence overseas. Our friends in Europe and the Far East depend on this U.S. military umbrella; it's about time they started paying their fair of this cost as well. Congress needs to keep burden-sharing a priority issue.

0102

EXECUTIVE OFFICE OF THE PRESIDENT

OFFICE OF MANAGEMENT AND BUDGET

WASHINGTON, D.C. 20503

THE DIRECTOR

INTRODUCTORY STATEMENT:
FOREIGN CONTRIBUTIONS FOR OPERATION
DESERT SHIELD/DESERT STORM

PRESENTED BEFORE

THE HOUSE COMMITTEE ON WAYS AND MEANS

BY

RICHARD G. DARMAN
DIRECTOR, OFFICE OF MANAGEMENT AND BUDGET

JULY 31, 1991

Chairman Rostenkowski, Ranking Republican Congressman Archer, and Members of the Committee:

It is a pleasure once again to appear before the distinguished Ways and Means Committee.

In response to your invitation, I am here to discuss foreign contributions to Operation Desert Shield/Desert Storm. I have provided the Committee with copies of the fifth report on "United States Costs in the Persian Gulf Conflict and Foreign Contributions to Offset Such Costs" (dated July 15, 1991). With this testimony I am also submitting the latest updates of tables associated with that Report. I believe you will find that this information responds to the questions put by Chairman Rostenkowski in his letter of June 14th.

To the extent that the Committee has further questions I -- and other representatives of the Administration who are here today -- would be happy to try to respond to them. But before doing so, please let me make five summary points, as follows:

(1) Foreign commitments have been very substantial. They total almost $54 billion. This is a large sum relative to any such prior financial burden-sharing; relative to total Desert Storm costs; and relative to our own early estimates of likely foreign contributions.

(2) Actual contributions received are now over $46 billion, about 85% of commitments. Almost $41 billion of this total has been received as cash contributions.

0103

(3) Detailed estimates of the incremental costs of
    Operation Desert Shield/Desert Storm for the period
    August 1, 1990-May 31, 1991 have been provided to the
    Congress as required by law. These estimates total
    $42.2 billion. But these are not yet estimates of full
    incremental costs. The Department of Defense estimates
    the likely total incremental costs to be about
    $61 billion. Total Congressional appropriations for
    incremental costs to date have been $46.5 billion. The
    pending supplemental request would bring that total to
    $49.5 billion.

(4) The outstanding commitments still to be received now
    total $7.89 billion. About 96% of this amount is due
    from Saudi Arabia and Kuwait, which have (to date)
    contributed $12.7 billion and $12.5 billion
    respectively.

(5) Although more remains to be done to assure fulfillment
    of foreign commitments, the record to date is one of
    truly remarkable contribution, cooperation, and
    achievement.

With that by way of introduction, I should be happy to turn
to such questions as the Committee may have.

Thank you very much.

Attachments:

-- "United States Costs in the Persian Gulf Conflict and Foreign
   Contributions to Offset Such Costs: July 15, 1991"
-- Updated tables

2

0104

EXECUTIVE OFFICE OF THE PRESIDENT
OFFICE OF MANAGEMENT AND BUDGET
WASHINGTON, D.C. 20503

THE DIRECTOR

July 15, 1991

Honorable Thomas S. Foley
Speaker of the House of Representatives
Washington, D.C.   20515

Dear Mr. Speaker:

Enclosed is the fifth report on United States Costs in the
Persian Gulf Conflict and Foreign Contributions to Offset Such
Costs, as required by Section 401 of P.L. 102-25. This report
was prepared in consultation with the Secretary of Defense, the
Secretary of State, the Secretary of the Treasury, and other
appropriate government officials. Previous reports have covered
the costs and contributions for the period beginning August 1,
1990, and ending on April 30, 1991, for costs, and May 31, 1991,
for contributions.

In accord with the legal requirement, this report provides
the following information:

   o the incremental costs associated with Operation Desert
      Storm that were incurred during May 1991;

   o the cumulative total of such costs, by fiscal year, from
      August 1, 1990, to May 31, 1991;

   o the costs that are nonrecurring costs, offset by in-kind
      contributions, or offset by the realignment,
      reprogramming, or transfer of funds appropriated for
      activities unrelated to the Persian Gulf conflict;

   o the allocation of costs among the military departments,
      the Defense Agencies of the Department of Defense, and
      the Office of the Secretary of Defense by category --
      airlift, sealift, personnel, personnel support, operating
      support, fuel, procurement, and military construction;
      and

   o the amount of contributions made to the United States by
      each foreign country during June 1991, as well as the
      cumulative total of such contributions. The report
      specifies the amount of cash payments pledged and
      received, provides a description and value of in-kind
      contributions pledged and received, and identifies
      restrictions on the use of such contributions.

0105

The costs reported to this point should be viewed as partial and preliminary for reasons noted in the enclosure. As required by Section 401 of P.L. 102-25, a sixth report will be submitted by August 15th. In accord with the legal requirement, it will cover incremental costs associated with Operation Desert Storm that were incurred in June 1991, and foreign contributions for July 1991. Subsequent reports will be submitted by the 15th day of each month, as required, and will revise preliminary reports to reflect additional cost estimates or reestimates.

Respectfully yours,

Richard Darman
Director

Enclosure

IDENTICAL LETTER SENT TO HONORABLE J. DANFORTH QUAYLE

COPIES TO: HONORABLE ROBERT C. BYRD, HONORABLE MARK O. HATFIELD, HONORABLE JAMIE L. WHITTEN, HONORABLE JOSEPH M. MCDADE, HONORABLE DANIEL K. INOUYE, HONORABLE TED STEVENS, HONORABLE JOHN P. MURTHA, HONORABLE SAM NUNN, HONORABLE JOHN W. WARNER, HONORABLE LES ASPIN, HONORABLE WILLIAM L. DICKINSON, HONORABLE JIM SASSER, HONORABLE PETE V. DOMENICI, HONORABLE LEON E. PANETTA, AND HONORABLE WILLIS D. GRADISON, JR.

-2-

0106

UNITED STATES COSTS IN THE PERSIAN GULF CONFLICT AND
FOREIGN CONTRIBUTIONS TO OFFSET SUCH COSTS

Report #5: July 15, 1991

Section 401 of P.L. 102-25 requires a series of reports on
incremental costs associated with Operation Desert Storm and on
foreign contributions to offset such costs. This is the fifth of
such reports. As required by Section 401 of P.L. 102-25, it
covers costs incurred during May 1991 and contributions made
during June 1991. Previous reports have covered the costs and
contributions for the period beginning August 1, 1990, and ending
on April 30, 1991, for costs and May 31, 1991, for contributions.

Costs

The costs covered in this and subsequent reports are full
incremental costs of Operation Desert Storm. These are
additional costs resulting directly from the Persian Gulf crisis
(i.e., costs that would not otherwise have been incurred). It
should be noted that only a portion of full incremental costs are
included in Defense supplemental appropriations. These portions
are costs that require financing in fiscal year 1991 or fiscal
year 1992 and that are exempt from statutory Defense budget
ceilings. Not included in fiscal year 1991 or fiscal year 1992
appropriations are items of full incremental costs such as August
- September 1990 costs and costs covered by in-kind contributions
from allies.

Table 1 summarizes preliminary estimates of Department of
Defense full incremental costs associated with Operation Desert
Storm from August 1, 1990, through May 31, 1991. The cost
information is shown by the cost and financing categories
specified in Section 401 of P.L. 102-25. Tables 2-9 provide more
detailed information by cost category. Costs shown in this
report were developed by the Department of Defense and are based
on the most recent data available.

Through May 1991, costs of $42.2 billion were reported by
the Department of Defense. The costs reported so far are
preliminary. This report includes an estimate of costs
identified to date of equipment repair, rehabilitation, and
maintenance caused by the high operating rates and combat use.
The report also includes some of the costs of phasedown of
operations and the return home of the deployed forces.

There are substantial costs that have not yet been reported.
These include equipment repair, rehabilitation, and restoration
that have not so far been identified, long-term benefit and

0107

disability costs, and the costs of continuing operations in the region. About 68,000 military personnel were in the region at the end of May, and approximately 72,000 reservists were still on active duty at that time. Significant amounts of materiel, equipment, ammunition and vehicles had not been shipped from Southwest Asia at the end of May. Materiel still in theater includes the large, heavy pieces of equipment which are costly and time consuming to prepare and transport. Combat aircraft continue to fly in the region and the U.S. forces will continue to remain in the region until all parties are satisfied with long term security arrangements. The costs through May plus the other costs not yet reported are expected by the Department of Defense to result in total incremental costs of over $61 billion.

Incremental Coast Guard costs of $3 million were incurred during this reporting period, with cumulative costs of $26 million through May to support military operations in the Persian Gulf.

Contributions

Section 401 of P.L. 102-25 requires that this report include the amount of each country's contribution during the period covered by the report, as well as the cumulative total of such contributions. Cash and in-kind contributions pledged and received are to be specified.

Tables 10 and 11 list foreign contributions pledged in 1990 and 1991, respectively, and amounts received in June. Cash and in-kind contributions are separately specified.

As of July 12, 1991, foreign countries contributed $8.0 billion of the $9.7 billion pledged in calendar year 1990, and $36.5 billion of the $44.2 billion pledged in calendar year 1991. Of the total $44.5 billion received, $39.1 billion was in cash and $5.4 billion was in-kind assistance (including food, fuel, water, building materials, transportation, and support equipment). Table 12 provides further detail on in-kind contributions.

Table 13 summarizes the current status of commitments and contributions received through July 12, 1991.

-2-

0108

Future Reports

As required by Section 401 of P.L. 102-25, the next report will be submitted by August 15th. In accord with the legal requirement, it will cover incremental costs associated with Operation Desert Storm that were incurred in June 1991, and foreign contributions for July 1991. Subsequent reports will be submitted by the 15th day of each month, as required, and will revise preliminary reports to reflect additional costs as they are estimated or re-estimated.

List of Tables

Table 1 - Summary, Incremental Costs Associated with Operation Desert Storm

Table 2 - Airlift, Incremental Costs Associated with Operation Desert Storm

Table 3 - Sealift, Incremental Costs Associated with Operation Desert Storm

Table 4 - Personnel, Incremental Costs Associated with Operation Desert Storm

Table 5 - Personnel Support, Incremental Costs Associated with Operation Desert Storm

Table 6 - Operating Support, Incremental Costs Associated with Operation Desert Storm

Table 7 - Fuel, Incremental Costs Associated with Operation Desert Storm

Table 8 - Procurement, Incremental Costs Associated with Operation Desert Storm

Table 9 - Military Construction, Incremental Costs Associated with Operation Desert Storm

Table 10 - Foreign Contributions Pledged in 1990 to Offset U.S. Costs

Table 11 - Foreign Contributions Pledged in 1991 to Offset U.S. Costs

Table 12 - Description of In-kind Assistance Received to Offset U.S. Costs as of June 30, 1991

Table 13 - Foreign Contributions Pledged in 1990 and 1991 to Offset U.S. Costs

-3-

0109

Table 1

SUMMARY 1/

INCREMENTAL COSTS ASSOCIATED WITH OPERATION DESERT STORM
Incurred by the Department of Defense
From August 1, 1990 Through May 31, 1991
($ in millions)
Preliminary Estimates

	FY 1990	FY 1991			Partial and Preliminary
	Aug – Sep	Oct – Apr	This period May	Total through May	Aug 1990 – May 1991
(1) Airlift	412	1,725	378	2,103	2,515
(2) Sealift	235	2,314	662	2,976	3,212
(3) Personnel	223	3,937	632	4,569	4,792
(4) Personnel Support	352	4,822	178	5,000	5,352
(5) Operating Support	1,210	11,680	278	11,958	13,168
(6) Fuel	626	3,263	372	3,635	4,261
(7) Procurement	129	8,272	68	8,339	8,468
(8) Military Construction	11	415		415	426
Total	3,197	36,429	2,567	38,996	42,194 2/

Nonrecurring costs included above 3/	201	11,855	662	12,516	12,718
Costs offset by:					
In-kind contributions	225	4,886	188	5,073	5,298
Realignment 4/	913	59		59	972

1/ Data was compiled by OMB. Source of data -- Department of Defense. This report adjusts earlier estimates to reflect more complete accounting information.

2/ The costs reported so far are preliminary. This report includes an estimate of costs identified to date of equipment repair, rehabilitation, and maintenance caused by the high operating rates and combat use. Additional costs for these categories will be reported as more information becomes available. The report also includes some of the costs of phasedown of operations and the return home of the deployed forces. However, certain long-term benefit and disability costs have not been reflected in the estimates. Those costs will be reported in later reports. The costs through May plus the other costs not yet reported are expected by the Department of Defense to result in total incremental costs of slightly more than $61 billion.

3/ Nonrecurring costs include investment costs associated with procurement and Military Construction, as well as other one-time costs such as the activation of the Ready Reserve Force ships.

4/ This includes the realignment, reprogramming, or transfer of funds appropriated for activities unrelated to the Persian Gulf conflict.

-4-

0110

Table 2

AIRLIFT

INCREMENTAL COSTS ASSOCIATED WITH OPERATION DESERT STORM
Incurred by the Department of Defense
From August 1, 1990 Through May 31, 1991
($ in millions)
Preliminary Estimates

	FY 1990	FY 1991			Partial and Preliminary Aug 1990 – May 1991
	Aug – Sep	Oct – Apr	This period May	Total through May	
Airlift					
Army	207	646	278	924	1,131
Navy	85	585	84	668	754
Air Force	114	470	10	480	595
Intelligence Agencies		1		1	1
Special Operations Command	6	24	7	30	36
Total	412	1,725	378	2,103	2,515

Nonrecurring costs included above		583	270	853	853
Costs offset by:					
In-kind contributions	7	78	10	88	96
Realignment 2/	6				6

1/ This includes the realignment, reprogramming, or transfer of funds appropriated for activities unrelated to the Persian Gulf conflict.

This category includes costs related to the transportation by air of personnel, equipment and supplies.

During this period over 1,300 redeployment missions were flown, returning over 104,000 people and 39,000 short tons of cargo to the U.S. and Europe. In addition, over 1,100 other missions were flown to carry supplies to U.S. forces still in the region.

-5-

0111

Table 3

SEALIFT

INCREMENTAL COSTS ASSOCIATED WITH OPERATION DESERT STORM
Incurred by the Department of Defense
From August 1, 1990 Through May 31, 1991
($ in millions)
Preliminary Estimates

| | FY 1990 | FY 1991 | | | Partial and Preliminary Aug 1990 – |
	Aug – Sep	Oct – Apr	This period May	Total through May	May 1991
Sealift					
Army	123	1,767	574	2,340	2,463
Navy	99	337	45	382	481
Air Force	12	194	42	236	248
Defense Logistics Agency		14	2	16	16
Special Operations Command	2	2		2	4
Total	235	2,314	662	2,976	3,212

Nonrecurring costs included above	57	694	229	924	981
Costs offset by:					
In–kind contributions	2	121	6	127	129
Realignment 1/	2				2

1/ This includes the realignment, reprogramming, or transfer of funds appropriated for activities unrelated to the Persian Gulf conflict.

This category includes costs related to the transportation by sea of personnel, equipment and supplies.

The previous October–April estimate has been reduced by $765 million, of which $442 million has been shifted to the operating support category. The balance represents refinement of previous estimates.

During this period a total of 64 ships (25 of them foreign flag ships) made redeployment deliveries. These vessels shipped over 282,000 short tons of dry cargo back to the U.S. and Europe. In addition, 170,000 short tons of petroleum products were transported to sustain U.S. forces still in the region.

-6-

0112

Table 4

PERSONNEL

INCREMENTAL COSTS ASSOCIATED WITH OPERATION DESERT STORM
Incurred by the Department of Defense
From August 1, 1990 Through May 31, 1991
($ in millions)
Preliminary Estimates

| | FY 1990 | FY 1991 | | | Partial and Preliminary Aug 1990 – May 1991 |
	Aug – Sep	Oct – Apr	This period May	Total through May	
Personnel					
Army	126	2,374	333	2,707	2,833
Navy	22	826	163	989	1,011
Air Force	75	737	136	873	948
Total	223	3,937	632	4,569	4,792

Nonrecurring costs included above		45	45	45
Costs offset by:				
In-kind contributions				
Realignment 1/	15			15

1/ This includes the realignment, reprogramming, or transfer of funds appropriated for activities unrelated to the Persian Gulf conflict.

This category includes pay and allowances of members of the reserve components of the Armed Forces called or ordered to active duty and the increased pay and allowances of members of the regular components of the Armed Forces incurred because of deployment in connection with Operation Desert Storm.

The previous October–April estimate has been reduced by $74 million in additional savings in Reserve component accounts.

At the end of May about 72,000 Reservists were still on active duty and about 68,000 people were still in theater.

-7-

0113

Table 5

PERSONNEL SUPPORT

INCREMENTAL COSTS ASSOCIATED WITH OPERATION DESERT STORM
Incurred by the Department of Defense
From August 1, 1990 Through May 31, 1991
($ in millions)
Preliminary Estimates

| | FY 1990 | FY 1991 | | | Partial and Preliminary Aug 1990 – May 1991 |
	Aug – Sep	Oct – Apr	This period May	Total through May	
Personnel Support					
Army	209	3,621	136	3,757	3,966
Navy	104	772	35	807	911
Air Force	24	386	6	392	415
Intelligence Agencies	2	9	1	9	11
Defense Logistics Agency	12	15	0 1/	15	27
Defense Mapping Agency		4	0 1/	4	4
Special Operations Command	2	7	0 1/	8	9
Office of the Secretary of Defense		9	0 1/	9	9
Total	352	4,822	178	5,000	5,352

Nonrecurring costs included above	4	994	44	1,038	1,042
Costs offset by:					
In-kind contributions	28	1,487	87	1,574	1,601
Realignment 2/	3				3

1/ Costs are less than $500 thousand.
2/ This includes the realignment, reprogramming, or transfer of funds appropriated for activities unrelated to the Persian Gulf conflict.

This category includes subsistence, uniforms and medical costs.

The previous October–April estimate has been increased by $108 million primarily to account for CHAMPUS costs.

In May, major costs were for subsistence and medical support.

-8-

0114

Table 6

OPERATING SUPPORT

INCREMENTAL COSTS ASSOCIATED WITH OPERATION DESERT STORM
Incurred by the Department of Defense
From August 1, 1990 Through May 31, 1991
($ in millions)
Preliminary Estimates

| | FY 1990 | FY 1991 | | | Partial and Preliminary Aug 1990 – |
	Aug – Sep	Oct – Apr	This period May	Total through May	May 1991
Operating Support					
Army	896	6,493	72	6,565	7,461
Navy	223	3,179	27	3,205	3,428
Air Force	68	1,930	177	2,107	2,175
Intelligence Agencies		1		1	1
Special Operations Command	15	26		26	41
Defense Communications Agency		1		1	1
Defense Mapping Agency	8	46	1	47	55
Defense Nuclear Agency		2		2	2
Office of the Secretary of Defense		3		3	3
Total	1,210	11,680	278	11,958	13,168

Nonrecurring costs included above		852	51	903	903
Costs offset by:					
In-kind contributions	167	1,576	23	1,598	1,765
Realignment 2/	698	12		12	710

1/ This includes the realignment, reprogramming, or transfer of funds appropriated for activities unrelated to the Persian Gulf conflict.

This category includes equipment support costs, costs associated with increased operational tempo, spare parts, stock fund purchases, communications, and equipment maintenance.

The previous October–April estimate has been increased by $226 million. This increase is the net effect of changes in the category in which costs are reported. Repair, rehabilitation, and maintenance costs of sealift assets are now reported under operating support while certain incremental in-country fuel costs previously reported in this category are now reported under the fuel category.

Costs reported during this period were primarily equipment maintenance and in-country operating costs.

-9-

0115

Table 7

FUEL

INCREMENTAL COSTS ASSOCIATED WITH OPERATION DESERT STORM
Incurred by the Department of Defense
From August 1, 1990 Through May 31, 1991
($ in millions)
Preliminary Estimates

| | FY 1990 | FY 1991 | | | Partial and Preliminary Aug 1990 – |
| | | | This period | Total | |
	Aug – Sep	Oct – Apr	May	through May	May 1991
Fuel					
Army	10	115	5	121	130
Navy	19	1,135	95	1,230	1,249
Air Force	137	2,005	270	2,275	2,412
Special Operations Command		8	1	9	9
Defense Logistics Agency	460				460
Total	626	3,263	372	3,635	4,261

Nonrecurring costs included above					
Costs offset by:					
In-kind contributions	21	1,072	62	1,135	1,156
Realignment 1/	60				60

1/ This includes the realignment, reprogramming, or transfer of funds appropriated for activities unrelated to the Persian Gulf conflict.

This category includes the additional fuel required for higher operating tempo and for airlift and sealift transportation of personnel and equipment as well as for the higher prices for fuel during the period.

Costs reported during this period were about equally divided between higher operating tempo and higher prices.

-10-

0116

Table 8

PROCUREMENT

INCREMENTAL COSTS ASSOCIATED WITH OPERATION DESERT STORM
Incurred by the Department of Defense
From August 1, 1990 Through May 31, 1991
($ in millions)
Preliminary Estimates

| | FY 1990 | FY 1991 | | | Partial and Preliminary Aug 1990 – May 1991 |
	Aug – Sep	Oct – Apr	This period May	Total through May	
Procurement					
Army	49	2,307	10	2,318	2,367
Navy	47	2,503		2,503	2,550
Air Force	32	3,324	57	3,381	3,413
Intelligence Agencies	1	13		13	13
Defense Communications Agency		0		0	0 1/
Special Operations Command		99		99	99
Defense Logistics Agency		4		4	4
Defense Mapping Agency		1		1	1
Defense Nuclear Agency		0		0	0 1/
Defense Systems Project Office		1		1	1
Office of the Secretary of Defense		21		21	21
Total	129	8,272	68	8,339	8,468

Nonrecurring costs included above	129	8,272	68	8,339	8,468
Costs offset by:					
In-kind contributions		155		155	155
Realignment 2/	119	47		47	165

1/ Costs are less than $500 thousand.
2/ This includes the realignment, reprogramming, or transfer of funds appropriated for activities unrelated to the Persian Gulf conflict.

This category includes ammunition, weapon systems improvements and upgrades, and equipment purchases.

The previous October–April estimates has been increased by $29 million to reflect refinement of costs for special purpose equipment to facilitate operations in Southwest Asia and a revision of costs for Army vehicle losses. Costs for May primarily reflect replacement of components on Air Force F-117 aircraft.

-11-

0117

Table 9

MILITARY CONSTRUCTION

INCREMENTAL COSTS ASSOCIATED WITH OPERATION DESERT STORM
Incurred by the Department of Defense
From August 1, 1990 Through May 31, 1991
($ in millions)
Preliminary Estimates

	FY 1990	FY 1991			Partial and Preliminary Aug 1990 – May 1991
	Aug – Sep	Oct – Apr	This period May	Total through May	
Military Construction					
Army	7	414		414	421
Navy					
Air Force	4	2		2	5
Total	11	415		415	426

Nonrecurring costs included above	11	415		415	426
Costs offset by:					
In–kind contributions		397		397	397
Realignment 2/	11				11

1/ Costs are less than $500 thousand.
2/ This includes the realignment, reprogramming, or transfer of funds appropriated for activities
unrelated to the Persian Gulf conflict.

This category includes the cost of constructing temporary billets for troops, and administrative and
supply and maintenance facilities.

There were no new costs reported in this category. There was a small decrease in the previously
reported October–April costs due to a reestimate of certain in–kind costs by CENTCOM.

0118

Table 10

FOREIGN CONTRIBUTIONS PLEDGED IN 1990 TO OFFSET U.S. COSTS 1/
($ in millions)

	Commitments			Receipts in June			Receipts through July 12, 1991			Future Receipts
	Cash	In-kind	Total	Cash	In-kind	Total	Cash	In-kind	Total	
GCC STATES	5,861	984	6,845				4,256	984	5,240	1,605
SAUDI ARABIA	2,474	865	3,339				886	865	1,751	1,588 2/
KUWAIT	2,500	6	2,506				2,500	6	2,506	
UAE	887	113	1,000				870	113	983	17 3/
GERMANY 4/	260	812	1,072				272	782	1,054	18 5/
JAPAN 4/	961	779	1,740				961	637	1,598	142 6/
KOREA	50	30	80				50	30	80	
BAHRAIN		1	1					1	1	
OMAN/QATAR		1	1					1	1	
DENMARK		1	1					1	1	
TOTAL	7,132	2,608	9,740				5,539	2,436	7,975	1,765

1/ Data was compiled by OMB. Sources of data: commitments -- Defense, State, and Treasury; cash received -- Treasury; receipts and value of in-kind assistance -- Defense.

2/ This is reimbursement for enroute transportation through December for the second deployment and for U.S. in-theater expenses for food, building materials, fuel, and support. Bills for reimbursement have been forwarded to Saudi Arabia.

3/ This is undergoing a final accounting.

4/ 1990 cash contributions were for transportation and associated costs.

5/ An accounting of in-kind assistance accepted by U.S. forces is under way.

6/ Resolution of balance is under discussion and should be resolved shortly.

-13-

0119

Table 11

FOREIGN CONTRIBUTIONS PLEDGED IN 1991 TO OFFSET U.S. COSTS 1/
($ in millions)

	Commitments 2/			Receipts in June			Receipts through July 12, 1991			Future Receipts
	Cash	In-kind	Total	Cash	In-kind	Total	Cash	In-kind	Total	
GCC STATES	27,146	2,941	30,087	700	178	878	19,575	2,941	22,516	7,571
SAUDI ARABIA	10,672	2,828	13,500		168	168	7,300	2,828	10,128	3,372
KUWAIT	13,474	26	13,500	700	8	708	9,275	26	9,301	4,199
UAE	3,000	87	3,087		2	2	3,000	87	3,087	
GERMANY	5,500		5,500				5,500		5,500	
JAPAN 3/	8,332 4/		8,332				8,332		8,332	
KOREA	100	175	275 5/	40	4	44	100	40	140	136 5/
DENMARK		6	6					6	6	
LUXEMBOURG		6	6					6	6	
OTHER	4	2	6		1	1	4	2	6	
TOTAL	41,082	3,130	44,212	740	183	921	33,511	2,994	36,505	7,707

1/ Data was compiled by OMB. Sources of data: commitments -- Defense, State, and Treasury; cash received -- Treasury; receipts and value of in-kind assistance -- Defense.

2/ 1991 commitments in most instances did not distinguish between cash and in-kind. The commitment shown above reflects actual in-kind assistance received unless specific information is available.

3/ 1991 cash contributions are for logistics and related support.

4/ The previously reported commitment has been reduced by $668 million, which has been paid to other coalition partners. A difference of understanding arose with respect to the Japanese contribution for 1991. On July 11th the President met with Prime Minister Kaifu and concluded that the difference in understanding was reasonable and Japan's payments were made in good faith with the agreed commitment. The President thereupon stated that "any differences that might have existed . . . have been resolved."

5/ The previously reported commitment has been corrected by a reduction of $30 million, which Korea paid to the U.K. The revision reflects an understanding between the United States and the Government of Korea that the terms of the Korean commitment allow this $30 million contribution to other members of the multinational forces. Future receipts are for in-kind assistance consisting of replenishment stocks for which delivery is now being arranged and transportation assistance, which is being drawn down as needed by U.S. forces.

-14-

0120

Table 12

DESCRIPTION OF IN-KIND ASSISTANCE RECEIVED
TO OFFSET U.S. COSTS AS OF JUNE 30, 1991

($ in millions)

	Calendar Year 1990	Calendar Year 1991
SAUDI ARABIA .... Host nation support including food, fuel, housing, building materials, transportation and port handling services.	865	2,828
KUWAIT .... Transportation	6	26
UNITED ARAB EMIRATES .... Fuel, food and water, security services, construction equipment and civilian labor.	113	87
GERMANY .... Vehicles including cargo trucks, water trailers, buses and ambulances; generators; radios; portable showers; protective masks, and chemical sensing vehicles	782	
JAPAN .... Construction and engineering support, vehicles, electronic data processing, telephone services, medical equipment, and transportation.	637	
KOREA .... Transportation	30	40
BAHRAIN .... Medical supplies, food and water	1	
OMAN/QATAR .... Oil, telephones, food and water	1	
DENMARK .... Transportation	1	6
LUXEMBOURG.. Transportation		6
OTHER .... Transportation		2
TOTAL	2,436	2,994

Table 13

FOREIGN CONTRIBUTIONS PLEDGED IN 1990 AND 1991 TO OFFSET U.S. COSTS
COMMITMENTS AND RECEIPTS THROUGH JULY 12, 1991 1/
($ in millions)

	Commitments			Receipts 2/			Future
	1990	1991	Total	Cash	In-kind	Total	Receipts
GCC STATES	6,845	30,087	36,932	23,831	3,925	27,756	9,176
SAUDI ARABIA	3,339	13,500	16,839	8,186	3,693	11,879	4,960
KUWAIT	2,506	13,500	16,006	11,775	32	11,807	4,199
UAE	1,000	3,087	4,087	3,870	200	4,070	17 3/
GERMANY	1,072	5,500	6,572	5,772	782	6,554	18 4/
JAPAN	1,740	8,332	10,072	9,293	637	9,930	142
KOREA	80	275	355	150	70	220	136
OTHER	3	18	21	4	17	21	
TOTAL	9,740	44,212	53,952	39,050	5,431	44,481	9,471

1/ Data was compiled by OMB. Sources of data: commitments -- Defense, State, and Treasury; cash received -- Treasury; receipts and value of in-kind assistance -- Defense.

2/ Cash receipts are as of July 12, 1991. In-kind assistance is as of June 30, 1991.

3/ This is undergoing a final accounting.

4/ An accounting of in-kind assistance accepted by U.S. forces is under way.

0122

Table 10 Updated as of July 29, 1991

FOREIGN CONTRIBUTIONS PLEDGED IN 1990 TO OFFSET U.S. COSTS 1/
($ in millions)

	Commitments			Receipts through July 29, 1991			Future Receipts
	Cash	In-kind	Total	Cash	In-kind	Total	
GCC STATES	5,844	1,001	6,845	4,256	1,001	5,257	1,588
SAUDI ARABIA	2,474	865	3,339	886	865	1,751	1,588 2/
KUWAIT	2,500	6	2,506	2,500	6	2,506	
UAE	870	130	1,000	870	130	1,000	
GERMANY 3/	260	812	1,072	272	782	1,054	18 4/
JAPAN 3/	961	779	1,740	1,045	567	1,612	128 5/
KOREA	50	30	80	50	30	80	
BAHRAIN		1	1		1	1	
OMAN/QATAR		1	1		1	1	
DENMARK		1	1		1	1	
TOTAL	7,115	2,625	9,740	5,623	2,383	8,006	1,734

1/ Data was compiled by OMB. Sources of data: commitments -- Defense, State, and Treasury; cash received -- Treasury; receipts and value of in-kind assistance -- Defense.

2/ This is reimbursement for enroute transportation through December for the second deployment and fo U.S. in-theater expenses for food, building materials, fuel, and support. Bills for reimbursement have been forwarded to Saudi Arabia.

3/ 1990 cash contributions were for transportation and associated costs.

4/ An accounting of in-kind assistance accepted by U.S. forces is under way.

5/ Resolution of balance is under discussion and should be resolved shortly.

0123

Table 11 Updated as of July 29, 1991

FOREIGN CONTRIBUTIONS PLEDGED IN 1991 TO OFFSET U.S. COSTS 1/
($ in millions)

	Commitments 2/			Receipts through July 29, 1991			Future Receipts
	Cash	In-kind	Total	Cash	In-kind	Total	
GCC STATES	27,146	2,941	30,087	21,125	2,941	24,066	6,021
SAUDI ARABIA	10,672	2,828	13,500	8,150	2,828	10,978	2,522
KUWAIT	13,474	26	13,500	9,975	26	10,001	3,499
UAE	3,000	87	3,087	3,000	87	3,087	
GERMANY	5,500		5,500	5,500		5,500	
JAPAN 3/	8,332 4/		8,332	8,332		8,332	
KOREA	100	175	275 5/	100	40	140	136 5/
DENMARK		6	6		6	6	
LUXEMBOURG		6	6		6	6	
OTHER	4	2	6	4	2	6	
TOTAL	41,082	3,130	44,212	35,061	2,994	38,055	6,157

1/ Data was compiled by OMB. Sources of data: commitments -- Defense, State, and Treasury; cash received -- Treasury; receipts and value of in-kind assistance -- Defense.

2/ 1991 commitments in most instances did not distinguish between cash and in-kind. The commitment shown above reflects actual in-kind assistance received unless specific information is available.

3/ 1991 cash contributions are for logistics and related support.

4/ The previously reported commitment has been reduced by $668 million, which has been paid to other coalition partners. A difference of understanding arose with respect to the Japanese contribution for 1991. On July 11th the President met with Prime Minister Kaifu and concluded that the difference in understanding was reasonable and Japan's payments were made in good faith with the agreed commitment. The President thereupon stated that "any differences that might have existed . . . have been resolved."

5/ The previously reported commitment has been corrected by a reduction of $30 million, which Korea paid to the U.K. The revision reflects an understanding between the United States and the Government of Korea that the terms of the Korean commitment allow this $30 million contribution to other members of the multinational forces. Future receipts are for in-kind assistance consisting of replenishment stocks for which delivery is now being arranged and transportation assistance, which is being drawn down as needed by U.S. forces.

0124

Table 12 Updated as of July 29, 1991

DESCRIPTION OF IN-KIND ASSISTANCE RECEIVED
TO OFFSET U.S. COSTS
($ in millions)

	Calendar Year 1990	Calendar Year 1991
SAUDI ARABIA .... Host nation support including food, fuel, housing, building materials, transportation and port handling services.	865	2,828
KUWAIT .... Transportation	6	26
UNITED ARAB EMIRATES .... Fuel, food and water, security services, construction equipment and civilian labor.	130	87
GERMANY .... Vehicles including cargo trucks, water trailers, buses and ambulances; generators; radios; portable showers; protective masks, and chemical sensing vehicles	782	
JAPAN .... Construction and engineering support, vehicles, electronic data processing, telephone services, medical equipment, and transportation.	567	
KOREA .... Transportation	30	40
BAHRAIN .... Medical supplies, food and water	1	
OMAN/QATAR .... Oil, telephones, food and water	1	
DENMARK .... Transportation	1	6
LUXEMBOURG... Transportation		6
OTHER .... Transportation		2
TOTAL	2,383	2,994

0125

Table 13 Updated as of July 29, 1991

FOREIGN CONTRIBUTIONS PLEDGED IN 1990 AND 1991 TO OFFSET U.S. COSTS
COMMITMENTS AND RECEIPTS THROUGH JULY 29, 1991 1/
($ in millions)

	Commitments			Receipts 2/			Future
	1990	1991	Total	Cash	In-kind	Total	Receipts
GCC STATES	6,845	30,087	36,932	25,381	3,942	29,323	7,609
SAUDI ARABIA	3,339	13,500	16,839	9,036	3,693	12,729	4,110
KUWAIT	2,506	13,500	16,006	12,475	32	12,507	3,499
UAE	1,000	3,087	4,087	3,870	217	4,087	
GERMANY	1,072	5,500	6,572	5,772	782	6,554	18 3/
JAPAN	1,740	8,332	10,072	9,377	567	9,944	128
KOREA	80	275	355	150	70	220	136
OTHER	3	18	21	4	17	21	
TOTAL	9,740	44,212	53,952	40,684	5,378	46,062	7,890

1/ Data was compiled by OMB. Sources of data: commitments –– Defense, State, and Treasury; cash received –– Treasury; receipts and value of in-kind assistance –– Defense.

2/ Cash receipts are as of July 29, 1991. In-kind assistance is as of July 29, 1991.

3/ An accounting of in-kind assistance accepted by U.S. forces is under way.

0126

STATEMENT OF THE HONORABLE SEAN O'KEEFE
COMPTROLLER OF THE DEPARTMENT OF DEFENSE
IN CONNECTION WITH COSTS AND CONTRIBUTIONS FOR THE GULF WAR
HOUSE COMMITTEE ON WAYS AND MEANS
JULY 31, 1991

Mr. Chairman, members of the Committee, I am glad to be here to discuss the contributions and commitments of America's coalition partners with respect to the costs of the Persian Gulf war.

The questions the committee asked are addressed in the statement of OMB Director Richard Darman. I am prepared to answer your questions on these or other questions.

With respect to identifying U.S. costs for the war, we in the Department of Defense used a rigorous process to ensure that we identified only costs that were truly incremental. By "incremental" we mean costs that were directly related to the Gulf crisis and were in addition to funds already budgeted for the forces involved. For example, incremental Desert Shield costs for an Army division were those that were over and above the budgeted amounts it would have spent if it had not deployed. The bulk of those incremental costs were due to the increased operating tempo and other preparations for possible combat under harsh environmental conditions.

Incremental costs are distinguished from total budgetary costs in that they were derived by subtracting previously budgeted funding. Incremental costs do not include previously budgeted funds for pay, training, maintenance, and equipment for active forces deployed to the Gulf area.

0127

STATEMENT OF
THE COMPTROLLER OF THE
DEPARTMENT OF DEFENSE

SEAN O'KEEFE

BEFORE THE

HOUSE COMMITTEE ON WAYS AND MEANS

IN CONNECTION WITH

DESERT SHIELD/DESERT STORM
COSTS AND CONTRIBUTIONS

JULY 31, 1991

0128

STATEMENT BY
HOLLIS S. MCLOUGHLIN
ASSISTANT SECRETARY
FOR POLICY MANAGEMENT
U.S. DEPARTMENT OF TREASURY
BEFORE THE COMMITTEE ON WAYS AND MEANS
U.S. HOUSE OF REPRESENTATIVES
July 31, 1991

Mr. Chairman and members of the Committee, I appreciate the opportunity to discuss the role that the Treasury Department has played in the burden sharing initiative to defray the costs of Operations Desert Shield and Desert Storm.

The Treasury Department has participated in an interagency effort along with the Department of State, the Defense Department, the National Security Council (NSC) and the Office of Management and Budget (OMB) to generate strong financial support from our allies. We have received support from our allies and coalition partners which has significantly reduced the budgetary cost to the American people of our efforts in the Gulf.

Allied commitments to the United States for 1990 and 1991 total nearly $54 billion. To date, we have received over $46 billion in cash and in-kind assistance from Germany, Japan, Saudi Arabia, Kuwait, the United Arab Emirates and Korea. This level of sharing the responsibility for the costs of military operations is unprecedented and demonstrates a solid international commitment to the successful efforts of the U.S.-led coalition to counter Saddam Hussein's aggression against Kuwait.

Treasury has helped to generate this support through its contacts with foreign officials and its on-going active participation in interagency consultations. As early as September 1990, Treasury Secretary Brady and Secretary of State Baker personally consulted a number of our allies in Europe, Asia and the Gulf region to discuss support for U.S. military actions in the Gulf.

I would like to comment specifically on Japan's commitment, as this issue was raised in the Committee's letter of invitation. In January, Finance Minister Hashimoto told Secretary Brady that Japan would contribute $9 billion to help offset incremental Desert Storm costs incurred in January-March 1991. We had asked that the entire $9 billion be in dollars and be disbursed to the United States. The Administration reported Japan's commitment to the Congress on this basis.

0129

Subsequently, Japan advised us that we had misunderstood its precise commitment. Japan said that it had intended all along to disburse part of its 1991 commitment to other coalition partners, as it had in 1990, and believed that this would be acceptable to the U.S.

On July 11, President Bush met with Prime Minister Kaifu and concluded that the difference in understanding was reasonable and that Japan's payments were made in good faith with the agreed commitment. The President indicated that "any differences that might have existed...have been resolved."

To date, Japan has contributed just under $10 billion to the U.S. to offset our military costs in 1990 and 1991. In addition, Japan has committed almost $1 billion to other multinational coalition partners, bringing its total contribution to the burden sharing effort to nearly $11 billion. These substantial payments represent a sizeable portion of this successful burden sharing effort.

Mr. Chairman, I would be happy to respond to any questions you or members of the Committee might have.

0130

TESTIMONY OF
EUGENE J. McALLISTER
ASSISTANT SECRETARY OF STATE
FOR ECONOMIC AND BUSINESS AFFAIRS
DEPARTMENT OF STATE
BEFORE THE
HOUSE WAYS AND MEANS COMMITTEE
ROOM 1102 LONGWORTH
WEDNESDAY, JULY 31, 1991
ON
"GULF RESPONSIBILITY SHARING"

MR. CHAIRMAN, MEMBERS OF THE COMMITTEE, THANK YOU FOR THE
OPPORTUNITY TO TESTIFY TODAY ON GULF RESPONSIBILITY SHARING
EFFORTS. WE BELIEVE THAT OUR EFFORTS TO ASSURE A FAIR
RESPONSIBILITY SHARING AMONG OUR ALLIES AND PARTNERS WERE AN
UNPRECEDENTED SUCCESS.

o   OVER $70 BILLION IN TOTAL FINANCIAL COMMITMENTS WAS
     RAISED. THIS $70 BILLION IN EXTRAORDINARY SPENDING IS
     GREATER THAN THE GDP OF A NUMBER OF COUNTRIES, INCLUDING
     GREECE, PORTUGAL AND YUGOSLAVIA.

o   IN THE SPHERE OF ECONOMIC ASSISTANCE, 26 COUNTRIES HAVE
     COMMITTED $16 BILLION IN 1990 AND 1991, MAINLY FOR THOSE
     "FRONT LINE" STATES CRITICAL TO THE SANCTIONS REGIME,
     NOTABLY EGYPT AND TURKEY. THIS EFFORT HAS BEEN COORDINATED
     THROUGH THE U.S.-LED GULF CRISIS FINANCIAL COORDINATION
     GROUP.

0131

o   IN MILITARY RESPONSIBILITY SHARING, OUR PARTNERS HAVE
    COMMITTED $54 BILLION TO THE U.S.:

    -- $9.7 BILLION IN 1990, OR 73 PERCENT OF THE $13.2
         BILLION IN 1990 INCREMENTAL COSTS; AND

    -- $44.2 BILLION FOR 1991 INCREMENTAL MILITARY COSTS.

o   IN ADDITION, CONTRIBUTORS TO RESPONSIBILITY SHARING HAVE
    ASSISTED OUR MILITARY PARTNERS. GERMANY, FOR INSTANCE,
    PROVIDED $822 MILLION TO THE U.K., AND JAPAN PROVIDED $330
    MILLION TO THE UK. GULF STATES -- KUWAIT, SAUDI ARABIA,
    AND THE UAE -- HAVE PROVIDED MORE THAN $5 BILLION TO
    SUPPORT OUR MILITARY PARTNERS.

LET ME BRIEFLY DESCRIBE THE STATUS OF DESERT SHIELD/DESERT
STORM CONTRIBUTIONS TO THE U.S.:

    --   GERMANY HAS DISBURSED ALL OF ITS DESERT SHIELD/STORM
         COMMITMENTS. GERMANY'S STRONG COMMITMENT TO
         RESPONSIBILITY SHARING WAS DEMONSTRATED BY ITS VERY
         RAPID DISBURSEMENTS OF MILITARY FINANCING IN SUPPORT
         OF DESERT SHIELD AND DESERT STORM. CHANCELLOR KOHL

0132

COMMITTED $5.5 BILLION FOR DESERT STORM. TWO MONTHS
LATER, ALL OF THAT COMMITTED FUNDING HAD BEEN
DEPOSITED IN THE DEFENSE COOPERATION ACCOUNT.

-- JAPAN HAS DISBURSED ALL OF ITS 1991 COMMITMENTS AND
WE ARE CONCLUDING THE FINAL ACCOUNTING OF 1990
DISBURSEMENTS.

-- KOREA, IN RECOGNITION OF ITS GLOBAL RESPONSIBILITIES,
ALSO CONTRIBUTED FINANCIALLY TO OFFSET OUR COSTS AND
HAS DISBURSED $220 MILLION OF ITS $355 MILLION DESERT
SHIELD/STORM COMMITMENTS. THE REMAINING ACCOUNT
CONSISTS OF IN-KIND SUPPORT FOR WHICH DELIVERY IS
BEING ARRANGED.

-- THE UNITED ARAB EMIRATES HAS DISBURSED ALL OF ITS $4
BILLION 1990 AND 1991 DESERT SHIELD/STORM COMMITMENTS.

-- KUWAIT HAS MET ALL OF ITS 1990 DESERT SHIELD
COMMITMENTS. KUWAIT ALSO HAS DISBURSED $10 BILLION
OF ITS 1991 DESERT STORM COMMITMENTS.

0133

-- SAUDI ARABIA HAS DISBURSED $12.7 BILLION OF $16.8
BILLION IN DESERT SHIELD/STORM PLEDGES. THIS IS THE
LARGEST AMOUNT, FOR BOTH DISBURSEMENTS AND PLEDGES OF
ANY COUNTRY.

IN SUMMARY, THE U.S. HAS RECEIVED $46 BILLION, OR 85 PERCENT,
OF THE $54 BILLION IN TOTAL COMMITMENTS. WE ARE CONFIDENT THAT
WE WILL RECEIVE ALL OF THE COMMITMENTS, IN A TIMELY MANNER.

0134

United States General Acc━ting Office

GAO

Testimony

For Release
On Delivery
Expected at
10:00 a.m. EDT
Wednesday
July 31, 1991

Allied Contributions in Support

of Operations Desert Shield and

Desert Storm

Statement of
Frank C. Conahan, Assistant Comptroller General
National Security and International Affairs
Division

Before the
Committee on Ways and Means
House of Representatives

0135

GAO/T-NSIAD-91-52

GAO Form 160 (12/87)

I appreciate the opportunity to testify today on the status of
allied contributions to support Operations Desert Shield and Desert
Storm and the use of these contributions to defray U.S. costs.   In
summary, we believe that the Office of Management and Budget's
(OMB) reports, for the most part, accurately reflect the status of
allied pledges and contributions.   However, we note that some
pledges have been revised, and the reported value of in-kind
support is, in some cases, based on estimated rather than actual
costs.

We believe that allied cash contributions should be sufficient to
finance U.S. funding requirements to pay for the incremental costs
of the war in the Persian Gulf and, that U.S. taxpayers' funds
will, therefore, not be needed.   We note that DOD's funding
requirements will be less than OMB's estimate of incremental costs
because, for example, some equipment lost during the war will not
be replaced, and other costs are being satisfied through in-kind
support furnished by our allies.

STATUS OF ALLIED CONTRIBUTIONS

Since the Iraqi invasion of Kuwait, the European Commission (EC)
and 49 countries have contributed support for the Persian Gulf
crisis.   These contributions include the deployment of military
forces to the Gulf region, cash transfers to the U.S. Treasury, in-
kind support to U.S. forces in Saudi Arabia and other Gulf states,

1

0136

and economic assistance to countries affected by the U.N. economic embargo against Iraq. Some countries have also provided other support, such as basing and overflight rights, military assistance to countries affected by the hostilities, and assistance to Kurdish refugees.

Military Contributions

During the Persian Gulf crisis, 36 countries sent ground, air, or naval forces or support units to the Gulf region. These forces participated directly in the multinational force or provided support by, for example, interdicting vessels suspected of violating the U.N. embargo, performing combat and combat support missions during Operation Desert Storm, and deploying medical personnel or chemical detection equipment.

Cash Contributions and In-Kind Support to the United States

Allied contributions to the United States have consisted of cash transfers to the Defense Cooperation Account[1] and in-kind support, including food, fuel, water, transportation, material, and facilities. Major contributors include Saudi Arabia, Kuwait, the United Arab Emirates, Japan, Germany, and Korea.

---

[1]Public Law 101-403 (Oct. 1, 1990), established this account to accept contributions to the Department of Defense (DOD), including money and proceeds from the sale of any property donated to DOD.

2

0137

As required by the Persian Gulf Conflict Supplemental Authorization
and Personnel Benefits Act, OMB is providing monthly reports on
contributions and incremental costs. In its latest report, dated
July 15, 1991, OMB reported that our allies had pledged about $54
billion and contributed about $44.5 billion, including $39.1
billion in cash and $5.4 billion in in-kind support. As of July
30, 1991, DOD had received an additional $1.6 billion in cash;
therefore, contributions are currently about $46.1 billion.

Table 1 shows the breakdown of pledges and contributions.

Table 1: Allied Pledges and Contributions to the United States
Dollars in millions

	Pledges			Contributions			Future	Percent of
	1990[a]	1991[a]	Total	Cash[b]	In-Kind[c]	Total	Receipts	Pledge Met
Saudi Arabia	$3,339	$13,500	$16,839	$ 9,036	$3,693	$12,729	$4,110	76
Kuwait	2,506	13,500	16,006	12,475	32	12,507	3,499	78
United Arab Emirates	1,000	3,087	4,087	3,870	217	4,087	0	100
Japan	1,740	8,332	10,072	9,376[d]	567	9,943	129	99
Germany	1,072	5,500	6,572	5,772[d]	782	6,554	18	99
Korea	80	275[e]	355	150	70	220	135	62
Other[f]	3	18	21	4	17	21	0	100
Total	$9,740	$44,212	$53,952	$40,683	$5,378	$46,061	$7,891	85

[a]1990 pledges covered August through December 1990. 1991 pledges covered January through March 1991.
[b]Cash contributions are as of July 30, 1991.
[c]In-kind contributions are as of June 30, 1991.
[d]Of these amounts, Japan and Germany specified that $961 million and $272 million, respectively, were for transportation expenses. Other countries did not place conditions on their contributions.
[e]Includes $25 million pledge under the 1990 pledge, but reserved for 1991.
[f]Includes Italy, Oman, Qatar, Bahrain, and Denmark.

3

0138

We believe that, for the most part, OMB's July 15, 1991 report accurately reflects the status of allied pledges and contributions. I would like to make some observations, however, regarding the Japanese and Korean pledges, the status of future receipts, and DOD's valuation of in-kind support.

Reductions in Pledges of Japan and Korea

In its earlier reports, OMB stated that allied pledges totaled about $54.6 billion. OMB recently revised this figure to about $54 billion to reflect a reduction in the 1991 Japanese and Korean pledges. According to administration officials, the pledges were reduced due to a misunderstanding between governments.

To our knowledge, no formal written agreements were signed regarding these pledges. According to administration officials, U.S. and Japanese officials met during January 1991 to discuss Japan's pledge for 1991. Japan pledged $9 billion in cash and U.S. officials believed that this pledge was solely for the United States. However, in early February 1991, the Japanese government issued a press release stating that the $9 billion was for financial support of the multinational forces, subject to the Japanese Diet's approval.

The Japanese Diet approved the pledge in March 1991, however due to a decline in the yen, the dollar value of the pledge had decreased

4

to about $8.532 billion. Of this amount, Japan disbursed $7.832 billion to the United States and $700 million to other countries. In July 1991, Japan contributed an additional $500 million to the United States to cover post-combat expenses, bringing the total to $8.332 billion. On July 11, 1991, President Bush met with Prime Minister Kaifu and accepted the Japanese government's position regarding the allocation of the 1991 pledge. OMB then reduced the pledge amount to $8.332 billion to reflect the actual amount paid.

The Korean government issued a statement on its 1991 pledge in January 1991 and specified that the pledge was $280 million "for the multinational force in the Gulf, the U.S. in particular." Korea had previously reserved $25 million of its 1990 pledge for 1991, therefore, the additional $280 million increased the total to $305 million. In February 1991, the Korean Minister of Defense, in a letter to Secretary Cheney, stated that the 1991 pledge was only for the U.S. government. However, in June 1991, the Vice Minister of Foreign Affairs, in a letter to the U.S. embassy charge d'affaires, stated that the pledge was for the multinational force, including the United States. In July 1991, the administration accepted this position, and OMB reduced the pledge by $30 million.

Status of Future Receipts

Of the $7.9 billion in future receipts, DOD expects to receive about $7.7 billion in cash, including $4.1 billion from Saudi

5

386 걸프 사태 미국 동향 4

Arabia; $3.5 billion from Kuwait; and up to $129 million from Japan. The remainder will be in in-kind support from Germany and Korea. Saudi Arabia has not provided a timetable for payment of its pledge, but DOD expects Kuwait to provide full payment by the end of fiscal year 1991. The exact amount of cash to be paid by Japan will be determined after final deliveries of in-kind material occur and the Japanese government pays suppliers. These deliveries consist of items, such as medical supplies, that were ordered but not delivered before hostilities ended and are now being shipped to stateside sites.

Germany has completed deliveries of in-kind support. The total of Germany's in-kind contributions, $782 million, does not reflect all of the costs Germany incurred to transport U.S. troops and equipment to German ports and overstates the value of certain vehicles. DOD officials are developing an estimate of transportation costs and have asked the German government to provide input. Our review of DOD's valuation showed that DOD inadvertently overstated the value of heavy transport vehicles and trucks by about $44 million. DOD plans to adjust the total to reflect an increase for the transportation costs and a reduction for the vehicles.

Korea's balance of $135 million reflects in-kind support due against its revised 1991 pledge of $275 million. The Korean government announced its 1991 pledge in January 1991, and since

6

0141

that time, DOD and Korean officials have been discussing U.S. requirements for in-kind support. To satisfy the balance, the Korean government intends to provide $85 million in airlift and sealift to transport cargo from the Persian Gulf and $50 million in in-kind material to replenish stocks drawn from inventories belonging to U.S. Forces, Korea, during Desert Shield and Desert Storm. Items offered include chemical protective clothing, vehicles, and gas masks.

DOD advised the Korean government that no additional airlift is required but that additional sealift assets may be needed. Since September 1990, Korea has provided four ships per month, and DOD estimates that it can use these ships through November 1991. Korea has offered additional ships, and DOD is reviewing this offer. DOD recently agreed to accept Korea's offer of $50 million in material, provided the items replace losses to U.S. Forces Korea's inventory for support of Desert Shield and Desert Storm and meet U.S. operational requirements and specifications. DOD has worked with the Korean government to ensure that these conditions are met and has revised the list of items initially offered. We are currently reviewing this matter.

Valuation of In-Kind Support

OMB has reported receipts of in-kind support valued at about $5.4 billion. This value is based on cost data compiled by the U.S.

7

0142

Transportation Command and the U.S. Central Command. When command officials did not have access to actual expenditures, they estimated the value using information provided verbally from local suppliers, prices paid under previously held U.S. contracts, and standard U.S. cost factors. As a result, the assigned value may differ from the actual cost incurred by the contributing country. For example, Central Command officials used a standard price per gallon to value fuel supplied to U.S. troops in Saudi Arabia based on the average price paid by DOD in September 1990 for jet fuel. The actual amount paid by the Saudi government is unknown.

Economic Assistance to "Frontline States" and Other Countries

In addition to cash and in-kind support to the United States, the EC and 24 countries pledged economic assistance to Turkey, Jordan, and Egypt, referred to as "frontline states," and to other countries affected by the economic embargo against Iraq. This support includes import financing grants, project assistance grants, and concessional loans. As of May 10, 1991, State reported that these pledges were about $16.1 billion for 1990 and 1991, and contributions were about $8.9 billion.

8

Table 2 shows the status of pledges and contributions.

Table 2: Economic Assistance to Frontline States and Other Countries
(as of May 10, 1991) Dollars in millions

Donor	Frontline states		Other countries[a]		Total	
	Pledge	Contribution	Pledge	Contribution	Pledge	Contribution
Gulf States	$6,168	$3,863	$3,636	$2,845	$9,804	$6,708
Saudi Arabia	2,848	2,188	1,833	1,463	4,681	3,651
Kuwait	2,500	855	1,184	763	3,684	1,618
United Arab Emirates	820	820	619	619	1,439	1,439
European Community	3,039	1,225	177	1	3,216	1,226
EC funds	805	624	0	0	805	624
France	200	0	30	0	230	0
Germany	1,195	462	137	0	1,332	462
Italy	650	37	9	0	659	37
Other[b]	189	102	1	1	190	103
Japan	2,126	803	481	0	2,607	803
Others	413	112	99	62	512	174
Korea	98	19	17	2	115	21
Norway	24	7	82	60	106	67
Switzerland	120	16	0	0	120	16
Other[c]	171	70	0	0	171	70
Total	$11,746	$6,003	$4,393	$2,908	$16,139	$8,911

[a]Bangladesh, Djbouti, Lebanon, Morocco, Pakistan, Somalia, Syria, and Tunesia.
[b]Belgium, Denmark, Ireland, Luxembourg, the Netherlands, Portugal, Spain, and
the United Kingdom.
[c]Australia, Austria, Canada, Finland, Iceland, and Sweden.

Other Types of Contributions

In addition to military, economic, and in-kind support, our
allies have contributed in other ways. For example, Germany
deployed a fighter squadron to Turkey and ships to the eastern
and central Mediterranean Sea and pledged about $2.7 billion in

9

0144

military assistance to Turkey, Israel, and the United Kingdom.
Also, some of our NATO allies and certain Gulf countries have
granted military basing and transit rights, and several countries
provided assistance to Kurdish refugees.

USE OF ALLIED CONTRIBUTIONS
TO DEFRAY U.S. COSTS

The United States has committed considerable resources to support
Operations Desert Shield and Desert Storm. We estimate that the
total cost of the operation exceeds $100 billion.   Our allies
have pledged about $54 billion, or about half, of the total cost.
The total cost is divided into three components. The first
component is the U.S. investment of about $50 billion to pay,
equip, and otherwise maintain a force of 540,000 personnel.
Second, we estimate up to $10 billion in other related costs,
such as the forgiveness of Egypt's $7 billion debt to the United
States.

The third component is the incremental costs of conducting Desert
Shield and Desert Storm, or those costs that DOD would otherwise
not have incurred, including combat costs. OMB reported that
these costs were about $42.2 billion from August 1990 through May
1991. OMB also reported that estimated remaining costs, such as
redeployment, personnel costs, and repair of equipment will be an
additional $19 billion--bringing the total incremental cost to

10

0145

about $61 billion. We are currently reviewing the basis for this estimate.

Incremental Costs Are Higher
Than Funding Requirements

While the United States has incurred substantial incremental costs to conduct Desert Shield and Desert Storm, there is an important distinction between these costs and funding requirements. Specifically, not all of the costs translate into new funding requirements. Funding requirements represent outlays that the United States has made or will ultimately be required to make, either from funds contributed by our allies or from U.S. taxpayers' funds. For example, the incremental costs reported by OMB include the value of equipment lost that will not be replaced, such as a B-52 aircraft, and, therefore, funding requirements would be less. Further, the costs include fuel and other items provided by our allies as in-kind support and, therefore, do not require any U.S. funding.

In contrast to a $61 billion estimate of total incremental costs, OMB reported incremental funding requirements for fiscal years 1991 and 1992 to be $47.5 billion. This figure does not include actual requirements of $2.1 billion funded with U.S. monies for fiscal year 1990. Combined, the total funding requirement through fiscal year 1992 is $49.6 billion. Of the $47.5 billion, $47.1 billion represents DOD funding needs and the other $400

11

0146

million represents miscellaneous funding needs for several other federal agencies, including the Departments of State, Veterans Affairs, and Education. Of the $47.1 billion in DOD funding requirements, $22.3 billion has been obligated through May 31, 1991. From May 31, 1991 through the completion of the operation, DOD expects to obligate an additional $2.4 billion for military personnel, $15.3 billion for operation support, including equipment maintenance and refurbishment, subsistence, and fuel, $5.4 billion for procurement, and $1.5 billion to replenish the stock funds. We are currently reviewing the basis for these funding requirements and reconciling the details to the total requirement.

To date, our allies have contributed about $40.7 billion in cash, and an additional $7.7 billion is expected, making about $48.4 billion available to meet U.S. funding requirements. Therefore, we believe that fiscal year 1991 and 1992 funding requirements can be fully financed from allied contributions without using U.S. taxpayers' funds.

— — — —

Mr. Chairman, that concludes my statement. I would be happy to respond to questions at this time.

(463812)

12

0147

관리
번호 91-2342

외 무 부

종 별 :

번 호 : USW-4252   일 시 : 91 0826 1847

수 신 : 장 관 (미일,미이,동구일)

발 신 : 주 미국 대사

제 목 : 걸프전 관련 미하원 군사위 보고서

연: USW-2501

금 8.26. 당관 박흥신 서기관은 RONALD BARTEK 하원 군사위 전문위원을 오찬접촉, 하원 군사위에서 작성중인 걸프전 관련 보고서 내용등 의회 동향을 탐문하고 최근 소련사태 관련 의견을 교환한바, 요지 아래 보고함.

1. 걸프전 보고서

- 하원 군사위는 ASPIN 위원장의 지시에 따라 60 페이지 분량의 걸프전 보고서를 작성중에 있으며, 동 보고서는 걸프전 배치 및 병참지원(1 차 보고서) 공중및 지상전 수행(2 차 보고서) 정보처리및 동 취약점(3 차 보고서)등을 다루게 될것임.

- 9 월초에 완료 예정인 1 차 보고서에는(2,3 차 보고서도 9 월중 완료 예정) 우방국의 BURDEN SHARING 문제가 다루어 질 것인바, 한국의 신장된 경제력에상응하는 국제적 역할증대 필요성을 강조하는 일반적 언급과 아국의 걸프전 지원과 관련 현금지원이 완료되고 잔여 물자및 수송지원의 구체적 소진방안이 양국정부간 협의중에 있다는 사실관계 언급 이외에는 특별히 한국관련 부정적인 내용은 없을 것임.

- 동 보고서가 완료되는 대로 당관에 송부 약속

2. FY 92/93 국방수권법안 관련 심의 동향

- 하기 휴회종료(9.11) 직후 FY 92/93 국방수권 법안에 관한 양원 합동 심의가 있을 것임.

- 동 법안중 우방국의 방위비 분담 증대를 위한 행정부의 협상의무와 분담금의 효율적 관리를 위한 우방국 상호 방위지불 계정 설립을 규정한 연호(USW-2501) DORGAN 수정안은 일부 문안에 대한 행정부의 아래 유보적 입장을 고려, 현재 상원측에서 문안 수정을 시도하고 있음.

. 우방국과의 방위비 분담 협상은 현재 국무부의 HOLMES 대사 책임하에 성공적으로

미주국	장관	차관	1차보	2차보	미주국	구주국	외정실	분석관
청와대	안기부							

PAGE 1   91.08.27   08:29

외신 2과 통제관 BS

0148

진행중이므로 불필요한 규정

. 동법안이 상정하고 있는 지불계정은 성격상 우방국의 걸프전 기여금 지불계정과 같은 형태로 운용할 수가 없으므로 현실적으로 가능한 문안으로 수정 필요

- 유럽 주둔 미군 병력을 FY 95 까지 10 만명(현재 16 만 5 천)으로 감축할 것을 주요 골자로 하는 연호 SCHROEDER 수정안은 당초 92 년 까지 동 수준 병력을 감축하도록 되어 있을 뿐 아니라, 법적 구속력이 있는 법안의 형태로 제출되었으나, 행정부의 강한 반대로 95 년(실제로 10 만명 수준으로 감축 예상년도)으로 수정, 법적 구속력 없는 SENSE OF CONGRESS RESOLUTION 형태로 채택된 것임.

3. 기지폐쇄 문제

- 연호(USW-4135) 기지폐쇄 조정위의 권한과 기능은 국내기지에 한정되어 있으나, 상당수의 상하의원들은 해외기지도 동 조정위의 권한에 포함시켜야 된다는 입장을 취하고 있음.

- 행정부가 해외기지 문제에 대한 의회의 간여에 반대하고 있고 다수의 공화당 의원들이 이러한 행정부의 입장을 지지하고 있어 상기 움직임이 법안화 하기에는 어려움이 있을 것이나, 해외기지 관련 예산 동결등 가능한 방법으로 금후 해외기지 폐쇄문제에 대해서도 의회가 영향력을 행사하려는 움직임이 증대 추세임.

4. 소련 국내정국

- 발트 3 국에 이어 우크라이나, 백 러시아 공화국등의 독립선언등 작금의 소련 국내사태는 여타 공화국의 잇따른 독립선언을 가속화 하여, 소련 연방의 실질적 해체를 더욱 앞당기는 상황으로 발전될 것으로 봄.

슬라브계 및 중앙아 공화국등 일부를 제외하고는 대부분의 공화국이 독립을 선언하게 될 것으로 보며, 이들과 연방과의 관계는 결국 현재의 EC 와 같은 경제연합체의 형태가 될 것이라는게 개인적 의견임.

- 우크라이나 공화국등이 독립이후 동 공화국 주둔 연방군 병력을 계속 자국의 통제하에 두겠다고 선언하고 있으나, 그렇게 되기는 어려울 것임. 현재의 병력중 자국민 이외의 병력은 철수시키거나, 아니면 연방과 일종의 주둔군 지위협정(SOFA)을 체결하는 방안은 가능하다고 봄.끝.

(대사 현홍주-국장)

예고: 91.12.31. 일반

일반문서로 재 ·19 (.(ㅅ.) ...

정 리 보 존 문 서 목 록

기록물종류	일반공문서철	등록번호	2012090554	등록일자	2012-09-17
분류번호	772	국가코드	IQ/US	보존기간	영구
명 칭	걸프사태 이후 미국.이라크 관계 동향, 1991-92				
생 산 과	북미1과/중동1과	생산년도	1991~1992	담당그룹	
내용목차	1. 1991 2. 1992				

0001

1. 1991

0002

외 무 부

종 별 : 지 급

번 호 : USW-3891 　　　　　　　　　　일 시 : 91 0805 1801

수 신 : 장 관(중동일,미일)

발 신 : 주 미국 대사

제 목 : 미-이락관계 현황(국무부 인사 조치)

　　대:WUS-3536, 연:USW-3113

　　금 8.5 당관 노광일 서기관은 국무부 이란-이락과 ALAN MISENHEIMER 이락담당관을 접촉, 미-이락관계 현황을 탐문하면서 GLASPIE 전 이락주재 대사의 거취를 알아본바, 동내용 하기 보고함.

　　1. 미-이락관계 현황

　　0 미국은 후세인 정권을 계속 국제적으로 고립시키고 동정권의 정통성을 무력화시키는데 중점을 두고 있으며, 미국내 각종 자산동결을 포함한 경제제재조치를 계속 시행하고 있음.

　　0 91.2. 이락측의 단교 조치후 미.이락 양국은 타국 대사관내 이익대표부를설치 운영중임.

　　- 이락측은 주미 알제리 대사관내 이익 대표부를 두고 있고, 동대표부내 이락 외교관 3 명이 활동

　　(1967 욤 키프르전쟁으로 미.이락 외교관계가 단절된 기간중 미국은 주이락벨기에 대사관에 미국 외교관 1 명으로 구성된 이익대표부를 운영한 전례가 있음.)

　　- 미국은 이락 주재 폴랜드 대사관에 이익 대표부를 두고 있으나 미국 외교관은 파견치않고 있으며 (폴란드 외교관 4 명으로 운영), 동이익대표부는 긴급 영사관계 업무 및 미국과 이중 국적을 보유하고 있는 아동(약 200 명 정도로 파악)에 대한 보호등 영사관계 업무와 미국대사관 시설 유지 및 고용원관리등 행정적 업무를 담당하고 있음.

　　2. GLASPIE 전 이락대사 동정

　　0 이락과 외교관계가 단절된 이상 원칙적으로 주이락대사직은 둘수가 없음.

　　0 GLASPIE 전 대사는 현재 다른 임무를 수해앟고 있고, 내부적으로 GLASPIE대사의

중아국 안기부	장관	차관	1차보	2차보	미주국	외정실	분석관	청와대

후임대사에 대한 인선이 완료된 상황이나 임용 절차를 취할 계획은 상금 없음.

  3. 제 3 국의 대이락 대사관 재개 문제

  0 미국은 제 3 국이 이락내 대사관을 재개하지 말것을 권유하고는 있으나, 동문제는 각국이 개별적으로 판단할 문제라는 입장임.

  0   다만,   미국으로서는   대사관이   재개되더라도   양국관계의   격을 낮추고(대사대리급)인원을 최소화시켜 동재개가 후세인 정권에게 줄수 있는 외교적 효과를 극소화시키기를 기대하고 있음.끝.

  (대사 현홍주-국장)

  예고:91.12.31 일반

외 무 부

종 별 : 지 급

번 호 : USW-4703   일 시 : 91 0919 1910

수 신 : 장 관(중동일,<u>미일</u>,미이,정안)(사본:주미대사)

발 신 : 주 미 대사

제 목 : 미군 중동지역 재배치(이락 대량 살상무기 사찰)

　대: WUS-4334

　1. 미국의 대이락 공격설과 관련, 주재국 언론, 국무부 및 국방부 발표내용을
종합, 하기 보고함.

　가. 행정부 발표

　. BUSH 대통령은 9.18 그랜드캐년에서 이락의 대량살상무기 사찰 목적으로 UN
헬기가 이락 영공을 비행할 때 미 공군기로 하여금 엄호 (ESCORT) 배행할 수있도록
하고, 또한 사우디측 요청에 따라 PATRIOT 미사일을 사우디에 배치키로결정하였다고
발표함.

　. BUSH 대통령은 상기조치는 이락측에 대해 위하려든 의도는 아니고, 이락내
대량살상무기의 철폐라는 UN 안보리 결의를 이락측이 이행하여야 한다는데 대한
미국의 단호한 결의를 보여주는 것이라고 언급하고, 동 조치로 인해 이락과의전쟁이
재발할 것으로 보지는 않다는다고 말함.

　. 금 9.19 국방부 정례 브리핑시 PETE WILLIAMS 대변인은 현재 비상사태계획
(CONTINGENCY PLAN) 을 수립중에 있고, 이는 여사한 상황 발생에 따른 당연한조치임을
설명함.

　. 동 WILLIAMS 대변인은 사우디측에 대한 PATRIOT 미사일 배치를 제외하고는
사우디에로의 미군병력 및 군용기의 재배치는 상금 없었음을 밝힘.(이에 반해미국내
일간지는 수일내 약 5 천명 상당의 미군이 사우디로 재배치될 것으로 보도함.)

　나. 당지 분석

　. 당지 언론은 동 조치는 이락측이 계속 대량살상무기 철폐라는 UN 안보리 결의를
준수치 않고있는 상황에서 바람직한 조치로 보고있으며, 동 조치로 인해 중동지역내
새로운 전쟁이 발발할 가능성은 희박한 것으로 보고있음.

중아국	장관	차관	1차보	2차보	미주국	미주국	외정실	분석관
정와대	안기부							

PAGE 1   91.09.20   08:56
　　　　　　　　　　　　　　　　　외신 2과 통제관 BS
　　　　　　　　　　　　　　　　　　　0005

. 동 조치는 이락측으로 하여금 UN 결의안을 무조건 수락한다는 문서를 받아내고 광범위한 UN 의 사찰을 실시케 해 위해 일종의 SBAER RATTLING 방안으로 보고있고 이락측도 결국에는 UN 의 무조건 사찰을 수락할 수 밖에 없을 것으로 보고있으나, 만약 이락이 계속 수락의사를 표명치 않을 경우, 이락의 쿠웨이트 침공시처럼 미측이 일정기간의 시한을 설정하고 동 시한내 이락측이 수락의사를 표명하지 않으면 무력사용을 포함, 모든 수단을사용하는 최후 수단을 채택할 가능성도 있다고 봄.

2. 동건 관련, 명 9.20 국무부 관계관과의 접촉 예정인 바, 동 내용 추보 예정이며, 상기 관련 기사 및 국무부 발표문은 USWF-3848 및 USWF-3849 로 팩스 송부함

(대사 현홍주-국장)

예고: 91. 12. 31 일반

일반문서로 재분류(19 . .)

PAGE 2

0006

빈호 : USW(F) - 3848
수신 : 장   관 (중동, 미원 미이)) 발신 : 주미대사
제무 : 걸프지역 미군 재배치 관련   (5 매)

STATE DEPARTMENT REGULAR BRIEFING BRIEFER: RICHARD BOUCHER
12:45 P.M. (EDT)   THURSDAY, SEPTEMBER 19, 1991

Q   Is there anything you can say about the diplomatic contacts which the administration is carrying out concerning the situation in Iraq?

MR. BOUCHER: The principal focus, George, remains in New York. We are -- with other members of the Security Council, as you know, -- we're actively engaged in efforts to assure Iraqi compliance with UN Security Council resolutions.

To remind you, Iraq is required under UN Security Council resolutions to comply with provisions demanding the destruction or rendering harmless of Iraq's nuclear, chemical, biological weapons capabilities and its ballistic missiles. The key element is Resolution 687, which set terms for the cease-fire with the assurance that Iraq could no longer pose a threat to international peace and security. The inspection teams are carrying out the mandate of the UN Security Council resolutions.

Furthermore, Iraq has long been on notice that the international community expects it to comply fully with the provisions of UN Security Council Resolutions 687 and 707. We expect Iraq to indicate its unconditional acceptance of Resolution 707. Members of the Security Council have conveyed to the Iraqi UN permanent representative the Security Council's demand that Iraq comply unconditionally with the requirement in UN Security Council Resolution 707 to allow UN helicopter flights in Iraq to assist UN inspectors in carrying out their responsibilities.

The Security Council president talked to the Iraqi representative, I believe, the night before last. Since then, we've been awaiting an Iraqi unconditional acceptance of the resolutions in writing. I think you've all seen various reports that speculate that there might be a response today. At this point, we have no firm indication of when the Iraqi response will come.

Q   Richard, (do you have anything ?) on the statements made by the United Nations ambassador of Iraq, Mr. Al-Anbari,

to the effect that his country is being subjected to threats and terrifying kinds of statements from these states.

MR. BOUCHER: I didn't prepare anything on that. I thought we'd rather deal with reality than various statements. The President yesterday said that we're not making threats, we're expressing our determination, a determination that's shared by other members of the international community to see that Iraq complies with mandatory resolutions of the Security Council.

3848 -1.

0007

Q   Richard, have you found any kind of indication for the kind of response that you expect from Iraq in his statements?

MR. BOUCHER: I -- the only thing I think we're looking for in his statements or statements from Iraq is the unconditional acceptance of the resolutions.

Q   Richard, a couple of questions. Yesterday you indicated that you would be watching Iraqi actions rather than words. Today you seem to indicate that an assurance -- a verbal assurance by them would suffice.

MR. BOUCHER: Jim, I didn't -- I don't think I indicated that yesterday. I said, in the end what matters is actions not words. Certainly one part of getting to the action, which means permitting the deployment of the helicopters without any conditions and their full use by the inspectors, that would be Iraq acceptance of that. The Security Council has requested the Iraqi assurances in writing, their unconditional acceptance of it, and that certainly would be one step on the way to the action that's necessary, and that's to permit the deployment of the helicopters.

Q   One other question. What would be the problem with letting Iraqi officials or officers aboard the UN helicopters, as the UN helicopters made their own way at their own speed across the Iraqi terrain?

MR. BOUCHER: Jim, the final arrangements for how the helicopters are used and, you know, whether there's an Iraqi navigator or something on board or not are things that the Special Commission and the inspectors can specify. The point here is that the Special Commission and the inspectors have to have the ability to conduct surprise inspections. They can't be allowed to be hampered and thwarted and hung up by Iraqi conditions, and that under the resolution the Iraqis have no right to establish any conditions.

Q   Richard, what do you make of the Iraqi assertions that there are minefields and other things around some of these sites that the UN team could stumble into and hurt themselves?

MR. BOUCHER: I hadn't seen those particular assertions. I don't have any particular comment on that, except I guess I would say that, you know, that's something the inspectors I'm sure will be aware of and deal with. If the Iraqis know of minefields, they could just tell them about it.

Q   Do you have any assessment of -- or expectation of an Iraqi response? I mean, some have said they are expecting compliance, an agreement to comply. I mean, do you have any other indications from other sources that --

MR. BOUCHER: I've said that, as you've seen, there's been various reports that expect some sort of Iraqi response today, but we have no firm indication of when the Iraqi response will come.

Q   Richard, there have been reports, some of them from United Nations officials, that the Iraqi forces are not doing terribly well against the Kurds in fighting around Kirkuk. Do you know anything about what's going on up there?

3848-2

0008

MR. BOUCHER: I haven't looked at the situation for about a week now. I think I'll just have to look for an update for you. As far as I know, we described the tensions as remaining high and I think that's still the case.

Q   Have any of the former allies that were in the coalition expressed any reservations about possible military action in Iraq?

MR. BOUCHER: You can -- you'll have to ask individual countries what their thoughts are, but I would refer you back to what the President said yesterday and that is we believe we would have the support of the international community, whatever was necessary to carry out the resolutions.

Chris?

Q   The potential escort mission the President spoke of yesterday, would that for one particular inspection team seeking to see particular things, or would it be an ongoing role that would go into months of all the various inspection teams doing all their various inspections?

MR. BOUCHER: I don't know, Chris. You can ask the Pentagon what is involved in the contingency planning and I expect they won't be able to tell you at this point.

Q   And could I -- another question. When -- you asked for free access by helicopter to basically all of Iraq, just doesn't the logistics of that really suggest that you would have to have a fairly major ground presence to fuel and service the helicopters and that sort of thing within Iraq?

MR. BOUCHER: I just don't know, Chris. Again, that gets into aspects of the Defense Department's contingency planning, and they will say as little as or as much as they want to about it.

Q   Richard, you indicated earlier that Iraq represents a threat to peace, certainly a threat to its neighbors. Is it still US policy that it's up to the Iraqi people to remove Saddam Hussein, or would the United States consider, in consultations with its allies, to speed up that process?

MR. BOUCHER: Frank, US policy remains that it's up for the Iraqi people to decide on their leadership and their government. We haven't changed our opinion of Saddam Hussein, and we certainly haven't changed our view that there can't be a normal relationship between Iraq and the rest of the world with Saddam Hussein still in power. The President yesterday was asked about the mission and what more might be added to the mission, and he spoke eloquently about two things. One is the fulfillment of the mission to get Iraq out of Kuwait, and the second was the continuing process under the UN resolutions to ensure the inspection and the destruction of Iraq's weapons of mass destruction, so that Iraq could no longer pose a threat to the region.

Q   A follow-up on the question. Do you consider Iraq as a threat to peace or the Middle East in the meaning of the peace process now going on?

3#4#-3

MR. BOUCHER: The question of the current state of Iraqi forces, I think, is something that the Pentagon has dealt with over time. Certainly I think the generals have said that they don't pose an immediate threat of invasion. But the situation with Iraq and the weapons that Iraq has developed and amassed is such that without the destruction of those weapons of mass destruction, the ultimate threat can't be discounted.

Q   I didn't make myself clear --

MR. BOUCHER: As far as the exact reflection on the peace process, I don't think I have any thoughts on that.

Q   Richard, could you tell us which of the allies in the coalition have said they will actively participate in the flights, the helicopter flights and protecting them?

MR. BOUCHER: No.

Q   Does the US have a reaction or a position on the UN decision to allow Iraq to begin selling oil again?

MR. BOUCHER: This is the implementation resolution for Resolution 706, which as you recall asked the Secretary General to come up with a plan

that would be approved by the Security Council. And the Security Council this morning adopted a resolution which authorizes the Secretary General to begin the implementation of Resolution 706. The US was pleased to cosponsor the resolution. It is aimed at beginning to bring relief to the people of Iraq, who have suffered under the repressive regime of Saddam Hussein. The resolution also provides for an initial contribution from Iraq to the compensation fund so that relief can also begin flowing at last to those outside Iraq who have suffered as a result of Iraq's unlawful invasion and occupation of Kuwait.

The third major benefit of the resolution is that it will generate funds for the work of the special commission, the boundary commission, and the return of Kuwaiti property still being held by Iraq.

The Security Council has repeatedly stated its concern about Iraq's non-compliance with Resolution 687, particularly with the work of the special commission. The Resolution will provide essential funding to help us ensure compliance, and it's entirely appropriate that the Iraqi government should be made to pay. It's also important to emphasize that the limited authorization for the sale of Iraqi oil is being made entirely within the existing sanctions regime which remains firmly in place. It does not in any way represent a weakening of the sanctions.

In this regard the crucial feature of the program, as mandated by Resolution 706 and detailed in the report and the recommendations of the Secretary General, is that no funds will ever pass into the hands of the Iraqi government. The sale of Iraqi oil and the procurement and distribution of relief supplies will be conducted under the supervision of the United Nations to ensure that the supplies reach those for whom they were intended.

0010

Q   Will Iraq have to accept this resolution for it be
implemented, or can you actually force them to comply?

MR. BOUCHER: I think Iraq has to accept the resolution in
order for it to be implemented as a practical matter. At this point
the Iraqis have neither formally accepted nor rejected the
resolution. As we said at the time, if Iraq has any sincere concern
about the fate of its people and the hardship that they are facing,
this is a way for them to see that the people get what they need.

Q   Anything on the hostage situation?

MR. BOUCHER: Nothing new for you.

Q   Richard, just to back up for a second, how will the goods
that are bought through this plan, how would they be distributed?

MR. BOUCHER: I don't have all the details of it at this point.
It's under a system that will be established by the report of the
Secretary General on the passage of the resolution.
I suspect that that kind of information will be available at the
United Nations.

Q   There seems to be a growing number of observers in this
country and abroad that the United States does not really have a
genuine interest in the removal of Saddam Hussein because of fear
that further destabilization of Iraq may not be in the best
strategic interest of the United States, and also because of
uncertainty that the removal of Saddam Hussein may lead to the
emergence or takeover of a group that may not be friendly to the
United States. Can you clarify this, please?

MR. BOUCHER: I don't quite know what you're talking about. I
think these issues have been addressed before. Our dislike for
Saddam Hussein and the ways in which he's led his country, I think,
has been something we've made no secret of. At the same time, we've
never called for the dismemberment of Iraq. What we've held forth
is that the people of Iraq should be allowed the opportunity to
choose their own government. And that remains our view.

Q   Richard, additional Patriots were sent to Saudi Arabia
because of their concern about the situation in Iraq. Has Israel
requested any additional help in that regard?

MR. BOUCHER: As far as the exact status of the Patriots, I
think you'd better check that with the Pentagon. And you can ask
Israel. I haven't heard of anything.

Q   Richard, back on the fighting around Kirkuk. Does the
United States have any evidence that the Iraqis are using air power
in any form that would violate the terms under which the coalition
forces withdrew?

MR. BOUCHER: I think the last time that we and the Pentagon
addressed that, the Iraqis hadn't been using air power. But I don't
have an update on it. I'll try to get you something.

7848-5

0011

USA(F) - 3849

경. 근 (중동1. 미일. 미이) -방신 - 주미대사

걸프지역 미군 재배치 관계   (10 매)

Bush Threatens to Send Jets To Back Up Iraq Inspections

By Ann Devroy and John Lancaster
Washington Post Staff Writers

President Bush yesterday sharply escalated pressure on Iraqi President Saddam Hussein to allow United Nations inspection and destruction of Iraq's hidden nuclear, chemical and biological arsenal, saying the United States is prepared to send warplanes to protect U.N. helicopters searching for the weapons.

In addition to placing some U.S.-based aircraft units on alert, Bush also said an unspecified number of Patriot missiles will be sent to Saudi Arabia at the request of King Fahd. "It's a safeguard," Bush told reporters during a trip to the Grand Canyon. The Saudis, he said, "don't want to feel threatened."

Senior American officials and Western diplomats described the U.S. actions as an effort to give military credibility to an ultimatum delivered to Saddam this week. The Iraqi leader was told that his government must give what one official called "absolute, written assurances" that the use of helicopters by U.N. inspectors—which Baghdad has tried to restrict—can proceed unimpeded and with no conditions.

Inspectors had said that their ground convoys in Iraq were insufficient for them to conduct surprise visits and aerial photography—particularly in light of Iraqi efforts to conceal storage sites and production facilities. U.N. resolutions governing the Persian Gulf War cease-fire authorize the inspectors to use their own aircraft in pursuit of their mission to find and eliminate Iraq's weapons of mass destruction.

U.S. officials said they anticipated an answer from Saddam by the end of the week. One official suggested that absent a satisfactory response, Bush would issue a public ultimatum with a deadline by which the helicopter flights into Iraq would begin.

Considerable numbers of U.S. warplanes, both on aircraft carriers and on the ground, remain in the Persian Gulf region following the war against Iraq, as do more than 35,000 U.S. service personnel. Pentagon officials denied reports of an imminent, large-scale deployment of U.S.-based planes.

Sources said, however, that the new deployment to the gulf of some aircraft could help drive home the message that Washington is serious about enforcing the U.N. resolutions. One unit mentioned for deployment was the 363rd Tactical Fighter Wing, composed of F-16s and based at Shaw Air Force Base in Sumter, S.C., according to a source.

The U.S. threat appeared to have the backing of both Britain and France, key allies in the Persian Gulf War and permanent members of the U.N. Security Council, and both countries were expected to participate in the air cover effort if it is needed. But diplomats in Paris and London expressed little enthusiasm for a new round of fighting, saying they believe Saddam will back down before he risks another air attack from allied forces.

Bush, Defense Secretary Richard B. Cheney and national security adviser Brent Scowcroft worked yesterday to dampen speculation that military moves are imminent. But they stressed that the helicopter flights are supported by the international coalition that fought the gulf war and will proceed with or without Iraqi acquiescence.

"There is no deadline" to execute the military orders to send new warplanes into the gulf," Bush said yesterday. "There's no threats. There's just determination . . . that he [Saddam] will comply to the letter of the U.N. resolutions."

U.S. officials continue to express amazement at Iraq's stubbornness in the aftermath of its devastating defeat in the war. In an interview recently, a Defense Department official sketched a portrait of an Iraqi military still wedded to its nuclear ambitions and possessed of surprisingly high morale.

Bush's efforts to force Saddam to back down were widely supported on Capitol Hill. Senate Minority Leader Robert J. Dole (R-Kan.) called the U.S. moves the "final warning" to Iraq, and others said the administration briefings matched public comments that the action envisioned was presently limited to enforcing the helicopter inspections.

Asked about imminent military action, Bush, who traveled to the Grand Canyon this morning to make an environmental speech, said, "I don't think it will come to that. I think the man will see that we are very serious about this, and he will do what he should have done in the first place: disclose and comply."

Cheney also played down the prospect of military action, telling reporters, "It's a prudent course for those of us in the Defense Department to be involved in planning for contingencies and that's exactly what we're doing."

Sept. 19, 1991
WP

3849 -1
0012

At the United Nations, Iraqi Ambassador Abdul Amir Anbari dismissed the situation as "a tempest in a teacup" and insisted Iraq had been fully cooperating with the United Nations. He said Iraq had been trying to arrange inspections that did not violate his country's national sovereignty.

But Bush and his senior aides described efforts to obtain Iraqi compliance as "pulling teeth, a grudging, resistant, difficult effort at every step." Bush said he was "fed up" with Saddam's resistance. The Iraqi leader, he said, "may be testing and probing" U.S. resolve on this, "but he knows better than to take on the United States of America."

A widespread impression was growing late yesterday that Iraq was on the verge of agreeing to the U.N. demands on the helicopter flights. At the United Nations, Iraqi envoy Anbari said, "The concerns of the United Nation's disarmament inspectors can be resolved by mutual understanding, not threats," Knight-Ridder reported.

Despite the presence of U.S. planes already in the gulf region, officials said any decision to provide air cover for the helicopter trips is likely to involve aircraft now based in the United States. "I don't know whether we have all the right kinds" in the region, a senior administration official said. "You don't escort a helicopter with a bomber or [a plane] off an aircraft carrier."

An Air Force spokesman declined to disclose the exact number of U.S. planes in the region, but said forces in Saudi Arabia there include the radar-evading F-117A bomber and the F-15E, both employed to considerable effect against ground targets during the war. As many as 150 more aircraft—including A-6 bombers and F-14 interceptors—are based on two aircraft carriers currently in the region, Pentagon officials said.

The helicopter inspection regime is the next stage in a weapon inspection effort that has included several ventures into Iraq by U.N. teams. The United States deployed a U-2 plane last month to gather better aerial intelligence in Iraq after a series of threats produced an agreement by Iraq that the high-altitude photo-reconnaissance plane could fly unimpeded, officials said. The helicopters were to carry inspectors to areas the U-2 flights

indicated might harbor hidden weaponry, an official said.

Iraq first said the use of the helicopters, which have been provided to the U.N. teams by Germany, would not be allowed. Baghdad then insisted on a series of what U.S. and other officials called "totally unacceptable conditions," including limits on areas of flights and requirements for certain notifications. If those conditions are not lifted, a senior U.S. official said, the helicopters will proceed "as if they are entering hostile territory" with all the military protection that involves.

The Patriot missiles will be sent to Saudi Arabia immediately, officials said. One senior official said Bush, in a lengthy discussion with King Fahd on Saturday, explained the need for the helicopter flights and air support and offered the missile battery as protection against any Iraqi retaliation with Scud missiles still believed to be in Baghdad's possession.

Scowcroft said the Saudis "feel uneasy, they feel exposed" and Bush called the move protective. Military officials refused to say whether Patriot missiles installed in Saudi Arabia during the war had been removed, or whether this amounts to an additional set.

Senior French officials in Paris told correspondent William Drozdiak they shared U.S. exasperation with Saddam's continuing lack of cooperation with the inspection teams. But given the escalating concern there with the Yugoslav and Soviet crises, there was a palpable lack of enthusiasm for renewed military action against the Iraqi regime.

In Britain, officials gave full backing to U.S. plans to possibly redeploy fighter planes to Saudi Arabia but refused to confirm that British planes would participate. "We don't get the impression we're going to war but we have not ruled out the use of force," a senior British official told correspondent Glenn Frankel.

In Congress, Dole took up the administration's threats to Saddam, noting in a speech to the Senate that "President Bush is making one last effort to deliver the message peacefully. If that doesn't work, it may be necessary to have the next message delivered by the United States armed forces."

Another Republican, Sen. Alfonse M. D'Amato (N.Y.), said, "I think the president has really given him

[Saddam Hussein] every opportunity; he had been more than patient. What you have to know is that when the president undertakes this type of action, what he's saying is, 'Saddam, you better tune up your hearing aid. We're not going to allow you to thumb your nose at the international community.' "

D'Amato echoed a sentiment that seemed to be reflected in public opinion polls and is common among GOP conservative. "My personal opinion is it would have been nice to have knocked out Saddam [during the war], but it didn't happen." he said.

Congressional leaders were given rush briefings yesterday after an early morning report by NBC News indicated imminent military action and movement of U.S. forces. No notice of any pending military move was given to congressional leaders previously, an official said, "because we haven't made the decision to move any forces yet."

In a letter Monday to House Speaker Thomas S. Foley (D-Wash.) and Sen. Robert C. Byrd (D-W.Va.), Bush suggested that military action against Iraq was possible if Saddam's government did not comply with the U.N. resolutions. "The United States will not tolerate the continuation of this situation and if necessary will take action to ensure Iraqi compliance" with the U.N. directives, Bush wrote in one of the periodic reports to Congress he is required to make under the terms of the January congressional resolution authorizing the use of force against Iraq.

Staff writers John E. Yang in Arizona and Helen Dewar, Guy Gugliotta, Tom Kenworthy and R. Jeffrey Smith in Washington contributed to this report.

Sept. 19, 1991
WP

7849-2
0013.

0014

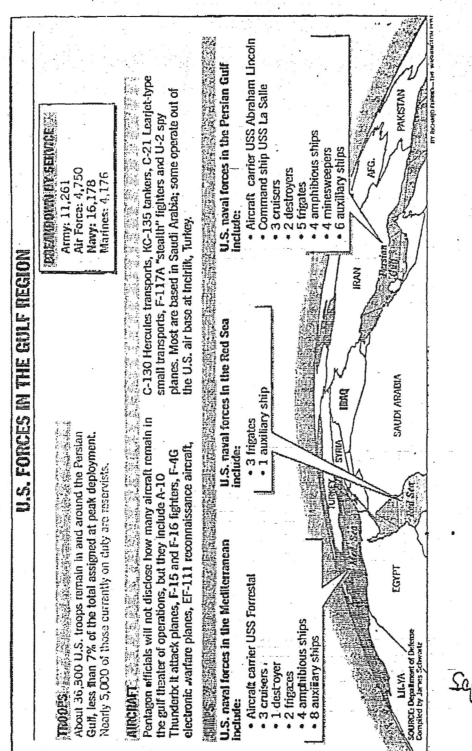

U.S. FORCES IN THE GULF REGION

TROOPS:

About 36,300 U.S. troops remain in and around the Persian Gulf, less than 7% of the total assigned at peak deployment. Nearly 5,000 of those currently on duty are reservists.

AIRCRAFT:

Pentagon officials will not disclose how many aircraft remain in the gulf theater of operations, but they include A-10 Thunderbolt attack planes, F-15 and F-16 fighters, F-4G electronic warfare planes, EF-111 reconnaissance aircraft,

C-130 Hercules transports, KC-135 tankers, C-21 Learjet-type small transports, F-117A "stealth" fighters and U-2 spy planes. Most are based in Saudi Arabia; some operate out of the U.S. air base at Incirlik, Turkey.

BREAKDOWN BY SERVICE:

Army: 11,261
Air Force: 4,750
Navy: 16,178
Marines: 4,176

U.S. naval forces in the Mediterranean include:

- Aircraft carrier USS Forrestal
- 3 cruisers
- 1 destroyer
- 2 frigates
- 4 amphibious ships
- 8 auxiliary ships

U.S. naval forces in the Red Sea include:

- 3 frigates
- 1 auxiliary ship

U.S. naval forces in the Persian Gulf include:

- Aircraft carrier USS Abraham Lincoln
- Command ship USS La Salle
- 3 cruisers
- 2 destroyers
- 5 frigates
- 4 amphibious ships
- 4 minesweepers
- 6 auxiliary ships

SOURCE: Department of Defense
Compiled by James Schwartz

LIBYA

EGYPT

TURKEY

SYRIA

IRAQ

SAUDI ARABIA

IRAN

AFG.

PAKISTAN

Red Sea

Persian Gulf

BY RICHARD FURNO—THE WASHINGTON POST

Sept. 19, 1991
WP

3849-3

U.S. WARNS IRAQIS IT WILL USE FORCE TO INSPECT ARMS

'PLENTY FED UP,' BUSH SAYS

He Authorizes American Planes to Provide Protection for U.N. Helicopter Flights

By ANDREW ROSENTHAL
Special to The New York Times

WASHINGTON, Sept. 18 — President Bush authorized American warplanes today to fly into Iraq to protect United Nations inspectors if President Saddam Hussein does not back down from his refusal to permit helicopter inspections of his military installations.

As he intensified a long-simmering diplomatic stalemate with Iraq into a new threat of force, Mr. Bush said he was "plenty fed up" with Mr. Hussein's defiance of United Nations Security Council resolutions and warned the Iraqi leader not to test American resolve once again.

But the President, perhaps mindful of the volatile political backdrop to his actions as the United States tries to arrange a Middle East peace conference, told reporters during a visit to the Grand Canyon today that he was confident there would be no outbreak of war.

U.N. Resolutions Cited

Mr. Bush said he was just doing some "prudent planning" on the strength of United Nations resolutions that he said permitted the further use of force to compel the destruction of Iraq's poison gases, Scud missiles and biological and nuclear weapons installations. He said he had no immediate plans for military action against Mr. Hussein.

"He knows better than to take on the United States of America," said Mr. Bush, whose words drew quick support from leading members of Congress.

Mr. Bush did not set a deadline for Iraqi compliance with the United Nations demand that its inspectors be allowed to fly into Iraq by helicopter. But it has been Mr. Bush's pattern in the last year to set deadlines and then follow with swift military action if they were not met, and officials said today

that an ultimatum to Baghdad was under consideration.

Baghdad Eased Position

In the months since the war ended, the United States has implicitly threatened Iraq with the use of force as Baghdad balked at complying with a series of United Nations resolutions that established the cease-fire in the gulf and set the conditions for a permanent peace. Each time, Mr. Hussein backed down.

They said the United States had been on the verge of issuing an ultimatum when Iraq eased its stand on the helicopters somewhat over the weekend, saying it would agree to the inspection flights under conditions that were deemed unacceptable by the American-led Western alliance.

In light of that shift, Mr. Bush's actions today were intended as a dramatic show of the West's determination to bend Baghdad to its will. Still, the move raised the specter of a renewed military confrontation with Iraq after less than seven months of the uneasy peace that followed the Persian Gulf war.

It also underscored the tenuous nature of the allied military victory over Iraq, which inflicted devastating damage on the Iraqi armed forces but left Mr. Hussein in power and set off armed conflict between Baghdad and ethnic and religious minorities in northern and southern Iraq.

A senior official traveling with Mr. Bush today said that some additional American forces would "definitely" be sent to Saudi Arabia within a day or two.

U.S. Forces in Region

By tonight, there was no sign of any new deployment of American forces to the gulf region, where there are still about 38,000 American troops, along with about 60 warplanes in Saudi Arabia and two aircraft carriers with more than 100 strike planes. There also are surface ships equipped with Tomahawk cruise missiles, which the United States used during the war against Iraq. American forces in Saudi Arabia were on a heightened state of alert today, Pentagon officials said.

Administration officials the White House plan was to prepare American fighters, along with British and French warplanes, to fly air cover for allied helicopters carrying United Nations inspectors and, if necessary, move to stop any Iraqi attack on the aircraft and then retaliate with strikes against Iraqi positions.

Mr. Bush said he also was sending a new supply of Patriot air defense missiles to Saudi Arabia, signaling that the kingdom had given its assent to a new allied military operation, perhaps from its territory.

Mr. Bush said he was confident that American warplanes would not have to go into action in Iraq once again to force Mr. Hussein to permit the United Nations inspections. A senior official said, "This is not Desert Storm II."

But Mr. Bush said: "I'm plenty fed up. I think the man will see we are very serious about this."

Mr. Bush added: "There's no, you know, threats, there's just determination. That's all there is, firm determination that he will comply to the letter of the U.N. resolutions. And it's not just the United States, a lot of other countries feel this way too."

Asked if he could foresee a situation that would set off a new war, Mr. Bush said: "I don't think Saddam wants any of that. I don't think he does."

He paused and said, "I'm confident he doesn't. Absolutely confident."

Comment by Dole

Senator Bob Dole, the Kansas Republican who is the Senate minority leader, said Mr. Bush was taking "the appropriate precautions."

Referring to Mr. Hussein, the Senator said, "His track record doesn't give anyone much hope that he will choose the sane and sensible course — voluntary compliance with an agreement to which, let us not forget, Iraq did agree."

He added: "President Bush is making one last effort to deliver the message peacefully. If that doesn't work, it may be necessary to have the next message delivered by United States armed forces."

Senator Alfonse D'Amato, Republican of New York, urged Mr. Bush to "deliver another message to Saddam Hussein: 'If you force us to commit troops to Iraq again, this time things will be different. This time, they'll be sent to bring you back dead or alive.'"

Attacks on Kurds

And Representative Les Aspin, the Wisconsin Democrat who chairs the House Armed Services Committee, said that in addition to forcing compliance with the United Nations inspections, Mr. Bush's warning today and the possible deployment of new forces to the gulf would also signal Mr. Hussein that he should not renew his attacks on the Kurds in northern Iraq.

"Saddam thinks we are so distracted by events in the Soviet Union and the demands of the Arab-Israeli peace process that we have forgotten about him," he said.

Sept. 19, 1991
NYT

3449-K
0015

Bush Is Sending Jets and Troops Back to Mideast

U.S. Move Increases Pressure On Iraqis to Cooperate In Weapons Inspections

By ANDY PASZTOR
AND GERALD F. SEIB
Staff Reporters of THE WALL STREET JOURNAL

WASHINGTON—President Bush authorized moving dozens of jet fighters and thousands of Air Force personnel back to the Middle East to force Iraqi President Saddam Hussein to cooperate with international weapons-inspection teams.

The F-15 jets, which are expected to arrive in the next few days along with tankers, Patriot air-defense missiles and other ground-support units, are intended to provide air cover—and perhaps even escorts over Iraq—for helicopters used by United Nations inspection teams. The move also sends a clear military warning to Saddam Hussein.

Mr. Bush and senior administration officials said an offensive strike against Iraq isn't imminent. But if Baghdad continues to impede inspection of its remaining facilities for chemical, biological and other weapons, Pentagon and other administration officials said, additional forces are likely to be sent to the region, giving Mr. Bush the option of ordering an attack.

Mr. Bush, while declaring that he was "plenty fed up" with Saddam Hussein's refusal to abide by the terms of the cease-fire that ended the Persian Gulf War, went out of his way to emphasize that he hasn't decided on offensive action and expects the Iraqi leader will back down before there is a military confrontation. Asked about the likelihood of renewed fighting, Mr. Bush told reporters during a trip to the Grand Canyon: "I don't think Saddam wants that. I'm confident he doesn't."

In fact, some administration officials said the chances of a strike have decreased slightly since last weekend, when Iraq began giving in to U.N. demands.

"This whole thing is precautionary," White House National Security Adviser Brent Scowcroft told reporters traveling with Mr. Bush. "If he [Saddam Hussein] will comply with the U.N. resolutions, there won't need to be an execute order."

Mr. Bush last weekend authorized the Pentagon to prepare to move as many as 5,000 U.S. forces back to the Saudi desert. Some of the U.S. units slated to be sent to Saudi Arabia won't arrive for some time under any circumstances, but the Pentagon's plans—dubbed "Operation Determined Resolve"—give Mr. Bush great flexibility to adjust the speed and size of the buildup depending on Baghdad's reactions.

Administration officials didn't talk about the decision to send forces back into the desert until yesterday, when NBC News reported that U.S. combat power was headed to Saudi Arabia. There currently are more than 36,000 U.S. forces in the Persian Gulf region, including nearly 5,000 Air Force personnel.

Iraq's ambassador to the United Nations, Abdul Amir al-Anbari, dismissed the latest tensions as "a tempest in a teacup," according to the Associated Press. He said Iraq has been cooperating with the U.N., but trying at the same time to protect its national security. Since the weekend, Iraq has softened its absolute refusal to permit U.N. helicopters to fly anywhere in the country and photograph suspected weapons-making or research facilities.

U.S. officials said the international inspectors intend to ignore any Iraqi conditions on helicopter flights that they find unacceptable, and that military action is likely only if Iraq tries to enforce all of its conditions.

In addition to the planes and crews already slated to go to Saudi Arabia, the Pentagon placed many more forces—including F-117 Stealth fighters, other frontline jet attack squadrons and Apache helicopters—on alert for potential deployment on short notice. The U.S. also has started preliminary discussions with some allies, including Saudi leaders, about possible offensive action if Iraq continues to obstruct inspections.

The decision to send Patriot batteries reflects Saudi and U.S. concern that Iraq still has large numbers of operational Scud missiles, partly because it has been able to salvage parts from some missile launchers damaged during the war. Although top Saudi officials privately are every bit as eager to get rid of Saddam Hussein as Mr. Bush, diplomatic sources said, a resurgence of the religious right in the kingdom has made them ambivalent about serving as a launching pad for a major attack.

Within the Bush administration, some officials long for an excuse to strike again at Iraq—perhaps even to attack the Iraqi strongman himself. But officials yesterday cautioned that the president and Mr. Scow-

Please Turn to Page A16, Column 1

Continued From Page A3

croft won't take such a step without a clear provocation. "What we're trying to do here is up the ante, . . . trying to force him to blink," said an administration official.

If Mr. Bush opts for offensive action, it isn't clear what the prime targets would be. Presumably, the White House would be intent on keeping civilian casualties as low as possible. But Pentagon planners and intelligence give the Iraqis high marks for dismantling and hiding large portions of the sophisticated weapons-making equipment that survived the war. Much of it is believed to be in fortified bunkers near populated areas.

Air Force Gen. Charles Horner, who would be in charge of any aerial attack on Iraq, acknowledged to reporters earlier this summer that it would take several days of sustained bombardment to show significant results. But he cautioned, "I'm not sure we really know" the current location of the most important equipment.

U.S. officials are particularly concerned about Iraqi deception involving its nuclear weapons program. Last month, a U.N. team found a factory 12 miles south of Baghdad that was manufacturing high-speed centrifuges used to produce highly enriched uranium. The factory's existence previously was unknown to Western intelligence agencies.

To avoid detection, the Iraqis also dismantled much of a second nuclear-related plant, and covered what remained with sheets of styrofoam, dirt and a deep layer of gravel, the inspectors found.

In still another instance, Iraq took much of the sophisticated equipment out of a uranium-processing plant, and removed identification labels and serial numbers identifying Western suppliers of remaining equipment. The inspection team concluded that Iraq had substantial outside help "beyond the supply of equipment and materials," probably including "continuing technical advice."

—*John J. Fialka contributed to this article.*

Sept. 19, 1991
WSJ

0016

Bush Rattles Saber: Will Iraq Flinch?

By R. W. APPLE Jr.
Special to The New York Times

WASHINGTON, Sept. 18 — By threatening to send American warplanes back over Iraq, President Bush is hoping to make President Saddam Hussein retreat and permit unfettered United Nations inspections, but if he fails, he will face few major diplomatic or political risks in taking direct military action.

News Analysis

Administration officials and other experts expressed doubt today that a new American initiative would disrupt the Administration's plans for a Mideast peace conference next month. In any event, these plans have been menaced by other developments, including the dispute over loan guarantees for Israel.

At first, the President and his senior advisers made clear, United States fighter-bombers would merely escort United Nations helicopters on inspection trips, but if that did not work, Mr. Bush would have to try other means to fulfill his pledge to prevent Iraq from amassing a nuclear arsenal.

The President's problem is whether military action would change much. During the Persian Gulf war air raids failed to destroy several of Mr. Hussein's nuclear and chemical weapons sites, and there is no reason to expect that they would do a lot better now. Punitive air strikes to "teach Saddam a lesson," as one official called them, are unlikely to break a man unbroken by the crushing defeat that the allies inflicted on Mr. Hussein earlier this year.

Coalition Remains Intact

The allied coalition remains more or less intact. The British, the French and the Soviet Union, the three key European allies during the gulf war, signaled that they were on board again in comments today, and Secretary General Javier Pérez de Cuéllar of the United Nations did likewise. Saudi Arabia has agreed to provide bases in return for Patriot missiles.

"I think the man will see we are very serious about this," the President said of Mr. Hussein. "He's not going to question our resolve on this."

Former Secretary of State Alexander M. Haig Jr. noted that Mr. Hussein had often backed down. On other occasions, however, "he has shown that he is quite capable of taking a very dangerous line and walking straight into the lion's mouth," Mr. Haig said.

Mr. Hussein has clung to power despite his concession of defeat in the Persian Gulf war on Feb. 28. And since early this summer, he has put repeated roadblocks in the way of international teams sent to Baghdad to check whether he has carried out a United Nations resolution calling for the de-

The President is taking few risks in threatening military action.

struction of Iraqi installations for the making of chemical, biological and nuclear weapons.

Inspectors Are Obstructed

Just as he proclaimed his intention during the war of surviving to fight another day, whatever the allies threw at him, the Iraqi leader seems determined now to cling to as much of his weapons capacity as he can by outwitting the inspection teams.

Again and again, the Iraqis have withheld information or access, the United Nations has issued warnings, and Baghdad has yielded a bit of ground. But the inspectors charge that the Iraqis have continued to hide or destroy critical equipment and to take other steps to avoid full detection of their attempts to make weapons of mass destruction. One inspector has been shot at and others have been obstructed in attempts to stage surprise inspections.

"I have no indication that they are modifying their position so far," Mr. Pérez de Cuéllar said today.

A July 25 ultimatum issued by the United Nations produced no result. Washington talked about "military options" but did nothing when the deadline passed without action, and today's statements by Mr. Bush, six weeks later, constituted an attempt to restore credibility to his threats.

A Clear Field at Home

On the domestic political front, Mr. Bush appears to have a clear field. On the record, Democratic leaders said nothing critical of the President's saber rattling, and one of the party's leading foreign-affairs specialists commented privately, "It would be another low-risk, high-tech operation, and of course there's no longer any threat that these regional things will turn into superpower confrontations."

Those who have been critical of the President's decision to end the war when he did argue that the current difficulties demonstrate anew the costs of failing to break Mr. Hussein's power and drive him from office when the moment was ripe. But the Democrats are not prepared to make that a major theme.

Recent polls suggest that much of the American public wants to concentrate on domestic issues (and indeed Mr. Bush was doing so today on his Western trip when he paused at the Grand Canyon to warn Iraq once again). But few politicians of either party doubt that the President could quickly rally the country behind a new military effort to insure that Mr. Hussein does not equip himself with nuclear weapons.

The yellow ribbons are still on doorways around the country, suggesting that the surge of patriotism of nine months ago is not yet spent, and T-shirts inspired by the gulf war are still selling well. Mr. Bush has shown conclusively that he can quickly focus the country's attention on foreign affairs when he seeks to, and to change the terms of political discourse.

"Our problem," another prominent Democrat said, "is that we are in a period of instability abroad. We don't have any candidates with foreign-policy credentials, and every time something like this happens, you can almost see the voters running for shelter to the Republicans and George Bush."

Sept. 19, 1991
NYT

3848-6

0017

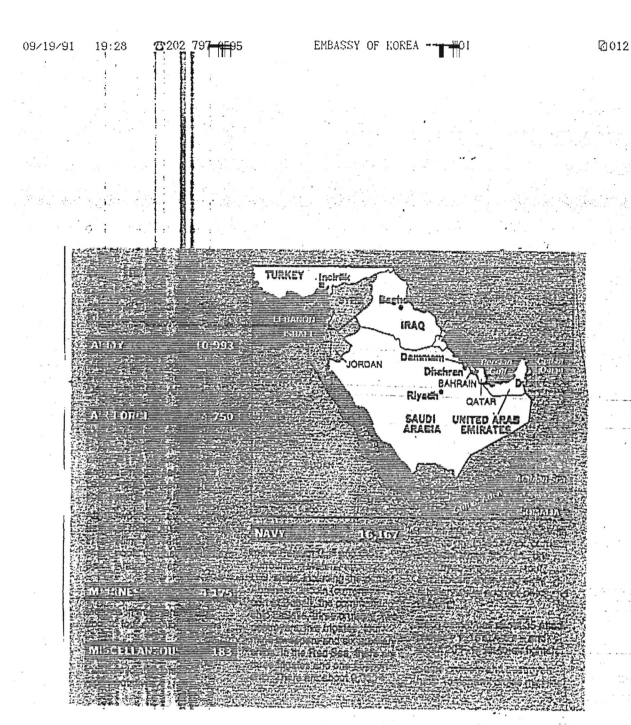

Sept. 19, 1991

3849-7

0018

US4(ㄷ) –

중   군   신신 ~ 주이덕사

(역)

Saddam: Boldness or Desperation?

Assertiveness Rebounds as Country and Regime Deteriorate

By Caryle Murphy
Washington Post Foreign Service

CAIRO, Sept. 18—Iraqi President Saddam Hussein's growing defiance of both the United Nations and his own people has now brought the most serious U.S. military threat to his regime since the Persian Gulf War ended with a cease-fire in February.

But Middle East diplomats are debating whether Saddam's new assertiveness reflects his growing confidence—or his desperation.

Saddam's political difficulties are evident throughout Iraq. According to Western analysts and Iraqis, his power has waned in both the Kurdish region of northern Iraq and the Shiite Muslim areas of the south. His stronghold remains the Sunni Muslim heartland of central Iraq, but even there, Iraqis say, his authority has eroded.

By any yardstick, Iraq's situation continues to deteriorate. It has no income and no prospect of getting any soon. Five months after the war ended, it remains isolated among its Arab neighbors. A recent fence-mending trip to Tehran by an Iraqi delegation resulted in no apparent easing of their tense standoff.

To his north, Saddam faces an unresolved situation with the Kurds, who have refused, after months of on-again, off-again negotiating, to sign the autonomy pact he was offering because of disagreement over who would control Kirkuk, a prosperous oil city. The Kurds also are skeptical that Saddam is sincere about democratic reforms in Iraq, and in a recent clash with Kurdish rebels, Saddam's forces reportedly did not fare well.

NEWS ANALYSIS

The Kurdish skepticism about Saddam's promises seems well founded. In a speech broadcast Monday, he reiterated that his ruling Arab Baath Socialist Party should continue in its vanguard role, and that there is no place for Western-style democracy in Iraq.

Anyone who adopted or admired Western values and attitudes, he said, "would not be allowed in any circumstances and conditions to take any post in leadership or direct the political, social and cultural life of the country."

His speech made no mention of a proposed new constitution or of the multi-party system he had previously pledged to introduce. This retreat from a position that has been touted to the masses by the official Iraqi media for months presumably took even his ardent supporters aback.

In the mainly Shiite Muslim south, Saddam faces an alienated, sullen populace. One international relief worker who received a recent report from Baghdad on the growing food shortages said his agency has been warned to prepare for the possibility of massive relief operations there unless the situation is eased.

In addition, Baghdad, as elsewhere in Iraq, is plagued with a major rise in crime, with armed men robbing shops even in the middle of downtown.

Saddam last Friday dismissed his prime minister, Saddoun Hammadi. The ousting of this longtime associate—one who has been in Iraq's leadership for 20 years—suggests a major disagreement between the two. Some observers suspect it may have been over whether to accept the U.N. Security Council resolution due for a vote this week, that would permit Iraq to sell oil under strict conditions in order to buy badly needed food and medicine.

Accepting this resolution, which Iraqi officials have condemned as impinging on Iraqi sovereignty, would be another humiliating move for Iraq's proud leader. But rejecting it would mean that he could be seen by his own people to be deliberately starving them.

His approach in recent months has been to push to the brink in evading and hindering the U.N. weapons inspection teams sent to Iraq to find and destroy his weapons of mass destruction.

Inspectors have complained that the Iraqis have hidden nuclear materials and that Scud missile transporters were reassembled after being destroyed. Most recently, in a violation of U.N. resolutions, the Iraqis prohibited the teams from using U.N. helicopters to search for hidden facilities. Although Iraq later said they could use them under certain conditions, it was the failure to give the inspectors free rein that prompted the United States to consider sending more warplanes to Saudi Arabia.

Every time Saddam backtracks, he stands to lose more credibility with his ruling entourage and his people. From Iraqi political history he can be aware that a leader who appears weak does not last long. "The character of this country," a veteran diplomat in Baghdad once said, "is that if you give one finger to your potential rival or friend, tomorrow you will lose your arm and the next day your head."

At the same time, Saddam may suspect that another U.S. air strike on his country would likely involve redoubled efforts to target him personally, according to the assessments of some Western and Arab officials. "If they can locate him, they will, and if they can get him, they will," one Arab diplomat said.

So most observers questioned predict that Saddam, as he has done in the recent past, will back down again.

Egyptian Foreign Minister Amr Moussa said in a telephone interview tonight, "We feel that Iraq, before anything happens, will cooperate. Its initial position was no helicopters will be flown. Now, they have accepted that they can be flown provided that one, two, three, four, I believe it's not the final position."

When the United States threatened military action before, in July, Egypt and Syria were not enthusiastic about the prospect of another wave of U.S. bombings of Iraq.

Asked whether Egypt is more supportive of U.S. military action now, Moussa replied: "We hope there will be no need for another strike. ... We definitely are in favor of total compliance by Iraq with the Security Council resolutions—and avoidance of another strike. The two together. But Iraq should apply the Security Council resolutions and should be brought to respect [them]."

Sept. 19, 1991
= WP

0013

3849-8

USW(F) -

장   견   발신 = 주미대사   [보안]
                                              [동경]

                                (역)

Measured Force on Iraq

President Bush has moved firmly but shrewdly to counter Saddam Hussein's persistent defiance of United Nations cease-fire resolutions. Yesterday he ordered American warplanes to prepare to escort U.N. helicopters should that be required to complete their arms inspection mission mandated by the Security Council.

The President has wisely resisted the temptation to bomb suspected weapons sites — an indiscriminate and probably futile approach. Instead, by backing up the U.N. mandate with an unmistakable threat of force, the President, in coordination with other Security Council members, reinforces respect for international law.

Mr. Hussein would be foolish to forget that Desert Storm was ended only on the basis of full compliance with U.N. resolutions requiring him to submit to full inspection and supervised destruction of his missiles along with any nuclear, biological or chemical weapons components.

The American planes are being made available to escort U.N. helicopters if Baghdad persists in obstructing their enforcement of these arms control provisions. The obstructions continue an Iraqi pattern of brazenly flouting cease-fire terms. These are not mere technical violations but a deliberate effort by Saddam Hussein to extract a psychological victory from the wreckage of military defeat.

Consider the record to date. Iraq has supplied inaccurate information about its missile stocks, enriched uranium supplies and chemical warheads. It refuses to acknowledge the existence of a biological warfare program that U.N. officials believe had reached at least the research stage. It has reyelded Scud missile launchers previously destroyed.

It has launched military incursions along the Kuwaiti border and fired weapons over the heads of U.N. inspectors seeking to visit a uranium enrichment facility. In the latest episode, it restricted helicopter inspections by imposing geographical, time and equipment limits on their flights.

Baghdad earlier this week began backpedaling on its helicopter restrictions, as it has done with other forms of non-cooperation. Yesterday's deployment of U.S. warplanes is intended to add muscle to diplomatic pressures.

There remain two schools of thought at the U.N. on how to deal with Saddam Hussein. One would follow the old U.N. traditions of deference to sovereign leaders. Some diplomats even now look for ways for the Iraqi dictator to save face, by easing the Security Council's terms for oil sales, for example, or downplaying Iraqi cease-fire violations.

But world peace and security would be better served by the second approach — putting the needed muscle behind U.N. resolutions. Those resolutions, if carried out effectively, could form the basis for a new world order based on collective security and international law. President Bush does well to advance that no longer utopian cause.

Sept. 19, 1991
NYT

3849-9

0020

The Right Reply to Iraq

IF MILITARY force is the only way to compel Iraq to comply with the U.N. resolutions, the United States will have to use military force again. Carrying out those resolutions fully, to the last dot, is essential. They would strip Iraq of all components of nuclear, chemical and biological weapons, as well as the missiles to deliver them. Possession of these weapons is the central issue in the rising tension between Iraq and the U.N.

Teams of U.N. inspectors have been in Iraq repeatedly since May looking for illicit weapons, locating secret factories and laboratories and assessing production capabilities. What they have already found is appalling. The Iraqis were much farther along in the development of nuclear weapons than the rest of the world had expected. They clearly had acquired the means to make biological weapons, and they had much larger stocks of chemical weapons than outsiders had estimated. But the inspectors do not believe that they are even close to the end of their job.

Now the Iraqis are challenging the inspectors' right—clearly stated in the resolutions—to use helicopters when and where they choose in their search for missiles. In response President Bush said yesterday that, if Iraq continues to resist, the United States will send more planes to its bases in Saudi Arabia and fly cover for the helicopters.

Iraq's ambassador to the U.N. explained that Iraq will try to work out procedures to allow the inspectors to operate without violating Iraq's "sovereignty." But Iraq's sovereignty was one of the victims of the battle in the desert. Iraq lost the war, and a defeated country's sovereignty is wholly conditional on the terms of the peace—in this case, those U.N. resolutions.

One reason for President Saddam Hussein's present tactics is to try to revise, retroactively, the truth that he and his army were beaten. Retaining some of the forbidden weapons is important to him not only as a military threat to Iraq's neighbors but as a demonstration to the cowed Iraqi people that Saddam is beyond the reach of even the mightiest governments in the world. If the U.N. resolutions were to be left unfulfilled, it is entirely probable that one of these weapons would shortly be used somewhere in the region simply as advertising; to demonstrate that Saddam Hussein had outsmarted and outlasted the alliance against him.

Iraq's regime is carefully testing the limits of American stamina and attention. President Bush is giving the right answer. In this desperately grave matter of Iraq's illicit weapons, there can be no question about the world's insistence on carrying out, completely, the U.N.'s terms.

Sept. 19, 1991.

WP

3849-10

0021

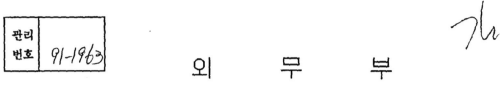

외　무　부

종　별 :

번　호 : USW-4725　　　　　　　　　　　　　　일　시 : 91 0920 1829

수　신 : 장관 (중동일,미일,미이,정안)사본:주시애틀(총)경유 주미대사-직송

발　신 : 주 미 대사

제　목 : 미군 중동지역 재배치설(UN 사찰및 이락 원유수출 결의안)

　　　대: WUS-4334

　　　연: USW-4703

　　　금 9.20. 노광일 서기관은 국무부 ALAN MISENHEIMER 이락담당관및 정보조사실
STEPHEN GRUMMON 중동담당관을 접촉, 연호 BUSH 대통령의 UN 헬기 엄호결정및작일의
이락산 원유수출 허가 UN 안보리 결의안에 대해 탐문한바, 동 내용 하기 보고함.

　　　1. 미군용기의 UN 헬기 엄호 비행

　　　0 이락은 UN 안보리결의 687 및 707 에 따라 대량 살상무기 철폐를 목적으로 UN
사찰을 무조건으로 수용해야 할 의무가 있고, 따라서 UN 사찰단의 헬기비행에 대해
조건을 부과할 수는 없으나 이락측은 이를 거부하거나 조건을 붙였음.

　　　0 이는 UN 결의안에 대한 명백한 위반으로서 미국을 위시한 주요 연합국은 UN 을
통해 동 문제를 조용히 해결하려고 노력하였으나, 이락측의 거부자세로 금번 BUSH
대통령의 미군기 엄호비행 결정이 내려졌음.

　　　0 금일 UN 에서 안보리 의장국인 불란서와 이락측이 접촉, 이락측에게 UN 헬기의
자유로운 비행을 포함 안보리 결의의 무조건 수용을 다시한번 종용할 예정으로
있으며, 이락측이 계속 거부하면 미국을 포함한 연합국측은 일정기간 시한을 설정하고
무력사용을 암시하는 수단을 사용할 수밖에 없을 것임.

　　　0 이락측이 UN 사찰을 거부하고 있는 것은 최근의 소련 쿠데타및 중동 평화회담
추진을 계기로 이락에 대한 연합국의 관심이 저하되었다는 판단하에 연합국측의
결의를 시험하고 있는 것으로 보여지며, 결국 이락이 헬기의 자유스런 비행을 포함
광범위한 UN 사찰을 수락할 수 밖에 없을 것으로 보고 있음.

　　　2. 이락 원유의 제한적 수출

　　　0 작 9.19 UN 안보리는 이락내 인도주의적 물품의 공급과 이락에 대한 배상자금

중아국	장관	차관	1차보	2차보	미주국	미주국	외정실	분석관
청와대	안기부							

확보를 위해 향후 6 개월이내 16 억불 상당의 이락 원유 판매를 허가하였음.(안보리 결의안 712 호)

- 상금 이락측은 동 조치는 이락의 주권 침해임을 들어 거부하고 있으나, 식량및 의약품 부족난을 해결할 다른 방안이 없으므로 결국 수락할수 밖에 없을 것으로 전망

0 동 원유 수출은 UN 측이 직접 관장을 하고 대금도 UN 이 관리하게 되며, 식량및 의약품의 구매및 국내배분은 기존 이락측의 시설및 유통망을 이용하게 될것임.

- 구매품목은 이락측의 소요판단을 보아가며, UN 이 결정하게 되나, 어느국가로부터 얼마만한 물량을 구매하느냐등의 상담은 이락측이 하게될 것임.(대금은UN 측이 직접 지급)

- 쿠르드족 및 시아파 밀집지역등 이락내 일부지역에 대해서는 UN 이 직접 구매물품을 배분하고, 기타지역에 대해서는 UN 의 감독하에 이락측이 물품을 배분하게 될 것임.끝.

(대사 현홍주-국장)

예고: 91.12.31. 일반

외 무 부

종 별 :

번 호 : USW-4726 　　　　　　　　　　　일 시 : 91 0920 1830

수 신 : 장관 (중동일,미일,미이) 사본:주시애틀총영사경유 주미대사(직송필)

발 신 : 주 미 대 사

제 목 : 미.쿠웨이트 군사협력 조약

대: WKU-0340

　금 9.20(금) 당관 노광일[84f금 9.20(금) 당관 노광일 서기관은 국무부 정보조사국 STEPHEN GRUMMON 중동담당관을 접촉, 미.쿠웨이크 군사협력 조약에 대해 탐문한바, 동 내용 하기 보고함.

　1. 주요내용

　0 향후 10 년간을 대상으로 미국은 쿠웨이트내 주요 군장비의 비축, 합동군사훈련 실시및 향후 비상사태를 대비한 미군의 공항및 항구 사용 방안을 규정함.

　0 군장비 비축규모및 장소, 합동군사훈련 실시회수등 구체적, 기술적 사항은 양국 군당사자간의 합의를 통해 확정함.

　0 쿠웨이트내 미군의 자동적 배치 또는 주둔을 규정하고 있지 않음.

　2. 미측입장

　0 동 조약은 행정협정 형식(상원 비준 불요)으로 작 9.19. 체니 국방장관과방미중인 AL-SABAH 쿠웨이트 국방장관간 체결됨.

　0 동 조약은 향후 걸프지역에 비상사태 발생시 미군의 개입을 원활히 하기 위한 군사물자의 사전배치등 주목적으로 한 군사협력에 대한 합의이지 쿠웨이트에 대한 안보공약(SECURITY GURANTEE)를 한 것은 아님.

　- 다만, 쿠웨이트내 비상사태시 미군의 개입을 상정함으로써 향후 쿠웨이트안보 위협국에 대한 억지효과는 있음.

　0 미국은 이와같은 군사협력 조약을 모든 GCC 국가와 체결할 예정이며, 가장 중요한 사우디와의 합의도 현재 잘 진행되고 있음.

　0 지난 걸프전 종전직후에 발표된 다마스커스 선언은 미국이 추구하는 GCC 국가와의 군사협력 조약으로 인해 의미가 없어졌다고 보지 않음.

중아국　　장관　　차관　　1차보　　2차보　　미주국　　미주국　　외정실　　분석관
정와대　　안기부

- 미국과 GCC 역내 국가와의 군사협력조약은 군사적 성격이 강한 반면, 다마스커스 선언은 걸프지역내 안전보장에 대한 아랍국(이집트및 시리아)내부의 정치적 지지효과가 있음. 끝.
  (대사대리-국장)
  예고:91.12.31. 일반

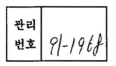

외 무 부

종 별 :

번 호 : UKW-1927   일 시 : 91 0920 1900

수 신 : 장관(중동일)

발 신 : 주 영 대사

제 목 : 미 공군의 이라크 재 공격설

대: WUK-1716

1. 당관 최참사관은 9.20 외무성 ELDON 중동담당관을 면담, 대호관련 주재국 입장을 타진한 바, 동인은 이락이 유엔 사찰에 완전히 응할 것을 기대하나 불응할 경우에는 미국의 군사조치 가능성도 배제할 수 없다하고, 미국이 조치를 취할 경우 영국도 같이 참여(ASSOCIATE)하게 될 것이라고 하였음

2. 당지 언론은 서방의 주목이 소련사태와 유고내전에 집중되어 있는 기회를 이용, 이락이 유엔사찰을 기피함으로써 미국은 이락에 대하여 새로운 경고를 하지 않을 수 없게 되었다고 보도하였는 바, 관련기사 별전 FAX 보고함

첨부: UKWF-0395. 끝

(대사 이홍구-국장)

91.12.31. 까지

홍채공통
: 홀군이 9시영을
좋것인지 ?

중아국	장관	차관	2차보	외정실	분석관	정와대	안기부

PAGE 1   91.09.21   09:34

외신 2과 통제관 EE

0026

주 영 대 사 관

UKW (F) - 0395

DATE:

수 신 : 장 관 (중동일)

발 신 : 주 영 국 대 사

제 목 : 미 공군의 이라크 재공격설

The Times (91.9.19, 1면)

US sends jets back to Gulf

From SUSAN ELLICOTT
IN WASHINGTON

THE United States will move extra air force units into Saudi Arabia as early as today in a final warning that Iraq must give access to United Nations teams to inspect Saddam Hussein's weapons of mass destruction or face military reprisals, White House officials said.

Last night Abdul al-Anbari, the Iraqi ambassador to the United Nations, said he was expecting to receive a "constructive" answer at any moment to the security council's demand that UN inspectors be allowed unrestricted use of their own helicopters.

Earlier President Bush's press secretary, Marlin Fitzwater, described the plans to send the units as "a precautionary measure". Mr Bush

said he did not expect any military action soon. "There is no deadline," he said.

"But I am thinking about seeing the will of the international community complied with ... I think the man will see that we are very serious about this. But I don't think it will come to that."

The warning is the latest in a series of leaks from the Bush administration this week designed to increase pressure on Saddam to comply with the UN resolutions. Mr Bush is seen as seeking to end Iraq's pattern of defiance on postwar issues before he addresses the UN on Monday about his vision for a new world order.

At issue is an Iraqi threat to forbid the inspectors from using any UN aircraft to fly around Iraq as they check compliance with a Gulf ceasefire agreement to eradicate all weapons of mass destruction — chemical, biological and nuclear.

Sources in Washington said that Iraq had appeared to be backing down on its dispute with the security council over access for nuclear experts to weapons sites. But the Gulf allies left no doubt that it is they who want to be in charge after Saddam's attempts to outwit them.

"We will not tolerate the continuation of this situation," President Bush told Congress in a message made public yesterday, "and, if necessary, will take action to ensure Iraq's compliance with the council's decisions."

Mr Bush obtained assurances from King Fahd of Saudi Arabia last weekend that America could move air force units on to Saudi territory, White House officials said. The deployments, including F117A Stealth fighters and F15E attack jets, are part of a new American strategy to force Baghdad to comply with the resolutions. The US has also agreed to a Saudi request for Patriot anti-missile systems to be deployed.

Unless Saddam backs down, America intends initially to draw personnel from the units as military escorts on the inspection flights. Further provocation, such as shooting at UN helicopters could lead to military action.
● New York: Thomas Pickering, the American ambassador to the UN, said that the allies did not have to observe the Gulf war ceasefire if Iraq failed to co-operate with the UN teams.

0027

$(3-2)$

The Times (91.9.19,11면)

US forced to give Iraq new warning

With the West's attention focused on the Soviet Union and Yugoslavia, Saddam has been able to reassert his authority, Michael Evans writes

The United States has been forced to threaten further military action against Iraq because of the growing confidence displayed by President Saddam Hussein in flouting the provisions of the United Nations ceasefire arrangements.

With the West focusing its attentions on the Soviet Union and Yugoslavia, the Iraqi leader has been publicly asserting his authority and demonstrating to the coalition governments that he intends to evade the restrictions imposed on him after his military defeat. He has bided his time, waiting for the departure of the majority of coalition forces before "flexing his muscles", as one British diplomatic source said yesterday.

Now, because of his persistent refusal to abide by the UN conditions for inspecting Iraq's nuclear and biological warfare facilities, the allies are forced to switch their attention back to Baghdad. RAF Jaguar jet fighters, as well as American F15s and possibly French aircraft, are expected to be involved in escorting UN helicopters into Iraq if Saddam continues to impose conditions on the use of UN helicopters for visiting nuclear sites in the country.

Saddam retreated from his initial refusal to permit UN helicopters inside Iraq but still banned them from flying over parts of Baghdad, either because he fears for his own safety or because there are facilities as yet undiscovered. But he also set other conditions: he wanted to ban aerial photography, to limit flights to two weeks, and to place Iraqi authorities on board the UN helicopters.

British and American diplomats are "fairly confident" that Saddam will capitulate, once he realises that the coalition is determined to see the UN ceasefire deal enforced. But eight Jaguar fighter-bombers sent to the Turkish base of Incirlik earlier this month to help protect Kurds in northern Iraq could be switched to helicopter escort duties if Saddam calls Washington's bluff. Defence sources said these aircraft, which were used with great effectiveness and suffered no losses throughout the Gulf war, could be redeployed with relative ease.

There has been close co-operation between the three Gulf coalition partners and they agree that further military action may be necessary. At this stage, the focus is on providing an escort for the UN helicopters, not attacking military targets if Saddam ever, if an escorting fighter were to be shot down, contingency planning includes the option of bombing some of the 45 nuclear and biological facilities pinpointed by satellites.

But the Ministry of Defence refused to make any comment yesterday, other than to say that Britain was prepared to take any steps to see that Iraq's weapons of mass destruction were destroyed, as ordered under the UN ceasefire arrangements. Saddam's obstructive attitude towards the UN inspectors is not the only example of his growing assertiveness since the end of the war. This week he made a point of declaring that there was no place for a Western-style democracy in Iraq. Although this was no great surprise, the statement was clearly intended to snub the West and to show President Bush and other coalition leaders that he was not going to be pushed around.

Last week he sacked Sadoun Hammadi, his prime minister, one of the more reasonable members of the Revolutionary Command Council, and negotiations with the Kurds, perhaps never undertaken with any sincerity, have come to an end. They now face renewed attacks.

0028

Financial Times (91.9.19,1면) (3-3)

Bush steps up pressure on Iraq

THE US yesterday announced it was ready to dispatch fighter aircraft to Saudi Arabia in order to force Iraq to comply with United Nations demands that it be given access to suspected nuclear and unconventional weapons sites.

The aim is to provide protective cover for UN helicopters searching for the sites of President Saddam Hussein's weapons of mass destruction, according to US and western officials, who said it did not signal the start of an offensive operation.

President George Bush, speaking in Grand Canyon, Arizona, said the US was determined that Mr Saddam comply with the UN mandate to inspect Iraq's nuclear facilities but damped speculation that military action was near.

"There are no threats, that's not what this is about," he said. "There's no deadline ... I'm confident he doesn't want a fight. I don't think it will come to that."

General Brent Scowcroft, Mr Bush's national security adviser, said the fighters would escort the UN helicopters should Mr Saddam continue to restrict their movements.

"It's an escort mission. If he will comply with the UN resolutions, there won't need to be an execute order," he said.

The dispatch of US fighters would escalate the long-running dispute between Iraq and the UN Security Council which has sought unsuccessfully to persuade Iraq to grant unconditional access to more than 40 sites suspected of harbouring chemical, biological and nuclear weapons.

However, a senior Pentagon official stressed that "there are no US military units on the way to the Gulf at this time", and the hope in Washington yesterday was that unanimous pressure from the UN would avert a confrontation.

UN diplomats became more optimistic yesterday that Baghdad would reach agreement on the operation of the helicopter units. Mr Abdul Amir al-Anbari, Iraq's UN envoy, described the inspection dispute as "a tempest in an empty cup of tea".

Iraq had said this week it would permit UN helicopter flights but imposed conditions which were unacceptable to the US, Britain and France, all permanent members of the Security Council.

The US has taken the lead on enforcing compliance, and has won support for its plan to send armed escorts to accompany the UN inspection teams from France and Britain.

Over the past few weeks, US intelligence has detected Iraqi efforts to hide or transfer nuclear-related equipment in a cat-and-mouse game with the UN inspectors, according to a US official.

US and other western officials said they hoped the prospective show of force would persuade Mr Saddam to "cave in" to UN demands.

The Security Council would settle for nothing less than "full, unfettered, unconditional" access for the UN inspection teams who are trying to identify and destroy all of Iraq's unconventional weapons.

This warning was reinforced by Mr Javier Pérez de Cuéllar, the UN secretary-general, who said that Gulf war resolutions permitted the use of military escorts for UN inspectors in Iraq. This comes into effect if the Baghdad regime fails to co-operate.

Pentagon officials said an alert order was issued to US aircraft units in the US and Europe, including F-117A Stealth fighters, F-15E jet fighters and aerial refuelling tankers.

These would complement the 26 US ships in the Gulf and surrounding area, which include the USS Forrestal and USS Abraham Lincoln aircraft carriers.

0029

SECRETARY'S MIDDLE EAST TRIP: BRIEFING HOST GOVERNMENTS

THE STATE DEPARTMENT HAS ASKED THAT WE PROVIDE THE
FOLLOWING INFORMATION ON SECRETARY BAKER'S RECENT
DISCUSSIONS ON THE ARAB-ISRAELI PEACE PROCESS IN MOSCOW
AND THE MIDDLE EAST:

-- BETWEEN SEPTEMBER 10 AND 20 SECRETARY BAKER
TRAVELLED TO THE SOVIET UNION AND THE MIDDLE EAST WHERE
HE HELD DISCUSSIONS ON THE ARAB-ISRAELI PEACE PROCESS
AND OTHER ISSUES WITH SOVIET, ISRAELI, PALESTINIAN,
EGYPTIAN, JORDANIAN, AND SYRIAN LEADERS.

-- THE FOCUS OF DISCUSSIONS WAS HOW TO NAIL DOWN
REMAINING ISSUES RELATED TO THE CONVENING OF AN OCTOBER
PEACE CONFERENCE AND DIRECT NEGOTIATIONS.

-- THE SECRETARY MADE CLEAR THAT A HISTORIC OPPORTUNITY
EXISTED FOR LAUNCHING DIRECT NEGOTIATIONS BETWEEN ISRAEL
AND THE ARAB STATES AND BETWEEN ISRAEL AND PALESTINIANS
TO ACHIEVE A COMPREHENSIVE SETTLEMENT OF THE ARAB-ISRAELI
CONFLICT AND URGED THE PARTIES NOT TO MISS THE OPPORTUNITY.

-- ALTHOUGH THERE ARE A NUMBER OF ISSUES THAT REMAIN TO
BE RESOLVED, THE SECRETARY FOUND ALL OF HIS
INTERLOCUTORS COMMITTED TO MOVING TOWARD THE CONFERENCE.

-- THE SECRETARY ALSO DISCUSSED WITH THE PARTIES IN THE
REGION ASSURANCES THAT THE UNITED STATES WAS PREPARED TO
PROVIDE ON ISSUES RELATED TO THE CONFERENCE AND TO
UNITED STATES POLICY.

-- IN THIS REGARD, THE SECRETARY MADE CLEAR TO ALL
PARTIES THAT THESE ASSURANCES WOULD NOT CHANGE US
POLICY AND WOULD NOT CONTRADICT THE TERMS OF
REFERENCE FOR THE CONFERENCE AND THE NEGOTIATIONS.
HE ALSO MADE CLEAR THAT THERE WOULD BE NO SECRET
ASSURANCES. ASSURANCES GIVEN TO ONE PARTY WOULD BE
KNOWN TO ALL THE OTHERS.

-- THE SECRETARY WILL CONTINUE HIS DISCUSSIONS WITH
HIS COUNTERPARTS AT THE UNGA NEXT WEEK IN NEW YORK
AND WILL BE DISCUSSING NEXT STEPS.

-- ALTHOUGH A DATE FOR THE CONFERENCE HAS NOT YET
BEEN AGREED UPON, THE UNITED STATES AND THE SOVIET
UNION REMAIN FIRMLY COMMITTED TO A PEACE CONFERENCE
IN OCTOBER.

SOVIET DISCUSSIONS

-- THE SECRETARY REVIEWED PEACE PROCESS STATE OF
PLAY WITH SOVIET FOREIGN MINISTER PANKIN. THE
SOVIETS REMAIN FULLY COMMITTED TO ALL THE
UNDERSTANDINGS PERTAINING TO THE CONFERENCE AND THE
PEACE PROCESS WHICH WERE REACHED BEFORE THE ATTEMPTED
COUP IN AUGUST.

-- THE SECRETARY REVIEWED WITH THE SOVIETS THE KE⬛
MODALITIES RELATED TO THE CONFERENCE AND FOUND
CONSENSUS AND SUPPORT ON BOTH SUBSTANCE AND PROCEDURE.

-- THE SOVIETS REMAIN COMMITTED TO A PEACE
CONFERENCE IN OCTOBER AND ARE CONFIDENT THAT THIS
OBJECTIVE IS ACHIEVABLE.

-- THE SECRETARY AND FOREIGN MINISTER PANKIN AGREED
TO MEET AGAIN AT THE UNGA ON SEPTEMBER 26 TO DISCUSS
NEXT STEPS.

ISRAEL

-- THE SECRETARY MET WITH PRIME MINISTER SHAMIR,
FOREIGN MINISTER LEVY, AND DEFENSE MINISTER ARENS TO
DISCUSS THE PEACE PROCESS AND ISSUES RELATED TO
ISRAEL'S REQUEST FOR LOAN GUARANTEES.

-- THE SECRETARY FOUND THE ISRAELIS COMMITTED TO THE
PEACE PROCESS AND TO MOVING FORWARD TO THE PEACE
CONFERENCE.

-- THE SECRETARY REVIEWED WITH SENIOR ISRAELI
OFFICIALS ISSUES RELATED TO THE CONFERENCE AND
PRESENTED A DRAFT LETTER OF ASSURANCES THE US WAS
PREPARED TO PROVIDE TO ISRAEL.

-- ON THE ISSUE OF LOAN GUARANTEES, THE SECRETARY
MADE CLEAR THAT THE BEST COURSE OF ACTION WAS TO
DELAY ISRAEL'S REQUEST FOR 120 DAYS AND REAFFIRMED
THE ADMINISTRATION'S DETERMINATION TO PURSUE THIS
APPROACH.

-- THE SECRETARY REAFFIRMED US SUPPORT FOR THE
ABSORPTION OF SOVIET JEWRY INTO ISRAEL AND RECOGNIZED
THE CHALLENGES ISRAEL FACED AT THIS TIME. AT THE
SAME TIME, HE UNDERSCORED THAT TO CONFRONT THIS
COMPLEX ISSUE NOW MIGHT MAKE IT MORE DIFFICULT FOR
ALL PARTIES TO MAKE THE DECISIONS STILL REQUIRED TO
MOVE FORWARD TO THE PEACE CONFERENCE NEXT MONTH.

-- THE SECRETARY REVIEWED WITH ISRAELI OFFICIALS SIX
ELEMENTS THAT COULD BE HELPFUL IN AGREEING TO A
DEFERRAL:

-   --THE ADMINISTRATION WOULD GUARANTEE A VEHICLE
FOR ACTION ON LOAN GUARANTEES AT THE END OF THE
120-DAY DEFERRAL PERIOD;

-   --THE ADMINISTRATION WILL COMMIT TO SEEK NO
FURTHER DELAY AT THE END OF 120 DAYS NO MATTER WHERE
THE PEACE PROCESS IS AS THAT TIME;

-   --THE ADMINISTRATION WILL RESTATE SUPPORT FOR THE
PRINCIPLE OF ABSORPTION AID TO ISRAEL;

0031

-     --THE ADMINISTRATION WILL COMMIT TO HANDLE
"SCORING" BY THE U.S. OFFICE OF MANAGEMENT AND BUDGET
(OMB) IN MOST REASONABLE POSSIBLE WAY CONSISTENT WITH
LEGAL REQUIREMENTS.

-     --THE ADMINISTRATION WILL MOUNT AN INTERNATIONAL
EFFORT AFTER JANUARY TO SOLICIT SUPPORT FROM OTHER
COUNTRIES FOR ABSORPTION AID;

-     --IF THERE IS COST TO ISRAEL ASSOCIATED WITH
DEFERRAL, THE US WILL AGREE TO OFFSET IT IN THE
ULTIMATE PACKAGE.

--   THE SECRETARY NOTED THAT THIS APPROACH WAS FAIR
AND REASONABLE AND URGED THE ISRAELIS TO ACCEPT IT.

--   GOI SAID IT WANTED TO AVOID A CONFRONTATION
BUT WASN'T PREPARED AT THIS TIME TO ACCEPT THE SIX
POINTS.

PALESTINIANS

--   ON SEPTEMBER 16, THE SECRETARY MET WITH
PALESTINIANS FROM THE WEST BANK AND GAZA TO REVIEW
PEACE PROCESS STATE OF PLAY AND TO DISCUSS THE
ASSURANCES THE US IS WILLING TO PROVIDE PALESTINIANS.

--   THE SECRETARY URGED PALESTINIANS FROM THE
OCCUPIED TERRITORIES TO BEGIN ENGAGING SERIOUSLY ON A
JOINT DELEGATION WITH JORDAN AND TO DO SO IN A WAY
THAT WOULD ALLOW THE PROCESS TO PROCEED.

--   THE SECRETARY REAFFIRMED HIS CONVICTION THAT THIS
PROCESS OFFERED A TREMENDOUS OPPORTUNITY FOR
PALESTINIANS THAT WOULD NOT COME AGAIN SOON AND URGED
THEM TO RESPOND PRACTICALLY ON THE ISSUE OF
PALESTINIAN REPRESENTATION.

--   IN THIS REGARD HE UNDERSCORED THE IMPORTANCE OF
FORMING A JOINT JORDANIAN-PALESTINIAN DELEGATION AND
URGED PALESTINIANS TO ENGAGE WITH THE JORDANIANS. HE
INVITED THE PALESTINIANS TO MEET WITH HIM IN AMMAN.

--   ON SEPTEMBER 20, THE SECRETARY MET WITH HANAN
MIKHAIL-ASHRAWI TO FOLLOW-UP ON THE ASSURANCE
EXERCISE. HE PRESENTED ASHRAWI WITH A US DRAFT
LETTER OF ASSURANCES.

EGYPT

--   IN HIS DISCUSSIONS WITH PRESIDENT MUBARAK, THE
SECRETARY FOUND CONTINUED EGYPTIAN SUPPORT FOR US
PEACE PROCESS EFFORTS AND OPTIMISM THAT THE
CONFERENCE CAN BE CONVENED NEXT MONTH.

0032

-- THE SECRETARY WILL BE CONSULTING WITH FOREIGN
MINISTER MOUSSA NEXT WEEK IN NEW YORK ABOUT NEXT
STEPS.

SYRIA
-- THE SECRETARY MET TWICE WITH PRESIDENT ASSAD ON
SEPTEMBER 18 AND 20 TO REVIEW THE PEACE PROCESS. THE
SECRETARY PRESENTED ASSAD WITH A DRAFT LETTER
OUTLINING THE ASSURANCES THE US WAS PREPARED TO
PROVIDE.

-- THE SECRETARY FOUND ASSAD COMMITTED TO ATTEND THE
OCTOBER CONFERENCE ON THE BASIS OF THE AGREED TERMS
OF REFERENCE AND INTERESTED IN FINALIZING THE
REMAINING CONFERENCE MODALITIES.

JORDAN

-- THE SECRETARY REVIEWED THE PEACE PROCESS AND
US-JORDANIAN RELATIONS WITH KING HUSSEIN ON SEPTEMBER
19.

-- THE KING REMAINS FULLY COMMITTED TO ATTENDING THE
PEACE CONFERENCE AND TO COOPERATING WITH PALESTINIANS
FROM THE OCCUPIED TERRITORIES IN PUTTING TOGETHER A
JOINT JORDANIAN-PALESTINIAN DELEGATION.

-- SECRETARY BAKER REVIEWED THE ASSURANCES THE US
WAS PREPARED TO PROVIDE JORDAN ON THE PEACE PROCESS
AND PRESENTED A DRAFT LETTER OUTLINING THOSE
ASSURANCES.

-- THE SECRETARY WILL CONTINUE HIS DISCUSSIONS WITH
JORDANIAN FOREIGN MINISTER NSOUR NEXT WEEK IN NEW
YORK.

LEBANON

-- ASSISTANT SECRETARY JOHN KELLY TRAVELLED TO
LEBANON FOR DISCUSSIONS WITH LEBANESE OFFICIALS ON
SEPTEMBER 14.

-- THE LEBANESE GOVERNMENT REAFFIRMED ITS DECISION
TO ATTEND THE PEACE CONFERENCE.

-- ASSISTANT SECRETARY KELLY REAFFIRMED US SUPPORT
FOR UNSC 425 AND FOR THE SOVEREIGNTY AND TERRITORIAL
INTEGRITY OF LEBANON. HE ALSO CALLED FOR THE
WITHDRAWAL OF ALL NON-LEBANESE FORCES FROM LEBANON.

0033

IRAQI VIOLATIONS OF ☰C RESOLUTIONS 687 AND 70☰

BEGIN TALKING POINTS:

-- WE ARE RELEASING TO YOUR GOVERNMENT A REPORT
ON IRAQ'S RECORD OF COMPLIANCE WITH UNITED NATIONS
SECURITY COUNCIL RESOLUTION, RESOLUTION 687. AS YOU
KNOW, 687 ENDED THE GULF WAR BY FORMALIZING THE
CESSATION OF HOSTILITIES BETWEEN THE COALITION AND THE
GOVERNMENT OF IRAQ.

-- THIS REPORT DOCUMENTS HOW IRAQ HAS REPEATEDLY AND
SYSTEMATICALLY VIOLATED THE REQUIREMENTS OF 687 WHICH
IT EARLIER ACCEPTED AS THE CONDITION TO ENDING THE
WAR.

-- IRAQ HAS MISREPRESENTED BOTH THE NUMBER AND SCOPE OF
DEVELOPMENT OF ITS WEAPONS OF MASS DESTRUCTION (WMD) -
CHEMICAL, BIOLOGICAL AND NUCLEAR - AND BALLISTIC
MISSILES.

-- IRAQ HAS USED DECEPTION AND CONCEALMENT TO PREVENT UN
SPECIAL COMMISSION INSPECTION TEAMS FROM LOCATING
MATERIALS AND EQUIPMENT SUBJECT TO ELIMINATION UNDER
RESOLUTION 687.

-- IRAQ HAS DENIED INSPECTORS FULL AND UNRESTRICTED
ACCESS TO FACILITIES COVERED UNDER RESOLUTION 687.

-- IRAQ HAS FAILED TO COMPLY WITH ITS OBLIGATIONS UNDER
ITS SAFEGUARDS AGREEMENT WITH THE INTERNATIONAL
ATOMIC ENERGY AGENCY (IAEA), THEREBY VIOLATING ITS
OBLIGATIONS UNDER THE NUCLEAR NON-PROLIFERATION
TREATY.

-- IRAQ HAS FAILED TO COMPLY FULLY IN RETURNING KUWAITI
PROPERTY OR IN REPATRIATING KUWAITI DETAINEES. IT
HAS RENEGED ON ITS PLEDGE NOT TO SUPPORT INTERNATIONAL
TERRORISM AND CONTINUES TO REPRESS ITS CITIZENS IN
VIOLATION OF RESOLUTION 688. IRAQ HAS ALSO DENOUNCED
THE KUWAIT/IRAQ BORDER SETTLEMENT PROCESS LAID OUT IN
UNSC RES 687.

-- IRAQ'S BEHAVIOR IN OBSTRUCTING, CONCEALING, AND
MISREPRESENTING ITS WMD AND BALLISTIC MISSILE
PROGRAMS TO THE UN SPECIAL COMMISSION AND IAEA IS
BEING ORCHESTRATED AT THE HIGHEST LEVELS OF THE IRAQI
GOVERNMENT. CONSEQUENTLY, WE CONCLUDE THAT IRAQ'S
INTENT IN SUBVERTING 687 REPRESENTS A POLICY AIMED AT
RETAINING A CAPABILITY FOR PRODUCING WEAPONS OF MASS
DESTRUCTION, INCLUDING NUCLEAR WEAPONS, AND BALLISTIC
MISSILES.

0034

-- IRAQ MUST NOT BE ALLOWED TO CONTINUE TO EVADE ITS
INTERNATIONAL RESPONSIBILITIES AND OBLIGATIONS UNDER
RESOLUTION 687. THE USG CONTINUES TO SUPPORT THE
EFFORTS OF THE UN SPECIAL COMMISSION AND THE IAEA TO
EXPOSE IRAQ'S ATTEMPTS AT CONCEALMENT AND BRING IT
INTO COMPLIANCE WITH 687'S PROVISIONS. WE CONTINUE
TO CALL ON IRAQ TO STOP VIOLATING THE PROVISIONS OF
THE CEASE-FIRE RESOLUTION AND TO GIVE COMPLETE
COOPERATION TO THE UN SPECIAL COMMISSION. WE ALSO
REITERATE OUR DETERMINATION TO TAKE WHATEVER ACTIONS
ARE NECESSARY TO ENSURE THAT THE OBJECTIVES OF THE UN
CEASE-FIRE RESOLUTION ARE ACHIEVED.

-- WE URGE YOUR GOVERNMENT TO JOIN US IN CONTINUING TO
SUPPORT STRICT ENFORCEMENT OF THESE UN RESOLUTIONS.

(END TALKING POINTS)

0035

IRAQI VIOLATIONS OF UN RESOLUTIONS 687 AND 707

(NOTE: THE U.S. GOVERNMENT, DOES NOT PLAN TO RELEASE THIS
PAPER AND REQUESTS THAT YOUR GOVERNMENT NOT RELEASE IT.)

SEPTEMBER 21, 1991

KEY JUDGMENTS

UN SECURITY COUNCIL RESOLUTION 687 DEMANDS THAT THE
GOVERNMENT OF IRAQ AGREE, UNCONDITIONALLY, TO
DECLARATION, INSPECTION, AND ELIMINATION OF ALL OF ITS
WEAPONS OF MASS DESTRUCTION (WMD) AND BALLISTIC
MISSILES. THE RESOLUTION ALSO DEMANDS THAT IRAQ RETURN
KUWAITI PROPERTY AND DETAINEES, CEASE ALL SUPPORT OF
INTERNATIONAL TERRORIST ACTIVITIES, AND DEMANDS THAT IRAQ
AND KUWAIT RESPECT THE INVIOLABILITY OF THE INTERNATIONAL
BOUNDARY BETWEEN THE TWO COUNTRIES AS SET OUT IN THE
AGREED MINUTES OF OCTOBER 4, 1963. A RELATED RESOLUTION,
UNSCR 688, DEMANDS THAT IRAQ CEASE REPRESSION OF ITS
CITIZENS.

THE IRAQI GOVERNMENT HAS REPEATEDLY VIOLATED THE
PROVISIONS OF THESE SECURITY COUNCIL RESOLUTIONS. THE
FIRST FOUR MONTHS OF INSPECTIONS BY THE UN SPECIAL
COMMISSION AND IAEA HAVE BEGUN TO ILLUMINATE IRAQ'S
COVERT PROGRAMS FOR WMD AND BALLISTIC MISSILES. FOR
EXAMPLE, IRAQ HAS:

O   MISREPRESENTED THE NUMBER AND SCOPE OF DEVELOPMENT OF ITS
WMD AND BALLISTIC MISSILES, THEN REVEALED THAT
INFORMATION, WHEN COMPELLED BY UN INSPECTIONS AND
INTERNATIONAL PRESSURE, CALCULATED TO AVOID FURTHER ACTION
BY THE SECURITY COUNCIL. AS AN EXAMPLE, THE CHART BELOW
SHOWS IRAQ'S PIECEMEAL APPROACH TO DECLARING ITS WMD AND
MISSILE FACILITIES.

DECLARATIONS OF SITES TO THE UN

	AS OF APR 18	AS OF JUN 18	AS OF SEPT 1
NUCLEAR	1	1	29
CW	8	11	12
BW	0	0	1
MISSILE	4	9	12

O   USED DECEPTION AND CONCEALMENT TO PREVENT UN INSPECTION
TEAMS FROM LOCATING EQUIPMENT SUBJECT TO ELIMINATION UNDER
RESOLUTION 687;

O   DENIED UN INSPECTION TEAMS FULL AND UNRESTRICTED ACCESS TO
FACILITIES ASSOCIATED WITH WMD AND BALLISTIC MISSILES; AND
IRAQ HAS NOT FULLY COMPLIED WITH THE REQUIREMENTS OF
RESOLUTION 687 TO RETURN KUWAITI PROPERTY OR REPATRIATE
KUWAITI DETAINEES. IT HAS VIOLATED ITS PLEDGE NOT TO
SUPPORT INTERNATIONAL TERRORISM AND HAS DEPLORED THE UN
PROCESS ESTABLISHED TO SETTLE THE BOUNDARY ISSUE.
FURTHERMORE, IRAQ CONTINUES TO REPRESS ITS CITIZENS IN
VIOLATION OF RESOLUTION 687 AND 688.

0036

O   THE IAEA BOARD OF GOVERNORS VOTED ON JULY 18, TO FIND IRAQ
IN VIOLATION OF ITS SAFEGUARDS AGREEMENT AND THUS OF THE
NON-PROLIFERATION TREATY-THE FIRST TIME IN THE AGENCY'S
EXISTENCE THAT SUCH A FINDING HAS BEEN MADE AGAINST A
MEMBER STATE. THIS WAS FOLLOWED BY A SEPTEMBER 20 MEETING
OF THE IAEA GENERAL CONFERENCE WHICH VOTED OVERWHELMINGLY
TO CONDEMN IRAQ FOR ITS ACTIONS.

THIS PATTERN OF BEHAVIOR RESULTED IN AN AUGUST 15 SECURITY
COUNCIL RESOLUTION (UNSCR 707) CONDEMNING IRAQ AND HOLDING IT
IN "MATERIAL BREACH" OF A NUMBER OF ITS OBLIGATIONS UNDER
RESOLUTION 687. (EXCERPTS FROM THE RESOLUTION ARE
APPENDED TO THIS DOCUMENT.)

BACKGROUND

ON APRIL 3, 1991, THE UNITED NATIONS SECURITY COUNCIL
APPROVED RESOLUTION 687, FORMALLY ENDING THE GULF WAR AND
LAYING THE GROUNDWORK FOR RESTORATION OF PEACE AND SECURITY TO
THE REGION. IN ADDITION TO REQUIREMENTS TO RESPECT KUWAIT'S
BORDER, RETURN STOLEN KUWAITI PROPERTY, REPATRIATE ALL
DETAINEES, AND REFRAIN FROM SUPPORT OF TERRORISM, AND SETTLE
ITS BOUNDARY WITH KUWAIT, THE RESOLUTION DEMANDED THAT THE
GOVERNMENT OF IRAQ:

O   AGREE, UNCONDITIONALLY, TO INTERNATIONALLY-SUPERVISED
ELIMINATION OF ALL OF ITS WEAPONS OF MASS DESTRUCTION
(WMD) AND BALLISTIC MISSILES, INCLUDING

--   ANY NUCLEAR WEAPONS OR NUCLEAR WEAPONS-USABLE
      MATERIAL;

--   ALL CHEMICAL WEAPONS AND BULK CW MATERIALS;

--   ALL BIOLOGICAL WEAPONS AND BULK AGENT;

--   ALL BALLISTIC MISSILES WITH RANGES IN EXCESS OF
      150 KILOMETERS; AND

--   FACILITIES, COMPONENTS, AND EQUIPMENT RELATED TO
      EACH OF THESE AREAS.

O   DECLARE THE LOCATIONS, AMOUNTS AND TYPES OF EACH OF THE
ABOVE ITEMS IN ITS POSSESSION AND AGREE TO URGENT, ON-SITE
INSPECTIONS.

IRAQ ACCEPTED THESE CONDITIONS IN RETURN FOR AN END TO
HOSTILITIES. THE UN CREATED THE SPECIAL COMMISSION WHICH,
ALONG WITH THE IAEA AND WORLD HEALTH ORGANIZATION, IS CHARGED
WITH IMPLEMENTING THE RESOLUTION'S MANDATES.

THIS DOCUMENT REVIEWS IRAQ'S RECORD OF PERFORMANCE UNDER
RESOLUTION 687 IN THE AREAS OF WEAPONS OF MASS DESTRUCTION,
BALLISTIC MISSILES, AND HUMANITARIAN CONCERNS.

0037

WEAPONS OF MASS DESTRUCTION

NUCLEAR WEAPONS AND NUCLEAR WEAPON-USABLE MATERIAL

REQUIREMENT: RESOLUTION 687 MANDATES THAT IRAQ DECLARE
THE LOCATIONS, AMOUNTS AND TYPES OF ALL FACILITIES AND
MATERIAL ASSOCIATED WITH ITS NUCLEAR WEAPONS-RELATED PROGRAM,
ACCEPT UNCONDITIONALLY THEIR REMOVAL, DESTRUCTION, OR RENDERING
HARMLESS BY THE IAEA WITH THE ASSISTANCE AND COOPERATION OF THE
UN SPECIAL COMMISSION, AND GIVE UNIMPEDED ACCESS TO THE IAEA
AND UN SPECIAL COMMISSION IN IMPLEMENTING THE RESOLUTION'S
PROVISIONS.

IRAQI ACTIONS: IRAQ'S ORIGINAL DECLARATION, PRESENTED TO
THE UN ON APRIL 18, STATED THAT IRAQ HAD NO NUCLEAR WEAPONS
PROGRAM, NO NUCLEAR WEAPONS-USABLE MATERIAL, AND THAT THE
ENTIRE IRAQI NUCLEAR PROGRAM WAS DEVOTED TO "PEACEFUL
PURPOSES." HOWEVER, THE RECORD OF THE PAST FOUR MONTHS SHOWS
THAT IRAQ CONTINUALLY MISREPRESENTED AND CONCEALED CRITICAL
ASPECTS OF ITS PROGRAM, OBSTRUCTED INSPECTORS AND DENIED THAT
THE PROGRAM IS ORIENTED TOWARD WEAPONS DEVELOPMENT.

MISREPRESENTATION OF NUCLEAR PROGRAM

O   IN LATE JUNE, UN INSPECTORS FOUND EVIDENCE OF A URANIUM
ENRICHMENT PROGRAM INVOLVING ELECTROMAGNETIC ISOTOPE
SEPARATION (EMIS). THIS DISCOVERY, ALONG WITH PREVIOUSLY
OBTAINED INFORMATION ON IRAQ'S NUCLEAR ACTIVITIES, LED
IRAQ TO DECLARE BOTH THE EMIS PROGRAM AND TWO OTHER
ENRICHMENT PROCESSES. HOWEVER, IRAQ MAINTAINED THAT THESE
PROGRAMS WERE DESIGNED TO PRODUCE FUEL FOR POWER REACTORS
AND RESEARCH REACTORS.

O   IN EARLY JULY, IRAQ ADMITTED TO A LARGE-SCALE EMIS
ENTERPRISE INVOLVING ENRICHMENT FACILITIES AT TARMIYAH AND
ASH SHARQAT, MATERIAL PRODUCTION FACILITIES AT AL-QA'IM
AND MOSUL, AND SEVERAL OTHER R&D FACILITIES.

O   AFTER THE INSPECTION VISITS, THE IAEA/SPECIAL COMMISSION
INSPECTION TEAMS ESTIMATED THAT, ONCE OPERATIONAL, THE
COMPLEXES COULD HAVE OPERATED A HUNDRED OR MORE ENRICHMENT
DEVICES (CALUTRONS) WITH A CAPABILITY TO PRODUCE UP TO 30
KILOGRAMS OF WEAPONS-GRADE URANIUM ANNUALLY.

O   IN LATE JULY, AFTER PERSISTENT QUESTIONS BY UN INSPECTION
TEAMS, IRAQ DECLARED A SIGNIFICANT CENTRIFUGE ENRICHMENT
DEVELOPMENT PROGRAM. IRAQ REVEALED A PRODUCTION FACILITY
AT AL-FARAT WHICH IT SAID WOULD BE ABLE TO MANUFACTURE 200
OR MORE CENTRIFUGES PER YEAR. A SUBSEQUENT IAEA/SPECIAL
COMMISSION VISIT PRODUCED EVIDENCE THAT LED TO AN
ASSESSMENT THAT THIS PLANT'S CAPACITY COULD BE AS HIGH AS
SEVERAL THOUSAND CENTRIFUGES PER YEAR.

0038

O   WITH EACH ADDITIONAL DECLARATION OF FACILITIES AND
EQUIPMENT, IRAQ HAS ADMITTED TO POSSESSING MORE NUCLEAR
MATERIAL, NOW AMOUNTING TO LARGE AMOUNTS OF URANIUM
FEEDSTOCK AND SMALL AMOUNTS OF UNSAFEGUARDED ENRICHED
URANIUM AND PLUTONIUM.

O   ON AUGUST 6, IRAQ ADMITTED TO PRODUCING UNSAFEGUARDED
PLUTONIUM. MAINTAINING THAT IT HAD NOT EARLIER REPORTED
THE EXTENT OF ITS PROGRAM FOR FEAR OF ITS BEING
MISUNDERSTOOD, IRAQ ADMITTED THAT IT HAD VIOLATED IAEA
SAFEGUARDS BY FABRICATING AND IRRADIATING NATURAL URANIUM
FUEL ELEMENTS IN ONE OF ITS SAFEGUARDED REACTORS AT TUWAITHA,
SEPARATING GRAM QUANTITIES OF THE RESULTING PLUTONIUM,
FAILING TO DECLARE ANY OF THESE ACTIVITIES TO THE IAEA,
AND THEN LYING TO UN INSPECTORS ABOUT THE OPERATION'S
EXISTENCE. IN SPITE OF THIS ADMISSION, IRAQ STILL
MAINTAINED THAT ITS MATERIAL PRODUCTION PROGRAMS WERE
SIMPLY PEACEFUL RESEARCH EFFORTS.

PATTERN OF CONCEALMENT

O   IRAQ STRIPPED LARGE AMOUNTS OF EQUIPMENT FROM BUILDINGS AT
TUWAITHA, TARMIYAH, AND AL-HAMATH AND THEN MISREPRESENTED
THE FUNCTIONS OF THOSE BUILDINGS TO INSPECTORS. ONLY WHEN
CONFRONTED WITH DISCREPANCIES BETWEEN THEIR DECLARATION
AND OBSERVABLE FEATURES SUCH AS ELECTRIC POWER, PLUMBING,
AND CRANE CAPACITIES -- OR WHEN CONFRONTED WITH
INCONSISTENCIES IN ITS PREVIOUS STATEMENTS -- DID IRAQ
ADMIT THE TRUE MISSION OF THE FACILITIES.

O   IRAQ BURIED EMIS EQUIPMENT BEFORE THE FIRST TEAM ARRIVED
AT TUWAITHA, UNEARTHED IT AFTER THE TEAM LEFT THE AREA,
LOADED THE EQUIPMENT ONTO TRUCKS, AND THEN COVERTLY
DISPERSED IT TO SEVERAL UNDECLARED LOCATIONS.

O   IRAQ ADMITTED HIDING ITS CLANDESTINE PLUTONIUM PRODUCTION
PROGRAM AT TUWAITHA FROM IAEA/SPECIAL COMMISSION
INSPECTORS DURING THE FIRST THREE INSPECTIONS BY PLACING
FUEL ELEMENTS ON TRUCKS AND RELOCATING THEM PRIOR TO
INSPECTIONS.

O   IRAQ RAZED NUCLEAR-RELATED STRUCTURES, AND REGRADED AREAS
AT MOSUL AND TUWAITHA TO HAMPER INSPECTORS.

O   AT TARMIYAH AND MOSUL, IRAQ PAINTED OVER WALLS AND DUMPED
THICK LAYERS OF GRAVEL IN AREAS WHERE RELEVANT MATERIAL
SAMPLES MIGHT HAVE BEEN OBTAINED.

O   AT TARMIYAH, IRAQ COVERED EMIS EQUIPMENT WHICH COULD NOT
BE EASILY RELOCATED WITH FRESHLY-POURED CONCRETE AND
SEVERAL FEET OF EARTH. IN SOME CASES, ENTIRE FLOORS OR
CEILINGS WERE REMOVED TO OBSCURE EQUIPMENT FOUNDATIONS AND
UTILITY CONNECTIONS, THUS DISGUISING THE TRUE PURPOSE OF
BUILDINGS.

0039

O   IRAQ BURNED DOCUMENTS AT BOTH TUWAITHA AND TARMIYAH AND
ADMITTED TO USING EXPLOSIVE CHARGES TO DESTROY EMIS
COMPONENTS AT SEVERAL REMOTE LOCATIONS TO PREVENT THE
MATERIAL OR EQUIPMENT FROM BEING VIEWED BY INSPECTORS.

OBSTRUCTION OF INSPECTION TEAMS

O   IRAQI OFFICIALS REPEATEDLY SOUGHT TO MISLEAD INSPECTORS
ABOUT THE PURPOSE AND FUNCTIONS OF BUILDINGS AT TUWAITHA,
TARMIYAH, AND ASH SHARQAT. IN THE FIRST CASE, A NUCLEAR
ASSOCIATION WAS DENIED; AT TARMIYAH THE FACILITY WAS
PORTRAYED AS A CHEMICAL PROCESSING FACILITY; AND AT ASH
SHARQAT THE BUILDING WAS DESCRIBED AS A COATING PLANT.

O   AT THE FALLUJAH TRANSPORTATION CENTER, INSPECTORS
REQUESTED ACCESS TO A TRUCK CONVOY PARKED INSIDE THE
FACILITY. WHILE BEING DENIED ACCESS BY IRAQI MILITARY
OFFICERS AT THE FRONT GATE, THE TEAM PHOTOGRAPHED THE
CONVOY LEAVING THE SITE THROUGH ANOTHER GATE. WHEN
INSPECTORS TRIED TO INTERCEPT THE CONVOY IN ORDER TO
INSPECT THE EMIS-RELATED CARGO, WARNING SHOTS WERE FIRED
OVER THEIR HEADS BY IRAQI SECURITY PERSONNEL.

O   AT ABU GHURAYB, INSPECTORS WERE DENIED ACCESS TO AREAS
WHERE EMIS EQUIPMENT WAS BEING STORED TEMPORARILY. IN
ADDITION, ONE INSPECTOR WAS DENIED MEDICAL CARE WHEN
REQUESTED.

INSISTENCE ON THE PEACEFUL INTENT OF THE PROGRAM

O   CONTRARY TO IRAQI CLAIMS THAT EMIS CONTRIBUTED TO IRAQI
ENERGY PRODUCTION,ENRICHMENT OF URANIUM USING
ELECTROMAGNETIC ISOTOPE SEPARATION REQUIRES FAR MORE
ENERGY THAN THE ENRICHED URANIUM PRODUCT COULD PRODUCE IN
A POWER REACTOR.

O   IRAQ CLAIMS THAT THE EMIS PROGRAM'S TARGET ENRICHMENT
(24) WAS, IN PART, DESIGNED TO PROVIDE FUEL FOR THE
SOVIET-SUPPLIED IRT-5000 REACTOR. YET THE SOVIETS HAD
ALREADY SUPPLIED FUEL FOR THE LIFETIME OF THE REACTOR AND
THE SIZE OF THE EMIS PROGRAM EXCEEDED ANY CONCEIVABLE
REQUIREMENT OF THE IRT-5000 REACTOR.

O   IRAQ WENT TO GREAT LENGTHS TO CONCEAL ITS URANIUM
ENRICHMENT AND PLUTONIUM PRODUCTION PROGRAMS, AS WELL AS
THE MATERIAL PRODUCED BY THOSE PROGRAMS, FROM THE IAEA AND
SPECIAL COMMISSION. BY FAILING TO DECLARE NUCLEAR
MATERIAL INVOLVED IN URANIUM ENRICHMENT AND PLUTONIUM
REPROCESSING ACTIVITIES AND BY FAILING TO PROVIDE DESIGN
INFORMATION ON FACILITIES WHERE MATERIAL WAS USED, IRAQ
DID NOT COMPLY WITH ITS OBLIGATIONS UNDER ITS SAFEGUARDS
AGREEMENT WITH THE IAEA, THEREBY VIOLATING ITS OBLIGATIONS
UNDER THE NON-PROLIFERATION TREATY.

0040

O   ON JULY 18, DR. HANS BLIX, DIRECTOR GENERAL OF THE IAEA,
STATED, "THE LARGE ENRICHMENT PROGRAM IN IRAQ WAS
CLANDESTINE. IT WAS NOT PLACED UNDER SAFEGUARDS AND NO
CONFIDENCE CAN ARISE THAT IT HAD PEACEFUL PURPOSES."

CONCLUSION

SINCE MAY, UN AND IAEA INSPECTIONS REVEALED IRAQ HAS
VIOLATED RESOLUTION 687'S NUCLEAR PROVISIONS IN SEVERAL
FUNDAMENTAL WAYS. IRAQ HAS FAILED TO DECLARE FULLY ITS
NUCLEAR-RELATED MATERIAL AND EQUIPMENT TO ACCEPT ELIMINATION
OF ALL OF THIS EQUIPMENT, AND TO PROVIDE COMPLETE INSPECTOR
ACCESS. INSTEAD IRAQ HAS:

O   REPEATEDLY MISREPRESENTED ITS NUCLEAR PROGRAM -- MOST
SERIOUSLY, FAILING TO DECLARE ITS NUCLEAR WEAPONS-RELATED
ACTIVITIES -- AND ACKNOWLEDGED PARTICULAR NUCLEAR
ACTIVITIES ONLY AFTER IDENTIFICATION BY INSPECTION OR
INTELLIGENCE;

O   CONCEALED PROSCRIBED ACTIVITIES AND EQUIPMENT, AND MADE
EFFORTS TO REMOVE, HIDE, DESTROY, AND COVERTLY RECOVER
EQUIPMENT; AND

O   BLOCKED UN INSPECTION TEAMS ACCESS BY MEANS UP TO AND
INCLUDING THREATS OF PHYSICAL FORCE.

IT IS NOW CLEAR THAT IRAQ'S NUCLEAR WEAPONS PROGRAM WAS
MULTIFACETED AND WELL-FUNDED. IT INVOLVED:

O   THOUSANDS OF WELL-EDUCATED SCIENTISTS AND ENGINEERS;

O   BILLIONS OF DOLLARS IN INFRASTRUCTURE;

O   ABOUT 30 RESEARCH, MANUFACTURING, STORAGE, AND PRODUCTION
SITES NATIONWIDE.

O   SEVERAL METHODS OF MANUFACTURING WEAPONS-GRADE MATERIAL
INCLUDING EMIS, GAS CENTRIFUGES, PLUTONIUM PRODUCTION, AS
WELL AS RESEARCH ON GASEOUS DIFFUSION, CHEMICAL, AND LASER
ISOTOPE SEPARATION TECHNIQUES.

CHEMICAL WEAPONS (CW)

REQUIREMENT: RESOLUTION 687 MANDATES THAT IRAQ DECLARE
ALL CHEMICAL WEAPONS (CW), AGENT STOCKS, AND RELATED
FACILITIES, PROVIDE FULL AND COMPLETE ACCESS TO UN INSPECTORS,
AND ACCEPT THE UNCONDITIONAL REMOVAL, DESTRUCTION, OR RENDERING
HARMLESS OF ALL CW MATERIAL, EQUIPMENT, AND FACILITIES.

IRAQI ACTIONS: THE RECORD SHOWS THAT IRAQ MISREPRESENTED
AND CONCEALED THE SIZE OF ITS PROGRAM.

0041

MISREPRESENTATION

O   IRAQ INITIALLY DECLARED ONE PRODUCTION AND STORAGE
FACILITY, EIGHT STORAGE SITES, 11,000 FILLED CHEMICAL
MUNITIONS, AND 1,000 TONS OF BULK AGENT AND PRECURSOR
MATERIAL. FOUR MONTHS OF UN PROBING ELICITED FOUR
ADDITIONAL DECLARATIONS WHICH DESCRIBED A MUCH MORE
COMPREHENSIVE PROGRAM:

--   46,000 AGENT-FILLED CHEMICAL MUNITIONS, INCLUDING
        2,100 MUNITIONS FILLED WITH MIXED NERVE AGENT'S;

--   79,000 UNFILLED MUNITIONS;

--   2,700 TONS OF BULK AGENT AND PRECURSOR MATERIALS;

--   3 ADDITIONAL CHEMICAL WEAPONS STORAGE SITES;

--   SEVERAL DUAL-USE CHEMICAL FACILITIES WHICH COULD
        AUGMENT IRAQ'S DEDICATED CHEMICAL WEAPONS PROGRAM.

O   AT SAMARRA, THE UN SPECIAL COMMISSION DISCOVERED EVIDENCE
OF THE CAPABILITY TO PRODUCE TWO UNDECLARED TYPES OF NERVE
AGENTS, GB AND VX. TO THIS POINT, IRAQ HAS REVEALED
PRODUCTION OF MULTIPLE TYPES OF CHEMICAL WEAPONS,
INCLUDING FOUR TYPES OF AGENT(SULFUR MUSTARD, GA-B-F,
MIXED SARIN AND VX).

O   CONCEALMENT

O   IRAQ REMOVED CW-RELATED DOCUMENTS FROM SAMARRA IN JUNE.
THIS REMOVAL WAS NOTED BY THE INSPECTION TEAM, WHICH FOUND
PILES OF ASH FROM FRESHLY-BURNT DOCUMENTS NEARBY.

O   INSPECTORS OBSERVED AREAS OF THE FACILITY WHICH HAD BEEN
RECENTLY ALTERED BY STREWING LIVE MUNITIONS AND RUBBLE IN
FRONT OF THE ENTRANCES TO PREVENT THEIR ACCESS.

CONCLUSION

SINCE JUNE, UN INSPECTIONS HAVE REVEALED THAT IRAQ HAS
VIOLATED RESOLUTION 687 BY FAILING TO: (1) FULLY DECLARE ITS CW
WEAPONS AGENT STOCKS AND RELATED FACILITIES; (2) TO PROVIDE
FULL AND COMPLETE ACCESS TO UN INSPECTORS, AND (3) TO ACCEPT THE
UNCONDITIONAL REMOVAL, DESTRUCTION, OR RENDERING HARMLESS OF
ALL CW MATERIAL, EQUIPMENT AND FACILITIES.

IRAQ'S PRE-WAR CW CAPABILITY, WHICH PRIOR TO OPERATION
DESERT STORM INCLUDED CHEMICAL AGENTS IN BOMBS, ARTILLERY
SHELLS, ROCKET WARHEADS, AND BALLISTIC MISSILES, WAS ONE
OF THE LARGEST IN THE WORLD. THIS, COUPLED WITH IRAQ'S
ATTEMPTS TO MISREPRESENT ITS CAPABILITY TO THE UN, IMPLIES
STRONGLY THAT SADDAM HUSSEIN'S INTENT IS TO CIRCUMVENT
RESOLUTION 687'S CHEMICAL WEAPONS PROVISIONS AND TO RETAIN A
CHEMICAL WEAPONS INVENTORY.

0042

BIOLOGICAL WEAPONS

REQUIREMENT: RESOLUTION 687 MANDATES THAT IRAQ DECLARE
ALL BIOLOGICAL WEAPONS (BW), AGENT STOCKS, AND RELATED
FACILITIES, PROVIDE FULL AND COMPLETE ACCESS TO UN INSPECTORS,
AND ACCEPT THE UNCONDITIONAL REMOVAL, DESTRUCTION, OR RENDERING
HARMLESS OF ALL BW MATERIAL, EQUIPMENT, AND FACILITIES.

IRAQI ACTIONS: IRAQ MAINTAINED IT HAD NO BIOLOGICAL
WEAPONS AND HAD CARRIED OUT NO RELATED ACTIVITIES. IT FAILED
TO ACKNOWLEDGE THE EXISTENCE OF A BIOLOGICAL WARFARE (BW)
PROGRAM AND AGENT STOCKPILES AND SUBSEQUENTLY ATTEMPTED TO
MISREPRESENT FACILITIES AND PROGRAMS AS LEGITIMATE BIOLOGICAL
RESEARCH FACILITIES FOR PEACEFUL OR PROPHYLACTIC PURPOSES.

FAILURE TO DECLARE PROGRAM

O   IRAQ DISCLOSED A BW RESEARCH PROGRAM AT THE SALMAN PAK
FACILITY ONLY AFTER THE ARRIVAL OF THE BW INSPECTION TEAM
IN EARLY AUGUST.

O   IRAQ DISCLOSED THAT IT WAS EXPERIMENTING WITH
MICRO-ORGANISMS THAT HAVE POTENTIAL OFFENSIVE MILITARY
APPLICATIONS:

--   BOTULISM (CLOSTRIDIUM BOTULINUM): CLOSTRIDIUM
         BOTULINUM PRODUCES A LETHAL TOXIN WHICH IS 10,000
         TIMES MORE POTENT THAN NERVE AGENT PER UNIT MASS.

--   ANTHRAX (BACILLUS ANTHRACIS): ONCE INHALED, SPORES
         GROW IN LUNGS, RELEASING A TOXIN WHICH IS FATAL IN
         MORE THAN 90 PER CENT OF TREATED CASES.

--   CLOSTRIDIUM PERFRINGENS: ATTACKS WOUNDS IN THE SKIN
         AND DESTROYS SKIN TISSUE, PRODUCING GANGRENOUS
         INFECTION WHICH CAN LEAD TO DEATH.

O   WHEN QUESTIONED FURTHER, IRAQ FINALLY ACKNOWLEDGED THAT
IT HAD UNDERTAKEN RESEARCH WHICH COULD HAVE HAD OFFENSIVE
MILITARY APPLICATIONS. IRAQ MAINTAINS, HOWEVER, THAT IT
HAS NOT WEAPONIZED BW AGENTS.

O   IRAQ CLAIMED THAT ITS BW RESEARCH PROGRAM, BEGUN IN 1986,
WAS TERMINATED IN AUGUST 1990 AND THAT ALL MATERIALS WERE
DESTROYED OR MOVED TO OTHER LOCATIONS. THE BW INSPECTION
TEAM, HOWEVER, FOUND CLEAR EVIDENCE AN EXISTING IRAQI
CAPABILITY TO PRODUCE WHAT HE TEAM'S LEADER CHARACTERIZED
AS "...VAST QUANTITIES OF BIOLOGICAL AGENTS". UN INSPECTORS
DISCOVERED THAT SALMAN PAK HAD THE CAPACITY TO PRODUCE
ENOUGH ANTHRAX WEEKLY TO CONTAMINATE AN AREA OF MORE THAN
600 SQUARE MILES.

O   IRAQ ALSO TURNED OVER TO THE INSPECTION TEAM A COLLECTION
OF 30 SAMPLES OF MICRO-ORGANISMS WHICH INCLUDED "STRONG
CANDIDATES" FOR BIOLOGICAL WARFARE AGENTS, SUCH AS
BRUCELLOSIS AND TULARAEMIA, THAT HAD NOT BEEN PREVIOUSLY
DECLARED.

0043

CONCEALMENT AND MISREPRESENTATION

O   IRAQ CLAIMED THAT ITS SALMAN PAK BW PRODUCTION FACILITY
WAS A "FOOD AND LIQUID INSPECTION AND ANALYSIS FACILITY,"
UNTIL CONFRONTED WITH EVIDENCE TO THE CONTRARY BY UN
INSPECTORS.

O   IRAQ HAD RECENTLY RAZED BUILDINGS AND SPREAD DIRT OVER
AREAS THAT WERE PART OF THE SALMAN PAK FACILITY, THEREBY
PREVENTING INSPECTORS FROM SAMPLING FOR TRACES OF
BW-RELATED MATERIALS.

O   INSPECTORS FOUND EVIDENCE OF REMOVAL OF CRITICAL EQUIPMENT
FROM BUILDINGS AND THE REMOVAL AND DESTRUCTION OF
DOCUMENTS AT SEVERAL IMPORTANT LOCATIONS WITHIN SALMAN PAK

O   UNEXPLODED ORDNANCE WAS RECENTLY PLACED AT BUNKER SITES AT
SALMAN PAK TO IMPEDE ACCESS. MUNITIONS WERE DIRECTLY IN
FRONT OF THE BUNKERS AND, DESPITE IRAQI EXPLANATIONS, THAT
THIS RESULTED FROM COALITION AIR STRIKES THE MATERIAL HAD
NONE OF THE DUST AND WEATHERING THAT CHARACTERIZED OTHER
UNEXPLODED ORDNANCE OF "DESERT STORM" VINTAGE.

O   DESPITE THE PRODUCT MANUFACTURER'S PUBLIC ASSERTION TO THE
CONTRARY, IRAQ CONTINUES TO CLAIM THAT ABU GHURAYB -- A
SUSPECTED BW FACILITY -- WAS A "BABY MILK" FACTORY. TO
SUPPORT THIS ASSERTION, IRAQ RELEASED A VIDEOTAPE OF
WORKERS AT ABU GHURAYB WEARING BLUE SMOCKS WITH "BABY MILK
FACTORY" STENCILED IN ENGLISH ON THE BACKS.

CONCLUSION

IRAQ HAS VIOLATED THE BW PORTIONS OF RESOLUTION 687 BY
FAILING (1) TO DECLARE BIOLOGICAL WEAPONS AGENT STOCKS AND
RELATED FACILITIES, (2) TO PROVIDE UN INSPECTORS FULL AND
COMPLETE ACCESS AND (3) TO ACCEPT THE UNCONDITIONAL
REMOVAL, DESTRUCTION OR RENDERING HARMLESS OF ALL BW
MATERIAL EQUIPMENT AND FACILITIES.

BALLISTIC MISSILES

REQUIREMENT: IRAQ IS REQUIRED TO DECLARE ALL BALLISTIC
MISSILES WITH RANGES GREATER THAN 150 KILOMETERS, RELATED MAJOR
PARTS, AND RELATED REPAIR AND PRODUCTION FACILITIES, PROVIDE
FULL AND COMPLETE ACCESS TO UN INSPECTORS, AND ACCEPT THE
UNCONDITIONAL REMOVAL, DESTRUCTION, OR RENDERING HARMLESS OF
ALL SUCH EQUIPMENT AND FACILITIES.

IRAQI ACTIONS: IRAQ INITIALLY DECLARED 52 SCUD MISSILES
AND SCUD VARIANTS AND 5 SITES FOR PRODUCTION, MAINTENANCE,
STORAGE, AND DEPLOYMENT. SUBSEQUENT INSPECTIONS REVEALED THAT
IRAQ HAD MISREPRESENTED ITS INVENTORY OF BALLISTIC MISSILES,
COMPONENTS AND FACILITIES AND ATTEMPTED TO DECEIVE INSPECTORS
AND CONCEAL MISSILES AND RELATED COMPONENTS FROM INSPECTION
TEAMS.

0044

MISREPRESENTATION OF EQUIPMENT INVENTORIES

O   IRAQ'S ORIGINAL DECLARATION FALLS HUNDREDS OF MISSILES
SHORT OF THE NUMBER THAT MAY REMAIN IN ITS INVENTORY.
AFTER SUBTRACTING THOSE MISSILES USED IN THE IRAN-IRAQ
WAR, THE GULF WAR, IN TEST FIRINGS AND THOSE WHICH WERE
DESTROYED BY THE SPECIAL COMMISSION FROM THE 819 WHICH
BAGHDAD ADMITS MOSCOW GAVE THEM, A LARGE NUMBER REMAINS
UNACCOUNTED FOR.

O   IRAQ'S ORIGINAL DECLARATION DID NOT INCLUDE FIVE TYPES OF
BALLISTIC MISSILES COVERED BY RESOLUTION 687 -- THE
AL-FAHD, THE AL-ABBAS, AND THE AL-HIJARAH, THE TAMMUZ I,
AND THE BADR-2000 (CONDOR II). DURING THE INITIAL
INSPECTION, NINE UNDECLARED AL-FAHDS WERE DISCOVERED AND
DESTROYED.

O   IRAQ INITIALLY FAILED TO DECLARE THE "SUPERGUN" -- AN
EXTREMELY LARGE ARTILLERY-TYPE LAUNCHER WHICH HAS THE
CAPABILITY TO LAUNCH MISSILES WITH WMD PAYLOADS TO RANGES
OF SEVERAL HUNDRED KILOMETERS. THE COMMISSION DECIDED, AND
COMMUNICATED TO IRAQ, THAT THE "SUPERGUN" THEREFORE FELL
WITHIN THE PROHIBITED WMD AND THAT IRAQ SHOULD HAVE
DECLARED IT UNDER RESOLUTION 687. IN FACT, IRAQ DENIED
THAT IT POSSESSED SUCH A WMD SYSTEM. IT WAS NOT UNTIL
MID-JULY THAT SITES AND EQUIPMENT ASSOCIATED WITH THIS
SYSTEM WERE DECLARED.

O   IRAQ UNDERSTATED THE EXTENT OF ITS MISSILE PRODUCTION AND
SUPPORT INFRASTRUCTURE BY FAILING TO DECLARE SIX
MISSILE-RELATED DEVELOPMENT AND PRODUCTION FACILITIES.

O   IRAQ DECLARED ONLY FOUR DECOY MISSILES DESPITE THE
EXISTENCE OF A LARGE QUANTITY BEFORE THE END OF OPERATION
DESERT STORM. SUBSEQUENTLY, AN INSPECTION TEAM FOUND AND
DESTROYED 11 UNDECLARED DECOYS.

O   IRAQ FAILED TO DECLARE LARGE AMOUNTS OF SCUD-RELATED
HARDWARE AND SUPPORT EQUIPMENT WHICH HAS BEEN DISCOVERED
AND TAGGED FOR EVENTUAL DESTRUCTION BY UN INSPECTORS.

EFFORTS TO DECEIVE INSPECTORS

O   DURING INSPECTIONS OF THE NASSR FACILITY, IRAQ PREVENTED
INSPECTORS FROM PHOTOGRAPHING SUSPECT AREAS.

O   AT THE SAME TIME THAT INSPECTORS WERE WITNESSING THE
DESTRUCTION OF PROSCRIBED MISSILES AT THE TAJI FACILITY,
IRAQI OFFICIALS WERE CONCEALING ADDITIONAL PROSCRIBED
MISSILE EQUIPMENT AT A SITE NEARBY.

O   IRAQ ATTEMPTED TO RE-BUILD WMD-RELATED EQUIPMENT
DISMANTLED UNDER SPECOM DIRECTION. INSPECTORS FOUND FOUR
SCUD/AL-HUSSEIN TRANSPORT TRAILORS PREVIOUSLY CUT IN HALF
AT TAJI WERE REWELDED TOGETHER AND MOVED TO AN UNDECLARED
SITE AT KHAN AL-MAHAWIL BARRACKS.

0045

O   IN VIOLATION OF SECURITY COUNCIL DEMANDS IN RESOLUTION
707, IRAQ HAS REFUSED TO COOPERATE WITH THE SPECIAL
COMMISSION IN ALLOWING UN HELICOPTERS TO OPERATE IN IRAQ
IN SUPPORT OF INSPECTIONS.

CONCLUSION

IRAQ HAS VIOLATED THE MISSILE PORTIONS OF RESOLUTION
687 BY FAILING TO DECLARE ALL BALLISTIC MISSILES COVERED
BY THE RESOLUTION, RELATED MAJOR PARTS AND FACILITIES,
FAILING TO PROVIDE FULL AND COMPLETE ACCESS TO UN
INSPECTORS, AND FAILING TO ACCEPT THE UNCONDITIONAL
REMOVAL, DESTRUCTION OR RENDERING HARMLESS OF ALL SUCH
EQUIPMENT OR FACILITIES.

IRAQ'S BALLISTIC MISSILE PROGRAM IS IMPRESSIVE.
USING A NATIONWIDE SYSTEM OF RESEARCH, DEVELOPMENT, AND
PRODUCTION FACILITIES, IRAQ HAS DEVELOPED THE INDIGENOUS
CAPABILITY TO MODIFY, PRODUCE, AND LAUNCH VARIANTS OF
THE SCUD MISSILE AND HAS MADE SIGNIFICANT PROGRESS
TOWARD PRODUCING ITS OWN LONG-RANGE SYSTEM.

IRAQ'S PRE-WAR MISSILE INVENTORY OF SOME 500 WAS
REDUCED BY ITS ATTACKS ON SAUDI ARABIA, BAHRAIN AND
ISRAEL AS WELL AS BY COALITION AIR STRIKES.
NONETHELESS, EVEN AFTER THE ELIMINATION OF 61 MISSILES
BY THE UN SPECIAL COMMISSION, SEVERAL HUNDRED ADDITIONAL
MISSILES REMAIN SOMEWHERE. THESE UNDECLARED MISSILES --
HIDDEN FROM UN INSPECTIONS -- WILL, IF ALLOWED TO
REMAIN, CONSTITUTE A SIGNIFICANT COVERT MISSILE FORCE.

IRAQI NONCOMPLIANCE WITH OTHER UN MANDATES

RETURN OF KUWAITI PROPERTY

WHILE PUBLICLY CLAIMING THAT IT IS PREPARED TO RETURN
STOLEN KUWAITI PROPERTY AS REQUIRED BY RESOLUTION 687, IRAQ HAS
PROVIDED ONLY AN INCOMPLETE LIST OF KUWAITI PROPERTY IN ITS
POSSESSION. IT RETURNED KUWAIT'S GOLD ONLY AFTER FOUR MONTHS
OF INTERNATIONAL PRESSURE.

IRAQ HAS YET TO RETURN OTHER KUWAITI PROPERTY, INCLUDING
CONTENTS OF ITS MUSEUMS, LIBRARIES, OR BILLIONS OF DOLLARS OF
KUWAITI MILITARY EQUIPMENT, INCLUDING HAWK AIR DEFENSE
MISSILES. RECENTLY IRAQI UNITS HAVE CROSSED INTO KUWAITI
TERRITORY AND REMOVED WEAPONS LEFT BEHIND DURING THEIR RETREAT
FROM THE EMIRATE AND HAVE ALSO SET UP OBSERVATION POSTS. IN
LATE AUGUST, KUWAITI FORCES DETAINED DOZENS OF IRAQI
PERSONNEL ENGAGED IN SUCH ACTIVITIES.

0046

REPRESSION OF IRAQI CITIZENS

REACTING TO IRAQ'S BRUTAL REPRESSION OF ITS CITIZENS,
ESPECIALLY THE SHI'A IN SOUTHERN IRAQ AND KURDS IN THE NORTH,
THE SECURITY COUNCIL PASSED RESOLUTION 688, WHICH DEMANDS THAT
IRAQ CEASE REPRESSION OF ITS CITIZENS AND ALLOW IMMEDIATE
ACCESS BY INTERNATIONAL HUMANITARIAN ORGANIZATIONS TO ALL THOSE
IN NEED OF ASSISTANCE IN IRAQ. WHILE IRAQ, UNDER THE THREAT OF
MILITARY ACTION BY COALITION FORCES, PULLED ITS MILITARY FORCES
BACK FROM SOME OF THE KURDISH AREAS IN THE NORTH, ITS POLICE,
INTELLIGENCE OPERATIVES, AND MILITARY FORCES HAVE CONTINUED TO
POSE A THREAT TO CIVILIANS.

IRAQ SIGNED A MEMORANDUM OF UNDERSTANDING WITH THE UN
SECRETARY GENERAL'S EXECUTIVE DELEGATE, PRINCE SADRUDDIN AGA
KHAN, ON APRIL 19 COVERING UN RELIEF EFFORTS THROUGHOUT THE
COUNTRY. IT PROMISED COOPERATION AND GUARANTEED THE UN ACCESS
TO ALL REGIONS WHERE RELIEF IS NEEDED. DESPITE THIS, SADRUDDIN
WAS INITIALLY DENIED ACCESS TO THE SOUTHERN MARSH REGION DURING
HIS JULY FACT-FINDING MISSION AND UN PERSONNEL ASSIGNED TO
ESTABLISH A FEEDING CENTER IN HAMMAR WERE EXPELLED IMMEDIATELY
AFTER HIS DEPARTURE. SADRUDDIN'S FORMAL PROTEST TO SADDAM
HUSSEIN WAS ANSWERED WITH A LETTER NOTING THAT IRAQ HAD NEVER
ACCEPTED RESOLUTION 688. IRAQI TROOPS, WHO HAD BEEN PULLED
BACK DURING SADRUDDIN'S VISIT TO THE AREA, WERE RETURNED TO THE
MARSHES IMMEDIATELY AFTER SADRUDDIN'S DEPARTURE FROM THE REGION
AND THE UN STILL HAS NOT BEEN ALLOWED ACCESS.

REPATRIATION OF KUWAITI DETAINEES

IRAQ AGREED TO RESOLUTION 687'S DEMAND THAT IT RELEASE
IMMEDIATELY ALL KUWAITI AND THIRD-PARTY DETAINEES AND PROVIDE
THE INTERNATIONAL COMMITTEE OF THE RED CROSS (ICRC) WITH ACCESS
TO SUCH DETAINEES. KUWAIT HAS STATED THAT IRAQ STILL HOLDS
ABOUT 2,422 KUWAITIS AND RESIDENTS OF KUWAIT AND THAT IRAQ HAS
RETURNED ONLY 206 ADULT DETAINEES SINCE THE CEASE-FIRE IN
APRIL. THE ICRC SAYS THAT IRAQ HAS NOT COOPERATED IN PROVIDING
ACCESS TO ALL PRISONS, CAMPS, AND INTERNMENT AREAS.

SUPPORT FOR TERRORISM

IN SPITE OF IRAQ'S STATEMENT -- AS REQUIRED BY RESOLUTION
687 -- THAT IT WOULD NOT COMMIT OR SUPPORT ANY ACT OF
INTERNATIONAL TERRORISM OR ALLOW ANY TERRORIST ORGANIZATION TO
OPERATE ON IRAQI TERRITORY, IRAQ STILL ALLOWS TERRORIST
ORGANIZATIONS TO OPERATE ON IRAQI TERRITORY.

SETTLEMENT OF KUWAIT/IRAQ BORDER

RESOLUTION 687 REQUIRED IRAQ TO ENTER INTO DISCUSSIONS
WITH KUWAIT BASED ON THE AGREED MINUTE OF OCTOBER 4, 1963 IN
ORDER TO SETTLE THE ISSUE OF THEIR BOUNDARY DEMARCATION. THE
RESOLUTION FURTHER PROVIDES THAT BOTH COUNTRIES WILL RESPECT
THE BORDER'S INVIOLABILITY. ALTHOUGH IRAQ ACCEPTED RESOLUTION
687, AT THE AUGUST MEETING OF THE BOUNDARY COMMISSION THE
IRAQI REPRESENTATIVE TO THE COMMISSION STATED THAT IRAQ
REJECTED THE WORK OF THE BOUNDARY COMMISSION AND ITS
DEMARCATION OF THE IRAQ-KUWAIT BORDER.

0047

EXCERPTS FROM UN SECURITY COUNCIL RESOLUTION 707
           PASSED UNANIMOUSLY ON 15 AUGUST, 1991

THE SECURITY COUNCIL...

CONDEMNS IRAQ'S SERIOUS VIOLATION OF A NUMBER OF ITS
OBLIGATIONS UNDER ... RESOLUTION 687 ... WHICH CONSTITUTES
A MATERIAL BREACH OF THE RELEVANT PROVISIONS OF RESOLUTION
687 ...

FURTHER CONDEMNS NONCOMPLIANCE BY THE GOVERNMENT OF IRAQ
WITH ITS OBLIGATIONS UNDER ITS SAFEGUARDS AGREEMENT WITH
THE INTERNATIONAL ATOMIC ENERGY AGENCY ... WHICH
CONSTITUTES A VIOLATION OF ITS COMMITMENTS AS A PARTY TO
THE TREATY ON THE NON-PROLIFERATION OF NUCLEAR WEAPONS OF
1 JULY 1968,

DEMANDS THAT IRAQ:

PROVIDE FULL, FINAL, AND COMPLETE DISCLOSURE ... OF ALL
ASPECTS OF ITS PROGRAMS TO DEVELOP WEAPONS OF MASS
DESTRUCTION AND BALLISTIC MISSILES WITH A RANGE GREATER
THAN 150 KILOMETERS ... WITHOUT DELAY ...

CEASE IMMEDIATELY ANY ATTEMPT TO CONCEAL OR ANY MOVEMENT
OR DESTRUCTION OF ANY MATERIAL OR EQUIPMENT RELATING TO
ITS NUCLEAR, CHEMICAL OR BIOLOGICAL WEAPONS OR BALLISTIC
MISSILE PROGRAMS ...

HALT ALL NUCLEAR ACTIVITIES OF ANY KIND, EXCEPT FOR USE OF
ISOTOPES FOR MEDICAL, AGRICULTURAL, OR INDUSTRIAL PURPOSE,
UNTIL THE SECURITY COUNCIL DETERMINES THAT IRAQ IS IN FULL
COMPLIANCE WITH THIS RESOLUTION AND PARAGRAPHS 12 AND 13
OF RESOLUTION 687 .... AND THE IAEA DETERMINES THAT IRAQ
IS IN FULL COMPLIANCE WITH ITS SAFEGUARDS AGREEMENT WITH
THAT AGENCY.

0048

미국은 이라크 지도자를 축출하기 위하여 더욱 적극적인 군사행동 검토중

(91.11.25.자 Washington Post 지 보도내용)

o 미 행정부는 걸프전의 완전치 못한 종결에 대한 민주당과 대통령후보들의
   비판에 직면하여, 후세인 이라크 대통령을 축출하기 위해 더욱 적극적인
   군사행동을 검토중이라고 미고위관리가 언급
   - 부시는 대통령 선거를 1년도 못남긴 시점에서 민주당측이 후세인의 계속
      집권을 걸프전 성과를 불식시키는데 이용할지 모른다고 우려

o 후세인 정권을 전복시키는 방안에는 이라크내 반군에 대한 군사훈련 및
   부품제공, 이라크 북부지역에 반군정부 수립지원등이 포함되어 있음

o 관계당국 및 관리들간에는 후세인 제거노력이 실행할만한 가치가 있을것인지
   여부에 대하여 논란

o 이러한 검토는 백악관 지휘하에 관계부처 회의에서 진쟁중인데, 후세인
   정권을 전복시키기 위한 이러한 계획이 실패할것이라는 미 정보전문가들의
   의견이 지배적
   - 계획이 성공하기 위하여는 미국의 이라크 내부정치에 대한 어느정도의
      리버리지와 이라크 반군내부의 연대가 이루어져야 할것인데 실질적으로
      두가지 다없음

o 미국내외 각계반응 및 입장
   ① 미하원 외무 소위원장 솔라즈의원(민주)와 상원 외무위원장 펠의원(민주)
      은 이라크 반군에 대한 적극적인 지원지지

   ② 국방부 고위관리도 경제제재 보다는 더욱 적극적인 대이락 조치 찬성하나,
      후세인 제거노력을 강화하는데는 가장 회의적

0049

- 최근 기자회견에서 중동문제 담당자는 후세인 제거를 위한 비밀계획이 현실성이 없으며 현존 반대세력이 후세인 정권을 탈취할수 있다고 생각 하는것은 망상이라고 일축

- 국방부 고위관리들은 미국의 목표는 최소한의 개입으로 현상황을 안정되게 유지하는 것이며 쿠르드인들은 자력으로 그들의 운명을 결정해야 한다고 언급

③ 국무부 관리들은 이러한 계획의 검토가 이라크의 새지도부를 창출하기 위한 간접 압력을 위주로 하고 있는 미국의 현전략(이라크의 계속적인 외교고립확보, 세계적 차원에서 엄격한 대이라크 경제제재유지, 이라크의 대량파괴무기 제조능력 제거등)을 재확인하는 선에서 결론이 날것으로 전망

- 11.20. 하원 외무소위에서 제레이언 국무차관보는 이라크내 반대세력 들과의 접촉을 넓혀 이라크의 복합사회적 성격을 대표하는 신정권이 창출될수 있도록 지원 노력을 계속하겠다고 언급

- 미국정책의 주요목표는 이라크 인민이 그들의 정부를 바꿀수있는 환경 조성에 있으며 후세인이 시아파와 쿠르드 반군단체들을 포용하지 못하고 있으므로 점차 권력기반이 약화될것으로 기대되나, 시간필요

④ 정보 당국자들은 최근 기자회견에서 최근의 미행정부 정책이 후세인 정권을 약화시키지 못했다고 언급

- 2주전 사위 '마지드'의 국방장관 임명과 1주전 이복형제 '하산'의 내무장관 임명등으로 미루어 후세인 체제 강화노력 계속

- 지난주 이라크 북부에서는 쿠르드족에 대한 식량선적 재개를 조건으로 쿠르드 게릴라들을 주요도시로 부터 철수시켜 이라크 정부군의 지위강화

- 종전이후 단한건의 쿠테타 또는 전복계획도 확인못함

- 미정보부 관리는 지속적이고, 광범위한 기반의 반군세력이 이라크내에 없으며, 어떠한 지원도 밑빠진 독에 물붓기일 것이라고 언급

0050

⑤ 독립서방 단체들은 경제 봉쇄제재 조치가 무고한 이라크 국민들만
괴롭히고 있다고 지적

⑥ 영국관리들은 이라크가 유엔 사찰과 감독에 대한 요구조건만 준수하면
영국을 비롯한 유럽국가들은 후세인 축출 노력에 지지 않겠다함

⑦ 터키는 터키국경을 위태롭게 할지도 모르는 쿠르드 독립국가 건설에
흥미가 없으므로 쿠르드 반군을 지원하는 자국내 미공군기지 사용허가
연장에 미온적

o 미 관리들은 각국의 대이라크 경제고립에 대한 관심이 ~~점소화~~ 시들해지고 있다고
우려표명

- 미국의 거센 항의에도 불구, 약12개의 유럽 상업은행등이 걸프전쟁중
동결된 수천만 달러의 이라크 외환을 최근 자유화 조치했음

- 1억1천만-1억2천 5백만 달러로 추정되는 영국은행헤제 외환을 포함한
자유화 조치된 기금들은 이라크의 식량 및 장비 수입에 큰도움이 되고
있어, 후세인이 유엔계획(석유수입에서 인도적 지원에 일정부분을
배당하고, 유엔이 동 인도적 지원의 공정한 국내배분을 감시)에 협조
하지 않고있음

0051

U.S. Weighs More Aggressive Campaign to Topple Iraqi Leader

By R. Jeffrey Smith and John M. Goshko
Washington Post Staff Writers

Frustrated by the inconclusive end of the Persian Gulf War and facing new criticism from congressional Democrats and presidential challengers, the Bush administration is reviewing proposals for a more aggressive U.S. campaign to force the overthrow of Iraqi President Saddam Hussein, according to senior U.S. officials.

The proposals, some of which have been floated by Iraqi opposition groups and U.S. lawmakers, include providing Iraqi rebels with such overt or covert assistance as military training and spare parts or helping to protect a provisional, alternative government that some rebels want to establish in northern Iraq.

There are differing views among officials and participating departments about whether any plan to oust Saddam is worth the effort. Looming over the discussions is the belief of U.S. intelligence experts that the plans would fail, largely because they depend on some degree of U.S. leverage over internal Iraqi politics and some degree of cooperation among Iraqi rebel groups. Both are virtually nonexistent.

"There are a lot of ideas out there . . . [and] I would not rule out that we would move in more aggressive ways" to destabilize Saddam's regime, said an official involved in the deliberations. "The [decision] process is very alive . . . and nothing has been rejected." The review is being conducted by an interagency committee under the direction of the White House.

Less than a year away from what President Bush hopes will be his election to a second term, he is increasingly concerned that Democrats will use Saddam's continued hold on power to tarnish the glow of the gulf victory, according to Republican sources.

Two weeks ago, for example, a potential Democratic presidential candidate, New York Gov. Mario M. Cuomo, who opposed starting the war last January, said that "in the end, [Bush] . . . made the worse deal. He had a war, killed people—he didn't, but the war did—and he fought it very well, except, in the end, he didn't get the objective, which was Saddam Hussein. And you can take pictures of Saddam Hussein now reviewing the troops."

Among those advocating a new U.S. policy is Rep. Stephen J. Solarz (D-N.Y.), a Foreign Affairs subcommittee chairman, who has urged direct aid to a coalition of anti-Saddam groups.

Solarz and Senate Foreign Relations Committee Chairman Claiborne Pell (D-R.I.) said they would support U.S. diplomatic recognition and military protection for a provisional government established by Kurdish, Shiite and Sunni rebels in the part of northern Iraq now monitored by the United Nations. The principal aim of the plan—first promoted here during a recent visit by Kurdish leader Jalal Talabani—would be to induce Iraqi army troops to defect to the rebels.

Some senior Defense Department officials—despite skepticism from the *Joint Chiefs of Staff*—also have pushed for a more active approach to the Iraqi problem than the current sanctions that sharply restrict Iraq's trade with the rest of the world. "A lot of people here have been uncomfortable about the state of affairs inside Iraq," one official said. "The last thing you want is a kind of Rhodesia [outcome] . . . where sanctions took years to have any effect. There is a lot of interest in finding more active roles" to play in Iraq, including helping disaffected Iraqi military officers.

Independent Western groups recently have complained that the sanctions are working against the wrong people, imposing grave hardship on Iraqi citizens, many of whom are reported suffering from food shortages and poor sanitary conditions.

A group of 15 Democratic and two Republican senators cited these hardships in a letter to Bush last Monday seeking strong U.S. actions to force Saddam's compliance with a U.N. plan for food distribution. Iraq refused to consent during negotiations in Baghdad last week with a U.N. representative, Prince Sadruddin Aga Khan.

British officials have said that as long as Iraq continues to comply with U.N. inspection and monitoring requirements, neither London nor other European capitals will support Western attempts to overthrow Saddam. And in Turkey, where permission for allied forces to operate from Turkish air bases in support of Kurdish rebels is due to lapse Jan. 1, there is little enthusiasm for actions that would embolden the Kurds in northern Iraq to press harder for an independent state that would threaten Turkish borders.

The U.S. military will not push for a formal extension of the Turkish agreement because experts do not accept Kurdish claims that Saddam's forces may move against them during the winter, officials said.

State Department policymakers have been among the most skeptical about stepping up efforts against Saddam. The idea of a covert action program to overthrow him was dismissed in interviews as "stupid," "out of touch with reality," and "Ollie North adventurism" by department officials who deal with the Middle East. To believe that any existing dissident movement or individual is now capable of wresting power from Saddam and his clique is delusion, they said.

"A lasting, broad-based coalition is not in the cards, and any supporters would be sucked in so deep they would never see the end of it," one intelligence official said. This intelligence assessment has changed little since shortly after Iraq's invasion of Kuwait in August 1990, when Bush authorized the CIA to

Nov. 25, 1991

position and to support the emergence of an Iraqi government representative of Iraq's pluralistic society."

Several U.S. and foreign officials said that to the best of their knowledge Washington is not now providing military assistance to the Kurdish, Shiite or Sunni rebel groups in Iraq that want to oust Saddam. It is continuing to support some anti-Saddam radio broadcasts, including Kurdish-language programs of the Voice of America, that were initiated during the war.

A senior military official, who spoke on condition that he not be identified, said the Joint Chiefs of Staff were skeptical about the feasibility of providing military aid or protection to the rebel groups. "I don't think there would be any interest in that at all. Our goal should be to ensure the situation remains stable with a minimum amount of U.S. involvement," he said. The official added that "we have already come to terms with the Kurdish problem. What they do for themselves will determine their fate."

U.S. government analysts said in interviews they have uncovered little evidence current administration policy has loosened Saddam's grip. His appointment two weeks ago of his son-in-law, Ali Hassan Majid, as defense minister and his appointment last week of his half-brother, Wathbin Ibrahim Hassan, as interior minister instead reflect an effort by Saddam to consolidate the ruling clique, possibly because of Saddam's growing paranoia or sense of isolation, the analysts said.

Several officials said the elevation of Majid, a brutal former governor of occupied Kuwait, may signal a coming crackdown against any discontented military officers as well as the Shiite guerrillas in southern Iraq. In northern Iraq, Saddam last week successfully pressured Kurdish leaders to order the withdrawal of guerrilla forces from key cities in exchange for a resumption of food shipments to the region, a move seen as strengthening the position of the loyalist Iraqi army during the winter.

U.S. intelligence agencies have been unable to confirm a single report from Iraqi exiles of coup attempts or plotting against Saddam since the war ended, administration officials said. A popular uprising remains at or near the bottom of the intelligence community's list of likely actions to unseat Saddam.

Nonetheless, the chief aim of U.S. policy remains, in the words of a senior State Department official, creating an "environment in which Iraqi people can change their government." He and others maintain that Saddam's inability to placate all of the Shiite and Kurdish rebel groups points toward a gradual erosion of his position. But Rep. Lee H. Hamilton (D-Ind.), who is briefed by intelligence officials in his role as chairman of the Foreign Affairs subcommittee on the Middle East, said in an interview that he believes it may be "more than a year before [Saddam] ... goes."

Meanwhile, U.S. officials describe a disquieting sign of flagging interest in economic isolation of Iraq. Over strong U.S. protests, roughly a dozen European commercial banks recently released tens of millions of dollars in foreign currency reserves frozen during the Persian Gulf War, the officials said.

The funds, including an estimated $110 million to $125 million released by British banks on Saturday, represent only a fraction of total Iraqi economic assets that remain frozen by U.S. allies, but they have helped Iraq purchase a growing share of the food and equipment imports it has declared within the past two months under U.N. rules. Iraq also has boldly announced its intention to buy as much food in the next year as it imported before the war.

Saddam "thinks he will get enough [imports] that he will not have to cooperate" with a U.N. plan to pay for humanitarian aid with Iraqi oil revenue and supervise its distribution inside the country, one U.S. government analyst said.

look for means or groups for overthrowing or destabilizing Saddam. Until the end of the gulf war, the CIA reported periodically that it had not found substantial or unified opposition to receive such assistance.

State Department officials say they expect the current review to result in a reaffirmation of support for current U.S. strategy, which relies on indirect pressure to bring about what officials refer to as "new leadership in Iraq."

There are three elements to the approach, officials said: Ensuring Iraq's continued diplomatic isolation; maintaining the strict economic sanctions and restraints on global economic trade with Iraq; and eliminating residual Iraqi capabilities to make weapons of mass destruction.

Asked last Wednesday about additional steps the administration might take, Assistant Secretary of State Edward P. Djerejian told a House Foreign Affairs subcommittee that "we will continue to broaden our contacts with the Iraqi op-

5151-2 (END)   Nov. 25, 1991 WP

발 신 전 보

분류번호	보존기간

번   호 : WUS-5395   911126 1820   종별 :

WUK -2143   WFR -2479
WKU -0485   WJO -0697
WUN -4085

수   신 : 주 ~~수신처~~ 대사. 총영사

발   신 : 장 관 (중동일)

제   목 : 미국의 대이락 정책

11.25자 '워싱턴 포스트'지 보도에 의하면 미행정부는 걸프전의 성과에 대한 종결에 대한 비난을 막기위해 후세인을 장관을 전복시키기 위한 강경조치들(이락내 반군세력에 대한 군사장비 및 훈련지원 또는 이락 북부지역에 반군정부 수립지원등) 을 검토중이라는바, 귀주재국측에 상기보도의 진위여부와 함께 현 이락정세 및 향후전망등에 대하여 상세탐문 보고바라며, 특기사항 있을시 수시 보고바람. 끝.

(중동아국장   이 해 순)

수신처 : 미, 영, 불, 쿠웨이트, 몰단, 유엔

92.6.10. 전문공개

보안통제

앙고재		기안자성명	과장	국장	차관	장관	외신과통제

0054

외 무 부

종 별 :

번 호 : USW-5851

일 시 : 91 1126 1918

수 신 : 장 관 (중동일,미일,미이)

발 신 : 주 미 대사

제 목 : 대이락 정책 검토

연: USW(F)-5151

대: WUS-5395

1. 11.25. 국무부 정례브리핑시 TUTWILER 대변인은 대호 WP 기사 관련 질문에 대해 하기 요지의 답변을 하였음을 우선 보고함.

- 현재 대이락 정책에 대해 검토(REVIEW)를 하고 있는 것은 사실이나, 이는 국무부가 실시하는 통상적 정책 검토의 일환으로 특별한 것이 아님.

- 미국은 후세인이 계속 집권해서는 안되며, 후세인이 계속 집권하는한 모든 대이락 제재 수단은 계속되어야 하며, 또한 이락이 UN 안보리 결의(687 및 688)상의 의무를 이행하도록 하기 위해 국제적 노력을 계속 경주한다는 기본입장을 견지하고 있음.

2. 동 관련 질의 응답 주요 부분은 별전 FAX(USW(F)-5195) 송부함. 끝.

(대사 현홍주-국장)

예고: 92.12.31. 까지

92. 6.30. 일반일 ㅈ

중아국 안기부	장관	차관	1차보	2차보	미주국	미주국	분석관	청와대

PAGE 1

91.11.27 10:40

외신 2과 통제관 CA

0055

Q   Yeah, another easy one. The Washington Post got excited today about the possibility that the administration isn't thoroughly pleased with the results of this invasion and that maybe some other things are going on. Let me just ask you basically: is there review going on on US policy toward Iraq, and --

MS. TUTWILER: Yes.

Q   Yes? Okay.

MS. TUTILWER: But, having said yes, our policies are always under review, and our policy on Iraq, yes, it goes under review,

as it does on any number of places around the world. It would be ridiculous to think that it doesn't. And the reason, obviously, that it's under review is to assure that it is being effectively -- as effective as possibly implemented.

Q   Well, is the administration pleased, satisfied with the results of its war against --

MS. TUTWILER: Of their own review?

Q   No, its war against Iraq. Have the goals been met? Apart from -- or more specifically, Saddam Hussein staying in power.

MS. TUTWILER: I'm not positive that the review is completed. I would also refer you to last Wednesday's testimony, where our Assistant Secretary, Ed Djerejian, spoke at length and in quite some detail about our policy. And as you know -- I'll restate parts of it -- our policy is that the Iraqi people deserve a new Iraqi leadership. We have made no secrets about that. You're familiar with all the many times the President has spoken to this. Saddam cannot be redeemed, and all possible sanctions must be maintained as long as he is in power. That is our standard policy.

We are dedicated to a coordinated international effort to ensure Iraq complies with its obligations under United Nations Security Council Resolutions 687 and 688. Pressures include our ongoing pressures, diplomatic isolation, economic sanctions, and support for the United Nations efforts to destroy Iraq's weapons of mass destruction and its ability to produce them.

Q   Is this a new review or part of an on-going review?

5195 -1

MS. TUTWILER: I think it's part of an ongoing review. I mean, I didn't ask if it's new, or --

Q I mean, when did it start? Do we know?

MS. TUTWILER: I don't know.

Q Is now the time to step up the pressure on Saddam Hussein? Is the government creeping toward a decision, or has the decision already been made to try and try a little harder to help the Iraqi people remove him from power?

MS. TUTWILER: Our policy, as you know, has never been targetted at one individual. That has not changed. We have said that he is a pariah, that there will be no normalization of relations with the United States, and that it is for the Iraqi people themselves to determine. But the Iraqi people, in our opinion, are the ones -- are the very ones who are being hurt by the continuing leadership of Saddam Hussein because of his isolation, the economic hardships, the embargo -- all of the things that we're all very familiar with.

Q (Off mike) -- a little bit, too. In this article, there's some discussion of whether a judgment has been reached as to whether you anticipate -- the US anticipates a new assault on the Kurds over the winter. Is this -- has the review gone to the point where you can tell us whether there is a decision, a judgment on that?

MS. TUTWILER: No.

Q Is there a parallel review of -- about US policy toward Iran, given the signs of --

MS. TUTWILER: Iran? I haven't asked. I'll be happy to ask.

Q Margaret, in his testimony, Mr. Djerejian said that the United States position was that Saddam Hussein was in a more brittle position because of recent redeployment, if you like, of his family members into key ministeries. That's not really very difficult -- different from anything that he's been doing over the past couple of years. And that was offered up as the reasoning for saying that he was -- his division was deteriorating and that his position was more brittle.

Is there anything more on that, because it doesn't really make sense that he's only doing things that he's been doing before, so then for you to say that the situation is getting worse?

MS. TUTWILER: Well, Ed is the expert. He is the Assistant Secretary of this region, and I'm certainly not going to take quarrel with his public testimony last Wednesday before the -- I believe it was the House Foreign Affairs Committee. So if you need a further elaboration of what he meant -- I haven't had an opportunity to read his entire testimony -- I'll be happy to refer your question to him.

5195-2

Q   Margaret, (there seems to be ?) an internal inconsistency
in what you say. You said the Iraqi people deserve a new leader,
Saddam Hussein cannot be redeemed. And yet in your next statement
you say US policy is not aimed at a single person. It sounds to me --

MS. TUTWILER: Not --

Q   It sounds to me like it is, in fact, aimed at removing him --

MS. TUTWILER: There's not a UN Resolution. I think there
were twelve of them originally that target

Saddam Hussein the individual. The United States has clearly
ernunciated our policy over the last -- what is it? -- more than a
year now, saying that Saddam Hussein is not a United States target,
wasn't why we built the coalition. In the same breath, the
President has said we would not weep buckets of tears if he's thrown
out, he's a pariah, the United States will not do normal business as
long as he's there. So, I mean, it is no secret, our views of
Saddam Hussein.

5195-3

미.영의 대이라크 정책관련 추이

91. 11. 28

1. 미행정부, 「후세인」 대통령 축출방안 모색(11.25.자 워싱턴 포스트지)

   o 미 행정부는 걸프전의 완전치 못한 종결에 대한 민주당 및 공화당
   일각의 비판에 직면, 이라크내 반군에 대한 지원을 주내용으로 하는
   「후세인」이라크 대통령 축출을 위한 적극적 방안을 검토중이나
   미 관계당국 및 관리들간에는 「후세인」제거 방안이 실행할만한
   가치가 있는지 여부에 대하여 이견.

   - 이라크인들이 새지도부를 창출할 수 있도록 간접압력을 행사하고
     있는 미국의 현정책 계속지지

   - 경제제재보다 적극적인 대이락 조치에는 찬성이나 후세인 제거
     노력 강화에는 회의적

   - 현재 이라크내에서 지속적이고, 광범위한 기반의 반대세력이 없어,
     어떠한 지원도 성공할수 없음

2. 미국무부 대변인은 11.25. 미국이 통상적 정책 검토의 일환으로 대이라크
   정책을 재검토중이나 「후세인」이라크 대통령을 축출하려하고 있다는
   언론보도는 부인

3. 주한 영국대사관의 외무부 비공식브리핑(11.26. 수교)

   o 「후세인」이라크 대통령의 당초 평화주장과 국내정치 민주화의지 및
   유엔과의 협력의사 표명등은 오직 시간을 벌기위한 기만적 책략이었음

   o 「후세인」은 대량파괴 무기개발과 관련하여 계속해서 유엔과 IAEA를
   기만하고있으며, 국내정치에 있어서도 민생, 쿠르드문제, 국내정치
   민주화등 각분야에서 국민의 고통을 외면하면서 폭압정권을 재건설하며
   핵무기를 제조하려 하고있어 이락 국내외를 막론하고 모두에게 위험한
   존재임.

0059

BRITISH EMBASSY

4 Chung-dong Chung-Ku Seoul Republic of Korea

Telephone 735-7341/3 735-7471/3
Facsimile (02) 733-8368
Telex K27320 PRODROM

Mr Chun Hae-jin
Director
Middle East Division
Ministry of Foreign Affairs
Seoul

Your reference

Our reference

Date   22 November 1991

Dear Director Chun

I enclose some briefing material from the Foreign and
Commonwealth Office on the situation in the Gulf, which I hope
will be of interest to you.

I should point out that the briefing paper on UN Security
Council Resolution 687 is for general briefing purposes and
should not be considered or quoted as British Government
policy.

Yours sincerely,

G A Harrison

SADDAM HUSSEIN: A CONTINUING MENACE

Saddam Hussein would like the world to think that he has changed; but it is clear that his protestations of peace, and his earlier statements of willingness to liberalise his regime and to cooperate with the United Nations, were aimed only at gaining time. His people continue to suffer all kinds of unnecessary deprivation, while he struggles to reassemble the oppressive and vicious apparatus he used for so long to terrorise them and to threaten the peace of the region. He dissembles and lies. His objective is to cow his people and to maintain his ability to produce nuclear bombs, chemical weapons and missiles to impose his will through terror, not only on his own hapless countrymen, but also on the whole region.

Saddam Hussein has lied repeatedly to the UN and to the International Atomic Energy Agency (IAEA) about his development of weapons of mass destruction. His regime has threatened, harassed and obstructed the UN inspection teams, to prevent them from uncovering illicit weapons, secret factories and laboratories and from assessing weapon production capabilities. His obstruction of the international observers is well documented, and his challenge to the UN over their inspectors' use of helicopters, and his detention of a UN inspection team in a Baghdad car park, are only the latest of his attempts to defy them and the international community. He persists because he sees the possession of abominable weapons as the most effective way of menacing neighbouring countries and gaining regional supremacy.

He could alleviate the hardships of the Iraqi people very easily but he does nothing. In Iraq there are shortages of food and medical supplies, of power generating equipment and of water treatment facilities, and there is a threat of serious epidemics. To help the Iraqi people, the UN Security Council passed Resolution 706, under which <u>Iraq would be able to export oil up to a value of $1,600 million over six months for the purchase of humanitarian goods</u>. The proceeds from the sale of the oil would be deposited in a UN-controlled account and used for, the Resolution states, "the purchase of foodstuffs, medicine and materials and supplies for essential civilian needs, ... and for all feasible and appropriate UN monitoring and supervision for the purpose of assuring their equitable distribution to meet humanitarian needs in all regions of Iraq and all categories of the Iraqi civilian population". So far no oil has been sold. Saddam Hussein has rejected the Security Council's reasonable conditions as an infringement of Iraq's sovereignty. He has chosen hunger and disease for the Iraqi people because he fears that UN involvement in the distribution

0061

of food and medicine in Iraq would reveal many odious facts about his regime.

Saddam has opened negotiations with the Kurds but has carefully avoided reaching agreement with them. His early apparent readiness to compromise has disappeared. The plight of the Kurds therefore remains precarious. Although, in early March, Saddam offered to resume talks with them, proposing autonomy on the basis of an improved 1970 agreement, it is obvious now that this was one of his attempts to fool the world. The international opprobrium he faced for the misery of the Kurdish refugees was hindering his efforts to persuade the UN to lift sanctions against Iraq, and, in addition, had brought multinational forces into northern Iraq to protect relief operations. Negotiations began in Baghdad in April and have continued on and off. The Kurds rightly see democratic reforms as a prerequisite for any agreement. When, in May, discussion was extended to cover constitutional change, Saddam agreed to abolish the Revolutionary Command Council (RCC), the prime instrument of his dictatorship, end the monopoly of the Ba'ath Party and hold free parliamentary elections within six months.

Widespread scepticism was well founded. Saddam appeared in his true colours on 13 September, dismissing Saadoum Hammadi, a Shi'ite whom he had elevated to Prime Minister in March, during the Iraqi army's brutal crushing of a rebellion by the country's Shias. Appointed to give the Government an appearance of respectability, Hammadi was said to have urged Saddam to introduce a more liberal and democratic system in Iraq. (Hammadi was also dropped from the RCC.) Saddam followed this on 16 September with a declaration that the Ba'ath Party would continue in its vanguard role and that there was no place for Western-style democracy in Iraq.

Saddam is determined to repress dissent at all levels, and continues to rely on a small inner circle of members of his Sunni clan, from his home village of Tikrit, in his attempts to control the whole of Iraq. He is not to be trusted. He is reconstructing a vicious, oppressive regime, ignoring the sufferings of Iraqis, and trying to build nuclear weapons. He is a danger to all, inside Iraq and outside Iraq.

0062

Background Brief

Foreign &
Commonwealth
Office, London

October 1991

UN SECURITY COUNCIL RESOLUTION 687: IRAQ:
WEAPONS OF MASS DESTRUCTION

The British Prime Minister, John Major, speaking in the House of Commons on 28 February 1991, the day when military operations in the Gulf were suspended, said:

> "Through the United Nations, we shall ..... seek a commitment from Iraq to destroy, under international supervision, all its ballistic missiles and weapons of mass destruction, and not to acquire such weapons in the future".

This was widely supported throughout the international community, concerned by Iraq's earlier use of such weapons against Iran and against its own Kurdish population, and by its threats to use them during the Gulf conflict. The Prime Minister's commitment was subsequently reflected in UN Security Council Resolution (SCR) 687, adopted by the Security Council on 3 April 1991.

Provisions of Section C of SCR 687

Section C of SCR 687 requires Iraq unconditionally to accept the destruction, removal or rendering harmless, under international supervision, of:

(a)   all chemical and biological weapons (CBW) and all stocks of agents, all related sub-systems and components, and all research, development, support and manufacturing facilities.

(b)   all ballistic missiles with a range greater than 150 kilometres, related major parts, and repair and production facilities;

(c)   all nuclear weapons, nuclear weapons-related material, and related sub-systems, components, research, development, support or manufacturing facilities.

Iraq was required to submit full declarations of the locations, amounts and types of all such items within 15 days of the adoption of SCR 687, to submit to immediate on-site inspections, and to

---

This paper has been prepared for general briefing purposes. It is not and should not be construed or quoted as an expression of Government policy.

0063

걸프사태 이후 미국.이라크 관계 동향, 1991-92 459

undertake unconditionally not to use, develop, construct or acquire such weapons of mass destruction (WMD) in the future.

SCR 687 set up a Special Commission which, with the International Atomic Energy Agency (IAEA), is to oversee the implementation of the provisions of SCR 687 Section C.

The UN Secretary-General appointed Ambassador Rolf Ekeus from Sweden as Executive Chairman of the Special Commission. Members were drawn from Australia, Austria, Belgium, Canada, China, Czechoslovakia, Finland, France, Germany, Indonesia, Italy, Japan, the Netherlands, Nigeria, Norway, Poland, the Soviet Union, the United Kingdom, the United States and Venezuela. They were selected on the basis of professional expertise and competence. The IAEA has established its own special Action Team chaired by Professor Zifferero of Italy to co-ordinate its work under SCR 687.

The work of the Special Commission and IAEA will comprise three phases: inspection, destruction and long-term monitoring. The Special Commission was mandated to carry out immediate on-site inspections of Iraq's CBW and missile capabilities, and to assist the Director-General of the IAEA in carrying out similar inspections of Iraq's nuclear capabilities, based on Iraq's declarations and any additional sites designated by the Special Commission itself. The Special Commission is responsible for the destruction of CBW items and for supervising the destruction by Iraq of its ballistic missile capabilities. The IAEA is responsible for the removal of all nuclear weapons-usable materials and for the destruction of Iraq's nuclear weapons capability.

The authority of the Special Commission and IAEA to carry out these tasks was confirmed by the UN Security Council in SCR 699 adopted on 17 June, which also required Iraq to bear the full costs involved. The Special Commission and the IAEA were also required by SCR 687 to develop plans to ensure the continued monitoring and verification of Iraq's compliance with the provisions of SCR 687 Section C. These plans have now been published as Security Council documents (S/22871/Rev 1 and S/22872/Rev 1) and approved by the Security Council in SCR 715, adopted unanimously on 11 October.

Progress so far

Inspections. The Special Commission and IAEA have mounted a major programme of inspections (see chronology). These have produced important findings about the scale, scope and sophistication of Iraq's WMD programmes and military infrastructure. The most significant discoveries so far have been the following:

(i) Nuclear weapons: Iraq initially claimed not to have a nuclear weapons programme, but the second IAEA nuclear inspection (22 June - 3 July), despite obstruction (including the firing of warning shots) and refusals of access to establishments, identified equipment mounted on lorries and tank transporters as calutrons - key components in the enrichment of uranium by electro-magnetic isotope separation (EMIS). After pressure from the Security Council and the despatch of a high-level mission to Baghdad, Iraq admitted on 7 July that it had three undeclared uranium enrichment programmes (EMIS, centrifuge-based technology and chemical separation).

This led the IAEA Board of Governors to condemn Iraq on 18 July for breaching its obligations under the safeguards agreement. The UN Security Council echoed this on 15 August in SCR 707, which also reinforced the rights and immunities of UN inspectors in Iraq, including the use of UN helicopters and aircraft on terms determined by the UN.

Subsequent IAEA inspections have unearthed further details about Iraq's nuclear weapon programmes, despite attempts at concealment. Iraq admitted to the fourth IAEA inspection team (27 July - 10 August) that it had irradiated undeclared fuel elements in a nuclear reactor, and separated small quantities of plutonium. The IAEA Board of Governors then concluded on 13 September for the second time that Iraq was in breach of its Non-Proliferation Treaty obligations. The sixth IAEA inspection (22-30 September) found clear documentary evidence of nuclear weapons development, including work on an implosion device. The Iraqis detained the inspectors for four days, forcibly removed documents in their possession, and only released them when it was agreed to produce a joint inventory of the documents seized. Iraq's behaviour was in flagrant breach of its obligations under SCRs 687 and 707.

(ii) Chemical weapons: Iraq's initial declaration of its chemical weapons (CW) capability identified the Muthanna State Establishment - known outside Iraq as Samarra - as its major CW plant. Muthanna was declared to consist of 16 sites, namely five research and development sites each with five laboratories; one sarin (nerve agent) and one mustard gas production plant; four intermediary production plants, and five munitions filling sites. Iraq said that all of these had been destroyed. As for munitions, Iraq declared at Muthanna: 6,920 120mm rocket warheads, 2,500 Saqr-30 missile warheads and 200 DB-2 gravity bombs, all claimed to be filled with sarin; 75 tonnes of sarin; 150 tonnes of tabun (another nerve agent) intermediate; 500 tonnes of phosphorus trichloride - a CW precursor; and 280 tonnes of mustard gas. Iraq also declared several other CW storage sites, mostly at airbases, each with a quantity of CW munitions: 336 sarin aerial bombs, 1,040 bombs and 105 artillery shells filled with mustard gas.

This substantially under-declared Iraq's CW munitions and facilities. Iraq did not, for example, declare its CW precursor production plants at Habbaniyah. Iraq has subsequently admitted to having some 46,000 filled CW munitions. Inspections have revealed that many of these munitions and chemical containers are leaking and unmarked, an indication of the hazardous nature of the

Special Commission's activities. Arrangements are now in hand to destroy these stocks and facilities.

(iii) <u>Biological weapons</u>: Iraq initially declared that it had no biological weapons (BW) and did not carry out any related activities. But during the first BW inspection (2-8 August), Iraq admitted that biological research activities for military purposes had begun in mid-1986. Research was undertaken at Salman Pak on bacillis anthracisa (anthrax), clostridium botulinum (botulin toxin) and clostridium perfringens (gas gangrene). Salman Pak was inspected and was found to have the capability to research, produce and store biological warfare agents, although no BW or filling facilities were found. The site had been extensively damaged by coalition bombardment, and inspection activity was further hampered by the levelling of key buildings by the Iraqis, who had also covered the area with a layer of earth. A second BW inspection took place from 20 September-3 October, adding to the Special Commission's knowledge of Iraq's BW related capabilities.

(iv) <u>Ballistic missiles</u>: Iraq's initial declaration of 52 missiles (51 Al Hussein, 1 Scud) and associated components and launchers was significantly below its actual holdings. Iraq subsequently admitted to a further 9 Al Fahad missiles (not operational). These declared missiles (and one more) have all been destroyed. But Iraq claimed to have had some 800 Scud missiles before the Iran/Iraq war. Even allowing for those used in research and testing and for the considerable number fired in that war, and for some destroyed by coalition bombing during the more recent Gulf conflict, there must still be large numbers concealed in Iraq. Inspections have revealed undeclared decoy and fixed launch pads but as yet no further missiles. Missiles and launchers are, of course, relatively easy to hide.

(v) <u>Supergun</u>: Iraq's initial declaration did not include the supergun, but it made a later admission on 17 July. Special Commission inspectors have now destroyed an assembled 350mm supergun and components for 350mm and 1000mm superguns, together with a tonne of propellant.

Although the scale and sophistication of Iraq's WMD programmes are clear, much remains to be uncovered. Of particular concern is Iraq's nuclear weapons programme. Important aspects of its BW and missile programmes (eg the nature of its research, development and production, capabilities and stockpiles) also remain to be clarified.

<u>UK contribution</u>

The UK has given full support to the Special Commission and the IAEA. A senior expert on chemical and biological defence is a full-time member of the Special Commission. The UK has so far provided over 30 experts and specialised CBW equipment and transport facilities for inspections, as well as information on Iraqi weapons programmes. For 1991/92, £1 million has been set aside to pay for UK support to the SPC and IAEA operations.

Future activity

The Special Commission and IAEA will continue their inspections well into 1992, when the problems of destruction work will begin to occupy more of their time and effort. The monitoring and verification of Iraq's compliance with SCR 687, under the strict compliance regimes approved by SCR 715, will be the key to preventing Iraq from redeveloping or reacquiring a WMD capability in the future. Success will depend on the determination of the international community to continue its support for the Special Commission and IAEA.

Lessons to be drawn

SCR 687 represents a major piece of practical UN arms control and disarmament activity of a kind never seen before. The authority of the UN has been significantly reinforced, and the Security Council has shown that it can react swiftly and positively to all attempts by Iraq to obstruct and delay the work of the IAEA and the Special Commission.

The practical experience gained during the Special Commission and IAEA inspections may also be of benefit in developing international measures to inhibit proliferation in other areas. In addition, whilst SCR 687 cannot necessarily serve as a model for other arms control efforts, the firm action taken by the UN against Iraq may deter other would-be proliferators (or at least limit their ambitions).

Iraq's programme to develop a nuclear weapons capability appears to have used almost exclusively facilities that had not been declared to the IAEA, and was therefore designed to circumvent the whole safeguards system. The fact that the Iraqi programme went undetected was not therefore a failure of the existing safeguards regime, but does point up the need to strengthen non-proliferation measures as a whole to deal more effectively with clandestine operations. A range of possible measures is being considered.

0067

CHRONOLOGY

April

3   UN Security Council adopted Security Council Resolution (SCR) 687.

18   Iraq made initial declaration of weapons of mass destruction (WMD).

22   Ambassador Ekeus appointed as Executive Chairman of the Special Commission.

May

15-21   UNSCOM* 1 - first IAEA nuclear inspection.

June

9-14   UNSCOM 2 - first CW inspection. Three British inspectors.

17   SCR 699 adopted, making Iraq liable for the costs arising from the implementation of Section C of SCR 687. SCR 700 (arms embargo) also adopted.

22-
3 July   UNSCOM 3 - second IAEA nuclear inspection. One British inspector. The Iraqis refused access to nominated sites in an attempt to conceal key equipment for their uranium enrichment programme; warning shots were fired when inspectors attempted to follow a convoy carrying this equipment.

28   President of the Security Council condemned Iraq's breach of its obligations under SCR 687 in obstructing UNSCOM 3.

30-
3 July   UN Secretary-General despatched a high-level mission to Iraq to demand Iraq's compliance with SCR 687.

30-
7 July   UNSCOM 4 - first ballistic missile inspection. One British (RAF) explosives ordnance adviser.

July

6-19   UNSCOM 5 - third IAEA nuclear inspection. Two British inspectors.

---

* United Nations Special Commission on Iraq - all dates relate to time spent in Iraq.

0068

7 July	Iraq declared three covert uranium enrichment programmes.
12	Demarche by the Permanent Five members of the Security Council asking, inter alia, for a full, final and complete disclosure by Iraq of all WMD programmes.
18	First IAEA Board of Governors condemnation of Iraq's breach of its Non-Proliferation Treaty obligations
18-20	UNSCOM 10 - second ballistic missile inspection, undertaken at short notice.
27- 10 August	UNSCOM 6 - fourth IAEA nuclear inspection. Two British inspectors.

August

2-8	UNSCOM 7 - first BW inspection. Five British inspectors. Concluded that Iraq had a biological research programme for military purposes (admitted by Iraq on 4 August).
8-15	UNSCOM 8 - third ballistic missile inspection. One British inspector.
15	Security Council adopted SCR 706, making provision for the costs of implementing SCR 687 to be drawn from revenues on Iraqi oil sold under UN supervision; and SCR 707, condemning Iraq's violations of obligations under SCR 687 and demanding that Iraq allow the Special Commission and IAEA to use their own aircraft for flights within Iraq.
15-22	UNSCOM 9 - second CW inspection. One British inspector.
31- 9 Sept	UNSCOM 11 - third CW inspection. One British inspector.
31- 5 Sept	UNSCOM 12 - fourth CW inspection. One British inspector.

September

6-12	UNSCOM 13 - fourth ballistic missile inspection. One British (RAF) explosive ordnance adviser. Terminated one week early by Iraq's refusal to allow the Special Commission to use its own helicopters.

0069

13 Sept   Second IAEA Board of Governors condemnation of Iraq's breach of its Non-Proliferation Treaty obligations.

14-22   UNSCOM 14 - fifth IAEA nuclear inspection.

20-
30 Oct   UNSCOM 15 - second BW inspection. Two British inspectors.

22-30   UNSCOM 16 - sixth IAEA nuclear inspection. Two British inspectors. Uncovered incontrovertible evidence of Iraq's nuclear weapons development programme. Inspectors held for four days by Iraqis in dispute over retention of documents.

October

3-9   UNSCOM 18 - fifth ballistic missile inspection, with UN helicopters. Two British inspectors.

6-
9 Nov   UNSCOM 17 - fifth CW inspection. Five British personnel on the team.

11   SCR 715, giving approval to the plans of the Special Commission and IAEA for long-term monitoring and verification of Iraq's compliance with SCR 687, adopted unanimously

0070

관리번호 91/1873

외 무 부

종 별 : 지 급

번 호 : JOW-0870

일 시 : 91 1202 1300

수 신 : 장관(중동일,중동이,기정)

발 신 : 주 요르단대사

제 목 : 미국의 대이라크 정책

대 WJO-697

12.1. 외무성 GHAZAWI 정무국장과의 면담등을 통해 본직이 파악한 현 이라크 일반정세 및 전망등은 다음과같음

가. 10.13-23 간 개최된 제 3 차 ARAB POPULAR POWER CONFERENCE 개회식에서후세인 대통령은 이라크가 경제 제재에도 불구하고 향후 20 년간 버틸 자신이 있다고 발표한바 있으나, 실질적으로 이라크는 극심한 식량과의 약품 부족현상에직면하고 있으며 유아 사망율도 걸프전 대비 380 프로 증가하고 있는 실정임.동기 개시와 함께 이라크는 약 30 억불 상당의 식품을 필요로하고 있으며 최근 이라크정부가 억류 영국인들을 석방함으로써 영국정부에 의해 동결되었던 해외 이라크 자산중 1.1 억미불 해제 시킨바 있으나 식량문제 해결에 큰도움을 가져오지 못하고있음

나. 부시 미대통령이 후세인 이라크 대통령 제거를 언급하고 있는것을 이라크측은 현재에 이라크내에 후세인대통령을 대체할수 있는 반정부 세력이 없음을 미국의 지도층이 인정하고 있는것으로 보고 있으며, 또한 이라크 방송매체들은 유엔제재에 대한 저항을 회교의 "성전"이라고 주장하면서 이라크내 반미, 반서구감정을 선동하면서 국민들의 불만을 돌리고, 후세인 대통령과 이라크정부에 대한 단결을 강조하고있음

다. 후세인대통령은 11.13.IBRAHIM HASSAN 자신의 이복동생을 내무장관으로임명하는등, 주요 각료직에 가까운 친족들을 배치하면서 자신의 정권유지를 위해 철저히 대비하고 있음

라. KURD 족 문제는 KURD 족내에 여러 단체가 존재하며 또 동파벌간에 단합이 이루어지지 못하고 있기때문에 실질적인 대이라크 정부 위협 존재가 되지 못하고

중아국 장관 차관 1차보 2차보 중아국 외정실 분석관 청와대
안기부

있음. 인근 터어키내에도 KURD 족이 거주하고 있으므로 터어키가 자국내 문제를
야기시키면서 이라크내 KURD 민족을 지원하지 않을것으로 보며 전열이 정비되지 않은
이라크내 소수의 KURD 민족으로서는 미국등 초강대국의 적극적인 특별지원이 없는한
이라크 정부군에 전면 대항, 후세인 대통령 정권을 전복시킬 가능성은 없다고
볼수있음. 끝
     (대사 이한춘-국장)
     예고:92.6.30

92. 6.30. 일반 ~

외 무 부

종 별 : 지 급

번 호 : KUW-0771   일 시 : 91 1205 1400

수 신 : 장관(중동일)

발 신 : 주 쿠웨이트 대사

제 목 : 미국의 대이라크 정책

대:WKU-485

1. 미국이 후세인을 제거하기 위하여 물리적힘(군사공격, 쿠르드나 시아이(SHIITE) 모슬림집단등 이라크의 반대세력 집단에 대한 무기공급등)을 쓸계획을 갖고 있는지는 확인할수 없으나, 쿠웨이트에서 이런 징후는 볼수없음.

2. 명년의 대통령선거를 앞두고 민주당측의 공격쟁점을 한가지 없애기 위해서 부시대통령은 사담을 빨리 제거해야될 필요가 있을것이라는 관측은 당지에서도 논의되고 있는 일임.

3. 그러나, 사담을 제거하는 일은 다음 몇가지 측면에 대한 고려 또한 중요함.

A. 실제적 측면

1) 직접공격:EC 의 지지가 의심스럽고, 아랍세계에서 반발이 예상되며(리비아에 대한 공격가능성에 대한, 이집트등 반응)그럼에도 불구하고 군사공격을해서 사담을 제거해도 이라크국민들의 대미 반감을 북돋아서 새로운 지배집단은여전히 반미, 과격집단이 될가능성이 많으므로(쿠웨이트 외무부미주국장은 지금 후세인이 당장 제거되면 후계세력은 오히려 더 과격한 성격을 띠게될것으로 생각되어 우려하고 있다고 말했음.)미국이 군사공격을 선택하기는 어려울 것임.공격하는 경우 쿠웨이트가 발진기지의 하나로 이용될수 있다는데(함제기에의한 공격이 주가될터이지만) 그런 징후는 없음.

2) 이라크의 반대집단 지원

가) 바스당 반대집단

우영국등 해외에 본거지를 두고 바스당 집권을 반대하고 있는 몇개의 집단이 있으나, 후세인정권의 장기간에 걸친 강력한 탄압으로 국내기반이 전혀없기 때문에 미국이 이들을 지원해서 후세인을 제거하기는 어려울것임.

중아국

나) 시아이

-HAKIMA 를 지도자로 하며 이란에 본거지를 두고, 이라크의 소수 종파(48 프로 전후)인 순니파로 부터의 해방과 이란과 같은 형태의 신정부 국가 수뇌부을 목표로 이란 지원하에 산만한 반전운동을 벌이고있음.

-미국이 이들을 지원하여 후세인 제거를 (559)(679)해도 조직된 세력이 아니어서 성공가능성이 의심스럽고 성공한다해도 이라크는 이란의 영향권으로 들어가게 되어 걸프지역의 정치적 불안을 가중시킬뿐더러, 이라크의 전통적 지배세력인 순니파의 반발로 내란이 야기되어 이라크의 부-------래할 우려가있음. 이는 걸프지역의 안정을 바라는 미국정책에 부합하지 않음.

다)쿠르드족

-터키와 이란(그정도는 다르겠으나 시리아)에 미치는 파급효과때문에 미국이 선택하기 어려울것임.

라)이라크 군대에 대한 지원

-미국의 가장 효과적인 선택일수는 있음. 당지 소문으로는 이라크군대는 사기도 저하되고 불만이 많아서 반정부세력화 할수 있다고함.

-그러나 후세인은 이점을 고려하여 군대를 주의깊게 관리하고 있고, 정예의전부력을 보유하고 있을뿐아니라 후세인에 대한 충성심에서 "전혀"문제가 없는소위 공화국수비대(REPUBLICAN GUARDS)가 군대를 제압하고 있기때문에 군의 반란은 어려운 사정이라고함.(HUSSEIN 은 최근 SWORD OF SADDAM 이라는 또 하나의 정보망을 조직하여 공화국수비대의 동향조차도 감시하고 있다고함)

3)시민봉기 가능성을 기대할수는 없다고봄.경제봉쇄에도 불구하고 바그다드시민들은 큰 불편없이 지내고 있다고하는 외신보도가 있고, 후세인은 이들을 경제적으로 될수있는대로 "안락"하게 해주어 불만에 의한 폭동을 예방하고, 지방이나 시골주민들에 대해서는 군사, 경찰력등에 의한 봉쇄와 선전으로 대처하고 있는데, 전체적으로 보아 후세엔에 대한 충성심이 있어서 당장 지도체재가 위협받고 있는 사정은 아닌듯함.

B. 전략적 측면

전략적 측면에서 고려할때 지역정세 안정의 핵심은 전과 다름없이 이란, 이라크, 사우디같은 주요국가간의 힘의 균형과 상호견제일 것임으로 이라크가 완전히 분해되거나 힘의균형 등식의 하나인자로서 전혀 역할할수 없게 되는것은 미국의

PAGE 2

0074

이익에도 도움이 안될것임. 한편 사우디는 이라크가 무력화할 경우 이란세력을감당하기 어려울 것임으로 이라크가 이란세에 대한 견제역할을 계속하기를 바라는 나머지 확실한 대안없이 후세인을 제거하는것을 주저할수도 있음. (당지영국대사관 정무참사관은 사우디가 화해밀사를 파송해서 후세인 타협을 시도하고 있다는 설이 있다고했음)

4. 이상과 같이보면 미국으로서는 결국 경제제재 조치를 계속하여 후세인의처지를 어렵게 만들고 "온건한" 반대세력이 후세인을 제거하도록 부추기는 방책이 최선의 선택일듯함. 이경우 "온건한" 반대세력은 정규군대에서 기대할수 있을것이라는 것이 당지관측임. 무력제거 운운은 민주당 선전의 예봉을 꺽기위한 정치적 제스쳐로서의 의도가 강할 가능성이 있음. 한편, 미국이 주도하는 경제제재조치가 장기화할경우 친위세력에 의한 갑작스런 제거 가능성도 있음.

그러나 이러한 사태 돌발전에 후세인은 경제제재조치를 늦추게하고 대외적인 숨통을 트기위한 노력으로서 실권을 장악한채 2 선으로 물러나고, 자기통제하에 있는 측근을 내세워 형식적인 유화제스쳐를 취할 가능성이 있다는 관측도 있는데, 미국도 이라크 봉쇄를 무한정 계속할수 없을것임으로 후세인의 후퇴제스쳐를 명분으로 삼아 사태를 적당히 마무리할 가능성도 있다고봄. 끝

(대사-국장)

예고:92.6.30. 일반

92. 6. 30. 일반

외 무 부

종 별 : 지 급

번 호 : KUW-0773

일 시 : 91 1206 1200

수 신 : 장 관(중동일)

발 신 : 주 쿠웨이트 대사

제 목 : KUW-0771의 재작성분(PART 1)

대:WKU-485

1. 미국이 후세인을 제거하기 위하여 물리적힘(군사공격, 쿠루드나 시아이(SHIITE) 모슬렘집단등 이라크의 반대세력 집단에 대한 무기공급등)을 쓸계획을 갖고있는지는 확인할수 없으나, 쿠웨이트에서 이런 징후는 볼수없음.

2. 명년의 대통령선거를 앞두고 민주당측의 공격쟁점을 한가지 없애기 위해서 부시대통령은 사담을 빨리 제거해야될 필요가 있을것이라는 관측은 당지에서도 논의되고 있는일임.

3. 그러나 사담을 제거하는 일은 다음 몇가지 측면에 대한 고려 또한 중요함.

A. 실제적측면

1) 직접공격: EC 의 지지가 의심스럽고, 아랍세계에서 반발이 예상되며(리비아에 대한 공격가능성에 대한, 이집트등 반응)그럼에도 불구하고 군사공격을 해서 사담을 제거해도 이라크국민들의 대미반감을 북돋아서 새로운 지배집단은 여전히 반미, 과격집단이 될가능성이 많으므로(쿠웨이트 외무부 미주국장은 지금후세인이 당장 제거되면 후계세력은 오히려 더 과격한 성격을 띄게될것으로 생각되어 우려하고 있다고 말했음) 미국이 군사공격을 선택하기에는 어려울것임.공격하는 경우 쿠웨이트가 발진기지의 하나로 이용될수 있을터인데(함지기에 의한 공격이 주가 될터이지만) 그런징후는 없음.

2)이라크의 반대집단 지원

가)바스당 반대집단

-영국등 해외에 본거지를 두고 바스당 집권을 반대하고 있는 몇개의 집단이있으나, 후세인정권의 장기간에 걸친 강력한 탄압으로 국내기반이 전혀없기 때문에 미국이 이들을 지원해서 후세인을 제거하기는 어려울것임:

중아국	장관	차관	1차보	2차보	외정실	분석관	정와대	안기부

91.12.07   01:54

외신 2과 통제관 FI

0076

나)시아이

-HAKIMA 를 지도자로하며 이란에 본거지를 두고, 이라크의 소수종파인(48 프로 전후) 순니파로 부터의 해방과 이란과 같은 형태의 신정국가수립을 목표로 이란지원하에 산만한 반정운동을 벌이고있음.

-미국이 이들을 지원하여 후세인 제거를 시도해도 조직된 세력이 아니어서 성공가능성이 의심스럽고 성공한다해도 이라크는 이란의 영향권으로 들어가게 되어 걸프지역의 정치적 불안을 가중시킬뿐더러, 이라크의 전통적지배세력인 순니파의 반발로 내란이 야기되어 이라크의 분열을 초래할 우려가있음. 이는 걸프지역의 안정을 바라는 미국정책에 부합하지 않음.

다)쿠르드 족

-터키와 이란(그정도는 다르겠으나 시리아)에 미치는 파급효과때문에 미국이 선택하기 어려울것임.

√ 라)이라크 군대에 대한 지원

-미국의 가장 효과적인 선택일수는 있음. 당지 소문으로는 이라크군대는 사기도 저하되고 불만이 많아서 반정세력화 할수있다고함.

-그러나 후세인은 이점을 고려하여 군대를 주의깊게 관리하고 있고, 정예의전투력을 보유하고 있을뿐아니라 후세인에 대한 충성심에서 "전혁"문제가 없는소위공화국 수비대(REPUBLICAN GUARDS)가 군대를 제압하고 있기때문에 군의 반란은 어려운 사정이라고함.(HUSSEIN 은 최근 SWORD OF SADDAM 이라는 또하나의 정보망을 조직하여 공화국수비대의 동향조차도 감시하고 있다고함.)

3)시민봉기 가능성을 기대할수는 없다고봄.경제봉쇄에도 불구하고 바그다드시민들은 큰불편없이 지내고 있다고하는 외신보도가 있고, 후세인은 이들을 경제적으로 될수있는대로 "안락"하게 해주어 불만에 의한 폭동을 예방하고, 지방이나 시골주민들에 대하여는 군사, 경찰력에 의한 봉제와 선전을 대처하고 있는데,전체적으로 보아 후세인에 대한 충성심이 있어서 당장 지도체제가 위협받고 있는 사정은 아닌듯함.(이상 PART 2 로 이어짐).

PAGE 2

0077

외 무 부

종 별 : 지 급

번 호 : KUW-0772

일 시 : 91 1206 1200

수 신 : 장 관(중동일)

발 신 : 주 쿠웨이트 대사

제 목 : KUW-773 의 PART 2

B. 전략적 측면

전략적측면에서 고려할때 지역정세 안정의 핵심은 전과 다름없이 이란,이라크,사우디같은 주요국가간의 힘의 균형과 상호 견제일것임으로 이라크가완전히 분해되거나 힘의 균형등식의 하나의 인자로서 전혀 역할할수 없게되는것은 미국의 이익에도 도움이 않될것임.한편,사우디는 이라크가 무력화할 경우 이란세력을 감당하기 어려울 것임으로 이라크가 이란세계에 대한 견제역할을 계속하기를 바라는 나머지 확실한 대안없이 후세인을 제거하는것을 주저할수도 있음.(당지 영국대사관 정무참사관은 사우디가 화해밀사를 파송해서 후세인 타협을 시도하고 있다는설이 있다고했음)

4. 이상과 같이 보면 미국으로서는 결국 경제제재 조치를 계속하여 후세인의 처지를 어렵게 만들고 "온건한" 반대세력이 후세인을 제거하도록 부추기는 방책이 최선의 선택일듯함. 이경우 "온건한" 반대세력은 정규군대에서 기대할수 있을것이라는것이 당지관측임.무력제거 운운은 민주당선전의 예봉을 꺽기위한 정치적 제스쳐로서의 의도가 강할 가능성이 있음.

한편 미국이 주도하는 경제제재조치가 장기화할경우 친위세력에 의한 갑작스런 제거 가능성도 있음. 그러나 이러한 사태 돌발전에 후세인은 경제제재조치를늦추게 하고 대외적인 숨봉을 트기위한 노력으로서 실권을 장악한채 2 선으로 물러나고, 자기봉제하에 있는 측근을 내세워 형식적인 유화제스쳐를 취할 가능성이 있다는 관측도 있는데, 미국도 이라크봉쇄를 무한정 계속할수 없을것임으로 후세인의 후퇴제스쳐를 명분으로 삼아 사태를 적당히 마무리할 가능성도 있다고봄.끝

(대사-국장)

예고:92.6.30.

92.6.30. 일반

중아국	장관	차관	1차보	2차보	외정실	분석관	청와대	안기부

外 務 部

관리번호 91/1905

종 별 :

번 호 : USW-6080

수 신 : 장 관 (중동일,미일)

발 신 : 주 미 대사

제 목 : 대이락 정책 검토

일 시 : 91 1209 1839

대: WUS-5375

연: USW-5851

금 12.9 당관 노광일 서기관은 국무부 MEISENHEIMER 이락 담당관을 접촉, 미국의 대이락 정책 현황에 대해 탐문한바, 동 내용 하기 보고함.

1. BUSH 대통령 정책에 대한 비난

- 최근 MARIO CUOMO 뉴욕주 지사등 일부 민주당 인사등 국내일각에서 미국이 GULF 전 당시 SADDAM HUSSEIN 을 제거하지 못한 것은 실책이라는 비난이 제기되고 있으나 이는 상황 종료후의 시점(HINDSIGHT)에서 있을 수 있는 비난에 불과함.

- 걸프전 개전당시 어느누구도 걸프전이 이처럼 신속히 최소한의 피해로 끝날 것으로 예상치 못하였으며, UN 안보리 결의도 이락의 쿠웨이트 철수외에 SADDAM HUSSEIN 제거를 목표로 하지 않았음은 주지의 사실임.

2. 대이락 제재 조치

- HUSSEIN 이 집권하는한 대이락 제재조치를 계속 실시한다는 미국의 기본 입장에는 변화가 없으며, 금일 오전 국무부 DAVID MACK 중동담당 부차관보가 이락 이익대표부 직원을 접촉할 시에도 이점을 명확히 밝혔음.

. 동 접촉시 MACK 부차관보는 이락북부 쿠르드족및 남부지역 시아파에 대한이락측의 탄압이 계속되고 있는 점에 대해 우려를 표명하고 HUSSEIN 이 집권하는한 미국으로서는 경제제재 조치나 미국내 이락 자산 동결 조치를 완화할 계획이 없음을 분명히함.

. 이에대해 이락 이익대표부측은 경제제재 조치로 인해 이락국민및 아동들이 심각한 식량및 의약품난으로 희생되고 있다고 주장하면서 제재조치 완화를 계속 요구하였음.

중아국 장관 차관 1차보 미주국 외정실 분석관 청와대 안기부

PAGE 1

91.12.10 09:39

외신 2과 통제관 CA

0079

- 미측으로는 이락내 식량및 의약품난은 HUSSEIN 측이 제대로 분배를 하지 않았기 때문에 발생하고 있는 측면도 있다고 보고 있으며, 이락내 식량및 의약품부족현상은 UN 안보리 결의안대로 UN 의 개입하에 이락산 원유판매를 통해 해결되어야 하지 대이락 제재조치 완화를 통해 해결할 수 없다는 확고한 입장임.

3. HUSSEIN 저항세력에 대한 지원

- 미국은 HUSSEIN 이 권좌에서 물러나야 모든 문제가 해결된다는 점은 공개적으로 언급하고 있고, 이락국민 스스로가 정부를 변경할수 있는 상황을 조성(CREATE THE CIRCUMSTANCES)하기 위해 다수 저항세력과 접촉을 하고 있음.

. 미국이 동 저항세력에 대해 무기를 공급하고 자금을 지원하는등 비밀공작(COVERT OPERATION)을 하고 있는지 여부는 성격상 공개적으로 확인해 주기는 어려움.

- 이락내에는 수많은 소규모의 HUSSEIN 저항세력 집단이 존재하고 있으며, 동 세력은 상호 규합점이 없이 각각 독자적으로 활동을 하고 있다는 점이 문제로제기되고 있는바, 미국으로서 우선 상기 HUSSEIN 저항 세력을 규합해서 하나의세력으로 만드는데 노력을 기울이고 있음.

. 12.5 국무부 DJEREJIAN 중동담당 차관보는 SAID JABR(HUSSEIN 전항세력의일원)와 면담, HUSSEIN 세력의 규합문제등을 협의한바 있음.

. 92.1 월 중순경 사우디에서 모든 반 HUSSEIN 집단이 참가하는 대규모 회의가 개최될 예정임.끝.

(대사 현홍주-국장)

예고: 92.6.30. 일반

92. 6. 30.

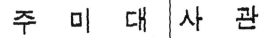

주 미 대 사 관

USW(F) : **5466**   년월일 : **91.12.11**   시간 : **14:10**

수 신 : 장 관 (중동일. 기보.)

발 신 : 주미대사

제 목 : 이락 국내정세

	보 안	
	해 제	

(출처 : NYT)

배부처	장관실	차관실	일차보	이차보	기획실	외정실	본석관	외전정	아즈	미주국	구주국	중아국	국기국	경적국	동상국	문활국	영교부	총무처	감사관	공보관	외연원	청와대	총리실	안기부	공보처
	/	/	/		/	/		/			O													

공보 보고 중함
각부 보사항 2개실

(5466 - 2 - 1)

외신 1과	
통 제	

0081

FOR POSSIBLE COUP IN IRAQ, U.S. PLANS

Seeing 'Strains' in Leadership in Baghdad, White House Is Planning Responses

By PATRICK E. TYLER
Special to The New York Times

WASHINGTON, Dec. 10 — The Bush Administration is reviewing military options on how the United States would respond to a coup in Iraq by senior members of the Iraqi armed forces, Administration officials said today.

The Administration has received recent intelligence reports of "serious strains" in the Iraqi leadership and wants to insure that President Bush is not caught without a plan of action, as he was during a coup attempt in Panama in October 1989, a move that preceded the invasion by United States forces two months later.

The military options, prepared by the Joint Chiefs of Staff over the last three weeks, would prepare the United States for a situation in which key officers in Iraq's armed forces might request support from Washington in an attempt to seize power from President Saddam Hussein.

The options are to be reviewed on Thursday at a high-level meeting of the so-called deputies committee of key Cabinet departments, which is headed by Adm. Jonathan T. Howe, the deputy national security adviser.

Timing of Military Plans

The planning comes as Mr. Bush's re-election bid is about to begin, and it seems likely to prompt critics to suggest that Mr. Bush is contemplating a foreign venture to divert attention from his domestic political troubles, or to insulate his re-election campaign from charges that the otherwise successful American military effort in the Persian Gulf war last winter failed to dislodge Mr. Hussein from power.

Some Democrats and Republicans have been urging the President to take stronger steps to remove Mr. Hussein and to avert a new humanitarian crisis in Iraq, where United Nations sanctions have led to widespread malnutrition among the poor, a condition that Mr. Hussein appears to be exploiting.

The military options were provided by Gen. Colin L. Powell, Chairman of the Joint Chiefs of Staff and the president's top military adviser. They were reviewed by Defense Secretary Dick Cheney before being sent to the White House late last week.

One potential dispute that emerged from the military review of coup "scenarios" posed by the White House centers on the issue of whether United States ground forces would be needed to back a successful coup attempt against Baghdad's current leadership.

White House Preference

The White House wants a military solution based only on air forces and naval forces, officials said, while General Powell is said to believe strongly that the removal of Mr. Hussein could not be guaranteed under any coup scenario without committing American ground troops, a decision that would present a politically debilitating and risky condition for the White House.

A classified discussion paper from General Powell is said to point out the difficulties of confronting the four Republican Guard divisions that ring Baghdad. While United States air forces might be sufficient to assist an Iraqi military coup by destroying and tying down loyalist forces, air power alone could not deal with every contingency or guarantee a final victory over Mr. Hussein, as one official described the military argument. The military review did not appear to be prompted by intelligence information indicating that Mr. Hussein's top officers were actually plotting against him.

"We have had intelligence information very recently that indicated some serious strains" within Mr. Hussein's inner circle, an Administration official said.

'Armed Conflict'

One intelligence report, received after Mr. Hussein changed defense ministers last month, described an incident of "armed conflict" between rival security forces of the new Iraqi Defense Minister, Ali Hassan al-Majid, a cousin of Mr. Hussein, and the relative he replaced, Hussein Kamel Hassan, who is Mr. Hussein's son-in-law.

The "conflict" resulted in "injuries and some deaths and was carried out in a revenge fashion" by Mr. Hassan's forces, the official said. The official added that other intelligence reporting indicated a general disaffection with Mr. Hussein among Iraq's traditional Sunni Muslim elite, which dominate the merchant class, the army and the upper ranks of the ruling Arab Baath Socialist Party.

By undertaking this review, however, the Administration may be hoping to foster the planning of a coup by keeping Mr. Hussein's regime under tight economic sanctions and by taking intrusive steps to remove or destroy all vestiges of Iraq's nuclear, chemical and biological weapons programs, as well as laboratories and factories taking part in ballistic missile work.

The military review was conducted in response to two specific scenarios posed by the National Security Council staff, officials said. Under one scenario, Iraqi military commanders began a coup attempt that bogged down and then asked for American assistance. Under a second scenario, Iraqi military leaders signaled to Washington they were ready to depose Mr. Hussein if the United States would provide support, particularly air support, since the Iraqi Air Force remains grounded as part of the allied cease-fire conditions imposed last winter.

To be successful in the removal of Mr. Hussein, General Powell is said to have forcefully argued, United States ground troops would be necessary and warned that the consequences of failure would undermine the long term gains United States foreign policy achieved with the gulf war victory.

91.12.11
NYT

5466-2-2

0082

외 무 부

종 별 :

번 호 : KUW-0788

일 시 : 91 12121400

수 신 : 장관(중동일)

발 신 : 주 쿠웨이트 대사

제 목 : 미국의 대이라크 정책

대:WKU-485

연:KUW-771

1. 이라크군의 쿠데타에 대비하기 위하여 미 참모 본부가 마련한 군사정책 (MILITARY OPTIONS)을 미행정부가 검토중임을 미행정부 관리가 언급한것으로 당지 언론이 보도함.

2. 이는 이라크 지도층 내부에 "심각한 긴장(SERIOUS STRAINS)"이 내재하고 있다는 최근정보를 바탕으로 한것이며, 이라크군 지휘관들이 훗세인을 축출하기 위하여 미국의 지원을 요청해오는 사태에 대비하기 위한것이라고함.

3. 이라크는 민간상인들을 통해서 요르단및 터어키로부터 식량, 의약품등의 물자를 밀반입하고 있는데, 이러한 밀무역이 안보리 경제제재를 극복해낼 정도의 큰규모는 아니나, 이때문에 이라크가 유엔의 인도적 제의를 계속 거부하고 있을 가능성이 있는것으로 보고있다고함. 끝

(대사-국장)

예고:92.6.30. 일반

① 훗세인 체제가 저도널 보고어떻게 됐읍니까? (보고서 2행)

② 이라크가 경제봉쇄 잘어 어떻게 리댁하고 있읍니까? (보고서 2,5행)

92. 6. 30. 민안

중아국	장관	차관	1차보	외정실	분석관	청와대	안기부

이라크가 경제 봉쇄에도 불구 지탱하는 이유

(워싱턴 포스트 바그다드 주재원보도)

91. 12. 14.
중동 1과

1. 지난 8월의 쿠웨이트 침공직후부터 16개월간에 걸친 유엔 제재조치에도
불구, 이라크는 식량구매와 부분적인 전후 복구사업을 계속하고 있는바,
이라크의 주요 수입원은 쿠웨이트 침공전부터 보유하고있던 금괴,
쿠웨이트로부터 약탈한 현금, 이라크 물품의 불법 교역으로 얻은 수입
및 해외 비밀자산등인 것으로 보임.

2. 이러한 재정수입을 배경으로 이라크는 유엔통제하에 16억불 상당의
원유 판매를 규정한 지난9월 유엔안보리의 인도적 제의를 거절하였는바,
이러한 재정수입으로 유엔의 제재조치를 얼마나 견딜수 있는지가 불확실
하므로 이라크의 정치장래를 예측하기 어려움.

3. 이라크 정부가 한달에 한번꼴로 열흘분 식량을 배급하고 있으나, 시중
상점에있는 작품은 민간기업들에 의해 수입되고 있음. 이라크정부는
외환, 관세, 수입허가에 대한 통제를 없애 민간기업에 의한 식량수입을
촉진하고 있는바, 대부분의 대외무역은 합법, 불법을 막론하고 후세인
친척 및 친지들에 의해 장악되고 있음.

4. 이라크가 비밀 재정수입이 있다는 것은 공습피해를 입은 일부 병원,
도시건강센타, 교량.통신소등의 계속적인 복구사업에서도 증명되고 있음.

5. 이라크는 요르단 아카바항등을 중개지로하여 석유제품과 트럭,
굴착장비등 중장비등을 불법 수출하고 있으며 쿠르드 게릴라들이 장악
하고있는 북부지역을 통해서도 터키 및 이란에 석유제품과 불도저,
크레인, 굴착장비등 중장비를 불법 수출하고 있음.

6. 한편, 이라크산 원유를 담보로 요르단이 크레딧을 제공하고 있으며,
알려지지않은 후세인의 비밀은행구좌 자산이 313억불에 이른다는 설도
있음.

0084

長 官 報 告 事 項

1991. 12. 14.
中東 1 課 (58)

題 目 : 「사담 후세인」 除去를 위한 美國의 對이라크 軍事措置 檢討說

最近 美言論은 美行政府가 軍事措置등을 包含, 보다 적극적인 「훗세인」 除去
方案을 講究中이라고 報道한바, 關聯 檢討意見을 아래 報告합니다.

공관의 보고에 기초함

---

1. 最近 美言論은 美行政府가 이라크內 叛軍에 대한 支援을 主內容으로하는
「훗세인」 逐出方案을 檢討中이며, 이라크 軍部에 의한 反「훗세인」
쿠데타 發生 可能性에 對備, 이를 支援하기 위한 軍事措置를 檢討中이라
보도함.(11.25字 워싱턴 포스트및 12.11字 뉴욕 타임즈)

2. 이와관련, 美國務部 **는 「후세인」이 執權하는한 對이라크 制裁措置를
계속한다는 基本立場에는 變化가 없으며, 美國이 定期的으로 對이라크
政策을 再檢討하고 있고, 多數 저항세력과도 接觸하고 있다고 말함으로써
軍事的인 方案도 檢討되고 있음을 示唆함. (駐美大使 報告)

3. 부시 行政府는 來年 大統領 選擧를 意識, 후세인 除去方案을 檢討中에
있는것으로 보이나, 施行 可能性 및 그 結果에 대해 行政府內 많은
異見이 尙存, 實現可能性은 稀薄함.

걸프戰때 앞두고 후세인을 제거하지 못한데 대한 國內一部 輿論의 비난을

4. 또한 美國으로서는 軍事行動의 경우 이라크 國民의 反美感情 高潮,
시아派 支援을 위한 이란의 影響力 增大등을 憂慮, 이라크 國民 특히
軍部의 反亂이 없는한 武力 介入은 어려울 것으로 보임. 또한 이라크
軍部內 갈등설에도불구, 現在 「후세인」의 軍部에 대한 장악도로 미루어
軍에 의한 反亂은 기대하기 어려운 것으로 알려짐.

5. 今番 美行政府의 軍事措置 可能性 檢討는 이라크內 反亂 可能性에 對備
하는한편, 이라크 軍部內 反후세인 勢力에게 美國의 支援을 示唆함으로써
反亂을 부추기는 效果를 노린것으로 보임.

0085

言論對策 : 해당무 끝

분류번호 문서번호	중동일 720- 3070	기안용지 (720-2327)		시 행 상 특별취급	
보존기간	영구·준영구 10. 5. 3. 1	장 관			
수 신 처 보존기간					
시행일자	1991. 12. 17.				
보존 기관	국 장		협 조 기 관		문 서 통 제 검열 발 송 인
	심의관				
	과 장	전 결			
기안책임자	임 현 재				
경 유 수 신 참 조		수신처 참조	발신명의		
제 목		미국의 대 이라크 정책관련 자료			

　　　최근 미언론은 미행정부가 적극적인 「사담 훗세인」 제거 방안을

강구중이라고 보도한바, 동 관련 장관보고사항을 별첨 송부하오니 참고

하시기 바랍니다.

　　첨 부 : 상기보고사항 1부.　　　끝.

　　수신처 : 주 미, 유엔, 터키, 이란, 쿠웨이트, 요르단, 대사

　　　　　　사우디

92. 6. 30. 일반

長官報告事項

1991. 12. 14.
中東 1 課(58)

題 目 : 「사담 훗세인」 除去를 위한 美國의 對이라크 軍事措置 檢討說

最近 美言論은 美行政府가 軍事措置등을 包含, 보다 적극적인 「후세인」 除去
方案을 講究中이라고 報道한바, 關聯 公館의 報告에 기초한 檢討意見을 아래
報告합니다.

1. 最近 美言論은 美行政府가 이라크內 叛軍에 대한 支援을 主內容으로하는
   「훗세인」 逐出方案을 檢討中이며, 이라크 軍部에 의한 反「훗세인」
   쿠데타 發生 可能性과 關聯, 이를 支援하기 위한 軍事措置를 檢討中이라
   보도함. (11.25.字 워싱턴 포스트 및 12.11.字 뉴욕타임즈)

2. 이와관련, 美國務部는 「후세인」이 執權하는限 對이라크 制裁措置를 계속
   한다는 基本立場에는 變化가 없으며, 美國이 定期的으로 對이라크 政策을
   再檢討하고 있고, 多數 저항세력과도 接觸하고 있다고 말함으로써 軍事的인
   方案도 檢討되고 있음을 示唆함. (駐美大使 報告)

3. 부시 行政府는 來年 大統領 選擧를 앞두고, 걸프戰時 「훗세인」을 除去치
   못한데 대한 國內 一部輿論의 非難을 意識, 후세인 除去方案을 檢討中에
   있는것으로 보이나, 成功 可能性 및 그 結果에 대해 行政府內 異見이 많아,
   實現可能性은 稀薄함.

4. 또한 美國으로서는 軍事行動의 경우 이라크 國民의 反美感情 高潮, 시아派
   支援으로 시아派의 勢力이 커지면 이란의 影響力 增大등을 憂慮, 이라크
   國民 특히 軍部의 反亂이 없는限 武力 介入은 어려울 것으로 보임.
   또한 이라크 軍部內 갈등설에도 不拘, 現在 「후세인」의 軍部에 대한
   장악도로 미루어 軍에 의한 反亂은 기대하기 어려운 것으로 알려짐.(주쿠웨이트대사

5. 따라서 今番 美行政府의 軍事措置 可能性 檢討는 일단 이라크內 反亂
   可能性에 對備하는 한편, 이를 言論에 흘린것은 이라크 軍部內 反후세인
   勢力에게 美國의 支援을 示唆함으로써 反亂을 부추기는 效果를 노린것으로
   보임.   끝.

0087

	분류번호	보존기간

발 신 전 보

WSB-1156   911224 1420 DW

번 호 : _____ 종별 : _____

수 신 : 주   수신처 참조   대사. 총영사

WKU -0531	WJO -0749
WUS -5826	WFR -2679

발 신 : 장 관 (중동일)

제 목 : 아랍권의 '후세인' 축출 동향

최근 베이루트발 UPI는 아래내용의 표제관련 보도를 했는바, 동 보도내용의 ~~진위여부~~ 및 관련사항등을 가능한 상세파악 보고바라며, 특이사항 있을시 수시 보고 바람.

- 아   래 -

ㅇ 레바논 일간지 '알디야르'가 사우디와 이란이 공동지원하는 '후세인' 정권축출 전략이 진행중이라는 보도와 때맞춰 '앗사드' 시리아 대통령이 12.22. 다마스커스 에서 이라크의 반'후세인' 회교 과격파 지도자 '하킴' 이란 혁명평의회 의장과 회담을 갖고 '후세인' 대통령을 비난했으며, '하킴'의장은 시리아와 '후세인' 축출전략을 논의 예정이라고 함.   끝.

(중동아프리카국장   이 해 순)

예 고 : 1992. 6. 30. 까지

수신처 : 주 사우디, (이란), 쿠웨이트, 요르단, 미국, 프랑스대사

※ 주 이란 대사만 현재 장비고장으로 비밀 전문 접수불가함.
   약 4-5일후 수리 완료 예정으로 사료됨. (대신사)

92. 6. 30. 인br

| | 보 안 통 제 | |

앙고재	기안자 성명		과 장 심의관	국 장		차 관	장 관		외신과통제
91 년 12 월 24 일 과									

0088

2. 1992

報 告 事 項

「사담훗세인」大統領 除去企圖說

題 目 : 美國의 對이라크 軍事措置 檢討說以後 關聯動向

91.11월말 美言論이 美行政府가 軍事措置등을 包含, 보다 積極的인 「훗세인」除去方案을 講究中이라는 報道를 한이후 最近 이라크內 反「훗세인」勢力에 의한 일련의 「훗세인」 除去企圖 움직임이 있는바, 同 關聯事項을 아래 報告 합니다.

1. 上記 言論報道와 關聯, 美國務部는 12월초 이라크內 多數 抵抗勢力과 接觸하고 있다고 말함으로써 軍事的 措置가 檢討되고 있음을 示唆하였으며, 어는 이라크內의 反亂을 부추기는 效果를 노린 것으로 評價되었음.

2. 이와관련 最近 다음과 같은 일련의 「훗세인」 除去企圖 움직임이 있음.

   ○ 「하킴」 이라크 回敎革命評議會(SAIRI)議長이 12월말 시리아를 訪問, 「앗사드」大統領과 「훗세인」 除去를 위한 協議 開催 (91.12.28.字 배이루트발 外信 및 1.5.字 駐이란 大使報告)

   ○ 이라크 反政 指導者들이 1.3.부터 시리아에서 會同, 「훗세인」除去 計劃 論議 (시리아發 外信 및 1.4.字 쿠웨이트 新聞) (駐쿠웨이트 大使報告)

   ○ 이라크, 쿠데타 主謀 將校 80명 處刑 (아테네發 外信)

   ○ 反政勢力들이 일부 高位將校들과 結託, 「훗세인」이 會議를 주재하던 空軍 司令部를 襲擊, 수명의 死傷者를 냄 (카이로發 外信)

3. 美國은 成功可能性이 가장 큰 이라크 國民 특히 軍部에 의한 自發的인 反亂을 誘導하기 위하여 反 「훗세인」 勢力을 糾合하는데 最大의 努力을 기울이고 있는바, 最近의 움직임은 이러한 美國의 努力 및 反亂時 支援을 시사한 美國政策의 結果로 보아나, 美國이 걸프戰이후 關係가 改善된 시리아등을 調整, 背後에서 積極的으로 作用하고 있을 可能性도 排除할수 없음.

4. 한편, 「팬암」機 爆破를 요요한 對리비아 制裁措置 關聯, 美國은 最後의 手段으로 軍事的 膺懲을 檢討할 수 있겠으며 이경우 中東平和會議에 미칠 惡影響등을 憂慮, 「카다피」除去를 위한 秘密工作을 구사할 可能性도 排除할수 없음. 끝.

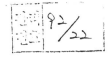

報 告 事 項

報 告 畢

1992. 1. 11.
中東 1 課 (2)

題 目 : 美國의 「사담 훗세인」 大統領 除去 企圖說

91.11월말 美言論은 「부시」行政府가 軍事措置등을 包含, 보다 積極的인 (강경한)
「훗세인」 除去方案을 講究中이라는 報道를 한바있으며 最近 이라크內 反
「훗세인」 세력에 의한 일련의 「훗세인」 除去企圖 움직임이 있는바, 同 關聯
사항을 아래 報告합니다. 은 이를 反映하는 것으로 보이는바
(反映)

1. 上記 言論報道와 關聯, 美國務部는 12월초 이라크內 多數 抵抗勢力과 接觸하고
   있다고 말함으로써 이라크 國內의 反「훗세인」勢力에 대한 軍事支援이 檢討되고
   있음을 示唆하였음.

2. 이와관련 最近 다음과 같은 一連의 「훗세인」 除去企圖 움직임이 있음.
   ○ 「하킴」 이라크 回教革命評議會(SAIRI)議長이 12월말 시리아를 訪問,
     「앗사드」 大統領과 「훗세인」除去를 爲한 協議 開催 (駐이란 大使 報告)
   ○ 이라크 反政 指導者들이 1.3.부터 시리아에서 會同, 「훗세인」除去 計劃
     論議 (駐쿠웨이트 大使 報告)
   ○ 이라크 政府 쿠데타 謀議 將校 80명 處刑 (아테네發 外信)
   ○ 反政勢力들이 일부 高位將校들과 結託, 「훗세인」이 會議를 주재하던
     空軍 司令部를 襲擊, 수명의 死傷者를 냄 (카이로發 外信)

3. 美國은 이라크에 대한 經濟制裁가 實效를 거두지 못하고 있으며 「훗세인」
   을 걸프戰直後 除去하지 못한데 대한 國內 批判 輿論이 大統領 選擧에 미칠
   影響을 考慮하여 「훗세인」 除去 工作을 推進하고 있는 것으로 分析됨.

4. 이러한 目標아래 成功可能性이 가장 큰 이라크 內部로 부터의 反亂을 誘導
   하기 위하여 軍部를 포함한 反「훗세인」諸勢力을 糾合하는데 最大의 努力을
   기울이고 있는 것으로 보임. 또한 美國은 걸프戰以後 關係가 改善된 시리아
   등을 調整, 背後에서 積極的으로 作用하고 있을 可能性도 排除할수 없음.

5. 한편, 「팬암」機 爆破 사건關聯, 美國은 리비아에 대해서도 軍事的 膺懲을
   排除하지 않고있으나, 이경우 中東平和會議에 미칠 惡影響등을 憂慮, 오히려
   「훗세인」除去와 類似한 「카다피」除去를 爲한 秘密工作을 試圖할 可能性도
   있다고봄. 끝.

0091

미국의 『후세인』 제거 노력
=======================================
(92.2.7.자 NYT 보도내용 요약)

o 『부시』 대통령은 『게이츠』 국장을 에집트, 사우디, 이스라엘 지도자들과
    『훗세인』 축출방안을 논의키위한 밀사로 파견했음
    - 각국지도자들과의 회담내용은 두가지로 구분할수 있는바, 이라크 『훗세인』
      대통령을 축출하기위한 비밀계획에 대한 논의와 유엔 안보리 승인하의 무력사용
      압력을 위한 공개 계획에 대한 논의임

o 미국은 유엔 승인하 이라크 군사목표에 대한 과시용 폭격을 심각히 고려하고
    있는데 이는 『훗세인』의 입지를 약화시켜 군부내 반정 세력을 고무하는 의도도
    있음
    - 현재 걸프지역에는 병력 25,000명, 전함 25척, 전투기 200여대의 미군병력 주둔

o 『부시』 대통령은 지난주 뉴욕 유엔 안보리 정상회담 기회를 이용, 이라크가
    유엔의 정전결의 위반을 계속하는 경우 좀더 강력한 제재조치를 취할것에 대한
    각국의 지지를 요청
    - 미국과 그의 동맹국은 유엔의 집요한 사찰이 『훗세인』의 입지를 약화시켜
      이라크내 쿠테타를 부추기도록 하려고 노력하고 있음 (유엔 사찰의 모든 조건은
      『훗세인』을 궁지에 몰아 넣도록 짜여져 있음)

o 『케이츠』 국장의 에집트 『무바라크』 대통령과의 회담에서는 팬암기 폭파사건
    관련한 대 리비아 제재조치도 논의되었는바, 에집트는 리비아에 150만의 노동자를
    보내고 있으므로 미-리비아 양국간의 알력을 해소시키기 위해 노력하고 있음

o 『케이츠』 국장은 주말에 리야드를 방문, 『파드』 국왕을 비롯한 사우디 고위
    관리들과 대 이라크 압력 강화방안 논의예정
    - 사우디는 『훗세인』이 건재하고 있는한 이라크의 대 사우디 보복 조치를 우려하고
      있음.

o 『부시』 행정부는 최근 수개월간 이라크 지도부 및 군부핵심에서의 균열을 최대한
    이용하기 위하여 반 『훗세인』 사전 계획 수립을 강화해 오고 있음
    - 미국관리들은 『훗세인』을 축출키 위한 방안들이 공개됨으로써 『훗세인』에
      대한 압력을 가중시킬수 있을 것으로 기대

0092

외 무 부

종   별 :

번   호 : KUW-0172   일   시 : 92 0315 1300

수   신 : 장관(중동일,사본:소병용대사)

발   신 : 주 쿠웨이트 대사대리

제   목 : 미군함정 걸프해역 배치(자응 제92-18호)

1. 미국항공모함 USS AMERICA 호(8 만본,80 대의 전투기적재)와 호위함 NORMANDY 호등 5 척으로 구성된 해군함대가 3.12 걸프해역으로 배치되어 대기중인것으로 보도됨.

2. 동함대의 걸프해역 배치는 이라크가 걸프전 휴전조건을 전면이행하도록 하기위한 군사적 압력 시위인것으로 보이는데, 금주중 이라크에 재입국할 유엔안보리 소속 휴전감시단의 활동에 대한 이라크측의 태도에 따라 군사제재조치 여부가 결정될것으로 보임.

3. 그간 이라크가 유엔 휴전감시단의 이라크내 활동(대량 살상무기저장및 제조공장 확인과 파괴)에 충분히 협조하지 않은것과 관련하여, 미국및 영국은 수차 이에대한 군사공격 거론등 강경입장을 취해온것으로 보아, 이라크가 이번에도비협조적일 경우 군사공격 가능성이 매우높은것으로 알려지고 있는데, 그러나 군사공격 경우에 그시기는 이슬람 금식기간이 끝나는 4 월초가 될것으로 당지외교단은 예상하고 있음.

4. 상기 미군함대 배치에 대하여 쿠웨이트 정부당국은 아무런 언급을 하지않고 있는데, 미국.쿠웨이트 양국은 3.1 부터 15 일간 양국 합동기동훈련을 실시중이며, 이에는 4 천명의 미해병대와 5 척의 미군함정이 참가하고있음. 끝

(대사대리-국장)

중아국   차관   1차보   2차보   중아국   분석관   안기부

주 영 ● 국 대 사 관

UKV(F) : 446   년월일 : 20716   시간 : 1802
수 신 : 장 관 (중동이, 미일, 구일)
발 신 : 주영대사
제 목 : 이라크 정세

보 안 / 봉 책 ┼   朱

(출처 :   )

THE TIMES   (6면, 3, 16. 1992)

US lines up strong Gulf strike force against Iraq

배부처	장관실	차관실	일차보	이차보	외정실	분석관	아주국	미주국	구주국	중아국	국기국	경제국	통상국	문협국	외연원	청와대	안기부	공보처	경기원	상공부	재무부	농수부	동자부	환경처
		/	/				/	/	0							/							

BY MICHAEL EVANS, DEFENCE CORRESPONDENT

THE Americans have assembled a powerful strike force in the Gulf region to renew military action against Iraq, if President Saddam Hussein continues to thwart United Nations efforts to eliminate his weapons of mass destruction. The firepower is only a fraction of that deployed for Operation Desert Storm, but Pentagon sources say it is "a composite" of everything used last year.

Since the end of the war, the Americans have maintained a strong presence in the area, acting as a continuing deterrent to Iraq and as a protective shield around Kuwait and Saudi Arabia. As a large part of Iraq's military capability was destroyed in the war, the size of the US strike force is probably sufficient to mount any operation against Iraqi targets without fear of heavy losses.

The US has 24,000 military personnel in the area, of which about 16,300 are at sea, 3,000 in the army and 5,000 in the air force. This compares with 430,000 US servicemen deployed for Desert Storm, but the main impact of the US military presence is in firepower. The US Navy confirmed yesterday that there were 20 American warships in the Gulf, the Gulf of Oman, and the northern Arabian Sea.

USS America, the sole aircraft carrier in the area, moved into the Gulf on Thursday. The carrier is escorted by three cruisers, four destroyers and two frigates. Apart from the 76 fixed-wing aircraft and helicopters on the carrier, there are an estimated 150 Tomahawk cruise missiles on the escort ships.

The US Navy deployment also includes a command ship, USS La Salle, believed to be in the Gulf, five amphibious ships and four support vessels. The amphibious ships, carrying 2,149 marines, are part of the 13th Marine Expeditionary Unit. Several reports have suggested that the marine force in

의신 1급 / 동 책

0094

US lines up ___ .

the Gulf has been increased to 7,000, but a US Navy official said the number of marines had remained at just over 2,000.

The British naval presence in the Gulf area consists of two warships, HMS York and HMS Beaver, and a support vessel, RFA Bayleaf. During the Gulf war, there were three warships.

There are believed to be about 200 US combat planes in Saudi Arabia and Turkey. They include nearly 40 F111F bombers, F16s and EF111A electronic jamming aircraft at Incirlik in Turkey. Aircraft based in Saudi Arabia at Dhahran, Riyadh, and the King Faisal base are believed to include 20 F117A Stealth fighters, about 50 F16s and 2 J-Stars, the US army's converted Boeing 707 spy planes which can pick out ground targets from more than 100 miles away.

The Pentagon confirmed that the American air force assets included a number of Stealth fighters, the most successful of the precision bombers in the Gulf War. The RAF has six Jaguar bombers and 2 VC10 tankers at Incirlik. Tornado aircraft at Cyprus and at RAF Brüggen in Germany could be deployed if a decision is made to renew air strikes. ▪

● Jerusalem: The Israeli government, stunned by news reports that it transferred American weapons and technology illegally to China and other Third World countries, bristled at the Bush administration yesterday (Ben Lynfield writes).

Ehud Olmert, the health minister, accused Washington of conducting a deliberate smear campaign against the Jewish state. "The goal is to slander the state of Israel publicly and internationally and to give the impression that Israel is harming U.S. interests," he said, emerging from a cabinet meeting/

446- Z-Z

0095

외　무　부

관리번호 92/259

종　별 : 지급
번　호 : USW-1430
수　신 : 장관(중동일,미일)
발　신 : 주미대사
제　목 : 대이락 제재동향

일　시 : 92 0320 1734

1. 국무부 TUTWILLER 대변인은 3.19 정례브리핑에서 최근 주재국 언론에 보도 되고 있는 대이락 군사제재 임박설 관련 질의에 대해 현재 미국은 유엔의 대이락 사찰에 주력하고 있을 뿐이라고 답변하고 군사조치 검토 여부에 대하여는 즉답을 회피함. 동인은 또한 지난 TARIG AZIZ 이락부수상 유엔방문시 EKEUS 유엔특별위 위원장에 의해 제시된 것으로 보도된 3.26 시한설에 대하여는 양자간 면담시 논의내용은 자신이 확인할수있는 사항이 아니나, 유엔 안보리 결의상으로는 여하한 시한도 명시되어있지 않다고 답변함. FITZWATER 백악관 대변인도 3.18 정례브리핑에서 상기 3.26 시한설을 부인하면서 유엔사찰팀이 이락에 입국예정인 3.21(토) 이 중요한 분기점이 될것이라고 언급하고 이락이 사찰에 응하지 않을 경우의 대안에 관하여는 여타 유엔회원국과 협의, 검토할것이라고 답변, 미국의 독자행동 가능성을 간접 부인함. WILLIAMS 국방부 대변인도 3.19 유엔 사찰팀 활동을 통한 해결이 가장 적절한 방안일것으로 본다고 언급, 군사제재 임박설을 부인함.

2. 상기와 같은 미행정부 각부처 대변인들의 공식부인 성명에도 불구하고 대이락 군사제재 문제에 관하여는 미행정부내에서 상당히 심각하게 논의되고 있는것으로 보도되고있는바 최근 주재국 언론에 보도되고 있는 주요 동향은 아래와같음.

가. POWELL 합참의장을 비롯한 고위 군부인사들은 대이락 군사공격이 미국에게도 큰 위험부담이 있을뿐 아니라 온건 아랍제국의 정치적 반발을 초래한다는이유로 반대입장을 취하고있음. 단, 국방부측은 군사공격에 대비한 상세 CONTINGENCY PLAN 은 이미 마련해 놓은 상태이며 실제로 최근에는 걸프만에서 상당한 미군병력 9USS AMERICA 항공모함등) 이동이 있었음. 반면 SCOWCRAFT 백악관 안보보좌관은 대이락 강경대응 입장을 취하고 있으며 부쉬대통령도 3.26-29 간 유엔사찰단의 활동이 아무런 성과없이 끝날 경우에는 군사조치도 불사한다는 방향으로기울여져 있는 (PREDISPOSED)

중아국	장관	차관	1차보	2차보	미주국	외정실	분석관	청와대
안기부								

92. 6. 30. 검토필

PAGE 1

92.03.21　09:15

외신 2과　통제관 BZ

0096

것으로 보도됨.

　　나. 그러나 당지 전문가들은 부쉬대통령이 여하한 결정을 내리던간에 국내 정치적으로 얻을 이득이 없으므로 (군사제재조치가 성공한다 하더라도 국내문제에대한 여론의 관심을 국외로 돌리기 위한 정치적 의도로 비판 받을 가능성), 군사조치 결정을 할경우에도 미국이 독자행동을 취하기 보다는 유엔의 추가 결의를봉한 COALITION 에의해 추진하게 될것으로 관측하고있음. 이와관련 미행정부는내부적으로 군사조치이외의 여타 제재조치도 검토중이며 동조치에는 15 억불로추상되는 이락의 국외자산동결 (부쉬대통령은 이미 국무부측에 여타국과 동건 협의토록 지시), 이락 인권상황에 대한 유엔사찰이 포함되어있는것으로 보도됨.

　　3. 당관 관찰

　　가. 미행정부측이 언론에 보도되고 있는 3.26 시한설을 공식부인하고 있음에 비추어 미국이 수일내에 대이락 군사조치를 취할 가능성은 희박한것으로 보이나 3.26-29 간 시행될 유엔사찰팀의 활동성과가 별무할경우 여하한 형태로든 대이락 강경제재 조치를 위한 적극적인 움직임이 있을것으로 판단됨.

　　나. 그러나 이경우에도 미국의 독자적인 군사조치는 국내 선거정국에 심각한 영향을 미칠뿐 아니라 그에 따른 정치적 부담도 올것이므로 유엔안보리의 추가 결의를 봉한 제재조치의 방식을 취할것으로 보임.

　　다. 동건관련 주재국 입장 파악을 위해 국무부 담당과장을 접촉 예정인바, 상세 추보 하겠음. 끝

　　(대사 현홍주-국장)

　　예고문: 92.12.31 일반

朱

주 미 대 사 관

USF(F) : 1774 년월일 : 92.3.23시간 : 17:25

수 신 : 장 관 (중동1, 미일)

발 신 : 주미대사

제 목 : 대 이락제재 동향 (국무부 브리핑)   (출처 : ANS)

보 안
통 제   함

21

STATE DEPARTMENT REGULAR BRIEFING   BRIEFER: MARGARET TUTWILER
12:10 P.M. EST   MONDAY, MARCH 23, 1992

     MS. TUTWILER: I believe the elections just happened yesterday,
that was March 22nd.

     Q   Margaret, do you have a reaction to -- do you have a
reaction to Iraq's apparent willingness now to make full, final, and
complete disclosure of their weapons program? For example, do you
believe that they are genuinely prepared to do this or are you
skeptical about it?

     MS. TUTWILER: I would put probably myself down in the
skeptical column.

     Q   (Off mike) -- details, can you elaborate a bit further on
that?

     MS. TUTWILER: I would just (know or note ?) because I am not
sure what is known publicly and what is not, to be honest with you,
but I would say that they don't exactly have a steady pattern of
follow through on things that they say they are going to do. This
is being obviously worked at the IAEA, it is being worked by the UN
special commission and all of us certainly hope that they do
promptly do what they have said they are going to do. They have
agreed to resolutions, they have sent letters saying they are going
to do these things, Tariq Aziz was just here saying they were going
to do them, so we'll see.

     Q   A follow up question. Has the special commission heard
back yet from the team that went over, arriving I believe on
Saturday?

     MS. TUTWILER: Heard back yet?

(1774 - 2 - 1)

외신 1과
등 제

0098

Q   Yes.

MS. TUTWILER: I am not sure that they have heard back, but you may know that -- I believe it was over the weekend, that the Iraqis sent a letter to the special commission. I don't have the details of that letter, you'd have to ask them, but there is why I put myself in the skeptical column. Here is another letter,

after a team arrives and after Tariq Aziz says all these things at the United Nations, then we have another letter that goes.

1774-2-2

0099

외 무 부

종 별 :

번 호 : USW-1548

일 시 : 92 0326 2017

수 신 : 장관(미일,중동일,중동이,기정) 사본: 국이완 대사

발 신 : 주미대사

제 목 : 대이락 제재 동향

연:USW-1430

당관 임성준참사관이 금 3.26 국무부 NEUMANN 이락, 이란과장을 면담 표제건에 관하여 파악한바 동요지 아래보고함(조태열 서기관, REUTHER 부과장배석).

1. 대이락 제재 동향

0 임참사관이 대이락 군사제재 임박설등 최근의 연론보도 내용에 대한 미행정부의 입장에 대해 문의한바 동과장은 아래와같이 답함.

- 후세인 정권을 상대로는 아무일도 할수없다는 것이 미국의 기본시각이며 후세인이 집권하고 있는한 이락에 대한 압력은 계속될것임. 그러나 후세인을 제거하는것이 미국의 정책목표는 아니며 미국은 지속적인 대이락 압력을 통해 궁극적으로는 이락내부 세력에 의해 후세인이 제거되기를 바라고있음.

-이락에 대한 군사제재 계획은 아직 없으나 그가능성은 배제하지는 않고있음(RULE OUT).

미국은 국제사회의 COALITION 을 통해 이락을 고립시키기위한 모든 외교적 압력수단을 계속 강구해 나갈것임 (우방국의 주이락 공관재개 및 고위정부인사 교류자재 요청등).

- 최근 TARG AZIZ 부총리가 유엔을 방문, 몇가지 약속을하고 돌아 갔으나 아직까지 아무것도 이루어진 것이없음. 유엔 사찰팀이 현재 이락에서 조사활동 중이나 이락은 여전히 미사일을 은폐하고 관련 사설파괴에 응하지 않고있음.

- 후세인은 압력이있을때만 굴복하고압력이 느슨해지면 물러서는 행태를 계속 반복해 왔는바 이락이 계속 유엔결의를 이행치 않을 경우에는 미국은 유엔을 통한 추가 조치(이락의 국외자산 동결등)를 검토할것임.

0 임참사관이 이러한 상황이 언제까지 계속될수있을 것으로 보느냐고 문의한데 대해

미주국 안기부	장관	차관	1차보	2차보	중아국	중아국	분석관	정와대

동과장은 구체적인 일정 (TIME FRAME)을 제시하기는 어렵다고 답하고 그러나 분명한것은 이락이 핵무기를 가지게될 상황은 용납할수 없다는 것이며 그경우에는 군사조치이외의 합리적인 대안이 없다는 것이라고 말함., 이와관련 REUTHER 부과장은 인도적인 고려도 간과할수없는 문제라고 말하고 현재 이락국민은 유엔 EMBARAGO 때문에 굶주리고 있는것이 아니라 이락정부가 모든 원조식량을 군대용으로 불법 비축하고 있기때문에 굶주리고있는 것이라고 강조함.

2. 동 유엔결의 이행을 위한 군사력 지원문제

0 임참사관이 이락이 유엔결의를 이행토록하기위해서는 군사력지원 (BACKINGFORCE)이 있어야 할것인바 현상황이 어떠한지 문의한데 대해, 동과장은 미, 영,불등의 공군력에 의한 공습능력은 상시 보유하고 있으며(터어키내의 공군기지 주둔) , 지중해. 걸프만의 항공모함과 우방제국의 걸프만 해군력 및 필요시 사우디등 걸프제국의 확고한 지원의사등을 유사시 (SHORT CHALLENGE) 대응능력은 확보되어 있다고 답변함.

0 임참사관이 여타국가의 추가지원없이 현재의 군사력으로 충분한지 문의한바, 동과장은 유엔 금지수역에서의 해상 검색활동에 참여하고있는 각국이 군함을 상시 배치하는데 어려움이 있어 ROTATION 방식을 취하고있다고 말하고 (영, 불, 카나다, 호주등이 참여중) 더많은 나라들이 참여할 경우 부담이 줄어들것이라고 답변함.

3. 미.이란관계

0 임참사관이 미국등 국제사회의 관심이 전후 이락처리문제에 쏠려있는 틈을 타서 이란이 이락의 세력약화를 기화로 역내 강대세력으로 재부상을 기도하고있는데 대한 경계론이 있음을 언급한데 대해, 동과장은 아주 중요한 문제를 지적 했다고 말하고 미국이 걸프전후 이락의 영토전(TERRITORIAL INTEGRITY)을 보장하고 쿠르드독립국 창설을 지지하지 않는 것도 바로 그러한 우려에 기인한다고 부언함.

0 그러나 동과장은 이란의 영향력 증대기도가 어느정도까지 어루어질지 (WHERE THE EVOLUTION EOMES OUT)는 아직은 분명치 않다고 말하고 중앙시아 회교공화국에 대하여는 아직 본격적인 영향력 확대노력이 있는것 같지않고, 오히려 동공화국들의 국내정세 안정에 더신경을 쓰고 있는것으로 보인다고 부언함. 동과장은 이어 사우디 등 걸프제국은 전통적으로 이란을 최대의 위협 (PRIMARY LONG-TERM THREAT)으로 보고있기 때문에 이란의 세력확대르 두려워하고있다고말함.

0 동과장은 최근 인질석방 문제에서 보여준 이란의 지원을 평가하고 있으나이란의

PAGE 2

지속적인 테러지원이 중단되지 않는한 미국과의 관계정상화는 어렵다고말하고 그러나 이란과 대화할 용의는 있다고 부언함.

임참사관이 현재도 이란과 대화를 하고있는지 문의한데 대해 동과장은 <u>제한된</u> <u>범위내에서 스위스를 통한 간접대화를 갖고있다고 답함.</u>

0 동과장은 이어 이란의 군산력이 위협적이진 않으나 북한으로부터의 스커드 미사일 수입, 핵무기 개발노력등 이란의 군비증강정책 (ARMAMENT POLICY) 은 예의 주시하지 않을수없는 고려요인 이라고말하고 북한의 대이란 무기수출이 언제까지 계속될 것으로 보느냐고 문의함.

이에대해 임참사관은 북한의 현경제 상황에서는 무기수출이 유일한 외화수입 원이브로 포기하기 어려울것으로 본다고 말하고 이락에 대해서와 마찬가지로 북한에 대한 국제사회의 압력을 강화해 나가야 할것임을 강조함. 끝(대사 현홍주-국장)

예고문: 92.12.31 일반

朱

외 무 부

종 별 :

번 호 : USW-1561   일 시 : 92 0327 1902

수 신 : 장관(미이, 미일, 중동일, 정특, 기정)

발 신 : 주 미 대사

제 목 : 하원 군사위 청문회

1. 하원 군사위 국방정책 연구반(반장: LES ASPIN 의원, 민주-위스콘신)은 "지역위협 및 1990 년대 국방 대책" 제하 일련의 청문회를 개최하고 있는바, 금3.27(금)에는 ROBERT GATES CIA 국장을 증인으로 출석시켜 중동 및 한반도의 정세에 관하여 청문회를 개최하였음. (당관 김형진 서기관 참석)

2. 동 청문회는 GATES 국장의 증언(증언문은 USWF-1863 로 FAX 송부함) 부분은 공개로, 이후 질의.응답은 비공개로 진행되었는바, ASPIN 의원과 BILL DICKINSON 의원(공화-알라바마)은 모두 발언에서 냉전이후 분쟁 발발의 위험이 가장높은 지역으로 중동과 한반도를 지적하고 동 지역에서의 안보위협 및 미군의 역할에 대한 GATES 국장의 견해를 요청한바, GATES 국장의 주요 증언 내용은 하기와 같음.

가. 중동은 향후 수년내 미국이 군사적으로 개입하게될 가능성이 가장 높은지역으로 특히 이락과 이란이 큰 위협이 되고 있는바, 이락은 걸프전 패배 및 UN 의 제재에도 불구하고 화학무기 원료 및 상당규모의 군사력을 보유하고 있으며, 제한적이나마 무기생산을 재개하고 있고 이란은 북한으로 부터의 스커드 미사일 구입등 90-94 년간 20 억불 상당의 무기를 외국으로 부터 구입할 계획으로 있으며 핵무기, 화학무기등 대량살상 무기개발 노력을 강화하고 있음.

나. 한반도는 미군의 실제의 적과 대치하고 있는 유일한 지역으로 북한은 병력의 전투준비도, 공군력, 병참등에는 약점이 있으나 남한에 대한 대규모 기습공격에 적합한 병력을 휴전선 바로 이북에 유지하고 있으며, 최근 기동력을 증강시켜 더욱 큰 위협이 되고 있음.

다. 더우기 북한은 핵무기 원료를 자체 생산할 수 있는 시설을 개발중에 있으며, 영변에 플로토늄 생산만계획위한 것으로 보이는 원자료 2 기를 건설, 1 기는 4 년전부터 가동중이며 보다 용량이 큰 1 기는 금년도 가동예정인바, 플로토늄 추출을

미주국	장관	차관	1차보	2차보	미주국	중아국	외정실	분석관
청와대	안기부							

92. 6. 30. 건도관 又

위한 핵연료 재처리 시설도 거의 완공단계에 있음.

라. 북한은 91.12 월 한반도 비핵화 선언에 합의하였음에도 불구하고 영변의 원자료 및 핵재처리시설의 존재 자체를 부인하고 있고 핵안전 협정을 상금 비준하지 않는등 핵개발을 계속할 조짐이 있어 제 3 국의 의심을 불식시킬만한 사찰을 받아들일 것인가에 대하여는 의구심이 있는바, 북한의 핵무기 개발은 임박하였으며 그것도 매우 임박(CLOSE, PERHAPS VERY CLOSE) 하였다고 봄. 북한의 핵무기 개발은 동북아 안보에 위협이 될뿐 아니라 북한이 외화를 얻기위해 핵물질 및 관련 기술을 외국에 수출할 가능성이 있기 때문에 더욱 우려가됨.

마. 장기적으로는 북한에 대해 과거 소련이 공급한 신무기 및 연료공급의 중단, 경제적 어려움등으로 북한의 남한에 대한 군사적 우위가 감소될 것이나, 단기적으로는 북한의 전략가들이 북한이 우위에 있을 때 남한을 공격하도록 권고할 수 있고 북한이 재래식 무기의 유지 및 현대화의 어려움으로 오히려 핵무기및 미사일 개발 노력을 강화할 수 있으므로 더욱 위험한 상황을 맞이하게 될 것임.

(대사 현홍주-국장)

92.12.31 까지

주 미 대 사 관

2370 Mass. Ave. N.W., Washington, D.C. 20008 / (202)939-5600 / Fax(202)797-0595

문서번호 미국(정)700- /202

시행일자 1992 . 4 . 28.

경유

수신 장 관

참조 미주국장

선결			지시	
접	일자시간		결재	
수	번호	25824	재	
처리자			공	
담당자			람	

제목 미국방부의 걸프전 결과 최종보고서

　　　　대 : WUS - 1967

　　　　연 : USW - 2121

　　　연호 표제보고서 사본 1부를 별첨 송부하니 참고하시기 바랍니다.

첨부 : 상기보고서 1부 (총3권).　　끝.

주 미 대 사

0105

TEXT OF PRESIDENT BUSH'S JULY 26 STATEMENT ON IRAQ'S
ACCEPTANCE OF THE EKEUS SOLUTION WITH HOST GOVERNMENTS FOLLOWS:

NOW, ON IRAQ. IRAQ'S BELATED ANNOUNCEMENT THAT IT WILL
ALLOW THE UNITED NATIONS SPECIAL COMMISSION TO CARRY OUT
AN INSPECTION OF THE AGRICULTURAL MINISTRY IN BAGHDAD DOES NOT
ALTER THE FACT THAT FOR SOME THREE WEEKS SADDAM HUSSEIN
FLAGRANTLY VIOLATED U.N. SECURITY COUNCIL RESOLUTION 687.

NOR DOES THIS ANNOUNCEMENT CHANGE THE FACT THAT IRAQ
DELIBERATELY AND CALLOUSLY HARASSED AND ABUSED THE U.N.
INSPECTORS SEEKING TO CARRY OUT THAT MANDATE: IMMEDIATE,
UNIMPEDED, UNCONDITIONAL, UNRESTRICTED ACCESS TO ANY
SIGHT THE U.N. DEEMS WARRANTED FOR INSPECTION, AND YES
NOW, ONCE AGAIN, SADDAM HUSSEIN HAS CAVED IN, AND WHILE
SADDAM HAS BENT TO THE WILL OF THE U.N., THE QUESTION
REMAINS WHETHER AFTER THIS DELAY A TRULY EFFECTIVE
INSPECTION OF THE MINISTRY IS STILL POSSIBLE. THE REAL TEST
OF HIS BEHAVIOR WILL BE IN FUTURE U.N. INSPECTIONS. BEHAVIOR
ALONG THE LINES WE'VE JUST WITNESSED WILL NOT BE TOLERATED.

SADDAM HAS LONG PURSUED A PATTERN OF WILLFUL NON-COMPLIANCE
AND OBSTRUCTION OF THE UNITED NATIONS SPECIAL COMMISSION. FOR
OVER A YEAR HE HAS LIED ABOUT THE EXTENT OF IRAQ'S WEAPONS OF
MASS DESTRUCTION PROGRAMS AND SOUGHT TO CONCEAL THEM FROM THE
UNITED NATIONS AND THE INTERNATIONAL ATOMIC ENERGY AGENCY.
NOW, THIS IS UNACCEPTABLE. IRAQ MUST AND WILL BE HELD TO THE
STANDARD OF FULL COMPLIANCE WITH SECURITY COUNCIL
RESOLUTION 687. SADDAM'S VIOLATION OF THE WILL OF THE
INTERNATIONAL COMMUNITY, AS EXPRESSED IN THE UNITED
NATIONS SECURITY COUNCIL RESOLUTIONS, CONTINUES IN OTHER
IMPORTANT AREAS. IRAQ HAS REFUSED TO PARTICIPATE IN THE
WORK OF THE IRAQ-KUWAIT BORDER COMMISSION. IRAQ HAS
REFUSED TO ACCOUNT FOR KUWAITI CITIZENS SEIZED DURING
THE OCCUPATION OF THE EMIRATE, AND TO RETURN PROPERTY
THAT WAS STOLEN BY THE OCCUPIERS.

IRAQ HAS NOT RENEWED THE MEMORANDUM OF UNDERSTANDING
WITH THE U.N. AND HAS STEPPED UP ITS HARASSMENT OF U.N.
OFFICIALS AND HUMANITARIAN AGENCIES OPERATING IN THE
COUNTRY. SADDAM HAS STEPPED UP HIS PERSECUTION OF THE
IRAQI PEOPLE IN FLAGRANT VIOLATION OF U.N. SECURITY COUNCIL
RESOLUTION 688 INCLUDING RECENT USE OF JET FIGHTERS AGAINST
THE SHI'ITES AND MAINTAINING A BLOCKADE OF THE KURDS.

0106

IRAQ HAS REFUSED TO ACCEPT U.N. SECURITY COUNCIL
RESOLUTIONS 706 AND 712, WHICH WOULD ALLOW FOR THE SALE
OF OIL FOR FOOD AND MEDICINE, CHOOSING INSTEAD TO HAVE
THE IRAQI PEOPLE SUFFER UNNECESSARILY, DENYING THEM
FOOD. THE INTERNATIONAL COMMUNITY CAN NOT TOLERATE
CONTINUED IRAQI DEFIANCE OF THE UNITED NATIONS AND THE
RULE OF LAW, AND THERE'S TOO MUCH AT STAKE FOR THE
REGION, FOR THE UNITED NATIONS AND FOR THE WORLD. I'LL JUST
TAKE A COUPLE OF QUESTIONS, JUST A COUPLE OF QUESTIONS HERE.

Q: DOES THIS MEAN THAT YOU FIND UNSATISFACTORY THE
SETTLEMENT THAT WAS MADE AT THE U.N. AND ARE REJECTING
IT, OR IS THIS A TEMPORARY SETTLEMENT OF THE PROBLEM?

PRESIDENT BUSH: NO, WE SUPPORT DR. EKEUS. HE HAS OUR
FULL RESPECT AND CONFIDENCE. AND SO THAT INSPECTION
WILL GO FORWARD, BELATEDLY SO--BUT IT WILL GO FORWARD. YES.

Q: DO YOU CONSIDER, MR. PRESIDENT, THAT THERE IS A NEED
NOW FOR SOME KIND OF ULTIMATUM, SOME KIND OF DEADLINE
GIVEN THEM, SOME KIND OF THREAT OF MILITARY AID?

PRESIDENT BUSH: SOME KIND OF THREAT OF --

Q: MILITARY ACTION -- PARDON ME.

PRESIDENT BUSH: YES, WELL, I DON'T KNOW THAT ANY MORE
IS REQUIRED RIGHT AT THIS MINUTE; I THINK EVERYONE KNOWS
THAT WE ARE DETERMINED TO SEE THESE RESOLUTIONS COMPLIED
WITH. WE ARE IN VERY CLOSE TOUCH WITH OUR ALLIES. THIS
STANDOFF NOW HAS BEEN RESOLVED BY HIS CAVING IN, BY HIS
BACKING DOWN. IN SPITE OF BLUSTER AND THREATS TO THE
CONTRARY. BUT THERE ARE MANY OTHER INSPECTIONS TO COME.

Q: DOES THAT MEAN, THEN, THAT THE CRISIS IN GENERAL
IS NOT OVER, THAT THERE WILL BE CONTINUING INCIDENTS
WITH SADDAM HUSSEIN?

PRESIDENT BUSH: WELL, THE WAY TO END THE CRISIS IS
FOR HIM TO FULLY COMPLY WITH THESE RESOLUTIONS I OUTLINED, AND
UNTIL THEN THERE WILL BE A LOT OF TENSION BECAUSE THE WHOLE
WORLD IS NOW MORE DETERMINED THAN EVER TO SEE THAT HE DOES
COMPLY, SO I CAN'T SAY THERE'S NO CONCERN -- NO REASON FOR
CONCERN ANY MORE AT ALL. THERE'S PLENTY OF REASON.

Q: MR. PRESIDENT, SOME U.S. MILITARY FORCES ARE EN ROUTE
TO THE REGION. IN VIEW OF THE AGREEMENT THAT HAS BEEN
WORKED OUT, WILL YOU ORDER THOSE FORCES TO STAND DOWN,
TO BE PULLED BACK, OR IS THAT MILITARY OPTION STILL OPEN?

0107

PRESIDENT BUSH: WELL, NORMALLY I DON'T DISCUSS THE
DEPLOYMENT OF MILITARY FORCES, AND I'M INCLINED TO STAY
WITH THAT RIGHT NOW. I DON'T THINK THERE WILL BE ANY
DRASTIC CHANGES IN EXISTING PLANS.

Q: MR. PRESIDENT, YOU SEEM TO BE SAYING THAT THE NEXT
TIME THERE WON'T BE ANY TIME FOR WARNING -- YOU'RE NOT
GOING TO LET ONE OF THESE CRISES BUILD UP LIKE THIS.
IS THAT WHAT YOU ARE TELLING US?

PRESIDENT BUSH: WELL, I DON'T -- YOU CAN INTERPRET IT ANY
WAY YOU WANT; ALL I'M TRYING TO DO IS EXPRESS THE
UNANIMOUS DETERMINATION OF THE SECURITY COUNCIL.

Q: DEPUTY SECRETARY EAGLEBURGER SAID TODAY HE EXPECTS
SECRETARY BAKER TO STAY AT THE STATE DEPARTMENT FOR A
LONG, LONG TIME. IS THAT YOUR VIEW AS WELL, OR IS HE
GOING TO MOVE TO THE CAMPAIGN CHARGE?

PRESIDENT BUSH: I HAVE NO COMMENTS ON THAT SUBJECT.

Q: MR. PRESIDENT, SADDAM HUSSEIN SAID TODAY THAT THE "MOTHER
OF ALL BATTLES" IS NOT OVER. WHAT DO YOU SAY TO HIM?

PRESIDENT BUSH: I SAY TO HIM, IF IT'S NOT OVER, HE
BETTER HOPE IT IS.

O: IS HE STILL A THREAT TO HIS NEIGHBORS IN THE
MIDDLE EAST?

PRESIDENT BUSH: NO, SADDAM IS A THREAT TO THE IRAQI
PEOPLE -- HE'S A THREAT TO HIS OWN PEOPLE. HE'S
BRUTALIZING HIS OWN PEOPLE IN FAILING TO COMPLY. AND HE
IS A THREAT TO PEACE AND SECURITY IN THE AREA -- THERE'S
NO QUESTION ABOUT ALL OF THAT. AND OUR ARGUMENT IS NOT
WITH THE IRAQI PEOPLE. I'VE SAID THAT SINCE DAY ONE OF
ALL OF THIS. AND I WILL REPEAT IT HERE TODAY: OUR
ARGUMENT IS WITH SADDAM HUSSEIN, THE BULLY, THE DICTATOR, THE
BRUTAL MERCHANT OF DEATH. AND THAT'S IT. AND IT IS NOT WITH
THE IRAQI PEOPLE. AND ONCE AGAIN HE HAS CAVED TN, AFTER A LOT
OF BLUSTER. BUT ALL I WANT TO DO HERE IS EXPRESS FOR THE
UNITED STATES OUR DETERMINATION TO SEE HIM COMPLY WITH THESE
RESOLUTIONS. WE HAVEN'T FORGOTTEN NOR HAVE THE OTHER MEMBERS
OF THE SECURITY COUNCIL.

0108

SO AGAINST A SOLID WALL HE ONCE AGAIN CAVED IN. I GUESS
THERE'S A CERTAIN HUMILIATION FACTOR FOR HIM WITH HIS
OWN PEOPLE, BUT I WOULD SIMPLY WE'VE JUST GOT TO LOOK
AHEAD NOW AND SEE THAT OTHER INSPECTIONS GO FORWARD AND
THAT HE COMPLIES WITH THESE RESOLUTIONS, THE SUBJECT OF
WHICH I DISCUSSED HERE A FEW MINUTES AGO. YES, LAST ONE HERE.

Q: IS THE THREAT OF FORCE NOT OVER UNTIL FULL COMPLIANCE
BEGINS?

PRESIDENT BUSH: I DIDN'T THREATEN ANYTHING -- THREATENED OR
CHANGED ANYTHING. THE OPTIONS THAT THE UNITED STATES AND OUR
PARTNERS HAVE AVAILABLE TO US ARE WELL-KNOWN, AND LET'S JUST
SEE THAT HE COMPLIES WITH THE RESOLUTIONS. I'M NOT HERE TO
THREATEN -- I'M SIMPLY HERE TO SAY THAT I'M GLAD THAT HE
CRATERED ONCE AGAIN ON THIS THREATENING -- BUT TO REITERATE
OUR DETERMINATION TO SEE THESE RESOLUTIONS COMPLIED WITH.
THAT'S ALL THAT THIS IS ABOUT. AND IT'S GOT TO BE DONE IN
TIMELY FASHION. AND I SALUTE MR. EKEUS. HE'S A COURAGEOUS MAN
AND HE WORKED HARD TO GET ACCESS TO THIS MINISTRY, WHICH HE
SHOULD HAVE HAD GIVEN TO HIM AUTOMATICALLY, BY VERY COMPETENT
PROFESSIONALS, VERY COMPETENT INSPECTORS. THANK YOU ALL VERY
MUCH.

0109

Embassy of
The Republic of Iraq
Seoul

سفارة الجمهورية العراقية
سيئول

Press Release

NO. 117-92

28/7/1992

NEWS HIGHLIGHTS FROM IRAQ

Week No. 30   Ending 26 July 1992

* Deputy Prime Minister, Mr. Tariq Aziz, met on July 19, Ambassador Rolf Ekeus, chief of the U.N Special Commission. During the meeting, Mr. Aziz stressed that Iraqi refusal of the inspection of the Ministry of Agriculture and Irrigation stems from the fact that this headquarter represents one of the symbols of the national sovereignty of Iraq. We are not refusing the inspection because the building falls within the interests of the inspection team as claimed by the Special Commission and for this very reason Iraq has, starting from the first day, invited Arab and foreign journalists and diplomats stationed in Iraq to visit the building and see for themselves, Mr. Aziz said.

Iraq is ready, separate from the mandate of the Special Commission, to invite a group of experts in the nuclear, chemical, projectile, and biological fields from countries of the Non-aligned Movement, from within the Security Council, or from other neutral countries to visit the headquarter of the Ministry to conduct an inspection of what it contains and ascertain the existence or absence of anything or any document related to the claims of the Special Committee, Mr. Aziz added.

* Commenting on the communique issued by the President of the UN Security Council concerning the murder of one of the UN guards in Duhok governorate, Foreign Minister, Mr. Ahmed Hussein, said on July 19, that Iraq is not responsible for the murder of the UN guard nor the other incidents which have occured to other UN representatives in the northern governorates of Iraq. The UN General Secretary and the Security Council know well that the government administeration is absent from the northern governorates, the Minister said.

The northern governorates have become an open area for the outlawed and irresponsible groups and that the American forces and its allies are the ones who are responsible for the chaos in the area, Mr. Hussein added.

* In a letter of protest submitted by the National Assembly to the Inspection Team which is forcing a siege on the

0110

building of the Ministry of Agriculture and Irrigation, the
Iraqi legislatives strongly condemned the immoral acts of
the Inspection Team which contradict the very principles of
international law and norms and the Human Rights Charter of
the UN.

* An official spokesman asserted, on July 23, that Iraqis
have every right to express their indignation against the
United States and Britain which have insulted them and
manipulated the United Nations to impose on the people of
Iraq an unjust blockade. The spokesman stressed that the
Iraqis were keen to see to it that no harm be done to the
Inspection Team who had been besieging the headquarters of
the Ministry of Agriculture and Irrigation, in cooperation
with security men who formed a human ring to protect the
Team. The spokesman also referred to the reports of Mr. Mark
Silver, the Team member as inaccurate and not honest, and
said that other members of the Team were fed up with crisis
created by their chief Rolf Ekeus and reluctant to act like
ordinary criminals.

On the other hand, Mr. Abdul Wahab Mahmoud, Minister of
Agriculture and Irrigation said in a press conference that
the Inspection Team left the site of the Ministry
voluntarily and all security measures were provided for the
Team. The Team's act of picketing in front of the building
of the Ministry is in contravention of all international
norms and laws, the Minister added.

* Ambassador Abdul Amir al-Anbari, Iraq's Permanent
Representative to the United Nations stressed on July 22,
that Iraq has fully cooperated with the International
Organization, but will not allow the inspection of the
Ministry of Agriculture and Irrigation because such an
attempt will be tantamount to humiliating Iraq and its
people. Any threat is, according to the UN Charter, an act
of aggression, Mr. Al-Anbari said.

* Parties and political forces in South America expressed
their solidarity with Iraq in confronting the imperialist
and Zionist attack against the country and urged for lifting
the unjust economic sanctions imposed on the people of Iraq,
said Comrade Abdul Ghani Abdul Ghafur, Member of the
Regional Command of Iraq of the Arab Ba'th Socialist Party.
Comrade Abdul Ghafur, who headed the Party's delegation to
the Political Parties Seminar in South America and
participated in the 3rd anniversary of the Sandinistan
Revolution in Nicaragua, said that he met with Mr. Daniel
Ortega former persident of Nicaragua who expressed his high
esteem of the leadership of President Saddam Hussein and
condemned the unjust sanctions against the children, women
and old men of Iraq.

* In a statement received by the Iraqi News Agency in
Amman/Jordan on July 25, the General Secrtariate of the
General Union of Al-Jazira People and the Front of National

0111

and Pan-Arab Struggle, said that the consequences of inviting the occupation forces to commit the aggression against Iraq by Al- Saud family have been reflected on the daily life of the Saudi people and have resulted in consuming the economy of the country and impoverishing the people of the country.

* In a message to President Saddam Hussein, the Tunisian Committee for Lifting the Sanctions Against Iraq condemned the recent crime of the American forces in burning the crop in northern Iraq. This crime demonstrates the scoundrel and cowardly nature of the American Administration and proves its frustration in trying to undermine the sovereignty of Iraq.

* Mr. Tariq Aziz, Member of the Revolution's Command Council, Deputy Prime Minister stressed in his press conference on July 24, that the fabricated crisis of inspecting the building of the Ministry of Agriculture and Irrigation is an American attempt to exploit the United Nations organs for the purpose of insulting Iraq. Previous attempts by the Americans are a stark proof, the Deputy Prime Minister said.

* The General Union of Arab Journalists called, in a statement on July 23, on the freedom-loving forces of the world to exert efforts to lift the inhuman sanctions against the people of Iraq. The Union also appealed to those forces to condemn the interference in Iraq's internal affairs and the vile attempts to undermine Iraq's national sovereignty and territorial integrity.

+ The Tunisian weekly "Unity" stressed in its July 25 issue, that indications and events have proved that a number of UN inspection teams' members in Iraq are agents of the CIA, with a mission to spy on Iraq. The attempt to inspect the Iraqi Ministry of Agriculture and Irrigation by foreign spies is an act in violation of the sovereignty of Iraq, the Weeky said.

* The Yemenite General Federation of Trade Unions called for immediate lifting of economic sanctions against Iraq.The Union also renewed in the final statement of the fourth session of its Central Council on July 23, its solidarity with the people of Iraq.

0112

관리
번호 92-2031

외 무 부

종 별 :

번 호 : USW-3767   일 시 : 92 0729 2010

수 신 : 장 관 (미일, 연이, 중동일)

발 신 : 주 미 대사

제 목 : 미 하원 외무위 청문회

　　1. 하원 외무위 유럽 및 중동소위 (위원장 : HAMILTON 의원)와 인권 및 국제기구 소위 (위원장 : YATRON 의원)는 금 7.29(수) EDWARD PERKINS 주 UN 대사 및 GEORGE WARD 국무부 국제기구담당 수석 부차관보를 증인으로 출석시켜 '페르시아만에서의 UN 의 역할 및 이락의 UN 결의 준수'에 관하여 공동으로 청문회를 개최하였음. (당관 김형진 서기관 참석)

　　2. PERKINS 대사는 모두발언에서 지난 2 개월간 SADDAM HUSSEIN 은 안보리의 결의를 공공연히 위반하여 왔으며, UN 의 권위에 대하여도 점점 심각하게 도전하고 있다고 언급하였으며, WARD 부차관보도 모두 발언에서 이락이 과거 눈속임으로 UN 의 요구사항을 회피하려던 것과는 달리, 최근에는 UN 의 이락 농무부 건물사찰 거부등 일련의 문제에 있어 UN 과 협조하기를 정면으로 거부하고 있어 걸프전 휴전 조건에 대한 의문이 제기되고 있다고 언급하였음. (상기 증인들의 증언문은 파편 송부 예정임)

　　3. 이어 계속된 질의.응답에서 HAMILTON 의원 (민-인디애나)은 대 이락 제재조치가 실패하는 경우 무력을 사용하는데 대해 UN 내 합의가 이루어져 있는지 또한 UN 후원하에 미국이 군사행동을 취할수 있는지 여부를 질문한 바, PERKINS 대사는 안보리는 이락으로 하여금 제재조치를 준수토록 해야 한다는데는 의견 일치를 보고 있으나, 현재로서는 관망자세를 취하고 있다고 답변하였으며, WARD 부차관보는 최근 이락 농무부 건물 사찰 거부와 같은 경우 미국이 무력을 사용할수도 있을 것이라고 답변하였음.

　　4. 한편 TORRICELLI 의원 (민-뉴저지)은 이락 농무부 건물 사찰과 관련 사찰단원 구성에 대해 이락과 협상을 한 것은 악선례를 남긴 것이라고 주장하였으며, LANTOS 의원 (민-캘리포니아)은 미국인이 이락 농무부 건물 사찰단에서 제외된 경위를 추궁한

미주국　　장관　　차관　　1.2차보　　중아국　　국기국　　분석관　　청와대　　안기부

PAGE 1

바, PERKINS 대사는 동 사태가 선례를 형성하지는 않는다고 답변하였으며 사찰단원 구성문제는 현장 사찰책임을 맡고 있는 EKEUS 대사가 결정한 문제라고 답변하였음.

5. 금일 청문회는 이락이 UN 결의를 계속 이행하지 않는 경우 미국의 무력사용 가능성을 타진해 보기 위한 목적도 있었던 것으로 보임. 또한 민주당측 의원들은 이락 농무부 건물 사찰에 있어서 승전국인 미국의 사찰단원이 패전국인 이락의 요구에 따라 사찰단에서 제외된 경위에 대해 강한 어조로 행정부측을 추궁하였는 바, 이는 민주당측이 금년 11월 대통령 선거를 앞두고 부시 대통령이 클린턴 민주당 후보의 외교경험 부족을 공격하면서 걸프전 승리를 자신의 치적으로 부각시키려는 노력을 전개하려는데 대해 걸프전 당시 SADAM HUSSEIN 을 제거하지 않는 것이 미국의 실책이었다는 일각의 여론을 확산시켜 상기 부시 대통령의 걸프전 승리 부각 움직임에 제동을 걸려는 측면도 있는 것으로 보임. 끝.

　(대사 현홍주-국장)

　예고 : 92.12.31. 까지

주 미 대 사 관

USW(F) : 5465   년월일 :   시간 :

수 신 : 장 관 (머인, 공동일)

발 신 : 주미대사

제 목 : 부시대통령, 对 이락 no-fly zone 발표   (출처 : FNS)

───────────────────────────────

STATEMENT BY PRESIDENT BUSH
THE WHITE HOUSE BRIEFING ROOM
WASHINGTON, DC

     And now I want to turn to the situation in Iraq. In recent
weeks and months, we have heard and seen new evidence of harsh
repression by the government of Saddam Hussein against the men, women
and children of Iraq. What emerges from eyewitness accounts, as well
as from the detailed August 11th testimony before the United Nations
Security Council of UN Human Rights Envoy Max Van der Stoel, is
further graphic proof of Saddam's brutality. We now know of Saddam's
use of helicopters and, beginning this spring, fixed wing aircraft to
bomb and strafe civilians and villages there in the south, his

3-1 page# 2   WEDNESDAY, AUGUST 26, 1992
execution last month of merchants in Baghdad, and his gradual
tightening of the economic blockade against the people of the north.
These reports are further confirmation that the government of Iraq is
failing to meet its obligations under United Nations Security Council
Resolution 688. This resolution, passed in April of 1991, demands
that Saddam Hussein end repression of the Iraqi people.

(5465 - 2 - 1)

0115

By denying access to UN human rights monitors and other
observers, Saddam has sought to prevent the world from learning of
his brutality. It is time to ensure the world does know. And
therefore the United States and its coalition partners have today
informed the Iraqi government that 24 hours from now coalition
aircraft, including those of the United States, will begin flying
surveillance missions in southern Iraq south of the 32 degrees North
latitude to monitor the situation there. This will provide coverage
of the areas where a majority of the most significant recent
violations of Resolution 688 have taken place. The coalition is also
informing Iraq's government that in order to facilitate these
monitoring efforts, it is establishing a no-fly zone for all Iraqi
fixed and rotary wing aircraft. This new prohibition will also go
into effect in 24 hours over this same area. It'll remain in effect
until a coalition determines that it is no longer required. It'll be
similar to the no-fly zone the coalition imposed on northern Iraq
more than a year ago.

I want to emphasize that these actions are designed to enhance
our ability to monitor developments in southern Iraq. These actions
are consistent with longstanding US policy toward Iraq. We seek
Iraq's compliance, not its partition. The United States continues to
support Iraq's territorial unity and bears no ill will towards its
people. We continue to look forward to working with a new leadership
in Baghdad, one that does not brutally suppress its own people and
violate the most basic norms of humanity. Until that day, no one
should doubt our readiness to respond decisively to Iraq's failure to
respect the no-fly zone. Moreover, the United States and our
coalition partners are prepared to consider additional steps should
Saddam continue to violate this or other UN resolutions.

$545-2-2$

주 미 대 사 관

USW(F) : 6376 년월일 : 92, 10. 6 시간 : 18:57

수 신 : 장 관 (미일, 중동일, 중동이)

발 신 : 주 미 대 사

제 목 : 이락건위자산동결조치)   (출처 : FNS)

보통 : 안제

──

STATE DEPARTMENT REGULAR BRIEFING
BRIEFER: RICHARD BOUCHER
12:18 PM   TUESDAY, OCTOBER 6, 1992

Q   The Iraqi regime has dismissed as illegal the recent Security Council resolution to seize the Iraqi oil assets, and -- saying that Iraq is going to press on to get the UN to allow it to sell $4 billion worth of oil. What is the US position on that, and --?

MR. BOUCHER: Our position is the position that we've always taken about this, and that's that Iraq has to comply with Security Council resolutions going right back to the very first ones, and that these steps that we've taken recently with the assets resolution were to borrow money to ensure that Iraq did pay -- for helping its people, for the compensation that it owes, and for other things, and that --. Iraq has been offered a means for many, many months now under Resolution 706 and 712 to export oil under carefully monitored conditions so that its oil revenues would pay for these things. But it hasn't taken up the offer. It hasn't accepted that UN resolution. And therefore other steps were necessary to deal with these conditions that were created by the Iraqi government.

Q   Are you leading the effort to implement that resolution?

MR. BOUCHER: We --

Q   Have you actually taken steps to do that?

MR. BOUCHER: The -- yes, we -- we're looking to put together a package that will implement the resolution fairly shortly. I guess I'd put it that way.

Q   Are you going to unveil that package soon, or --?

MR. BOUCHER: I'm not -- I can't promise when we will, but I'm sure we'll be glad to report to you on this progress as we go forward.

(6376 - 1 - 1)

외신 1과
동 제

배부처 장관실 차관실 일차보 이차보 외정실 분석관 아주국 미주국 구주국 중아국 국기국 경제국 통상국 문협국 의연원 청와대 안기부 공보처 경기원 상공부 재무부 농수부 동자부 환경처 과기처

0117

걸프사태 이후 미국.이라크 관계 동향, 1991-92 513

외교문서 비밀해제: 걸프 사태 37
걸프 사태 미국 동향 4

초판인쇄 2024년 03월 15일
초판발행 2024년 03월 15일

지은이 한국학술정보(주)
펴낸이 채종준
펴낸곳 한국학술정보(주)
주 소 경기도 파주시 회동길 230(문발동)
전 화 031-908-3181(대표)
팩 스 031-908-3189
홈페이지 http://ebook.kstudy.com
E-mail 출판사업부 publish@kstudy.com
등 록 제일산-115호(2000. 6. 19)

ISBN 979-11-6983-997-6 94340
      979-11-6983-960-0 94340 (set)